Flash & Director
Designing Multiuser Web Sites StudioLab

Antonio Gould
Thomas Blaha
Gaz Bushell
Justin Clayden
Charles Forman
Geoff Gaudreault
Stef Lewandowski
Mauricio Piacentini
Anthony Rowe
Steve Webster
Jon Williams

friendsof

DESIGNER TO DESIGNER™

Flash & Director

Designing Multiuser Web Sites StudioLab

© 2002 friends of ED

First Published 2002

Trademark Acknowledgments

friends of ED has endeavoured to provide trademark information about all the companies and products mentioned in this book by the appropriate use of capitals. However, friends of ED cannot guarantee the accuracy of this information.

Published by friends of ED
30 Lincoln Road, Olton, Birmingham. B27 6PA. UK.

Printed in USA

ISBN: 1-903450-44-6

Flash & Director

Designing Multiuser Web Sites StudioLab

Credits

Authors
Thomas Blaha
Gaz Bushell.
Justin Clayden
Charles Forman
Geoff Gaudreault
Antonio Gould
Stef Lewandowski
Mauricio Piacentini
Anthony Rowe
Steve Webster
Jon Williams

Content Architect
Matthew Knight

Editors
Dan Squier
Julie Closs
Libby Hayward
Andrew Tracey
Adam Dutton

Author Agents
Jez Booker
Chris Matterface

Additional Material
Doug Brown
Manno Bult

Project Manager
Jenni Harvey

Technical Reviewers
Ryan Adams
Simone Baboni
Manno Bult
Matt Gadd
Gareth Heyes
Stef Lewandowski
Steve Parker
Vibha Roy
Todd Simon
Gabrielle Smith
William Thompson

Graphic Editors
Matthew Clark
Katy Freer

Indexer
Fiona Murray

Cover Design
Deb Murray

Managing Editor
Dave Galloway

Proof Readers
Dev Lunsford
Julia Gilbert

Special Thanks to
Nick Manning
Jez Booker

Illustration
Chris Matterface

Thomas Blaha   http://www.ncimedia.com/

Thomas has been involved in computing and media since the early 1980's and began working with Director as a hobby while attending graduate school in 1993. It became a fulltime career in the fall of 1994, when he started North Coast Interactive, Inc., a development company focusing on the Business-to-Business communication needs of the Industrial marketplace. Since its inception, he's been involved in the development of leading edge projects (ranging from interactive CD-ROMs to eCommerce websites) for companies both large and small.

Justin James Clayden   www.coolfusion.com.au

Justin lives at the beach in sunny Coledale, where there is surfing to be done that has little to do with the Internet. Justin's Masters thesis deals with 'avatars' by seeking to categorise them. When he's not writing theses, building avatars, or surfing waves, Justin likes to record music and write games. Justin is the founder of Cool Fusion Multimedia, an entity which provides coursework and educational software to a number of Australian Universities. Oh yeah, and he likes astronomy.

Justin would like to thank the following people for their assistance on this project: Margie Rahmann for helping me free up time to do it, Alan Queen for his great chapter on the Multiuser Server in 'Director 8.5 Studio and finally, friends of ED. Happy coding, and remember - go outside sometimes!

Charles Forman   http://www.setpixel.com   cforman@setpixel.com

Charles Forman is an art director, developer, and strategist in Chicago, Illinois. He is president of SetPixel Corp, which focuses on effective solutions through gaming and other high response models. SetPixel also releases enlightening articles, demos, and source based on strong concepts rather than the loose, general application of technology. Charles has given speeches on high-level Director/Lingo topics, and has been featured on the front page of the Chicago Tribune, on HOW Magazine's Top 10 list and in numerous Director books. Contrary to the picture, Charles Forman is not evil. Well, not very.

Geoff Gaudreault   http://www.zanpo.com

Geoff Gaudreault is a new media designer and freelance artist based in Washington, DC. He began his career in computer graphics as an architectural perspectivist. He has done renderings for the Smithsonian, Andersen Consulting, and many others. He has been designing interactive applications for the past two years, participating in projects for companies like the Discovery Channel, Great American Restaurants, and the Washington Post. His latest personal project is Zanpo.com, an online virtual city built with Macromedia Flash.

Antonio Gould   http://www.3form.co.uk

Antonio Gould spent his formative years in Cardiff, Wales before heading off to the bright lights of Birmingham, England to study Maths and Artificial Intelligence. After spending three years knee deep in numbers and strange squiggles he emerged and decided to drop everything and start making websites. After working for a number of years in various agencies and roles, he set up 3form Digital Media with Stef Lewandowski. The company specialises in youth based music and television sites, and Flash work. They have worked for clients such as Sprite, Universal Music, and Toni and Guy. When Antonio's not squinting in front of his monitors he enjoys eating, playing music, and eating.

Stef Lewandowski http://www.3form.co.uk

Stef Lewandowski is creative director of UK-based 3form, and is one of that peculiar breed of people who show equal enthusiasm for both web programming and graphic design. After studying Computer Science at Birmingham University he worked as a freelance designer and as a creative director before forming 3form with Antonio Gould. He has worked on websites as varied as Birmingham Museums and Art Gallery and a snowboarding park for Sprite. As well as spending far too much time in front of a computer screen he has other interests including running club events, video-art, VJing, photography, and writing music.

Mauricio Piacentini http://www.tabuleiro.com

Mauricio Piacentini is a co-founder of Tabuleiro Produções, a software and games development company located in São Paulo, Brazil. Tabuleiro has produced games and interactive pieces for a large number of websites since it started its operations in 1994, including all of the most important Latin American portals. The company line of products for Director and Authorware includes Nebulae MultiUserServer, ShapeShifter3D, DirectMediaXtra, WebXtra, StreamingMediaXtra, MpegXtra and DrawXtra. Tabuleiro products are currently used by thousands of developers in more than 60 countries around the globe. Mauricio holds a degree in Communications and Arts from the University of São Paulo.

Anthony Rowe and Gaz Bushell squid s o u p http://www.squidsoup.com

Anthony is co-founder and a director of squid s o u p, a leading interactive design group based in London. His background includes stints as a teacher, as a flamenco guitarist, and as a long distance single-handed sailor. Gaz Bushell's first degree was in sculpture and he is now the soup's chief coder. squid s o u p is a group of interactive designers, artists and musicians that specialise in surprising yet intuitive interactive design solutions. Clients include Levi's, Intel, PlayStation, Macromedia and Audi. Their work has been shown at the ICA, Sonar and SIGGRAPH.

Steve Webster

Steve Webster spends most of his time tinkering with scripting, backend and Flash technologies, or writing about tinkering with scripting, backend and Flash technologies. Being clearly masochistic in nature, he's been programming since he was knee-high to a grasshopper and can currently be found plotting his route to world domination. Steve would like to thank his girlfriend Nicki for her saint-like patience while he was once again "that bloke locked away upstairs".

Jon Williams http://www.shovemedia.com

Jon first got involved with Flash 2.0 because he didn't know how to do rollovers in JavaScript and thought it was simpler. He started scripting heavily with Flash 4 while attempting to build interactive, modular presentations, and has now been involved in web projects ranging from broadcasting basketball tournaments to corporate site makeovers. He wants to be a superhero, and reckons that the future of Flash is "some 14-year-old kid with a dialup in Kansas with way too much free time."

Flash & Director Designing Multiuser Web Sites StudioLab

Table of Contents

Table of Contents

11

12

13

14   An advanced application   395

Table of Contents

Introduction

Welcome! friends of ED are excited about the opportunities that packages like Macromedia's Flash and Director offer the web landscape, and this means that we're particularly excited about the opportunities for new web experiences offered by multiuser applications that use Flash and Director.

You can get by on the Web without interacting with other people, but it's a lot more fun and productive when you *can* interact with other people. It becomes more alive, more interesting, and more like the global village that we were all promised the Web would be. This book will let you create applications that could be anything – whiteboards that people all over the globe can simultaneously scribble on, or chat rooms where you can pull faces at other users.

The information contained within these pages will steadily give you the skills to go out and develop your own exciting, enticing multiuser web applications. It won't only give you the skills you need, but an accurate picture of the current landscape and the tools at your disposal.

Where to go

The job of this introduction is to welcome you aboard, show you some of the layout styles that we've used, and make sure that you know where to find some assistance when you start talking back to your computer out of sheer frustration.

The first thing you should do after reading this is to read the first chapter. It'll help you to get your bearings and set you off in the correct direction. It covers the basic concepts behind multiuser environments, and compares Flash and Director. It may be that you bought this book purely for Flash, or purely for Director, but take a look at this section before deciding what you need – you may well be surprised!.

You may not have both Flash 5 and Director on your machine. In fact that's quite likely. Don't worry – if you want to have a go with the other, Macromedia will oblige. As you probably already know, they provide 30-day free trials of all of their products, so you just need to point your browser at www.macromedia.com, and you'll find free downloads of both Flash and Director.

Layout Conventions

We've tried to keep this book as clear and easy to follow as possible, so we've only used a few layout styles to avoid confusion. Here they are...

- Practical exercises will appear under headings in this style...

Build this Movie now

...and where we think it helps the discussion, they'll have numbered steps like this:

1. Do this first
2. Do this second
3. Do this third, etc...

- When we're showing code blocks, we'll use this style:

```
Mover.startDrag (true);
Mouse.hide ();
```

- Where a line of code is too wide to fit on the page in the Flash section, we'll indicate that it runs over two lines by using an arrow-like 'continuation' symbol:

```
if (letters[i].x_pos == letters[i]._x &&
➡      letters[i].y_pos == letters[i]._y) {
```

Lines like this should be typed as a single continuous statement.

- In the Director section, we use the Lingo continuation symbol:

```
mycallback=gMultiuserClient.setNetMessageHandler   \
            (#defaultmessageHandler, script "main")
```

Unlike Flash, you can include this symbol when you type the code into Director, and things will still work fine – Director recognizes the symbol, and simply appends the next line to the end of the previous one. Whether or not you use them depends on how neat you want your code to look.

- When we discuss code in the body of the text, we'll put statements such as stop in a code-like style too.

- When we add new code to an existing block, we'll highlight it like this:

```
Mover.startDrag (true);
variable1 = 35;
```

- When we need to draw attention to a few lines within a large section of code, we'll use ellipsis points ... to mark where we've abbreviated the code.

- Pseudo-code will appear in this style:

```
If (the sky is blue) the sun is out
    Else (it's cloudy)
```

- Where we want to point out text that appears on your screen, we'll use this emphasized style: menu name

- Interesting or important points will be highlighted like this:

> This is a point that you should read carefully.

- File names will look like this: `mydirectorfile.dir`

- Web addresses will be in this form: www.friendsofed.com

- New or significant phrases will appear in this **important words** style

Code download

All of the code source files for this book can be downloaded direct from the friends of ED website at www.friendsofed.com. Go to the `books` section, find this book, and the code option will appear as a tab on the left-hand side. You'll notice that you can also find the errata page for the book here. We hope that it will include nothing, but we know we're not perfect, so check before you start the book.

If you have any problems with the source files, then please contact us using one of the methods detailed below and we'll do our best to help.

Support

If you have any questions or problems with the book, check out our web site: there's a range of e-mail addresses there (or you can use `feedback@friendsofed.com`) that you can contact for help. Please get in touch: we like talking to you.

There are also a host of other features up on the site: interviews with designers, samples from our other books; and a message board where you can post your own questions, discussions, and answers (or just take a back seat and look at what everyone else is talking about). If you have any comments, problems, or suggestions, write to us. It's what we're here for and we'd love to hear from you.

Chapter 1

Why Multiuser?

The idea of this introduction chapter is to investigate why we might want to add multiuser capabilities to our sites in the first place, looking at how a realized multiuser environment can benefit different aspects of your site. Along the way we'll use some real-world examples to back up our theories.

As we said in the introduction, we fully realize that you are very probably coming to this book with a preference for, or more experience of either Flash or Director. With this in mind, we'll look at the differing capabilities that Flash and Director have to offer us as developers, weighing up the pros and cons of each and finding out how we can choose the best tool for the job.

Finally, we'll take a close look at some of the key technical concepts that you'll need to know about before setting off proper on the journey to multiuser guru-dom! If this all sounds a little scary then don't worry – we'll take it slow and make sure we've got the grounding we need to really get the most out of the remainder of the book.

Hmmm... where can I use this wonderful technology?

Before we set off on our journey proper, it's worth taking some time to think about the benefits that multiuser interactivity can bring to the sites you design and develop.

Among the factors that are most important in a web site's continued survival, gaining and retaining visitors has to be top of the pile. So-called "sticky" content is the Holy Grail of every web developer around the globe, meaning that we're often having to go to increasingly extreme lengths to achieve that goal.

When people place such a high value on attracting and keeping traffic, surely the introduction of the potential to interact with others is a valuable factor? But multiuser is just limited to online gaming, right? Let's take a look at some of the areas where it can be used.

E-commerce

One particular area that could benefit from multiuser content is that of e-commerce. As we all know, one of the great advantages of selling goods or services online is that customers can wander by any time of day or night for a spot of retail therapy.

One of the things you lose in all this, however, is one of the key things that traditional bricks and mortar companies hold dear – customer interaction. With customers being the most fickle of beings, if they can't find the information they need on your site then they'll be winging their way to your rivals faster than you can say, "there goes another one".

Adding multiuser capabilities can help here by allowing your customers to ask questions of your staff (or even other customers) during the sales process, something which has largely been ignored in the online world.

Research has shown that over 90% of online shoppers want some sort of human interaction available during the purchasing process. Without this, the world of e-commerce will stagnate into little more than a collection of catalogue retailers, as opposed to a global high street able to really compete with the established bricks and mortar industry.

Online Conferences

Another exciting possibility for multiuser connectivity is the ability to set up online conferences. Macromedia itself uses the Shockwave Multiuser Server to create online conferences in which a number of guests can provide information to users in a question and answer format.

This technology is being heavily used by TV stations to allow viewers to chat with the stars or creators of top programs, and can equally be used by businesses in the same manner.

Business Presentations

This is yet another exciting application for multiuser content. Multi-location businesses that would generally hold a physical meeting to discuss business matters can now take advantage of online multiuser content to meet "virtually", saving money and time.

Anything here is possible, from streaming audio and video to collaborative whiteboards where designers and developers can get together and thrash out ideas on a virtual canvas – this could even be used for business brainstorming sessions.

According to Macromedia,

"BP Amoco uses the Shockwave Multiuser Server to enable a global audience of employees to experience and participate in live company presentations. Recently, petroleum engineers in a shed on a UK oilfield delivered a presentation that included synchronized slides, demonstrations and animations in real-time to participants. The server also enabled participants to chat live with one another and to vote on issues."

I can only assume that the shed was either on an oilrig or floating in the North Sea, because there's no oil in my back yard, just a really nice shed. But either way, the fact that BP were at sea illustrates the incredible potential here.

Learning

Multiuser environments are collaborative, and collaboration is good for learning. Having such a collaborative environment on the Web allows distance teaching, and tutoring. This could be used for learning from remote places, or perhaps whilst in hospital. It also means experts on subjects, who perhaps live far away from the class, can be consulted for a lesson. I'm sure this would save an awful lot of money on flights and hotels for the esteemed professor.

It also provides whole new ways of teaching, such as "just in time" or on the spot learning. For example, say that your nephew just can't work out his algebra homework, and there's a really good documentary on the stag beetle on TV that you really don't want to miss. He could log into such a class and get help on the subject, allowing you to gain knowledge of the stag beetle's strange mating habits.

Entertainment

Probably the most prolific use of multiuser content is in the entertainment arena. In addition to online multi-player games, a common use for this technology is to develop chatrooms where visitors to your site can talk to one another.

One of the most famous systems in existence has to be Habbo Hotel, from Finnish outfit Sulake. http://www.habbo.com

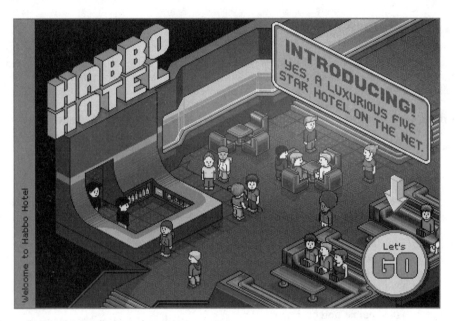

According to the media bumph:

"Habbo Hotel is a chill-out space where you can hang out with your friends. Guests are represented in the hotel by a personal figure called a Habbo. This hotel is primarily for teens in the UK, but everyone is welcome."

In essence, each user is represented by their chosen Habbo, which they can dress and style as they desire. They can then roam, point - and click - style, throughout the Habbo Hotel. There is a huge number of common areas in which you can meet and interact with other users, even playing games such as battleships with them. You can also create yourself a private space where you can invite a select few to peruse your nice décor and admire your style and sensibility... or not, as the case may be.

Having looked at an example of Director strutting its stuff, I guess we'd best balance up with a look at a similar system developed using Flash. In this case, we're going to take a look at Dubit.co.uk, developed by LightMaker Technologies. This is a multi-award winning site that allows you to roam the streets of a virtual city, interacting with others.

According to LightMaker, Dubit.co.uk is:

"...an "immersive 3D environment" that exploits most of the TotalMediaTechnology TM functionality.

There are games, SMS gateways, live interactive animated 3D chat, streaming MP3s and online information and advice. Visitors can shop on Dubit securely.

The site is targeted at 11 to 17 year olds with an interface and the type of interactivity they want."

Digging a Little Deeper...

Now that we know why we might want to add multiuser capabilities to our sites, we're going to explore the underlying technologies that make this possible. If this all sounds a bit too tricky then don't fret – we're not embarking on a masterclass in advanced networking. We're just going to get ourselves where we're in a position to appreciate the different options available to us, and to understand when me might want to choose one over the others.

The technical term for the stuff we're looking at in this section is **network topologies**. If you're not familiar with the theory of basic computer networking, then you may not have heard that term before. Basically, it refers to the different ways in which several computers can be physically joined (or networked) together.

There are a great variety of network topologies in existence, some commonly used and others extremely specialized, but thankfully only a few of those are relevant to us as web developers. The ones we'll be focusing on here are:

- Client/Server

- Peer-to-Peer

- Hybrid

Client/server

In a client/server network, each machine connected to the network is either a client or a server, and each client is connected to a central server which handles all the processing and relaying of data.

This is a commonly used topology and is the essence of most of the connections we make on the Internet. Unfortunately this system is susceptible to failures, especially server - based failures. If the server falls down, then all communications between the clients are lost.

Another disadvantage to this model is that if a sufficiently large number of clients are connected to the server, the server can become bogged down with requests. This means that the network will operate slowly and could cause problems for time-critical applications.

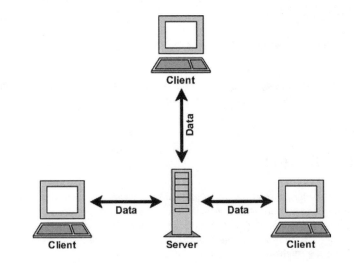

Peer-to-peer

With the peer-to-peer network topology, we have each client connecting to each of the other clients. The obvious implication of this is that in a large network each client could have many hundreds of connections, which could result in a slower network. In addition, each client needs to know the identity of the other clients in order to be able to connect and communicate.

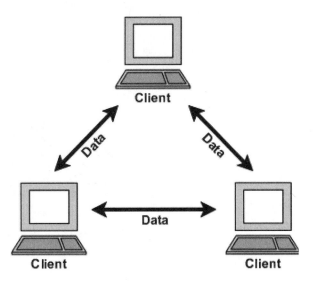

This technology is used in the popular file sharing protocol Gnutella (and Napster, for those of you who remember it) and is highly robust. The failure of one or more clients will not bring the entire network down, meaning that a peer-to-peer network is unlikely to suffer from the problems a client/server network would experience in the event of a server failure.

Hybrid networks

Technically speaking, a hybrid network topology is one that combines the features of any two or more individual topologies. For our purposes we're going to be a little more specific and say that a hybrid network is one that uses a combination of client/server and peer-to-peer network topologies.

As previously mentioned, the main problem with client/server networks is that the entire network is reliant on the server to do all the work of relaying data from one client to the others. This can put a tremendous strain on the server if a great number of clients are connected or if the processing work that the server has to perform is complex.

On the other side of the fence, peer-to-peer networks are limited by the fact that each client must know the identities (i.e. the IP addresses) of the other clients on the network. This is fine if the identities of the clients, and the number of clients seldom changes, but this is unlikely to be the case. The idea of combining the client/server and peer-to-peer topologies to create a hybrid network is to remove the aforementioned limitations to create a better network.

The basic plan would be for each client to initially connect to the server to register its identity and to fetch the identities of all currently registered clients. The client can then establish individual connections with the other clients on the network and communicate with them using those connections. It's important to note that the connection to the server would need to remain open so that it can update the client with the identities of any new clients that register.

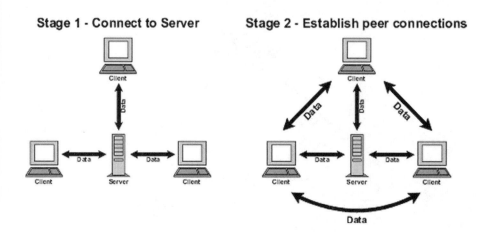

Using this method means that the client only needs to know the identity of the server before it can connect to the network, obtaining a list of its peers from the server. The load on the server is reduced because the clients themselves handle the bulk transfer of data.

Lines of Communication

In addition to the physical way in which the computers concerned are connected, we also need to know the ways in which the processes running on those computers communicate with one another.

As we've said, each computer acts as both a client and a server with peer-to-peer networks. If we were to choose this topology for a given application then we would be responsible for writing the routines to both issue requests and respond to requests from other clients.

However, the client/server model offers a number of possibilities. First, we have the traditional connection method used when accessing a web site. The client will generate a request for a document (an HTML page for example), which will be sent to the server by way of a temporary connection. This connection is then closed.

The server will process this request, creating a connection to the client over which it will transfer the requested document (should it be found) or an appropriate response.

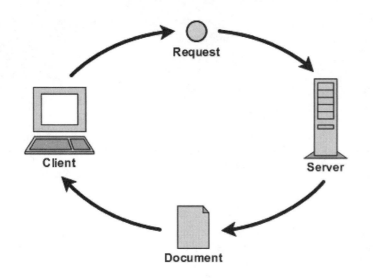

We use this type of connection every day and take it for granted, but it's a highly efficient system for delivering content both over a small network and the wider Internet. This method is generally slower than the alternative (which we will investigate in a moment), often taking up to 10 seconds for the server to respond to a request.

The other way that the client/server interaction can be handled is by way of a persistent two-way connection between the client and the server – generally known as a socket connection.

The advantage of this method is that, because the connection is persistent, the response from the server is generally much quicker than using the traditional method outlined above. This means that the connection is suitable for time - critical applications such as collaborative whiteboard projects and multi-player games.

That said, a number of persistent connections to any one server can slow the whole system down. Unlike the traditional model, where connections are being made and broken as and when they are needed, clients using the socket model remain connected. This also introduces the problem of client limits, since a server cannot be expected to handle an unlimited number of client connections.

Socket connections are often referred to as "realtime connections", whereas the traditional HTTP method connections are also known as "non realtime connections".

In this book we will investigate these methods as used in multiuser environments for Flash and Director. The traditional method, however, will be modified slightly with server-side code, which will make the requests more dynamic and interactive.

Director versus Flash

"If you only have a hammer in your toolbox, you tend to think of every problem as a nail." I'm not sure where I've heard that, but it rings very true for the way in which many web developers tackle problems.

With all of the hype that's surrounded Flash over these past few years, you'd be forgiven for thinking that every slick multimedia site on the Web is a product of Flash. In fact, many of those sites will have been developed in Director, and would have required a superhuman effort to develop in Flash.

The truth is that it's a case of picking the right tool for the right job. Cracking a nut with a sledgehammer is pure overkill, while trying to knock a wall down with a nutcracker will be a long and unforgiving task. Investigating the problem, and then picking the right product to solve that problem will make our lives nice and easy as developers.

So, just what are the differences between these two Macromedia heavyweights? Follow me and all will be revealed...

A brief history

Before we kick off with a comparison between these two fine contenders for your multiuser pleasure, it's worth studying their background.

Director started out its life on the Apple Macintosh as a product called VideoWorks Interactive, way back in the 1980s, and was originally intended to create multimedia presentations bound for CD-ROM. Macromedia as we know it today was born out of this product, and to this day Director continues to be its flagship product.

Director was ported to DOS/Windows 3.1 in 1994, and has gone from strength to strength since. With the advent of the Shockwave web browser plug-in, and the recent inclusion of 3D rendering technology, Director is truly a multi-format multimedia application.

Flash, on the other hand, started out as a product called Animator from a company called FutureSplash. It was developed specifically for the Web, enabling developers to include vectored artwork and animation in their sites. Animator gradually gained some high profile customers, not least of all the mighty Microsoft Network.

Macromedia acquired FutureSplash and renamed its groundbreaking product Flash. As Flash matured, its capabilities were expanded, and the explosion in interest for it came about with the advent of Flash 4. With a slick interface, a powerful but simple scripting language, and the carpet deployment of the new Flash plug-in, developers were able to construct some truly awesome sites.

High Noon at the Multiuser Corral

Now it's time for the showdown you've all been waiting for. Time to rip the hoods from Flash and Director and take a peek at what they're made of and what they can do for us. Contenders, ten paces on my count, and then you turn and **draw...**

Macromedia Flash

Macromedia Flash currently has a couple of ways to deliver multiuser connectivity for your web sites.

Firstly we have the `loadVariables()` function and its derivative `loadVariablesNum()`. These functions will basically initiate an HTTP connection to a given URL and read the data returned. The target for these functions can either be a simple text file or a server-side script (such as one written in PHP), which will then be processed by the server and the output sent back to the Flash movie.

In either case, we need to make sure that the data that's presented to the Flash movie is in a format that it can understand. Basically, the data present in the text file or returned by the server-side script needs to be presented in the following URL - encoded format:

```
&var1Name=value&var2Name=value&var3Name=value
```

The data is read in as name/value pairs, with each name and value being separated by '=', and each name/value pair separated by an ampersand '&'. Once this data has been loaded in, it is then available within the Flash movie as individual variables.

If the target of the `loadVariables()` call is a server-side script, then information can be passed from the Flash movie to this script using either the GET or POST methods available in standard HTML forms. This allows the script to customize its response depending on the information passed into it, and is the key to creating basic multiuser applications.

The downside to this is that up to a minute can pass between requesting the data and receiving it, especially if the server is extremely busy. The fastest response you can generally expect is around two seconds. This means that the multiuser capabilities of Flash with `loadVariables()` is limited to turn - based games.

For this reason, Macromedia introduced the concept of sockets in Flash 5 with the XMLSocket object. This heralded a breakthrough for multiuser Flash developers who had been stuck with slow and cumbersome HTTP-based connections until that point.

Although those three sacred letters have been appended to the beginning of the object name, it is important to realize that the XMLSocket object is capable of sending and receiving any data that can be represented textually. In addition to this, it has the ability to process the incoming data as XML, and this is why it's been named the way it has.

The main deficiency in this technology is the fact that the XMLSocket in Flash cannot accept connections from the outside world, only make them. This means that Flash is incapable of creating a peer-to-peer based network and you need a dedicated server program to relay messages between the clients.

Since reinventing the wheel is generally a bad idea (unless your wheel is better than the rest, of course) it's worth investigating some of the existing socket server programs designed to work with the Flash XMLSocket object. Here are the URLs of just a few of them...

- Swocket: http://swocket.sourceforge.net

- Fortress: http://www.xadra.com/

- MoockComm: http://www.moock.org/chat/

You can find a more complete list of socket servers at the following URL...

http://www.tupps.com/flash/faq/xml.html

Another downside to socket-based connections in Flash is that they're limited to connections only within the same subdomain as that on which the Flash movie resides. This restriction was added to the Flash plug-in as a security measure but is the bane of most Flash developers who have ever worked with the XMLSocket object.

For example, if the Flash movie is located at myserver.com, and the socket server is running on mysocketserver.com, any attempt to connect to the socket server will be refused by the Flash plug-in. If the socket server were also running on myserver.com then the connection would be allowed.

Finally, another Flash plug-in security measure prevents any connection attempted to a port number lower than 1024. Port numbers below 1024 are generally used for common web services such as HTTP (port 80), ftp (port 21) and telnet (port 23). For this very same reason, many firewalls will block any attempt to connect to port numbers above 1024, meaning that many servers have to be manually configured to allow such connections.

Macromedia Director

Director, on the other hand, has a wealth of options available to it via the Multiuser Xtra. It is able to create peer-to-peer and client/server connections and is not restricted in the same way that Flash is.

In addition to this, Director 8.5 is shipped with the much-improved version 3 of the Multiuser Server application, which is designed to work with Director and allow connections between clients. It also has the potential for server-side scripting.

For the purposes of this book, we've concentrated on giving you a firm foundation in the use of the excellent Multiuser Server shipped with Director, but there are also third-party servers available. One example of this would be FUSElight, a free cross-platform server available from Sulake, the creators of Habbo Hotel and Mobiles Disco. More information on this and the other Director options can be found in Chapter 15.

The Journey Has Only Just Begun...

This chapter should have given you an initial taste of the exciting potential for multiuser applications, and some ideas of how you might start to implement these ideas. This is just the appetizer to the main course, so keep reading.

Chapter 2

Non-Realtime Connections

When you think of multiuser applications, you probably first think of realtime situations such as networked games or online chatrooms. We'll be looking at realtime connections in the next few chapters and seeing how useful they can be, but it's important to realize that this isn't the only way to achieve multiuser connectivity in Flash.

For instance, a forum is undoubtedly a multiuser application, but there's no need for it to be kept updated in realtime in the way that a racing game or a chat room would. It needs to check for messages, but it doesn't need to do this continually – if it only checks every few minutes or so, you're not going to notice. In fact, unless the necessary resources are available on the network and on your server, you may find realtime connections impractical.

In this chapter we're going to take a look at the important world of non-realtime techniques, and how we can use them to make a perfectly good multiuser application with some simple ActionScript and a little server-side magic.

Server-side scripting – an overview

In a standard client/server setup for the Web, a client program (usually a web browser) opens a connection to a server, requests a file, the server returns the file to the client, and the connection closes. This is the kind of connection we use to send our main SWF to the user when they connect to our multiuser site.

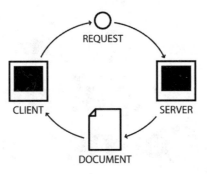

With server-side scripting enabled, the client can request a script file on the server, and the server's response is to execute that script and send back the results. According to the instructions within the script, these results can take just about any form: an HTML page, an XML document, Flash variables, an image, a PDF document – almost anything. Once the results are sent back, the connection closes.

What's particularly interesting about these scripts is that they can draw in information from all sorts of external sources: other web pages, databases on the server, and so on. We can even send them variables along with our requests.

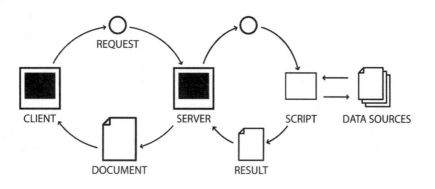

Just to make things a little clearer, let's consider a simple example. I'm sure you're quite familiar with search engines, and how they can be used to track down information on the Web. My own particular favorite can be found at www.google.com, and if you navigate to this page and search on the term "Macromedia Flash", you'll be redirected to a list of relevant sites. Look at the address at the top of your browser, and you should see the following URL:

http://www.google.com/search?q=Macromedia+Flash

We can break this down into two parts: the first indicates the page we want to look at, and in this case it's Google's search page:

http://www.google.com/search

This page actually just consists of a script on their server, and that script is designed to search their gargantuan list of web sites for any text matching the particular words we just submitted. The words have been attached to our request as a **query string** that reads:

?q=Macromedia+Flash

So, Google's search script essentially just compares two sources of information: the user input and the Google database itself. It then takes the results and sends them back to the client in the form of an HTML page that we can quickly scan and use to click through to sites of interest.

The best thing about server-side scripting is that it allows us to create our web content dynamically. We can customize and adapt content to suit the time of day, to reflect different users' preferences, to automatically display a list of the latest news, to run searches, and to generally keep sites up-to-date – all without having to edit them by hand.

What's more, it isn't just HTML web pages that stand to benefit from server-side scripting. We can also write scripts that pass data back to Flash clients, and significantly raise the bar on what we can do with them – that's what this chapter is going to be all about. However, before we go into the mechanics of server-side scripting for Flash, let's take a quick look at PHP, the scripting language we're going to be using. We'll consider how and why it came about, and contrast it with a couple of its competitors.

The History of PHP

Rasmus Lerdorf conceived the original PHP language in late 1994, when he put together a collection of Perl scripts to keep a record of visitors to his online résumé. The idea really caught on among visitors to his site, and in response to popular demand, he released them into the public domain in 1995 under the moniker "Personal Home Page Tools".

Over the next few years, use of PHP grew rapidly, and the number of developers involved with the PHP project grew along with it. At the time of writing, we're up to version 4 of PHP, which has access to a large number of third party add-ons, some of which even include functions for dynamically generating SWF files from scratch.

There are a couple of important things to note about the PHP engine (the program that actually executes PHP scripts on behalf of the web server):

- Firstly, it's an **open source** project. In case you aren't familiar with this term, the main practical upshot of this is that it's freely available for anyone to use, either commercially or otherwise. It's also under continuous development by people collaborating across the Internet to build it into a first-class web platform. There are many web sites around which offer free scripts for you to use – anything from HTML-based bulletin boards and search programs to multi-player Flash engines.

- Secondly, it's available for use on both Windows *and* Unix-based platforms (including MacOSX).

You can download PHP from http://www.php.net, where you'll also find a wealth of information about it and associated third-party tools.

Alternative Server-Side Scripting Languages

PHP isn't the only server-side scripting language available to you for interaction with Flash movies, and depending on your particular circumstances, it may not be the best choice. Some of the other most popular server-side technologies currently bidding for space on your web server are:

- Active Server Pages (ASP)

- ColdFusion (CFM)

- Java Server Pages (JSP)

- Perl (CGI)

Let's take a quick look at the relative pros and cons of each, and round the section off with a summary of PHP for good measure.

Active Server Pages (ASP)

Microsoft developed ASP in the late 1990s. ASP works in a similar fashion to PHP in that each page contains a mixture of HTML and script elements. These script elements can be written in JScript (the Microsoft implementation of JavaScript), JavaScript, or VBScript.

ASP relies on the Component Object Model (COM), a set of standards laid out by Microsoft for the interfacing of system components. ASP works by creating instances of these server-side components and interacting with them through the COM interface.

Apart from its inbuilt compatibility with other COM-based applications, the main advantage of ASP is its ease of use. A developer with just a little experience of VBScript or JavaScript can jump straight in and create a powerful, data-driven site within just a day or two.

The most obvious drawback of ASP is that it will only run on a Microsoft web server running on a Microsoft operating system. It's possible to replicate a lot of its functionality on a Unix-based web server (using Chill!Soft for example), but no other mainstream operating systems support or adhere to Microsoft's COM standard. Since this is the system that underpins the whole functionality of ASP, non-Windows systems have an immediate handicap. Another disadvantage is that certain overheads involved with communication between COM components can lead to slower operation compared to other server-side scripting languages.

ColdFusion (CFM)

ColdFusion was originally developed by Allaire as an alternative to the server-side scripting technologies that were available. ColdFusion differs from almost all other server-side languages in that it's tag based, meaning that it looks a lot like existing HTML and XML documents. The actual language used is called ColdFusion Markup Language (CFML), and its documents (referred to as **templates**) have a .cfm extension.

The main problem with ColdFusion is one of cost: licenses for the ColdFusion Server application are not cheap (upwards of $999 at the time of writing). However, you can find many third party hosting companies that will offer ColdFusion Server as part of their packages.

Earlier this year, Macromedia and Allaire completed their long-anticipated merger, so you can expect to hear a lot more about ColdFusion in the future. It is already rumored to be the technology behind the next generation of Generator-type applications from Macromedia, so it looks like we could all be getting fairly cozy with ColdFusion sometime soon.

Java Server Pages (JSP)

Sun Microsystems developed JSP as an alternative technology to ASP, providing a way to embed components in the script and to have them do their work to generate the resulting page that is sent of the web browser. JSP pages can contain HTML, Java code and JavaBeans (Java components).

Its main advantage is similar to that of ASP, in that it lets you integrate your dynamic web pages with existing Java-based business systems. Its main disadvantage is that the active code is written in Java. You'll hear many novice developers expressing the opinion that Java is a difficult language to grasp; however, you may well find that the extra effort pays off in the long term, as it opens up the doors to a rich programming environment.

Perl (CGI)

Perl is another open source language, and is well known as the granddaddy of all server-side web scripting languages. It has been used for many years to implement what is known as a Common Gateway Interface (CGI). CGI is probably the most widely supported technology on the web, and, scripts written in Perl can run on virtually any web server/operating system combination you care to throw at it.

The big drawback of CGI scripts is that they are very resource-intensive. Every time a script is invoked, a new process is created on the server – effectively a new program being run, complete with memory allocations and so on. It's not hard to imagine what happens to a server when a large number of CGI requests are received simultaneously... everything grinds to a halt!

PHP

The main advantage of PHP is that it's an open source project. This means that, like Perl, it is available for almost every web server/operating system combination. PHP doesn't suffer from the performance disadvantages of Perl, making it ideal for all types of web sites. The large community of developers using and improving PHP ensures its continuing success as one of the most popular and efficient server-side scripting technologies in existence.

PHP Basics

This is going to be a quick crash course in PHP, so it will just be a taster of what you can do with the language, and will hopefully give you a few ideas of your own. If you want to find out more about PHP, you might like to check out some of the other books in the friends of ED bookcase that devote themselves purely to the subject of Flash and PHP.

PHP files are essentially just ASCII (or **plain text**) files, just like HTML documents; so first of all, you will need a text editor that can save text files. It doesn't need to be anything fancy, and I would personally recommend using HomeSite, BBEdit, Notepad, or one of the other free text editors available.

You will also require access to a PHP-enabled web server. If you have your own server, then simply download the relevant files from www.php.net and check out the PHP installation appendix at the back of the book. Otherwise, you should find out from the relevant owner/administrator/technical support staff whether the server you'd like to use already supports PHP, and if not, perhaps you can even persuade them to install it for you!

Let's take a look at a simple PHP script:

```
<?
  print ("Hello World!");
?>
```

Type the above into a blank text document, save the file as hello_world.php and upload it to your web server. To see it in action, you now just need to open your browser and call up an address like http://www.somewhere.com/path/to/hello_world.php (replacing www.somewhere.com with the address of your own site, and path/to/ with the folder into which you uploaded the file). The following should now appear in your browser:

Ok, so now for a quick run-down of the structure of this simple script:

■ The first and last lines contain matching <? and ?> tags. These tell the PHP processor that everything in between should be interpreted as PHP code, and processed by the PHP engine rather than just sent to the browser and interpreted there. You can put any number of these tag pairs into a page, and intersperse them with HTML, XML or Flash variables code. However, in this example, and all of the others in this chapter, we shall only be using one piece of PHP per document, so you don't need to worry about this.

■ Within these tags we have a single line, which looks much the same as a function call in ActionScript. As you'd expect, the command print simply outputs its argument to the browser — in this case, the string *Hello World!* The results of all PHP print statements are sent to the browser consecutively, so multiple print statements will still only generate one page of output. For instance:

```
<?
for( $myCounter = 0; $myCounter < 10; $myCounter++ ) {
  print ( "Hello World!<br>" );
}
?>
```

I'm sure you will be familiar with the structure of a simple `for` loop such as this, and all this does is print out ten lines of `Hello World!` with a `<br>` tag in-between each line. The reason we have to use a `<br>` tag rather than a carriage return is that the browser interprets our output as HTML, so we must format our output using HTML tags. This has implications when we use PHP to output text to Flash, which can interpret both methods, depending upon whether a text field is set to accept HTML or not.

PHP uses variables in a similar way to Flash, in that PHP is a non-typed language – in other words, any variable can contain any type of data. Unlike many other languages, you don't have to declare a variable as being of a specific type (string, integer, floating-point number, and so on), so any PHP variable can hold any type of data – we say it's **loosely typed**.

> Being loosely typed is both a good and a bad thing. It helps you write code much faster, and more flexibly: you don't need to figure out in advance what variables should be what type; you're also free to make changes as you go along. Perhaps you want to specify an important parameter with greater accuracy than you'd originally intended (adding decimal points and the like) – no problem, just change the numbers and the variable will cope. However, this freedom also means you need to be careful and consistent with your use of variables: loosely typed variables can cause tremendous headaches and logic errors, especially when it comes to debugging your code.

We distinguish a variable name by use of the dollar symbol $. In the last example, we set a variable $myCounter to 0, and then looped round, incrementing it each time. As you can see, the structure of the language is remarkably similar to ActionScript at this level.

Just like ActionScript, we can define functions with multiple parameters, which can return certain values:

```
<?
function replicate($myText, $numTimes) {
  $tempString = "";
  for( $myCounter = 0; $myCounter < $numTimes; $myCounter ++) {
    $tempString .= $myText."<br>";
  }
  return($tempString);
}

$myString = replicate("Hello World!", 10);
  print ( $myString );
?>
```

In this example, I have created a simple function that accepts a string and an integer as arguments, and returns the string replicated that number of times with a `<br>` tag after each item.

As with ActionScript, we define functions using the `function` keyword, specify arguments in parentheses, and use the `return` keyword to return a result. We can use the function later on by calling it by name and with the correct arguments.

You will notice that there are a number of areas in which the syntax for PHP differs from ActionScript, and there is an example of this here. When we wish to concatenate two strings together in ActionScript, we use the + operator, whereas in PHP we use the . (dot) operator. You can see two examples of this in the code above – the `.=` operator is used to successively append a new string to an existing string, and the `.` operator is used to append `<br>` to each successive line.

This particular distinction is one that reflects a fundamental difference between the two languages: ActionScript is inherently object-based, and uses dot notation to reference different objects, properties and functions. In contrast, PHP does not have any kind of object-oriented structure built into it.

To fully understand what happens when a PHP script is executed have a look at the source of the page as the browser sees it. You'll notice that all of the PHP code has disappeared, leaving just the text that we put in the call to the `print` function.

Now that we've got a handle on the basics, let's start looking at how we can put this to use.

Loading External Data

The simplest way to make a Flash movie interact with a PHP script is to use the ActionScript functions `loadVariables` and `loadVariablesNum` to send movie data to the PHP script. If we design this script to send associated data back to the movie, we can start down the road to creating some truly dynamic Flash applications.

The syntax of the `loadVariables` command is as follows:

```
loadVariables(url, target [, variables])
```

where:

- `url` is a URL (either absolute or relative) where the variables are located

- `target` is a level or movie clip to receive the variables

- `variables` is an optional argument specifying a method for sending variables

When the `loadVariables` command is called, the Flash plug-in fetches the file identified by `url` and the variables are loaded into our Flash movie. In order for this to succeed, the variables and their values must be specified within the file in the following format:

```
&var1name=value&var2name=value&var3name=value...
```

For each of these name and value pairs, a variable is created on the timeline specified by target. These variables can then be used in the Flash movie in the same way as we would use a normal variable created using ActionScript. An example would be displaying these variables in a textbox.

Tic Tac Toe in Flash

Now that we know more than we ever wanted to know about setting up non-realtime connections in Flash, it's time to put all that knowledge to the test. To do this, we're going to build a multiuser Tic Tac Toe game. To whet your appetite, take a look at the screenshot of the finished product.

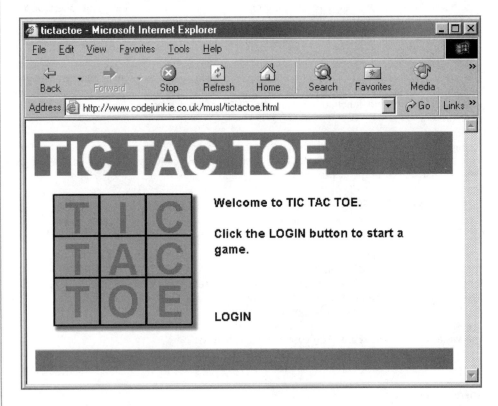

By the end of the chapter you should be in a position to develop your own non-realtime multiuser applications or to extend the example given.

Tic Tac Toe Know-How...

If you're not familiar with the game of Tic Tac Toe then this next bit is for you – you can't design a game without knowing how to play it. If you're a veritable Tic Tac Toe grand master, then you might want to give your eyes a rest and skip this section.

Tic Tac Toe, also known as 'noughts and crosses', is a simple two-player strategy game and is played on a 3x3 grid. Each player is assigned a token (o or x) and takes it in turns playing their token in an empty cell.

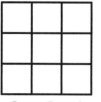

Game Board

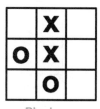

Playing...

In order to win the game, a player must have three of their tokens in a straight line. The line can be a vertical, horizontal or diagonal one, as illustrated below...

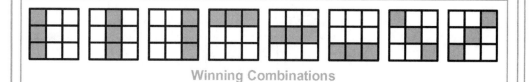

Winning Combinations

In addition to trying to create a winning line of their own, each player must try and block the attempts of his or her opponent to do the same. If all the cells are occupied with tokens but no player has a winning combination then the game is declared a draw.

A master plan

Before we actually roll up our sleeves and get our hands dirty, let's take a step back and look at what we're trying to accomplish. Designing an application before you start to build it is generally a good idea – it'll prevent many a headache!

The basic steps we'll need to go through in the game are:

1. Wait for the user to log in to server.
2. Read the game data from server.
3. If we already have 2 players, inform the user that the game is full and return to Stage 1.
4. If we are the first player then we need to wait for another player to join the game.
5. Wait for the current player to make their move.
6. Change the current player.
7. Check to see if game is over (i.e. won, drawn or quit). If so, return to Stage 1
8. Otherwise, return to Stage 5.

We can visualize these steps using the flowchart shown below.

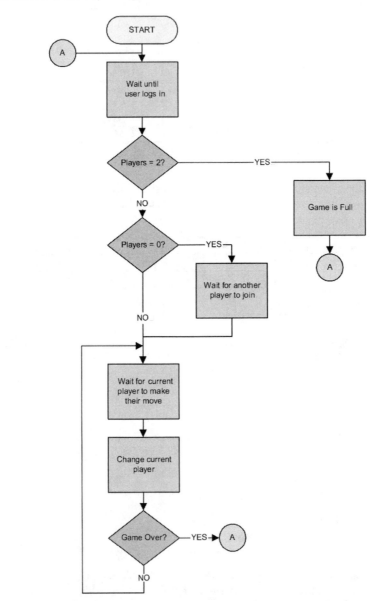

This may seem an elaborate way of doing things, but it is necessary to keep the data we're using up to date. It's important that each client checks the server for updated information and updates the board appropriately or they won't be able to see which squares are free for them to place a counter on.

Building a board for the game

The first thing we need to do is to set out the frame and layer structure for the movie.

1. Create a new movie, and add the layers and frame labels shown in the screenshot. Don't worry about the rest, we'll be adding that as we go along, but make sure you get the four frame labels (Start, Login, Waiting, Play Game) in the right order.

We'll now work through each of the sections of the movie (as denoted by the frame labels) in turn.

2. The Background layer is common to all of the sections, and in my movie I've provided a simple design – it's worth spending a little time giving your application some character by getting creative here.

3. Next up is the Board MC layer. As the name may suggest, this layer will hold the main game board. Since we're after the ultimate in usability, we want to let the player place their token on a cell by simply clicking on that cell. For this we'll need some buttons, so create a simple button as an outlined square like the one pictured overleaf.

Symbol Properties

Name: Cell Button

Behavior:
- ○ Movie Clip
- ● Button
- ○ Graphic

OK
Cancel
Help

4. Now create another eight instances of the button, and use the Align tools to make sure that they are evenly spaced.

Align

In Tr St Fi Align

Align:

Distribute:

Match Size: Space:

To Stage:

5. Select all the buttons and hit F8 to convert them into a movie clip, and give it the name Board:

Symbol Properties

Name: Board

Behavior:
- ● Movie Clip
- ○ Button
- ○ Graphic

OK
Cancel
Help

6. We now we need to go in and make some important modifications to our Board movie clip, so double-click on our instance on the main stage.

7. You can see from the screenshot that I've added a layer above and below the original layer (which I've named Buttons). The bottom layer, Shadow, contains a simple drop-shadow effect for the board. You can leave this out if you like, but I think it looks pretty cool!

8. Before we take a look at the Textboxes layer, we need to add some ActionScript to our buttons to make them do what we want.

As you can see, the code is pretty simple – it's just a call to a function on the _root of our movie, which is where all the clever stuff will be done. You'll need to change the number passed to the clickCell function for each button, working left to right, top to bottom.

The numbers shown in the next couple of screenshots are just to illustrate how you should name your textboxes and shouldn't actually be present in the movie clip!

9. Once that's done, we can move on to the Textboxes layer. As the name suggests, we're going to have some a dynamic textbox for each cell of the game board in this layer, and use them to display the player tokens once they've been placed.

Place nine dynamic text boxes on the screen, one over each number. Name each one slightly differently, staring with `cell1` in the top left hand corner and going left to right, top to bottom just as we did with the button code. Make sure that each textbox is wide enough to display the X and O characters that we'll be using.

10. When creating the textboxes, ensure that the Selectable checkbox is cleared – aside from causing problems with the underlying buttons, there's no reason why the player should need to select any of the text.

11. With all that sorted, it just remains for us to go back to the main movie and give the instance of the Board movie clip an instance name of `Board`, so we can reference it with our ActionScript.

We also need to attach some ActionScript to the instance of Board. This is necessary because we'll be using the loadVariables command to read game data from the server, as well as sending game data back to the server. In order to ensure that the server has responded to our request we'll stop the main movie whenever we make a call to loadVariables to which we need to know that the server had responded. We'll then use an onClipEvent handler to get it all going again.

12. Add the following code to our instance of Board:

```
onClipEvent(data) {
    if (_root.gameEnd == false) {
        _root.play();
    }
}
```

What we're doing here is checking to see if a game is being played. If it is then we start the movie playing again when a response to a loadVariables call is received.

Having done all that, it's time for us to start making the game work. We'll begin by focusing on the four parts of gameplay individually, and see what Actions we need to define specifically for each one. Since the beginning is always a good place to start we'll kick off with the **Start** section.

Starting the game

1. Begin by adding some a `stop` action to the Actions layer to halt the movie on the start frame once it's loaded so that it doesn't go merrily off on its own.

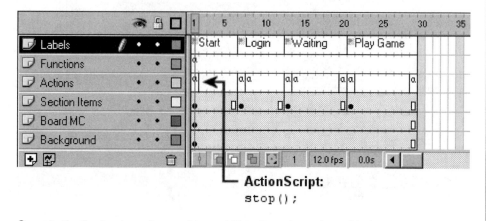

ActionScript:
```
stop();
```

2. In the Section Items layer, add a multiline dynamic textbox with the name status.

Welcome to TIC TAC TOE.

Click the LOGIN button to start a game.

LOGIN

Text Options

Dynamic Text
Multiline
Variable:
status
☐ HTML
☐ Border/Bg
☑ Word wrap
☐ Selectable
Embed fonts:

3. Add a button to enable the user to attempt to create or join the game, and attach the following simple ActionScript:

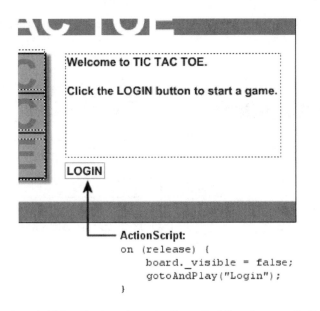

ActionScript:

```
on (release) {
    board._visible = false;
    gotoAndPlay("Login");
}
```

All we're doing here is hiding the board movie clip so that the player can't alter it while the movie is going through the motions, and then forwarding the user to the Login section, which we'll look at now.

Logging in

1. Starting with the Section Items layer, copy the status text box from the previous section so that we can keep the player informed as to what is happening, as shown.

2. For the Actions layer, we need to add the following ActionScript to the frame immediately under the Login label. This will get the current state of the game from the server.

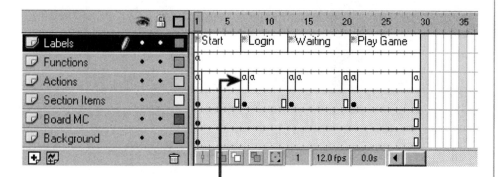

```
// Set status text
status = "Connecting to server, please wait";

// We're starting a new game
gameEnd = false;

// Request game data from server
board.loadVariables("variables.txt?" add
➥int(Math.random() * 1000000));

// Halt until loaded
stop();
```

This code updates our status text so that the user knows what's going on. It also updates our gameEnd variable to false, so that any response to a loadVariables call will get the movie playing again, and loads the game data from the server. We then halt the movie to wait for the server response.

There are a couple of things to notice about the loadVariables call. Firstly, we've actually called loadVariables with reference to our board movie clip instance. This is so that any data returned from the call will be loaded into that particular movie clip. Secondly, you'll see that we're adding a random number onto the end of the name of our data file. We do this so that the web browser does not feed us a cached version of the file, and we can be sure our data is up-to-date

Since the movie was halted at the end of the previous frame, we can safely assume that by the time we come to the next frame the game data has been loaded from the server.

3. We need to add rather a lot of code to the next frame in the Actions layer. Here's the first section:

```
// If no players are playing...
if (board.noPlayers == 0 || board.noPlayers == null) {
// Player takes the "O" token, and has the first go
thisPlayer = "O";
board.nextMove = "O";
```

If the number of players currently playing is zero (or null), then we must be the first player in the game. We set our token to O and given ourselves the first go, and also set up some other important variables that will be stored on the server.

```
// Set number of players
board.noPlayers = 1;

// This variable will be set to 1 if the game is quit
board.gameQuit = 0;
```

We clear the board (using a function that we haven't written yet) and then call loadVariables to store the game state on the server.

```
// Set all of the cells to be blank
clearBoard();

// Store the current game state
board.loadVariables("write_variables.php", "POST");
```

Finally we go to the Waiting section to wait for another player to join the game.

```
// Now we have to wait for the other player to join
gotoAndPlay("Waiting");
```

You'll see that the file we're calling with loadVariables is actually a PHP script. We'll create this script later to write the game data to our variables.txt file.

4. Still in the same script, moving on to the next section:

```
} else if (board.noPlayers == 1) {

  // If a player is waiting, player takes "X" token
  thisPlayer = "X";

  // Set number of players
  board.noPlayers = 2;

  // Store the current game state
  board.loadVariables("write_variables.php", "POST");

  // Let's play!
  gotoAndPlay("Play Game");
```

If there's already a player waiting to play a game, we assign ourselves the X token and tell the server that we now have a full compliment of players for the game. We then go to the Play Game section to commence battle!

5. Finally, add:

```
} else {

  // Otherwise, we have 2 players playing already
  status = "Sorry, the game is full";
  gotoAndStop("Start");
}
```

If the number of players is not equal to 0, and not equal to 1, then we must already have 2 players in the game. In this case we inform the user that the game is currently full and send them back to the beginning of the movie.

While we're waiting...

It's time to tackle the Waiting section. This is where the player will be sent if they are the only player logged in. We'll hold them here and constantly check the game data to see if another player has joined the game.

1. Before we deal with all that, we need to handle the bits and bobs on the Section Items layer. Basically, we have our trusty old status textbox and a shiny new ABORT button that the player can use if they no longer want to wait for another player, as shown.

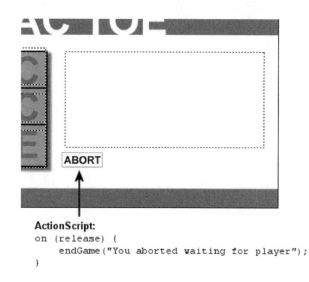

ActionScript:
```
on (release) {
    endGame("You aborted waiting for player");
}
```

2. Add the ActionScript you see to your ABORT button. This snippet of ActionScript calls the endGame() function (which we'll create on the Functions layer shortly) to set the status text, perform a few cleanup tasks and then drop the user back in the Start section.

3. Our code for the first frame of the Waiting section is pretty similar to its equivalent in the Login section:

```
// Set status text
status = "Waiting for another player to join...";

// Request game data from server
board.loadVariables("variables.txt?" add int(Math.random() *
➡1000000));

// Halt until loaded
stop();
```

All we do here is set some status text, load the game data from the server and halt the movie until a response is received.

4. On the following frame we see if we've got enough players to start a game yet. If so, we go to the **Play Game** section. Add the following code to do this:

```
// If we've got enough players to start game...
if (board.noPlayers == 2) {

    // ...let's play!
    gotoAndPlay("Play Game");
}
```

5. We now leave a 5-frame gap so that we're not hammering the server with requests for the game data. At the end of the gap we loop the movie back to the Waiting frame for another request:

```
// Carry on waiting
gotoAndPlay("Waiting");
```

Play the game

Now, onto our final section: Play Game. This is where the game will be played, so there's a fair amount of game logic referenced here, though most of it is contained in various functions on the Functions layer.

1. The Section Items layer is an exact duplicate of that in the Waiting section, except that the ABORT button now sets a variable that will be stored on the server (in order to tell the other player that we've quit) and passes a different message to our endGame function. Add this code to the button:

ActionScript:
```
on (release) {
    board.gameQuit = 1;
    endGame("You have quit the game");
}
```

2. The ActionScript on the first frame of this section sets the _visible property of the board movie clip to true so that we can see it and sets the status text according to whose turn it is next:

```
// Show game board
board._visible = true;

// Set status text accoring to next player
if (board.nextMove == thisplayer) {

  status = "Make your move...";
} else {

  status = "Opponent's move...";
}
```

Once again, we have a frame gap (7 frames this time) so that we're not hammering the server with game data requests. On the final frame of this section we have some code to calculate what to do next depending on the state of the game.

3. As before, we'll take this in logical chunks. We begin by calling the function checkGameWon to find out if anyone has won the game yet. If they have, we call the now infamous endGame function to clean up the game, passing it a message to tell us who won the game.

```
// Check to see if the game has been won.
winningToken = checkGameWon();

// If it has...
if (winningToken != false) {

    // End the game with winning message
    endGame(winningToken add " wins the game!");
```

4. If the game hasn't been won, we need to establish whether the game is a draw. If so, we call the endGame function with an appropriate message:

```
} else if (checkGameDraw() == true) {

    // If the game is a draw, end game.
    endGame("The game was a draw!");
```

5. If the game is neither a win nor a draw, we need to find out whether the other player
    has quit. If this is the case, we end the game with a suitable message:

    ```
    } else if (board.gameQuit == 1) {

        // If the other player has quit, end game.
        endGame("The other player has quit the game!");
    ```

6. Finally, if the game is has not been won, drawn or quit, then we need to carry on
    playing. If it's not our turn to make a move then we're waiting on the opposing player
    to make their move. In this case we need to fetch the latest game data from the server.
    We then loop the movie back to the Play Game frame and start all over again.

    ```
    } else {
        // Otherwise, if it's not our turn...
        if (board.nextMove != thisPlayer) {
            // Request game data from server
            board.loadVariables("variables.txt?" add
                                    ➤ int(Math.random() * 1000000));
        }

        // Carry on playing
        gotoAndPlay("Play Game");
    }
    ```

Defining our functionality

With construction of the movie now 99% complete, we just need to define all the functions that
we keep seeing about the place and we're finished. These all belong on the first frame of the
Functions layer.

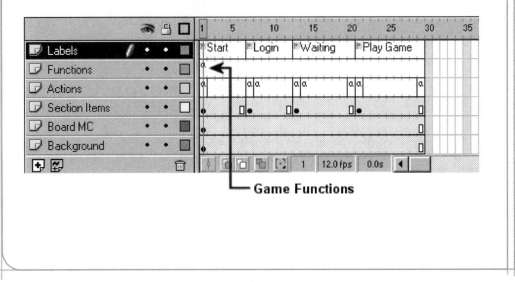

— Game Functions

1. The first function we need to create is called `clickCell`; this is the function we call from the buttons in the Board movie clip. This function will make sure that it's our turn to have a go, that the chosen cell is not already occupied, and then register the move with the server:

```
function clickCell(cellNumber) {
    // If it's our turn to move...
    if (board.nextMove == thisPlayer) {

        // ...and if the cell is empty...
        if (board["cell" add cellNumber] == "") {

            // ...put player's mark in cell
            board["cell" add cellNumber] = thisPlayer;

            // Change active player
            if (thisPlayer == "O") {
                board.nextMove = "X";
            } else {
                board.nextMove = "O";
            }

            // Store new information on server
            board.loadVariables("write_variables.php", "POST");

            // Set status
            status = "Waiting for server response...";

            // Halt the movie
            stop();
        } else {

            // If cell already occupied, inform user
            status = "You must choose an empty cell";
        }
    } else {

        // If it's not out turn, inform user
        status = "It's not your go";
    }
}
```

2. The `clearBoard` function uses a simple `for` loop to clear all of the textboxes in the board movie clip instance. It's used to reset the board at the start of a new game:

```
function clearBoard() {

    // Loop through each cell on the board
    for (count = 1; count <= 9; count++) {
```

```
        // Clear cell
        board["cell" add count] = "";
    }
}
```

3. endGame is a function that we've met several times already, and it's used to clean up the game data ready for the next game, and set the status text so that the user knows what's going on:

```
function endGame(statusText) {
    // Set status text to inform user why game has ended
    status = statusText add "\n\nGame Over!";

    // Set flag variable so we know game has ended
    gameEnd = true;

    // Reset number of players in the data file on server
    board.noPlayers = 0;
    board.loadVariables("write_variables.php", "post");

    // Go back to the start to wait for next game
    gotoAndStop("Start");
}
```

4. checkGameWon is used to determine whether any one player has 3 of their tokens in a straight line, and is called from the final frame of the Play Game section. On discovering that one of the players has a winning line, it returns that player's token. Here's the first part of the function:

```
function checkGameWon() {
    // Check for horizontal line...
    for (count = 1; count <= 9; count += 3) {
if ((board["cell" add count] == board["cell" add (count + 1)]) &&
➥ (board["cell" add (count + 1)] == board["cell" add (count +
2)])) {
            if (board["cell" add count] != "") {
                return board["cell" add count];
            }
        }
    }
```

5. As you can see, we have a nested pair of for loops that we're using to check for a horizontal line of tokens. We now perform the same check for vertical lines:

```
    // Check for vertical line...
    for (count = 1; count <= 3; count++) {
        if ((board["cell" add count] == board["cell" add (count +
3)]) && ➥
            (board["cell" add (count + 3)] == board["cell" add
(count + 6)])) {
```

continues overleaf

```
        if (board["cell" add count] != "") {
            return board["cell" add count];
        }
    }
}
```

6. This section checks for lines along each of the diagonals:

```
// Check for diagonal line...
if ((board.cell1 == board.cell5) &&
➡(board.cell5 == board.cell9)) {
    if (board.cell1 != "") {
        return board.cell1;
    }
}
if ((board.cell3 == board.cell5) &&
➡(board.cell5 == board.cell7)) {
    if (board.cell3 != "") {
        return board.cell3;
    }
}
```

7. Finally, if no winning lines are found then we return `false`:

```
// If no winning line found, return false
return false;
}
```

8. `checkGameDraw` will check to see if the game has been drawn. For our purposes, we'll assume that a game has been drawn if all of the cells on the game board are occupied by a token:

```
function checkGameDraw() {
    // Assume that game is a draw
    gameDraw = true;

    // Then, loop through each cell of the board
    for (count = 1; count <= 9; count++) {

        // If the current cell is blank...
        if (board["cell" add count] == "") {

            // ...the game can't be a draw
            gameDraw = false;
        }
    }
    // Return findings
    return gameDraw;
}
```

We can safely assume that a full board represents a draw because this function is only called once we've established that the game has not been won. The drawback to this is that we won't spot an unwinnable game until the board is full. However obvious it may be, the players will need to keep playing to the bitter end in order to declare the game a draw. As it doesn't take too long to finish a game of Tic-Tac-Toe, this is a fairly minor problem for our users to contend with.

The PHP magic

With all our client-side Flash business out of the way, we now just need to create the PHP script that will update our variables.txt file with the data passed to it.

The PHP part of the game effectively acts as a go-between for the two players. When a user makes a move, the updated game data is sent to this script. It then writes these variables into the text file and exits. When the user requests the current board state, it's just a matter of loading in the variables from the text file that has been written by the PHP script – simple!

Here's the complete listing for our script. Add it to a blank text file, and save it to your working directory as write_variables.php:

```php
<?
   // Add all posted fields to text file in Flash variables format
        $filename = "variables.txt";

   // Go through all  posted variables and add them to a string
   $queryString = "";

   foreach($HTTP_POST_VARS as $key => $value) {
       $queryString .= "&" . $key . "=" . $value;
   }

   // Open the file for writing
   $variableFile = fopen ($filename, "w");

   // Write the variable data to the file
   fwrite($variableFile, $queryString);

   // Close the file
   fclose ($variableFile);
?>
```

We're using much more complicated PHP code in this function than we've met previously, some of which may not look familiar to you. Let's take it from the top.

We start by specifying the name the file that we're going to write to:

```php
        $filename = "variables.txt";
```

When we send the current state of the board to this script, we use the POST method (which allows us to send a lot more data than its GET counterpart). We also only send the variables contained within the board object, so that we can keep the file small and simple. $HTTP_POST_VARS is a global array used by PHP to hold all the variables posted to the script. This is where the data received from Flash are stored, so we extract the name and the value of each:

```
$queryString = "";

foreach($HTTP_POST_VAR as $key => $value) {
    $queryString .= "&" . $key . "=" . $value;
}
```

The foreach loop here runs through each of the variables that were sent to the server, and appends them to $queryString in a URL-encoded format.

The final three lines handle writing the data into a file:

```
// Open the file for writing
$variableFile = fopen ($filename, "w");

// Write the variable data to the file
fwrite($variableFile, $queryString);

// Close the file
fclose ($variableFile);
```

First, we use the fopen command, which accepts two arguments: a path to the file we want to open (in this case variables.txt, which is in the same directory as our script resides); and a method (which in this case tells the function to open the file in "write" mode. The fopen command returns an identifier for the file that we have just opened, so that if we have multiple files open, we can be sure that we're writing into the correct file.

We use the fwrite command to write data into the specified file. In this case we specify the PHP variable $queryString, which we've used to hold our Flash-formatted variables.

Once we've finished using a file, it is a good idea to use the fclose command so that other users can have access to it. Only one user can write into a file at a time, so keeping a file open for too long can slow down multiuser applications.

Testing

In order to run the game, I would advise setting up a couple of computers, using two browsers on your machine, or maybe phoning a friend and asking them to try the game out with you.

You will need to upload a copy of the published SWF, the PHP file, and the `variables.txt` file to your web server, and ensure that they are all in the same directory. You then need to make sure that the permissions are set correctly so that PHP is allowed to write the `variables.txt` file. You can do this using your FTP client, and changing the permissions to "777" if you are using Linux. (This has a number of security implications, since it allows anyone to write or alter files in this area of the site, so you may want to speak to your server administrator for advice.)

Once you have uploaded the files, simply type the appropriate web address into your browser, and start playing. You may get problems if you use the back and forward or reload buttons in your browser for obvious reasons, so I'd advise against this! Also, avoid closing browsers without logging off first. If this happens, and the game thinks it's full constantly, the easiest thing to do is delete all the information from your `variables.txt` file.

Wrapping things up

You now have a solid understanding of the server-side scripting approach to interacting with a web server using Flash, and you should be able to see how your own multiuser projects can take advantage of server-side technologies.

We're going to continue into the more glamorous world of realtime Flash multiuser applications in the next few chapters, starting with a comprehensive introduction to XML and how we can use this in the next chapter. Don't forget non-realtime approaches though – it is a valuable part of your design skills, whether as part of an overall plan that includes both realtime and non-realtime approaches for different parts of a site, or just for the sake of simplicity.

Chapter 3

Introduction
to XML

Chances are, you've already heard of XML. You may even have dabbled with it, in which case this chapter will largely serve as a refresher for what you know already. Either way, there's no escaping its gradual advance on just about every aspect of application design – it's getting into everything, and Flash is no exception! That being the case, there's still a great deal of confusion as to what it's actually good for: a lot of people will describe it as a powerful, flexible 'data storage format', which rather makes you wonder what databases are good for. No, it's not really designed for efficient storage of data. However, it's very good for **transporting structured data** from one place to another, and that's what we're interested in.

Let's start by considering a cheeseburger. When you see the word 'cheeseburger', what do you picture in your head? It's probably some sort of unhealthy fast-food item wrapped in tinfoil that you picked up last week at the drive-through. Most people know what a "cheeseburger" is, as that word has a pretty universal meaning. But, what if we had to describe a cheeseburger without using the word 'cheeseburger'? We could describe it by listing out the parts that make it up, like so:

"Cheese, meat-like patty, a sesame-seed bun, lettuce, ketchup, and a pickle."

But imagine you were on the phone to a person who has never heard of cheeseburgers, and had to tell them how to assemble one? You could just list the ingredients, but who knows what they'd get on the other end? They may end up with some weird 'cheeseburger a la mode', with the cheese, meat, and condiments all stacked up on top of a whole bun. Good luck picking that up!

That list says nothing about how those items should be arranged, or what they have to do with one another. The person on the other end may even think that a cheeseburger is simply all of those items arranged neatly on a platter. Clearly, what we'd have to do is describe to them the relationships between these items, like this:

"Meat, cheese, lettuce, ketchup, and a pickle all nestled inside a sliced sesame-seed bun."

Here, we clearly demarcate the bun as a container for all of the other items. Likewise, all of the other items are contained within the bun. What does all this have to do with XML, you may ask? Well, quite a lot as it happens.

What exactly is XML?

XML stands for eXtensible Markup Language, and is designed to give you a simple way to bundle up data so that each element not only describes itself, but also its relationship to other elements. It was designed by the World Wide Web Consortium as a flexible markup language whose rules can be easily extended or even redefined for a whole range of purposes. As the W3C put it, XML is "a common syntax for expressing structure in data".

In case you're still mystified, let's quickly clarify what we mean by a **markup language**. Markup is a term that's been used in the print industry for centuries, and refers to the symbols added to source text that indicate how it should be presented on the printed page. Over the last decade, the growth of the Web has put markup on everyone's radar, relying as it does on the HyperText Markup Language, known to us all as HTML. Of course, this is one very familiar example of a *non-extensible* markup language: it features a small, well-defined collection of symbols (referred to as **tags**), most of which deal specifically with text formatting of one kind or another.

These markup tags are common to both HTML and XML, and can take three forms: opening tags (`<tag>`) mark where you want formatting to start, and closing tags (`</tag>`) mark where it should end. This enclosing pair of matched tags constitutes an **element**, and the block of content between them forms the **contents** of that element. The third type of tag (`<tag/>`) is used when there isn't any content to put between the opening and closing tags – a line break `<br/>` for example – and is therefore referred to as an **empty element**.

HTML is a language that defines a specific set of tags and a particular purpose for each. With tag names like `<b>` for bold, `<i>` for italic, and `<p>` for paragraph, it's fairly obvious that it's primarily designed to help us apply formatting to passages of text. By contrast, XML is a **meta-language**, which is really just a fancy way of saying 'a language for creating languages'. Let's look at a very simple example of an XML document, which might be useful for sending data around inside a shoot 'em up game:

```
<player1>
  <message>Hello world</message>
  <fire_gun />
</player1>
```

As you can see, the element called `player 1` contains elements called `message` and `fire_gun`. The `message` element itself contains the text data "Hello world" while `fire_gun` is an empty element with no contents at all. We could send this XML to everyone playing the game, and the meaning would be clear: player one has sent out the message "Hello world" and fired off his gun.

If we make the analogy to a real spoken and written language, XML provides us with rules of grammar and syntax, but leaves us to define our own vocabulary. Each word in the language corresponds to a particular element, which we can use as a container for data or for other elements. If we invent a new type of element, we can simply add it to our list of possible elements, thereby extending our vocabulary (hence the word **extensible**).

What's more, we can apply our custom markup systems to just about any task we can think of. With XML, we can define our own vocabulary of elements for dealing with a particular subject or field, and apply that vocabulary with a strict format defined by the rules of XML formatting. This vocabulary that we develop is all declared and described in a **Document Type Definition**, or **DTD**. This is a file that lists the entire vocabulary of elements and attributes that we wish to use in our XML document, and specifies how they are related and how they should be used.

Any XML-based markup system that is developed for a specific use can be referred to as an **XML application**. An enormous number of XML applications have already been defined, and are in use today in a multitude of venues and on a variety of scales. There have been applications written to describe music (MusicML), chemical and molecular structures (CML), vector graphics (SVG), sports data, and statistics (SportsML).

Putting XML to good use

Hopefully, you can now start to see why XML can be useful. Just in case you're still a little skeptical, let's use our fast food example to demonstrate one of the many ways XML can be put to use. Let's pretend for a moment that XML never existed, and that we had to describe our cheeseburger to another computer somewhere out on the Internet. We'd probably send the data in the form of name/value pairs, like this:

```
cheeseburgeritem1="cheese"
cheeseburgeritem2="meat_patty"
cheeseburgeritem3="lettuce"
cheeseburgeritem4="ketchup"
cheeseburgeritem5="pickle"
```

Well, that's each of the ingredients covered, but we don't know how they relate to one another. We certainly know each of the ingredients belongs to the cheeseburger, because each variable name starts with the string "cheeseburger". But, we still have the same problem that we did before, and our computer is bound to make a mistake building our perfect burger. So, how do we tell the computer that the bun is the container for all of the other items? We could do something like this:

```
cheeseburgeritem1="bun"
cheeseburgeritem1subitem1="cheese"
cheeseburgeritem1subitem2="meat_patty"
cheeseburgeritem1subitem3="lettuce"
cheeseburgeritem1subitem3="ketchup"
cheeseburgeritem1subitem4="pickle"
```

The client application would have to be smart enough to take substrings of the variable names, and figure out that all of the variables that began with the string "cheeseburgeritem1" actually belong inside that item. As you can see, this is already getting rather cumbersome. What if we wanted to go another level deep, and describe all of the miscellaneous ingredients that go into that mysterious meat patty? Heaven forbid!

Let's look at our cheeseburger again, this time described in terms of XML:

```
<cheeseburger>
  <bun>
    <cheese />
    <meat_patty />
    <romaine_lettuce />
    <ketchup />
    <pickle />
  </bun>
</cheeseburger>
```

As you can see in the XML snippet above, everything is enclosed within the `<cheeseburger>` tags. So, we know that all of the XML within those tags belongs to the `<cheeseburger>` element. Inside that is the `<bun>` tag, which encloses all the elements that go inside the bun. So, by using this syntax, we have successfully defined the relationships between the parts of the cheeseburger.

XML Attributes

One crucial aspect of XML that we've not touched on yet concerns the use of element **attributes**. These let us assign properties to particular elements, and therefore make them a great deal more versatile. We can specify an attribute within an opening tag (or an empty element) with the following syntax:

```
<tagname attribute="value">
```

What use is this? Well, let's consider our original example once again – let's say, for instance, that we'd like to add some mustard to our cheeseburger. The tags we've defined so far don't allow for mustard, and although there's nothing to stop us adding a `<mustard>` tag, let's stop for a moment and think ahead. What about other condiments that we may want to accommodate in the future? Barbeque sauce? Salsa? Mayo? Peanut butter? Given that we're unlikely to ever formulate a definitive list, we're at risk of having to update our schema with new tags every time a new trend hits town. As our list of tags gets steadily longer and longer, where do we draw the line?

We can get a far more future-safe arrangement by replacing the very specific `ketchup` tag with a more generic one called `condiment`. We can then give it an attribute that allows us to specify the particular condiment we're interested in. Here's how it might look:

```
<cheeseburger>
  <bun>
    <patty type="beef" />
    <cheese type="cheddar" />
    <condiment name="ketchup" />
    <condiment name="mustard" />
    <lettuce type="romaine" />
  </bun>
</cheeseburger>
```

As you see, it's not just the condiment tags that stand to benefit from this treatment. In principle, we could now cope comfortably with requests for vegetarian burgers topped with Emmental cheese. Ultimately, you can arrange the information in whatever manner you choose – it is only good or bad to the extent that it serves your particular needs. Whether you define a particular bit of data as an attribute or as a separate element depends entirely on what you intend to do with it. Good questions to ask are:

- Does this unit of data have the possibility of changing its form?

- Does this unit of data have other units of data contained within it?

If the answer to either of these questions is 'yes', then you'll probably want to represent that unit of data as an element. On the other hand, if it's a self-contained little morsel of data that could take a whole variety of values, then it probably makes sense to define it as an attribute.

Writing well-formed XML documents

In order to write XML that can be read by any parser, it must be **well-formed**. This means it follows the proper syntactical rules set down in the XML specification, and while these rules aren't hard to understand, they are fairly strict. Some, we've already covered implicitly, but there's no harm in spelling them out once more before we take the plunge and start putting our XML into use.

Declaration and the single root

A well-formed XML document must start with an **XML declaration**, which looks like this:

```
<?xml version="1.0"?>
```

As you can see, the syntax used is slightly different to that which we've seen so far. That's because this isn't an XML element, but an instruction to the XML parser. In fact, the XML parser that's built into the Flash plugin isn't nearly as strict as most, and doesn't actually require you to include this declaration. However, it's worth putting in so that other XML parsers can handle your document, should the need arise.

Well-formed documents should also have just **one root element**, in which all the document's other elements are contained. Once again, the Flash XML parser really isn't picky about this rule, but others certainly are. Internet Explorer will return an error if you try to render the following XML:

```
<Album artist="Bjork" title="Debut">
  <Song>Song Name</Song>
  <Song>Song Name</Song>
</Album>
<Album artist="Bjork" title="Post">
  <Song>Song Name</Song>
  <Song>Song Name</Song>
</Album>
<Album artist="Bjork" title="Homogenic">
  <Song>Song Name</Song>
  <Song>Song Name</Song>
</Album>
```

In order for this XML to constitute a well-formed document, I'd need to place it within a single root element, and add a declaration at the top:

```
<?xml version="1.0"?>
```

```
<Boxset>
  <Album artist="Bjork" title="Debut">
    <Song>Song Name</Song>
    <Song>Song Name</Song>
  </Album>
  <Album artist="Bjork" title="Post">
    <Song>Song Name</Song>
    <Song>Song Name</Song>
  </Album>
  <Album artist="Bjork" title="Homogenic">
    <Song>Song Name</Song>
    <Song>Song Name</Song>
  </Album>
</Boxset>
```

What's in a name?

Element names must conform to the following guidelines:

- They must start with either a letter or an underscore, and continue with letters, digits, hyphens, underscores, and periods.

- They must not start with the sequence 'XML' in either capital or lowercase letters.

- They cannot contain spaces. A space delineates the end of an element name and the beginning of the first attribute. So, if you had an element named big dog, then the XML parser would assume it was an element named big, whose first attribute was called dog. On discovering that there was no value specified for dog, it would then return a fatal error.

Once your element conforms to these guidelines, you also have to make sure that each attribute within your element has a unique name. For example, the empty element player shown below is badly formed:

```
<player name="bob" color="red" color="blue">
```

Note that, unlike HTML, all attribute values *must* be specified within quotation marks.

Matching, case-sensitive tags

Each non-empty element must have a **matching pair of opening and closing tags**. The following snippet of XML shows a well-formed non-empty element.

```
<excerpt book="A Tale Of Two Cities">
  It was the best of times, it was the worst of times...
</excerpt>
```

This also applies to an empty element like `<tag></tag>`, except when the abbreviated form `<tag />` is used. It's important to remember that element names are case-sensitive, so the following element is badly formed:

```
<EXCERPT book="A Tale Of Two Cities">
  It was the best of times, it was the worst of times...
</excerpt>
```

Careful with that markup!

Text elements (like our passage from Dickens above) cannot contain markup. If we were to throw in certain characters such as `<`, `&`, or `>`, the XML parser would confuse them for markup, and either parse our XML incorrectly, or (more likely) reject it outright as badly formed.

Of course, this is quite easy to prevent if we're creating our XML by hand, or from known elements. If we're generating it on the fly though (as we will do very shortly), we may well need to take precautions. Say that you had a Flash movie that took input from a text field and inserted it into an element within an XML document. Now say the user entered the following:

```
This is really <BLINK>FUN!</BLINK>
```

By adding this text straight into the XML file, you'd effectively create a new, unwanted element called `BLINK`.

Fortunately, you can use the Flash function `escape` to convert your string to a URL-encoded format, turning all the special markup characters into hexadecimal escape sequences. So, to ensure that users can't modify your XML structure, you simply need to escape the input text before it's added to the XML document, like this:

```
textfield = escape(textfield);
```

Now, the input text shown above would be in encoded form, and look like this:

```
This%20is%20really%20%3CBLINK%3EFUN%21%3C%2FBLINK%3E
```

If we need to display the text later on, we just pass the encoded string to the `unescape` function, which will convert any escaped characters back to their original formats:

```
textfield = unescape(textfield);
```

Nesting

When elements sit one inside another, it is called nesting. In order for an element to nest correctly inside another, it must close with an ending tag before its parent element, like this:

If it doesn't, then the elements are said to 'overlap', like this:

These overlapping elements mean that we no longer have a clear data structure. We can no longer say that the country element contains the state element, or even vice-versa.

As you may be aware, most web browsers allow HTML tags to overlap quite freely. Since the precise structure of HTML isn't nearly as important as the finished result, they are designed to be very tolerant so that it's as easy as possible to knock together a simple web page that looks just the way you want it to. By contrast, XML has explicitly defined structure at the top of its priorities – overlapping elements defeat the object and render it unusable.

> You might wonder why someone couldn't design a parser that automatically closed any child elements on reaching a closing tag for the parent to fix this problem. They could, but they'd be doing nobody any favors. If the parser's assumption ever proved wrong, it would quite happily go and build an incorrect data structure for your XML. All sorts of things could then go wrong without so much as a warning. No XML parser should be set to automatically fix malformed XML – it should only ever report it.

So it's important to be careful when building your documents, and to keep a track of how all your elements nest. Formatting your XML by indenting your nesting elements helps (although it introduces **whitespace** into your document, which we will cover a bit later).

Making your own application

Since XML is so flexible, there's virtually no limit to the number of ways to write an XML application. Basically, each application has its own language that is defined by its particular specialized pursuits.

Whether your application is for an auction site, a mammalogy database, a fast food restaurant, or multiuser chat room, you'll need to define a vocabulary that best suits your needs. Not only will you need to pick words that accurately define the data that you are trying to encapsulate, but you'll need to define a structure in your XML that best defines the real-world relationships between those elements.

For instance, let's say we were building an application for diet planning and training. In this application, we want to be able to define a day's worth of meals, and count up the nutritional values of every food in each meal. We'd be tracking important nutritional information like calorie intake, fat, cholesterol, and sodium.

Now, there are many different ways we can start to plan this. Often I like to start with the simplest element and work my way out to the big picture. In this case, our simple element will be a single portion of food.

```
<FOODITEM/>
```

Now that food will have certain properties, like a name and a size. We can define those properties as attributes of our XML element:

```
<FOODITEM name="Ham, honey baked" weight="230"/>
```

Now, since our weight is a numerical value, we'll need to define what sort of unit this weight is measured in. We can add that as an attribute as well:

```
<FOODITEM name="Ham, honey baked" weight="230" units="grams"/>
```

This food will also have certain nutritional values that we want to track. Now we have a decision to make. Do we want to add these as attributes, or as elements contained within our food element? This is a decision you'll have to make often, and it is a part of defining the structure for your new language.

Since nutrients will most likely have their own attributes, like name, value, and unit, we'll probably want to make these elements contained inside our food element, like so:

```
<FOODITEM name="Ham, honey baked" weight="230" units="grams">
   <NUTRIENT name="Calories" value="250" units="kcal"/>
   <NUTRIENT name="Fat" value="30" unit="grams"/>
   <NUTRIENT name="Cholesterol" value="25" units="mg"/>
   <NUTRIENT name="Sodium" value="140" units="mg"/>
</FOODITEM>
```

Now, since we are trying to teach good diet habits, we don't want this food sitting by itself in a vacuum, do we? We don't want our clients scavenging their refrigerators at all times of the day whenever they feel the urge! We need to teach them to organize these foods into nice square meals where they sit down and eat like civilized people.

So, we'll need a 'meal' element. And that meal shall have a name. And that meal shall contain all of the foods that are a part of that meal.

```
<MEAL name="Dinner">
  <FOODITEM name="Ham, honey baked" weight="230" units="grams">
    <NUTRIENT name="Calories" value="250" units="kcal"/>
    <NUTRIENT name="Fat" value="30" unit="grams"/>
    <NUTRIENT name="Cholesterol" value="25" units="mg"/>
    <NUTRIENT name="Sodium" value="140" units="mg"/>
  </FOODITEM>
  <FOODITEM name="Peas" weight="50" units="grams">
    <NUTRIENT name="Calories" value="100" units="kcal"/>
    <NUTRIENT name="Fat" value="5" unit="grams"/>
    <NUTRIENT name="Cholesterol" value="0.5" units="mg"/>
    <NUTRIENT name="Sodium" value="79" units="mg"/>
  </FOODITEM>
  <FOODITEM name="Rice" weight="150" units="grams">
    <NUTRIENT name="Calories" value="45" units="kcal"/>
    <NUTRIENT name="Fat" value="1" unit="grams"/>
    <NUTRIENT name="Cholesterol" value="0" units="mg"/>
    <NUTRIENT name="Sodium" value="98" units="mg"/>
  </FOODITEM>
</MEAL>
```

Now, you can see we're starting to define a real language here. So far, we've got three different element names, and many different attributes. We can take it even further by defining food types, like beverages, foods, or condiments. Or, we can define a calorie limit for each meal, and set it as an attribute in the meal element. The possibilities are endless.

This example shows how we examine the concepts and activities of a typical field of interest, and build a language around them. We also examine the relationships between those things, activities, and concepts, and build our XML structure in a way that echoes those relationships. Let's develop this a little bit further.

XML, Flash, and the DOM

As we've seen, XML gives us a simple yet powerful way to represent hierarchical data structures. However, it doesn't dictate how this data should be displayed. This separation of content and presentation allows for the same data, stored in an XML document, to be presented in the manner of your choosing.

We all know what an excellent tool Flash is for displaying content on the web in a myriad of different ways. It isn't tied down to the rigid, static formatting of HTML. With the advent of ActionScript, and its evolution into a real object-oriented programming language, Flash has become an even more powerful tool for manipulating various forms of data and graphical elements. Previous versions of Flash allowed for the import of dynamic data as a basic string of variables. These variables were all stored in one place, either in the root of a movie, or a movieclip, all given equal importance. With Flash 5, you can now import XML, and Flash will automatically parse it, and build a tree of objects that will be accessible via the XML object methods in ActionScript. This "tree of objects" is what's known as the DOM (**Document Object Model**).

Now, when I say model, what do you picture in your head? Aside from fashion models, you might be picturing a model airplane, or model train set. A model is the physical manifestation of something else, correct? The Document Object Model is simply a schematic representation of the relationships that exist between the elements in an XML document. Drawn on paper, it looks like a tree upended, with the trunk at the top, and the leaves at the bottom.

The most common analogy to the XML DOM is a family tree. Let's look at a simple family tree written as XML, and represented in a DOM.

Our family tree in XML looks like this:

```
<Parent>
  <Child>
     <Grandchild/>
     <Grandchild/>
  </Child>
  <Child>
     <Grandchild/>
     <Grandchild/>
  </Child>
</Parent>
```

Our DOM looks like this:

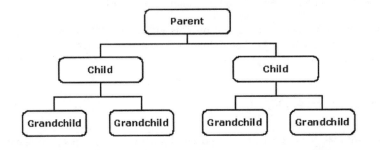

I mentioned before that Flash **parses** XML. Parsing means to break something down into its component parts, and state the semantic interrelationships between those parts. What Flash does when it parses XML, is to check if your XML is well-formed (that is, whether it makes sense according to the rules of XML), discover the relationships between all of the elements, and then build an nested tree of **nodes** based on those relationships, populating them with the data contained in the XML.

So, what is a node? Well, each of these branches of the tree of objects is a node. Every component part of an XML document is a node (including elements, text, and even the space between tags). Any node in the tree can have nodes within (**child nodes**), and all but the root will have a **parent node** containing it.

Flash recognizes two node types: **element nodes** and **text nodes**. We only used the former in the example above. It's not important for you to understand the technical details of how this works, but it is important to understand the way the Flash holds the XML data.

The best real-world analogy of this would be scaffolding, or an intricate framework for a concrete casting. This tree of nodes is simply a container to hold your XML data. This container is built in such a way as to retain the original relationships created by the hierarchical structure of your XML document. This way, your whole XML document, or parts within your XML document can be rebuilt and output without losing any of its structure. Often, we display this structure in the format of a flowchart like the one you see opposite.

Navigating the tree

So, once we build this tree, how do we get what we need out of it? Say we need to find a specific bit of information, or a series of nodes buried deep within a cascading hierarchy of elements. Can we refer to it by name? Not exactly, so let's refer to our famous cheeseburger example and see how we do this. I've modified the cheeseburger slightly to make the hierarchy a little more complex, so I've placed the condiments within their own element.

```
<cheeseburger>
  <bun>
    <patty type="beef"/>
    <cheese type="cheddar"/>
    <condiments>
      <condiment name="ketchup"/>
      <condiment name="mustard"/>
    </condiments>
    <lettuce type="romaine"/>
  </bun>
</cheeseburger>
```

Now let's say we want to refer to the condiment named 'mustard' using ActionScript. You might think that we can use standard Flash object referencing, like so:

```
cheeseburger.bun.condiments.condiment
```

Unfortunately, it doesn't work that way. For one, there are two condiments, so you would have two objects with the same name, which would be bad. Secondly, even though the Flash environment and the XML DOM are both very object-oriented, they are two different animals. Flash cannot automatically assume what to do with your document, as that would limit its usefulness and versatility. It is best to merely build a container for your document, and allow you ways to access the data within it.

In order to refer to a particular XML element, we have to list out the 'directions' or the path we took to get to that object. It's akin to describing your address as a relative location from a landmark. Let's say I lived near the shopping mall, say 2 blocks south, and one block east. If I were to describe my address using XML object syntax, it would look like this:

```
mall.south.south.east
```

Now, we all know how to navigate based on the cardinal directions, but how do we navigate an XML tree? Well, basically, we can think of it in the following way. 'Up' and 'down' transverses between parent and child, and 'right' and 'left' will go from sibling to sibling.

The `XML.firstChild` property will bring us to the first child of a level in an XML tree. If you go back and have a look at the cheeseburger XML, you will see that `XML.firstChild` will bring us to the root element, `<cheeseburger>`. The `<cheeseburger>` element contains a child element, `<bun>`, which contains four elements. To get to the `<bun>` element, we would enter:

```
bun = XML.firstChild.firstChild
```

Now, we want to point to the third child element within the bun element. Unfortunately, there is no `thirdChild` property in Flash, so we'll need to go to the first child in the element and go 'sideways' to the third child. We do this by using the `XML.nextSibling`. To get to the first child of the bun, we enter:

```
bun.firstChild
```

And then, to get to the third child, we need to go to the next sibling's sibling, like so:

```
condiments = bun.firstChild.nextSibling.nextSibling
```

Almost there! Now we are at the `<condiments>` element. To get to the mustard, we need to go 'down' one level and 'sideways' one element. We'll add a `firstChild` and `nextSibling` to our rather long reference:

```
mustard = condiments.firstChild.nextSibling
```

Seems kind of awkward, doesn't it? Well, actually, you'll find it really does cut the mustard. You can basically point to any location in an XML document by using combinations of `firstChild` and `nextSibling`. It works well in your functions, too, because you can use ActionScript to build loops that dynamically assemble these references, and also use referencing to point to locations within these documents.

We'll explain this in further detail later. Now that we've learnt how to point to specific nodes within a document, what can we actually do with them? For a start, we can use the following properties to read data from them, and even manipulate that data:

- **nodeName** is a property that exposes the **name** of whichever node was used to call it.

- **nodeValue** is a similar property, which exposes the **value** of whichever node was used to call it. Only text nodes have a value, which takes the form of a string containing the text within the node.

- **nodeType** returns an integer denoting the type of the calling node. Flash only recognizes two node types: element nodes (1) and text nodes (3).

■ **attributes** exposes a collection of name/value pairs that correspond to the attributes held in a calling node. You can access attribute values using either of the following two forms of syntax:

```
myXMLnode.attributes.attributename
myXMLnode.attributes["attributename"]
```

Now, before we get too bogged down in object—oriented programming theory, let's start applying all we've learned about XML to a Flash application.

Bringing XML into Flash

To provide an example that you may actually see in a multiuser environment, we're going to construct an XML document that's typical of what you might see being passed to a client in a chat room application. We'll build a room, put a few guests in it, and allow a place within the XML structure for them to send messages back and forth. For now, we'll simply put it into a file manually for learning purposes. We don't need to worry about server set-ups or dynamically generating XML yet.

1. Like HTML, you don't need any special software to make XML documents. All you need is a simple ASCII text editor, like Notepad or SimpleText. So, fire up your favorite editor, and plop in the following chunk of XML:

```
<?xml version="1.0"?>
<Chatroom name="Bobs Diner">
  <Guest name="Felix">
    <Message/>
  </Guest>
  <Guest name="Olive">
    <Message>Hello there, do you like Spinach?</Message>
  </Guest>
  <Guest name="Chappy">
    <Message/>
  </Guest>
</Chatroom>
```

You can see that our XML starts with the root element Chatroom. This is our all-encompassing root element, which will contain all the information there is concerning the room, and we've given it the name, "Bob's Diner". There are three guests in this room, Felix, Olive, and Chappy. Felix and Chappy are both pretty quiet at the moment, and aren't saying anything. They have the ability to speak, because we've defined the 'Message' element into which they can place their suave and clever remarks. However, it seems that Olive is the only one trying to make conversation. Her message element contains the text, "Hello there, do you like Spinach?"

2. Save this file as `chatroom.xml`, taking care to ensure that your editor doesn't sneak in the extension `.txt` whilst you're not looking.

3. You've now created your first XML file. Simple, huh? If you want to make sure that it's well-formed, you might like to load it up in Internet Explorer (version 4.0 or later), which has its own built-in XML parser. It will parse your XML, display it with proper indentation, and even pretty it up with syntax coloring. This is a very handy way to verify your XML quickly.

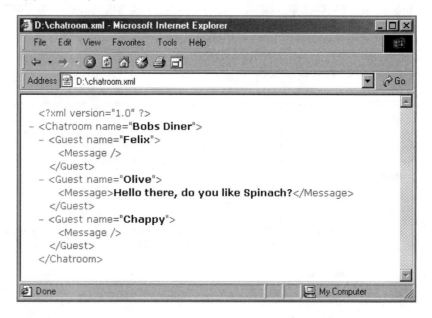

Let's bring our XML into Flash.

4. Open Flash, start a new movie, and save it in the same location as you saved your XML file.

5. Create two layers in your main timeline, one called actions, and the other called graphics.

6. In the first frame of the actions layer, input the following code:

```
chatXML = new XML();
```

This creates a new XML object called *chatXML*. We need to define this object as an XML object before populating it with XML, so that it can inherit all the properties and methods of the XML class.

7. Add this line of code underneath the one you've just added:

```
chatXML.load("chatroom.xml");
```

This loads data from the specified text file, and imports our XML document into the XML object, where it is parsed and converted into the XML object tree.

> *The argument we provide to the XML object's load method can actually point to any source of XML: with a URL as its argument, we could load up data from any XML document on the Internet; it could even point to a server–side script that returns XML.*

8. Test the movie, and the XML should load into the Flash movie. Unfortunately, you won't see any results, because we haven't actually told the movie to doing anything with it yet. If you debug your movie, you can view all the variables in your document to see the loaded XML. Don't look too closely at the actual contents of the XML file in the debugger, though. The debugger is small and crowded, and doesn't always display your XML properly. So, for now, we'll work on another way to display our XML in Flash.

9. Select the graphics layer, and create a text field on the stage. Use the Text Options panel to set this field to hold multiline, dynamic text, and check the Word Wrap check box. In the Variable field, enter the variable name *output*, and expand the text box to fill your stage.

Our movie now has a text field that will display whatever string has been assigned to the variable output. In theory, we could go straight on and use the XML.toString method to string-format all the XML data held in chatXML, and assign this string to output. However, there's rather an important issue we really ought to deal with first.

Much like loading variables, loading XML is an **asynchronous** operation. This means that the loading process doesn't necessarily coincide with the timing in the movie, and the movie won't stop playing to wait for the XML data to turn up. If we simply assigned XML.toString to a variable without checking whether it had loaded, we'd have no guarantee that there was any XML there at all. Luckily for us, there are two ways to verify that data has been successfully loaded into the XML object.

The first is to take a look at the XML.loaded property, which is only true once the XML has been loaded. This is a simple, robust way to check, but, since the load operation is asynchronous, it requires you to build a loop in your movie that constantly checks the value of this variable.

The second is to use the XML.onLoad event handler, which is automatically executed whenever an XML document is loaded into an XML object. By default, no function is assigned to this event handler, but you can do so by using the following syntax:

```
myXML.onLoad=myHandlerFunction;
```

In this case, myHandlerFunction is the name of a function that will be executed just as soon as a call to myXML.load has completed. Let's use this latter method to build a handler that places our XML document's contents into the text field we just created.

To finish off our exercise, add the highlighted code below to the first frame of your actions layer:

```
chatXML = new XML();
chatXML.onLoad=chatXMLonload;
chatXML.load("chatroom.xml");

function chatXMLonload (success) {
    if (success) {
        output = chatXML.toString();
    }
}
```

In our first new line of code, we tell Flash to call the function chatXMLonload whenever the chatXML object raises an onLoad event (which it does whenever a call to its load method is completed). Note that we don't place parentheses after the name of the function, because we are **assigning** the function object to the onLoad event handler, rather than **calling** the function to execute.

We follow up by defining the function itself, which needs to take a single argument called success. When this function is called, it will be passed a Boolean value that indicates whether or not the chatXML.load call was successful. So, if the XML has been loaded, success is true, and we can go ahead and parse it into output.

Now test your movie. If you did everything right, you should be able to see the contents of the XML document displayed on the stage, as illustrated in the screenshot:

```
Movie1.swf                                              _ □ ×

    <?xml version="1.0"?>

    <Chatroom name="Bobs Diner">

    <Guest name="Felix">

        <Message />

    </Guest>

      <Guest name="Olive">

        <Message>Hello there, do you like Spinach?</Message>

      </Guest>

      <Guest name="Chappy">

        <Message />
```

Dealing with whitespace

You may have noticed that our output seems to be missing a couple of tags from the bottom – in fact, they're still there, but simply running outside the limits of our text field. This is partly due to a number of additional spaces in the parsed XML, which arise because of the way Flash interprets all the **whitespace** (carriage returns, spaces, and tabs) that we used to keep our original document nicely formatted and readable.

Whitespace is a perfectly valid part of an XML document. The way you format your XML document, including the elements and text within it, are all a part of the XML structure. In order to retain the integrity of this structure, and to reproduce it, XML parsers must acknowledge all of the text and formatting within the document.

By default, the Flash XML parser will retain every bit of whitespace in a document, keeping it tucked away in text nodes between elements. This is great news if you want to send XML back to the server, as it will retain all its original formatting. Unfortunately, this can have rather unexpected effects on the node hierarchy – let's look at how the whitespace in chatroom.xml affects the intended hierarchy.

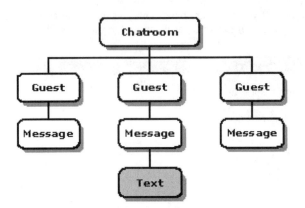

The first figure shows how we intended our document's hierarchy to look, while the second shows how it actually is, in light of the whitespace we've used to make it more readable. Note that the gray boxes denote text nodes, while white boxes correspond to elements, and whitespace is abbreviated to 'WS' in the second figure:

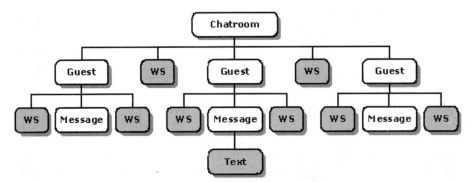

As you can see, the seemingly innocent whitespace actually changes the object hierarchy quite radically. We clearly need to acknowledge its presence in some way. There are four ways we can deal with it.

Firstly, you can construct your XML without any extraneous whitespace, effectively writing the entire document in a single continuous line. This is certainly the most efficient method, not to mention the easiest to implement. If the XML in question is going to be sent back and forth between a client and a server (that is, it's not intended to be read by people), then this is quite an effective option. However, it's not advisable if the documents need to be edited by hand, as it makes the XML exceedingly difficult to follow, especially if there are a lot of nested elements.

Secondly, you can code around the whitespace. If you know in advance how your XML will be structured, and where the whitespace is going to appear, you can program your code to skip over it. Alternatively, you can build checking routines into your code that look out for instances of whitespace and skip over them automatically. This is usually a painful, cumbersome process, which will probably slow down your processing considerably.

Thirdly, you can use the XML.ignoreWhite property. Simply set this property to true before loading your XML, and *voila!* no whitespace. This is a wonderfully easy way to get rid of your whitespace. The only problem is that this property was only implemented as of Build 41 of the Flash 5 player. If you know that every member of your target audience has that build (or a more recent one) then you're in luck – otherwise, you're in trouble. Furthermore, the Flash authoring environment shipped with Build 30, and can't be updated, so even you won't be able to test your movie properly from within Flash.

Finally, you can strip out the whitespace on the client side. There have been many functions written that will automatically traverse your XML and remove all those pesky whitespace nodes automatically. This is my own preferred method, so let's return to our chatroom example again, and take a look at a how we might construct a function that will do this for us.

Removing whitespace from our chatroom

1. Select the first frame of the actions layer (where we placed our code before), and add the following function, which locates and removes empty text nodes from within a specified XML object:

```
function clearwhite (thisXML) {
    // Run this function on siblings
    if (thisXML.nextSibling != void(1)) {
        clearwhite(thisXML.nextSibling);
    }
    // Check to see if current node is a text node
    if (thisXML.nodeType == 3) {
        var empty = true;
        // If text contains ASCII characters above 32, it is not
        // empty
        for (i=0; i<thisXML.nodeValue.length; i++) {
            if (thisXML.nodeValue.charCodeAt(i) > 32) {
                empty = false;
                break;
            }
        }
        // If the current node is an empty text node, delete it
        if (empty) {
            thisXML.removeNode();
        }
    } else {
        // Run this function on child nodes
        if (thisXML.firstChild != void(1)) {
            clearwhite(thisXML.firstChild);
        }
    }
}
```

There's one method here that we've not seen before: **removeNode** simply deletes a specified node (and all its child nodes, grandchild nodes, and so on) from its parent XML object. The parent's structure is automatically updated, so there's no risk of leaving a 'hole'. For instance, if we deleted the second child from a parent node with three children, the third child would automatically become the second child.

> This clearwhite function is a recursive function. In other words, it is a function that calls itself. You call it once, sending it your entire XML document. It operates on one element at a time, but then calls itself to run on the siblings and children of each element. It executes, and then filters down from the root of your XML all the way to the deepest element in your XML tree. Admittedly, the clearwhite function is a bit complex for your first function that manipulates XML. But, since whitespace is often the first issue you run into when bringing Flash into XML, a function like this is often the first one you need to implement.

2. We want this function to be executed on chatXML as soon as it's been loaded with data, so we need to call it as part of the handler function chatXMLonLoad, sending chatXML as an argument. To do this, add the highlighted line below to the chatXMLonLoad function:

```
function chatXMLonload (success) {
    if (success) {
        clearwhite(chatXML);
        output = chatXML.toString();
    }
}
```

3.   Check that your script in the first frame of the actions layer looks like the one shown.

```
Frame Actions                                                        ×
Movie Explorer   Frame Actions                                    ?  ▶
+  −   Frame Actions                                               ▼ ▲
chatXML = new XML();
chatXML.onLoad=chatXMLonload;
chatXML.load("chatroom.xml");

function chatXMLonload (success) {
    if (success) {
        clearwhite(chatXML);
        output = chatXML.toString();
    }
}

function clearwhite (thisXML) {
    // Run this function on siblings
    if (thisXML.nextSibling != void(1)) {
        clearwhite(thisXML.nextSibling);
    }
    // Check to see if current node is a text node
    if (thisXML.nodeType == 3) {
        var empty = true;
        // If text contains ASCII characters above 32, it is not empty
        for (i=0; i<thisXML.nodeValue.length; i++) {
            if (thisXML.nodeValue.charCodeAt(i) > 32) {
                empty = false;
                break;
            }
        }
        // If the current node is an empty text node, delete it
        if (empty) {
            thisXML.removeNode();
        }
    } else {
        // Run this function on child nodes
        if (thisXML.firstChild != void(1)) {
            clearwhite(thisXML.firstChild);
        }
    }
}
Line 18 of 37, Col 33                                               ⊕
```

4.   Test your movie, and you'll see that all the XML is compressed into one long string. In fact, the line may well wrap onto several lines since it's so long, but that's just a matter of how it's presented – resize your Flash client and you'll see that it is actually just one line.

```
◈ Movie1.swf                                                    _ □ ×

<?xml version="1.0"?><Chatroom name="Bobs Diner"><Guest
name="Felix"><Message /></Guest><Guest name="Olive"><Message>Hello
there, do you like Spinach?</Message></Guest><Guest
name="Chappy"><Message /></Guest></Chatroom>
```

Case Study: An XML broadcast

So far, we've seen how XML can be used to describe large, complex data structures. Not only can XML be used to store data, it can also be used to transmit queries and messages between different platforms and servers.

Using XML, you can encapsulate data and messages inside XML tags, and send them to a server that 'speaks XML'. That is to say, a server that understands the XML syntax and can parse it. Most likely this is a script or program that understands the particulars of your specific application's syntax, so that it knows what to do with the XML once it is parsed.

Let's say you're building a Flash-based front-end for an auction site, and you're using XML as a medium for all client-server transmissions. A typical query you'd send to the server might be:

```
<GETITEMS category="Mittens" shownum="3">
```

First of all, you will you need to build a front-end that understands your particular application, and can build these strings of XML to send to the server. You will also need a server-side script that can parse the XML, and know that GETITEMS means to return a list of all items that are in the Mittens category. Your server would respond with the number of items in the shownum attribute, in this case three:

```
<ITEM Name="Mittens, Cotton Knit" price="10">
<ITEM Name="Mittens, Gore-tex" price="25">
<ITEM Name="Mittens, Leather" price="40">
```

You can see how encapsulating your data in XML not only gives you the data, but also tells you what the data means. It's a very simple, robust, and convenient way to transmit data. In this case, you would use the sendAndLoad method of the XML class to send your XML and parse the response from the server.

Certain servers often have a predetermined vocabulary for you to use, especially those that are written for a specific task such as a real-time chatroom. XML socket servers are one such type of server. These servers allow persistent socket connections between client and server, which are real-time connections that have almost no latency issues. These servers are specifically tuned for real-time applications like chat. We'll go further in depth into XML socket servers in later chapters, but for now we are going to focus more on working with XML to communicate between client and server.

In order to demonstrate this, we are going to set up a simple Flash movie in which we have virtual clients, who can communicate via a virtual server. We'll be able to spawn as many clients as we want, and they'll all be able to send messages to each other. All of the messages will be transmitted in XML format.

For simplicity's sake, we are going to keep all of our communications internal to the Flash movie. We have yet to talk about servers and possible server configurations, so setting up and using a real server is a bit too much to swallow for this exercise. Our virtual server is going to be at the root of our movie, and our clients will be linked movie clips that can be attached dynamically at our request.

Building a UI

Before looking at the code that makes it all work, let's start by setting up the graphical interface elements for our movie.

1. Create a new movie in Flash, add two new layers to the main timeline (giving us a total of three), and rename them actions, text, and graphics.

2. Let's define a simple button. We'll be using this for a variety of different purposes, so make it as generic as possible. Select the graphics layer and draw a circle that's 16 pixels in diameter, with no text in it or anything to hint at a particular function – I've used a gray fill and black stroke.

3. Select both elements (stroke and fill) of the circle graphic, group them together, and hit F8 to convert this group into a symbol, which you should give a generic name such as Generic Button.

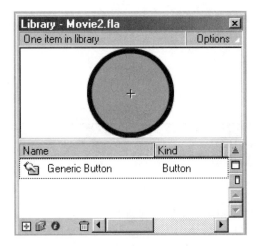

4. You should still have an instance of the button on the stage, so drag it to the bottom left-hand corner. This button is what we'll use to launch our virtual clients. Our clients will connect to our server, so don't let the fact that this is in the same place as our virtual server confuse you – all will be revealed.

5. Since it's not yet obvious what this button is for, we'll need to add a description. On the text layer, create a static text field that reads Add Client and center it below your button. You may like to place a "+" symbol on top of the button symbol to further reinforce its function.

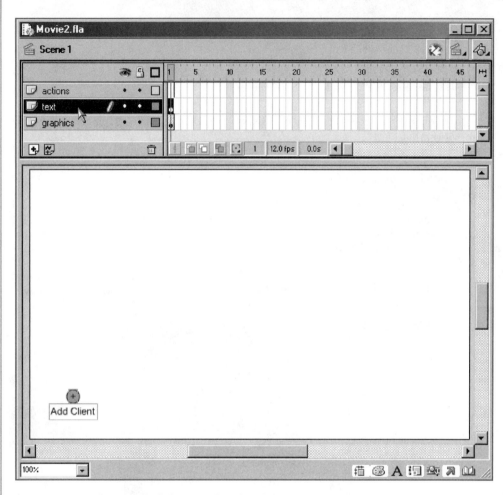

Now, let's start building our client interface.

6. In the main timeline, create a simple gray box with rounded corners, around 130 pixels wide by 180 pixels tall.

7. We want the client to be a movie clip that we attach later on, so select the box and its outline, group them together, and make them into a movie clip called client.

8. In the Library panel, right-click on the new movie clip and select Linkage.... Choose to export this symbol, and give it the ID client.

Now this movie clip will be exported along with our movie, and it can be attached to the stage by means of the attachMovie method. If you wish, you can now delete the movie clip from the stage and work on it by opening it from the library.

9. Double-click on the client symbol's entry in the library, so that you can edit it from its own timeline. You should see a single layer there, which you should rename background. Add three more layers above that layer, calling the topmost layer actions, the second text, and the third buttons.

10. Move the gray box so that the top left-hand corner is at (0,0) on the client stage. Use F8 once again to turn it into a button, and name it dragwindow. You won't need to make any rollover states for this button, as it will simply be used to let us to drag the virtual client to any position on the stage.

11. Still working on the client symbol's stage, drag two instances of the generic button onto the buttons layer. Place one in the upper-right hand corner of the background graphic, and one in the lower right-hand corner.

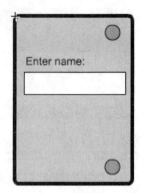

12. Select the text layer, and use whatever font you like to place an "X" on the top button, and a ">" over the bottom one. The former will be our "close" button, whilst the latter will be used to submit and send items.

We have a fairly nice little interface. You may even wish to drop a shadow under our interface to give it that 3D look that's so popular these days. Your client timeline should now have four layers (or maybe five if you've decided to add the shadow effect), and be just one frame long. Here's how mine looks so far:

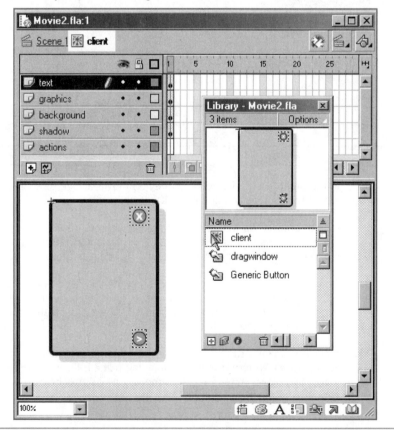

13. Add a new frame to each of the layers, and create a keyframe on frame 2 for the layers actions, text, and buttons. We're going to have two frames in this movie: the first will be a login screen where a user can enter their name; the second will be the screen on which the actual chatting takes place.

14. On the text layer in frame 1, create an input text field for the variable username. Make sure to check Border/Bg under the Text Options panel, so that it's clear this is an input text field, and place it roughly in the center of the interface.

15. Just above this, place a static text field that reads Enter name:. Next to the bottom button, place a static text field that reads Join. It should look a little like the one shown.

In frame 2, we need text fields for our username, the text display for the chat session, and a place to type messages.

16. Create a dynamic text field, link its contents to the variable username, and place it at the top of the dialog. Just below this, create a dynamic text field that can show at least five lines of text, so make sure its properties are set to multiline and word wrap. Since we want to display HTML formatting here, check the HTML check box in the Text Options panel. Add a static text field just underneath, reading Display.

17. Below this, create an input text field, and link it to the variable message. This is where we will input the message text we wish to send. A static text field here that reads Input will help to clarify its purpose. For both of these fields, you should make sure that Border/Bg is checked.

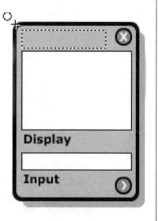

18. Finally, we need to add a movie clip to the second frame of the client timeline. This movie clip will contain no graphics, but its use will soon become fairly evident. Create a new movie clip called dummy and drag this movie clip into the second frame of your client timeline. It will look like a little dot with a registration mark, and when you deselect it, it will look like a circle. You can put it anywhere, but put it in a place where you can easily get to it.

That's it for the graphical interface portion of our exercise.

Building the code

Now, on to the code! We'll start with the client movie clip, our virtual client, and then build the virtual server in the root timeline.

1. In the first frame of the client timeline, in the actions layer, we're going to add three functions. The first is called initClient, and simply initializes variables in our movie:

```
function initClient () {
    username = "New User";
    display = "";
}
```

We're initializing two variables, username and display. By default, username is set to "New User" when we launch a new client.

2. Our next function, receiveMessage, will be our handler for all messages received by the virtual server.

```
function receiveMessage (messageXML) {
    var fromuser, fromtext;
    //
    // parse message into XML object
    var XMLreceived = new XML(messageXML);
    //
    // Get username and message text from XML nodes
    fromuser =
XMLreceived.firstChild.firstChild.attributes.username;
    fromtext =
XMLreceived.firstChild.firstChild.firstchild.nodeValue;
    //
    // Output to display in HTML format.
    display += "<B>"+fromuser+":</B> "+fromtext+"<BR>";
}
```

This function takes a string of XML and parses it into the XML object hierarchy. To keep things simple, we are going to assume we know the basic structure of our XML message beforehand, which is as follows:

```
<MESSAGE>
<USER username="Name of User">This is my message
</USER></MESSAGE>
```

Once we've parsed the XML, we pull the data we need out of nodes in known locations in our XML. We get the user's name and the text message from the XML object, and then output it to our display field in HTML format. Notice that we are appending the new message text to the display text field, so that all of our old messages remain.

3. Our final function to add to this frame is called sendMessage. This function will take an argument that is a string containing the text we want to send:

```
function sendMessage (stringtosend) {
    var usernode, textnode;

    // make a new XML object to place message
    var XMLtosend = new XML("<MESSAGE/>");

    // create a node for the username
    usernode = XMLtosend.createElement("USER");
    usernode.attributes.username = username;

    // create a text node for the message
    textnode = XMLtosend.createTextNode(stringtosend);

    // append text node as a child of the user node
    usernode.appendChild(textnode);

    // append user node to XMLtosend
    XMLtosend.firstChild.appendChild(usernode);

    // send to the 'server'
    _root.broadcast(XMLtosend.toString());
}
```

This function builds an XML message in the format that was shown before. It starts by creating a new XML object, whose root node is called MESSAGE. It then creates a new node called USER and applies the username attribute to that node. Then a new text node is created, using the string of text sent in the argument. The text node is appended to the user node, and then the user node is appended to the MESSAGE node in our new XML object (along with the text node). Then, the whole thing is converted into XML source and sent to our virtual server.

4. We want to execute the initClient function right away, so we'll call that in the first frame as well. We'll also add a stop so that we don't go to the second frame before the client enters his username:

```
initClient();
stop ();
```

The screenshot shows how your code should look in the first frame of the client timeline:

```
Frame Actions                                                              [x]
 Movie Explorer   Frame Actions                                         (?) ▶
 +  -   Frame Actions                                                    ▼ ▲
function initClient () {
    username = "New User";
    display = "";
}

function receiveMessage (messageXML) {
    var fromuser, fromtext;
    //
    // parse message into XML object
    var XMLreceived = new XML(messageXML);
    //
    // Get username and message text from XML nodes
    fromuser = XMLreceived.firstChild.firstChild.attributes.username;
    fromtext = XMLreceived.firstChild.firstChild.firstchild.nodeValue;
    //
    // Output to display in HTML format.
    display += "<B>"+fromuser+":</B> "+fromtext+"<BR>";
}

function sendMessage (stringtosend) {
    var usernode, textnode;

    // make a new XML object to lpace message
    var XMLtosend = new XML ("<MESSAGE/>");

    // create a node for the username
    usernode = XMLtosend.createElement("USER");
    usernode.attributes.username = username;

    // create a text node for the message
    textnode = XMLtosend.createTextNode(stringtosend);

    // append text node as a chld of the user node
    usernode.appendChild(textnode);

    // append user node to XMLtosend
    XMLtosend.firstChild.appendChild(usernode);

    // send to the 'server'
    _root.broadcast(XMLtosend.toString());
}

initClient();
stop ();
```
```
Line 43 of 45, Col 1                                                       ⊕
```

5. The close button needs to have code to close the client window. In the actions for the close button, in both keyframes, place the following code:

```
on (release) {
    this.unloadMovie();
}
```

6. In frame one, the send/submit button will take us to the second frame, where the chat occurs. In this frame, in the actions for the send/submit button, place the following code:

```
on (press) {
    gotoAndStop (2);
}
```

7. In the second frame we'll use our send/submit button to submit our text messages to the server. In frame two, in the actions for the send/submit button, place the following code:

```
on (press) {
    sendMessage(message);
    delete message;
}
```

This will call the sendMessage function, sending as the argument the text in the message text field. After the function is called, the text is cleared from the field, so new messages can be written.

8. Remember that dummy movie clip we made earlier? Well, we are going to use that to monitor our display text field to make sure that it is always scrolled to the bottom. Select the movie clip, and give it the following code:

```
onClipEvent (enterFrame) {
    _parent.display.scroll = _parent.display.maxscroll;
}
```

That code will execute on every frame, and ensure that the scroll of our display is always set to maxscroll. In other words, it will always be scrolled to the bottom.

9. Before we finish with the client movie clip, we need to make it draggable, so that we can put each instance where we like, and multiple instances won't end up obscuring each other. Select the background object, and attach the following code:

```
on (press) {
    this.swapDepths(_root.depth);
    startDrag ("");
}
on (release) {
    stopDrag ();
}
```

We're now done with the client, and have only to build our virtual server! You'll be glad to hear that this isn't much more complicated than writing a single function to broadcast messages to all the clients in our movie.

10. Navigate back to the main timeline (that is, not the client) and place the following code into the first frame of the actions layer:

```
// initialize variables
depth = 0;

function broadcast (messageXML) {
    for (name in this) {
        if (typeof (this[name]) == "movieclip") {
            if (this[name]._name.substring(0,6) == "client") {
                this[name].receiveMessage(messageXML);
            }
        }
    }
}
```

The function broadcast takes a string of XML source as its argument, and sends it to the receiveMessage function of every instance of the client movie clip.

11. Nothing is going to happen in our movie unless we place some actions in the original Add Client button on the main stage. This button will simply attach the client movie clip at an incremental depth, and scoot it down and left so as not to overlap any of the other clients that may have just been spawned. Add the following code to our button:

```
on (release) {
    depth++;
    this.attachMovie("client","client" + depth, depth);
    setProperty ("client" + depth, _x, depth * 20);
    setProperty ("client" + depth, _y, depth * 20);
}
```

12. As you can see, we increment our depth variable, attach a client at that depth, and then move it slightly. That's all there is to it! Now you can test your movie, or publish it and run it in a browser. You can launch as many clients as you wish, and they all can talk to each other. Pretty cool, eh?

Our setup here is rather different to what you'd find if you were using a real server. In that event, you could attach these receiveMessage functions to onLoad event handlers, and have them automatically parse the XML when it arrives, and wouldn't need to convert your XML to a string when you sent it. The XML.send method automatically serializes your XML into a string of XML source and sends it.

The setup is slightly different, but in most respects, the way we deal with the XML, and the actual structure of the XML that we're sending back and forth is very similar to that which you would see in a real setting.

This is a fairly simple server. It doesn't do any parsing of XML, so it doesn't really understand what it is getting. It just reflects everything to every client that has been attached to it. A real XML server could parse the XML, understand a variety of different tags, and do different things based on those tags.

For instance, it could parse out the message tag, and read an attribute that was the name of the user to send the message to. So, then you could send private messages as well as broadcasting messages to everyone. You could have tags that request a list of users in the chat room, or send special system messages for logging on and off. The possibilities are endless.

You should now have a fairly good idea of how XML can be used within Flash to enrich a whole variety of applications. In the next chapter, we'll learn more about how we can apply this to real-time connections, using the XML Socket Object.

Chapter 4

Persistent Connections for Realtime Interaction

All the multiuser applications that we've built so far have used a web server to provide a link between each of our client SWFs. That is, the web server would give all the separate instances of the SWF (one for each user) access to a common source of information that represents the current state of our multiuser environment. Well, not always **totally** current.

As we've seen, the sort of connection used by web servers is non-persistent. It's less what you'd normally think of as a connection, and more akin to a kind of relay race in which you spend most of your time waiting for a team-mate to get round the track and hand you back the baton. Fairly useful, but not much good for the sort of real-time interaction we all dream of seeing in our multiuser applications. Think about how much fun Quake would be if everyone had to take it in turns to move about and take potshots at one another...

Now think again! We can't promise the full splendor of Quake, but we can move some way along the path to that sort of interaction by learning how to use persistent connections to get our SWFs talking to each other. In the course of this chapter, we're going to look at using **sockets** to do just this, and develop a simple chat room application to illustrate just what's possible with this approach. So, without further ado, let's get started!

Introducing sockets

We want to create a persistent connection between our client SWFs so they can exchange information in real-time. Essentially we want to set up a **dedicated** link between them through the medium of the Internet.

Sockets provide us with a very straightforward way to do just this, especially since Flash 5 includes a ready-made socket class – XMLSocket, which we'll look at in a moment – and therefore makes it very easy to incorporate them into our movies.

However, the sockets themselves are only one part of the picture: we still need an appropriate server for our movies to connect to – a **socket server**. Once that's set up, a user can connect to the server and the two will remain connected. Unlike previous examples, a movie won't need to open up a brand new connection every time it wants to communicate with the server. With the simplest server, each client connected to the server can send data to the socket server, which will then forward the data to each machine connected to the server. This is known as a **relay server**, and can be seen in the following diagram.

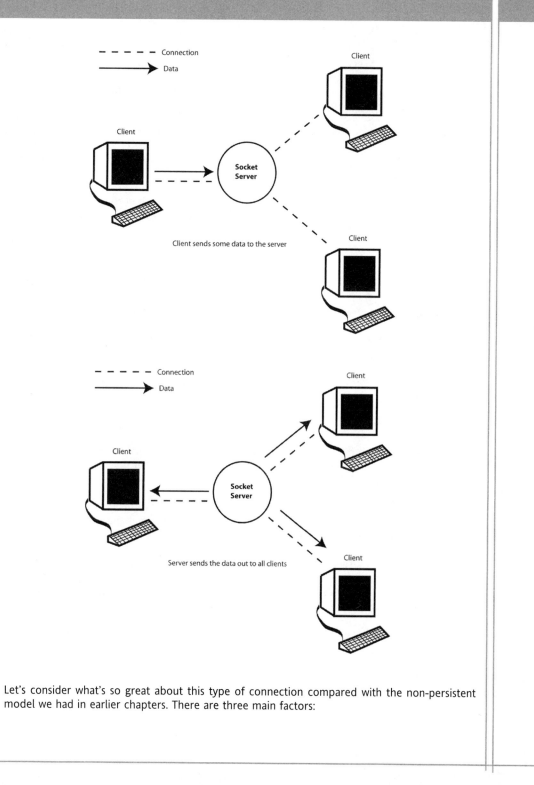

Client sends some data to the server

Server sends the data out to all clients

Let's consider what's so great about this type of connection compared with the non-persistent model we had in earlier chapters. There are three main factors:

- Socket connections allow data to flow freely in both directions. Unlike the web server, the socket server can send information to clients without having to wait for them to make a request. This means that a socket server can prompt movie updates as soon as they're necessary, rather than leaving clients to check in periodically in case there's a change and they need to update themselves.

- The repeated process of opening and closing connections to a web server can slow down the whole communication process. Sockets therefore make it far more economical to pass small chunks of data more frequently, which is ideal for real-time interaction.

- In multiuser systems it's often important to know who is currently connected to the system. Using a persistent connection allows us to retain this information.

Socket Servers

There are a number of socket servers available, and each has its advantages and disadvantages.

Flash Nexus – this is probably the best socket server available, and has been programmed with Flash specifically in mind. It's free to download, and has a very powerful graphical interface with multi-user capabilities including database access, multiple rooms, user registration, and more. However, it isn't cross-platform, and requires a Windows-based PC to run.

CommServer (by Derek Clayton) – this is an entry-level socket server that is again free to download. It's built in Java, so it is cross-platform and widely supported but doesn't have the power of other socket servers – it simply accepts a message and broadcasts that message to all clients that are logged in.

AquaServer (by Brandon Hall) – this falls somewhere between CommServer and Flash Nexus. It is built in Java making it cross-platform and widely supported; but it doesn't have the graphical interface offered by Flash Nexus.

Fortress (by XadrA) – is a powerful "all-singing all-dancing" server, and is not free. It's open-standards based, and has facilities to serve all kinds of devices simultaneously (mobile phones, personal computers, games consoles..). You can find out more about it at www.XadrA.com.

There are other Socket servers available (Flash Oracle and FlashNow, for example), but we are going to use CommServer because it's cross platform and very simple to use. If you intend to be working solely on a Windows server, then it might be a good idea to investigate Flash Nexus after you've seen how CommServer works.

Setting up the CommServer

Here, I'm going to take you through the process of installing the server and associated software. CommServer has three requirements, which are:

- You must have a free TCP port above 1024.

- You must have a Java Development Kit (JDK) or a Java Runtime Environment (JRE) installed on your computer.

- Your computer must be able to run Java programs.

Let's take a look at how to make sure that your machine satisfies these criteria. We'll assume that you're going to be working on your own computer for the moment - if you want to use this server in a web environment, you'll need to contact your ISP.

Installing Java

The first step is to install the JDK or JRE, both of which are freely available to download from www.javasoft.com. If you know that you already have Java installed on your computer, then you can skip this step. Some new operating systems, such as Mac OS X, come with a JDK already installed as standard.

Open your web browser and go to www.javasoft.com/products. There should be a list of product groups - choose the latest Java platform, standard edition, and then select the correct download for your operating system.

The JDK can be quite large, so you may need to wait for a while. Once you've downloaded it, follow the specific instructions for installing the software on your operating system. This is generally quite straightforward.

Installing CommServer

The next step is to install the CommServer Java application, which you can download from http://www.moock.org/chat/moockComm.zip. Unzip the file and place it somewhere on your hard disk in its own directory.

On most platforms you need to run the next command from a command line, such as the MSDos prompt on a Windows machine. At your command prompt, change to the directory in which you have stored the commserver files like this: cd myDirectory.

On a Macintosh machine under OS 9, there is no command line, so you will need to use the Jbindery program instead, which is covered in the documentation that comes with CommServer.

The next step is to start the server, so type the following command:

```
java CommServer 1025
```

If you are working on a Mac under OS 9, you need to drag the CommServer.class file onto the Jbindery application, type "COMMSERVER" into the "command" text area, and "1025" into the "arguments" text area.

Hopefully you should get a message something like the following:

Attempting to Start Server
Server Started on Port 1025

If you encounter a problem, take a look at the Java documentation and the help file that comes with CommServer.

The Flash XMLSocket class

Along with the more general XML support that we looked at in the previous chapter, Flash 5 introduced **XML sockets** to the Flash user. These have proved nothing short of revolutionary for ambitious Flash developers: not only do they allow us to set up persistent connections with an absolute minimum of fuss, but they also let us send and receive our data in XML format.

To establish a persistent connection between a Flash movie and a server, we simply need to create an XMLSocket object in the movie. Let's take a quick look at its methods and the types of events that it can handle.

Method	Purpose
connect()	Attempts to establish a connection with a server
close()	Terminates the connection
send()	Sends an XML fragment to the server

Events	Purpose
onConnect	Raised when a connection attempt finishes
onData	Raised when data is received, but before it is parsed as XML
onXML	Raised when received data has been parsed into an XML Object
onClose	Raised when the connection is closed by the server

Using a persistent connection to the socket server

Let's take a look at how we actually go about using an XMLSocket in Flash, and see what steps are required to make it do something useful. We'll start by setting up our connection.

Connecting to the server

1. Create a new Flash movie, name the default layer Actions, and put a `stop` command in Frame 1.

2. We need to create a new XMLSocket object, using the class constructor. Place this code under the `stop` action:

```
mySocket = new XMLSocket();
```

3. Connecting to the server is ultimately just as simple to achieve using the `connect` method:

```
mySocket.connect("192.168.10.175", "1025")
```

The two arguments specified refer to the socket server's location on the network, and the network port number through which it's communicating. You'll notice that my own test machine uses the IP address 192.168.10.175 to identify itself on the network, so that's what I'm using to point to the socket server. When it comes to publishing your application on the Web, you'll probably need to be a little less specific about where the socket server is located. In this case, you can simply specify the domain in which the server is running – for example:

```
mySocket.connect("http://www.somewhere.com", "1025")
```

4. If everything's gone to plan, our movie should now be able to establish a connection to the socket server, as shown:

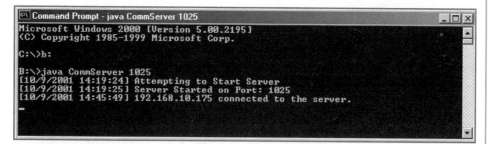

Catching connection errors

Well, the connection is working, but it doesn't actually **do** anything! Crucially, there's nothing in our movie to indicate whether or not the connection's been successful.

There are two phases in the connection process that we need to check for. The first is that a connection attempt has been started by Flash. The second is that a connection has been attempted with the server, and this is either successful or unsuccessful.

We can use the `connect` method to check for the first phase. The `connect` method returns a Boolean value indicating whether or not the connection attempt has been started successfully, returning `true` if it has, and `false` if not. Generally speaking this phase will be successful unless there is some kind of internal misconfiguration. We can therefore build a test for this condition into our code. Place this code under what you have written:

```
if( mySocket.connect("192.168.10.175", "1025") == false)
{
  trace("Error connecting");
  gotoAndStop("Error");
}
else
{
  trace("Connecting");
  gotoAndStop("Connecting");
}
```

As we've already noted, the XMLSocket object raises an `onConnect` event when a successful connection is established. This event can be used to let us know if we have successfully connected to the server. To make use of this, we just need to define a handler function for this event.

Defining a handler for the onConnect event

The first new line of code we need to add assigns a handler function called `handleConnect` to the `onConnect` event raised by `mySocket`.

```
stop();

mySocket = new XMLSocket();
mySocket.connect("192.168.10.175", "1025")

mySocket.onConnect = handleConnect;
```

> When defining an object's event handlers in this way, I've noticed that it's rather a common mistake to put brackets after the name of the function– for example, the following three examples are all wrong:
>
> ```
> mySocket.connect() = handleConnect;      // Wrong!
> mySocket.connect = handleConnect();      // Wrong!
> mySocket.connect() = handleConnect();   // Wrong!
> ```
>
> As you can see, the correct way to do it doesn't feature any brackets at all.

The `onConnect` handler is automatically passed a Boolean argument (which we've picked up as a parameter called `success`) that indicates whether the connection attempt was successful or not. Since you're dealing with a remote system, it's never wise to assume that the connection will succeed, so it's good practice to check for this whenever you use an XMLSocket.

The function itself simply uses trace calls to indicate the success (or otherwise) of the attempted connection:

```
function handleConnect(success)
{
  if (success)
    { trace("Connection successful"); }
  else
    { trace("An error occurred!"); }
}
```

Add this to your miniature movie beneath the code you have already, and give it a test run (CTRL+ENTER). You should now see the first signs of life from the movie – hopefully they'll look like this:

Okay, it's really not that impressive. However, we do now have the means to respond to the success or failure of the socket connection. From here, it hardly takes any effort to show our results to an end user – we just add a couple of messages to the stage and a gotoAndStop call for each one:

```
stop();

mySocket = new XMLSocket();
mySocket.connect("192.168.10.175", "1025")

mySocket.onConnect = handleConnect;

function handleConnect(success)
{
   if (success) {
      trace("Connection successful");
      gotoAndStop("Succeeded");
   } else {
      trace("An error occurred!");
      gotoAndStop("Failed");
   }
}
```

So, there are two points at which we can check for errors: our initial attempt to connect to the server, and when the onConnect event is raised.

Now that we have a connection to the server, let's start doing something with it.

Sending and receiving data via the server

As we saw in the previous chapter, XML provides us with a tremendously simple way to pass around sets of hierarchical data, such as we often find in our heavily object-based Flash projects. Flash stores XML in a handy node structure, letting us use dot notation to access specific parts of that structure.

So far, we've set up a connection between our movie's socket and the socket server (which for all practical purposes might easily be on the other side of the world). Now we want to communicate with the server, and broadcast our presence to anyone else that might happen to be hooked up to it.

Sending data with send

You probably won't be surprised to learn that we can use the XMLSocket send method to send data to the socket server. Likewise, it shouldn't come as a great shock to discover that we need to bundle that data into an XML object in order to send it – after all, that's what XML sockets are designed to work with.

In fact, the send method only takes one argument – the XML object containing the data we wish to send:

```
mySocket.send(someXML);
```

You should already be familiar with XML objects from the last chapter, so let's create a very simple one as follows:

```
someXML = new XML("<USER>Joe Bloggs</USER>");
```

If you add these two lines to your script, you should succeed in sending the name "Joe Bloggs" to the socket server as the value of a node called "USER". Fine, except that our movie isn't listening out for data, so you won't see any indication that it's actually worked.

Receiving XML objects with onXML

This isn't a problem – all we need to do is write a handler for the onXML event, and any data being broadcast by the server will be passed into it as an argument in the form of an XML object. The handler function below simply streams the contents of this object into a string, which it sends to the Output window:

```
mySocket.onXML = handleXML;

function handleXML(theXML)
{
   // XML has been received by Flash. Process it here
   trace( "XML received: " + theXML.toString() );
}
```

Add this to your script, and test the movie once again – you should now see the following:

```
Output                                            ×
                                          Options
Connecting
Connection successful
XML received: <NUMCLIENTS>1</NUMCLIENTS>
XML received: <USER>Joe Bloggs</USER>
```

What's this? We only sent one XML object, but it looks as if we've received two! You may even find (if you have a particularly sluggish connection to the server) that the XML received from the first object appears *before* the "Connection successful" message triggered by onConnect. So what's going on?

Well, it's obvious that we're not the only ones generating data here. Since we've just connected to the server, you won't be that surprised to discover that the server itself has sent out a message. The message in question contains a single XML node "NUMCLIENTS", whose value indicates how many users are currently connected to the server. It's sent out whenever someone connects to (or disconnects from) the server, so that any other connected clients can keep track of who else is online at any given moment. This is a very useful bit of data, and we'll be making substantial use of it very shortly.

> You might like to try duplicating the send call, or even removing it, just to demonstrate to yourself that the <NUMCLIENTS> message isn't sent in response to your own message, as it may initially appear to be.

The onXML handler isn't actually the first place you can get your hands on data received by the socket. Your XMLSocket will initially deal with string-formatted XML data, and then use a default handler function called onData to parse this string into the XML object we pick up in the onXML handler. While you can normally get by just fine without knowing anything at all about the onData handler, you can occasionally get some slight speed increases in your Flash movie by writing your own version, and parsing the raw XML yourself.

In this case, we've used the XML object's toString method to format the objects' contents in a readable form – effectively reversing the effect of the default onData handler. In fact, we could have got exactly the same results by writing our own onData handler and simply outputting the string-formatted XML that gets passed to that. Either way, this format obviously makes it easy for us to read all the XML messages received, and for that reason can prove very useful for monitoring application status and debugging.

As we saw in the last chapter, a different set of priorities kicks in when we start wanting to manipulate our data. Particularly when working with more complex data hierarchies, it's much, much simpler to be able to treat them as objects. We can apply this to our current example very easily – each of the XML objects we've received has just one node, so we just grab the values of each one:

```
function handleXML(theXML)
{
  // XML has been received by Flash. Process it here
  rootNode = theXML.firstChild;

  trace( "NodeName received: " + rootNode.nodeName.toString() );
  trace( "NodeValue received: " + rootNode.firstChild.
nodeValue.toString() );
}
```

As you'll recall from the last chapter, the value we're trying to access is actually held inside a text node within the root node we're looking at. In order to read the node value, we therefore need to access the value held in its `firstChild` node. Don't worry if this seems strange at first: there are plenty of examples in this and subsequent chapters that should help make this seem a little more natural.

Update the `handleXML` function as shown, and test the movie – you should see the following output:

Essentially, we're simply pulling properties off the root node of each XML object. As we learned in the last chapter, the node value needs a little more persuading than the node name, due to the way that Flash XML objects store element values. Besides this, there's very little to it, mainly because we know in advance exactly what the XML is going to look like (and it's not exactly what you'd call complex), and we're treating all the data we receive in exactly the same way. In practice, we may well need to be ready for a whole range of different possible inputs, figure out what sort of data we've been sent, and then decide what to do with it.

Presenting received data in the movie

Let's add some dynamic text fields to the Messages layer of our movie – specifically in the Succeeded frames – and use them to display the data we've received. In the screenshot, I've added some static text labels to mark the dynamic fields `userCount` and `userName`:

Now we just need to update the `handleXML` handler function so that it passes received data to these variables. In some applications, you can be absolutely certain of the structure of any message you're going to receive, and you can therefore search through each object's XML in a systematic fashion.

A less efficient, but much more flexible approach is to take each XML object received, scan through its top-level nodes, and take specific actions whenever you match specific `nodeNames`. If unexpected nodes are encountered, they'll simply be ignored, and this makes for a robust program that can handle bad data without going to pieces. This approach also makes it very easy to add new functionality to the application without having to go through a lot of tedious recoding. All in all, it has quite a lot going for it!

As we've seen, all XML objects have a `firstChild` property, which corresponds to the first node in the object. We start with this node, and then use the `nextSibling` property of that node to traverse the top-level node structure.

```
function handleXML(theXML)
{
  // XML has been received by Flash. Process it here
  rootNode = theXML.firstChild;

  do {
    if(rootNode.nodeName == "NUMCLIENTS")
    {
      // NUMCLIENTS node found
      userCount = rootNode.firstChild.nodeValue + " user(s)
online";
      trace( "Number of clients: " +
rootNode.firstchild.nodeValue.toString() );
    }
    else if(rootNode.nodeName == "USER")
    {
      // USER node found
      userName = rootNode.firstChild.nodeValue + "just connected
to the server";
      trace( "New client name: " +
rootNode.firstchild.nodeValue.toString() );
    }
  }
  while ( childNode = childNode.nextSibling )
}
```

When we test our SWF, we'll see the received information presented within the movie itself, just as we'd expect.

You can see the user count in the movie itself, so you might like to open up a few more instances of the SWF and see for yourself that the <NUMCLIENTS> value does indeed rack up as each user connects to the server. You'll see the count update automatically in every instance, and if you check out the Output window on your original Test Movie instance, you can see that the user name gets sent out each time. Now try closing all these extra SWFs, and watch the user count drop again:

```
Connecting
Connection successful
Number of clients: 1
New client name: Joe Bloggs
Number of clients: 2
New client name: Joe Bloggs
Number of clients: 3
New client name: Joe Bloggs
Number of clients: 4
New client name: Joe Bloggs
Number of clients: 3
Number of clients: 2
Number of clients: 1
Number of clients: 2
New client name: Joe Bloggs
Number of clients: 3
New client name: Joe Bloggs
Number of clients: 2
Number of clients: 1
```

Closing the connection to the server

What happens when we're done with our socket connection? Well, that depends on who wants to break things off first: the Flash client or the socket server. Say we encounter freak network conditions that prevent any kind of data getting through, and your movie loses its connection to the server. Alternatively, the server crashes completely, and can't transmit any more data. Either way, when the socket in your movie loses its connection to the server, it raises an onClose event. You can therefore write a handler that will output some kind of error message, or perhaps ask the user to attempt a new login. Here's how we might define a simple handler:

```
mySocket.onClose  = handleClose;

function handleClose()
{
  trace("Error: the connection has closed");
  gotoAndStop("Error");
}
```

It's quite easy to test this – just create a new Error frame, run the movie, and shut down the server!

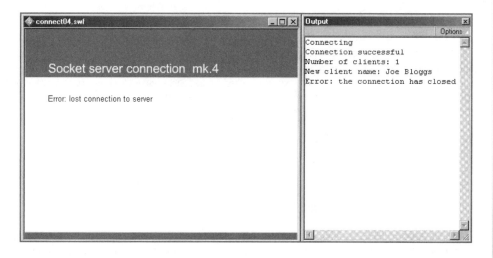

Okay, so we've got the "lost server connection" scenario covered. But what if our users want to disconnect for themselves? Well, we've already seen that the socket server will register a client breaking off their connection (even if they simply shut down the client SWF) by bumping down the user count – what more do we need?

Let's consider a practical scenario: say we've a bunch of twenty friends logged into an online chat room. Everyone's chatting away happily, and Bill spots that it's well past time he went out to meet his date for the evening. He quickly shuts down his computer and heads out for a night of fun and frolics. Everyone else spots that the user count has dropped by a count of 1, but none of them know **who** it was that just left! When Pat and Jon then ask him to help them resolve a difference of opinions, they can't be sure whether he's thinking very deeply about their problem or has simply gone away...

So closing SWFs isn't exactly the most civilized way to break off your connection – how about we build a 'Quit' button into our movie? We can then use it to send out a quick message saying something like "Joe Bloggs has now left the server". If we add a call to our XML socket's `close` method, we can use this to break off the connection as well.

```
function quitServer()
{
  // Put the userName variable into an XML object
  closeXML = new XML(userName);
  closeXML.nodeName = "USERLEFT";

  // Send the XML object to the server
  mySocket.send(closeXML);

  // Close the XMLSocket connection
  mySocket.close();

  // Redirect to the Offline frame
  gotoAndStop("Offline");
}
```

The first part of the function sends an XML object to the server, informing other users of the fact that this particular user has quit the server. We put the `userName` variable into a node called `USERLEFT`, so that the resulting XML will look like `<USERLEFT>Joe Bloggs</USERLEFT>`. We then close the connection to the server using the `close` method and send the user to the Offline frame.

We now need to wire up a Quit button on the "Succeeded" frame with the following script:

```
on(release)
{
  quitServer();
}
```

Finally, we need to add a little to our message handling script. When an active client receives one of these `USERLEFT` nodes, we want a message to appear on their screens, telling them that the specified user has left. Inside our function `handleXML`, we want to add the highlighted lines:

```
do {
  if(rootNode.nodeName == "NUMCLIENTS")
  { ... }
  else if(rootNode.nodeName == "USER")
  { ... }
  else if(rootNode.nodeName == "USERLEFT")
  {
```

```
            // USERLEFT node found
            userLeft = rootNode.firstChild.nodeValue + "has left the
        ➡ server";
            trace( "Client quit: " +
        ➡ rootNode.firstchild.nodeValue.toString() );
        }
    }
    while ( childNode = childNode.nextSibling )
}
```

Writing more complex XML objects

Let's again consider a number of users talking to each other in an online chat room. Each user will be able to send messages to all of the other users in the room. The XML for this might be structured as follows:

```
<USER>Joe Bloggs</USER><MESSAGE>Hello World!</MESSAGE>
```

This indicates that user "Joe Bloggs" has sent a message to the group saying "Hello World!" We might consider putting this message into an XML object as follows:

```
myXML = new XML("<USER>Joe Bloggs</USER><MESSAGE>Hello
➡World!</MESSAGE>");
```

In theory, that's all well and good. In practice though, you're going to be taking the user name and message text from object properties within your client application. Consequently, this isn't the most versatile way to do things – you might well end up with something like:

```
myXML = new XML("<USER>" + name + "</USER><MESSAGE>" + message +
➡"</MESSAGE>");
```

As we know, Flash treats XML in an object-oriented fashion. Although it takes up a few more lines of code, it's ultimately far more flexible to put together the XML node structure using an object-based approach.

Let's apply this to our user-message example. Start by creating an XML object called userXML to contain the first node "USER". Give it the value "Joe Bloggs", and set its nodeName property to "USER":

```
userXML = new XML("Joe Bloggs");
userXML.nodeName = "USER";
```

If you use the toString method to trace this to the output window, you'll see:

```
<USER>Joe Bloggs</USER>
```

Now do exactly the same thing for the "MESSAGE" node:

```
messageXML = new XML("Hello World!");
messageXML.nodeName = "MESSAGE";
```

We now have two XML objects, and need to specify them as nodes within a single XML hierarchy. The easiest way to do this is to create a new XML object and apply the `appendChild` method for each one:

```
myXML = new XML();
myXML.appendChild(userXML);
myXML.appendChild(messageXML);
```

Now that the object is prepared, we just need to send it to the server:

```
mySocket.send(myXML);
```

Of course, this will give you just the same results as the string-based definition. However, you should find that this basis proves very rewarding when your XML structures start to get more complex. In fact, we now have all the building blocks in place to create a full-blown application, and that's precisely what we're going to spend the rest of the chapter doing.

A multiuser chat room

A chat room, in case you're unfamiliar with the term, is an area of a web site which will allow a number of users to send messages to each other, and to have a virtual conversation with a number of other people logged in to the same web site.

Let's take a look at what it should look like:

The Flash movie will contain a number of sections:

- A login frame, where the user is asked to log in to the site

- A frame telling the user that the movie is connecting

- An error frame, in case there is a problem connecting

- A chat frame (which is what you can see above) where the user will be able to type in a message to be sent

- A frame to show that the chat session has finished

Building the chat room

We're going to go through this step by step, so let's start by building the graphical content that we need, before writing the code to manipulate everything.

1. Start a new movie, and make it 400 x 300 pixels. Set up the timeline with four layers, as in the screenshot. Add the labels Login, Connecting, Error, Chat, and Offline to frames 1, 10, 20, 30, and 40 of the top layer.

2. On the bottom layer, you need to place all of the background graphics that will stay looking the same throughout the movie. I've used a very plain style, with a couple of gray boxes and a title - but feel free to be a bit more inventive.

XML Chat Client

3. If you haven't done it already, add keyframes to correspond with the labels you created in step one on the next layer up (labeled Content in the screenshot). In the first frame, add an input box for the user to type in their user name, and a short explanation.

4. Still in the same frame, create a simple OK button, and attach the following ActionScript to it:

```
on(release)
{
    if(!(username eq ""))
    { chatConnect();}
}
```

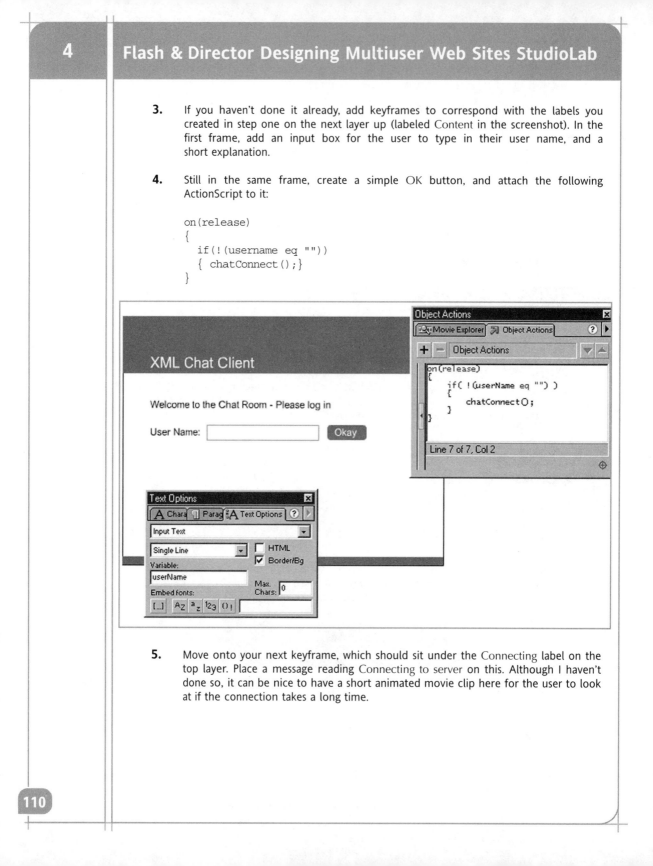

5. Move onto your next keyframe, which should sit under the Connecting label on the top layer. Place a message reading Connecting to server on this. Although I haven't done so, it can be nice to have a short animated movie clip here for the user to look at if the connection takes a long time.

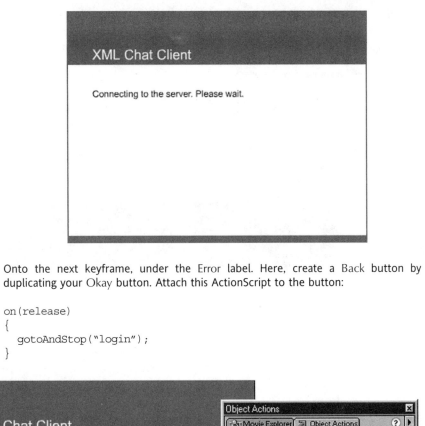

6. Onto the next keyframe, under the Error label. Here, create a Back button by duplicating your Okay button. Attach this ActionScript to the button:

```
on(release)
{
    gotoAndStop("login");
}
```

7. The Chat frame is next, and this is the most important frame in the movie - this is the frame where the user actually does the chatting. You need to create four text boxes as shown in the screenshot, and set their properties as shown in the individual boxes. In particular, make sure that you check the HTML option of the `chatDisplay` and `messageText` text boxes.

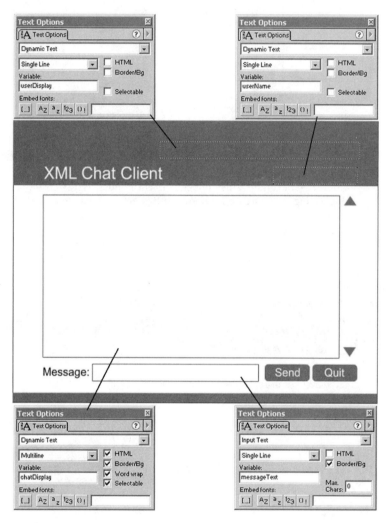

8. Now, still on the same keyframe, we need to create some simple buttons. First of all, we need some buttons to control the scrolling of the main text window, so create a simple scroll button, and place two copies of it to the right of the window to allow users to scroll up and down. Then, create buttons called Quit and Send at the bottom right of the screen. Add the scripts shown in the screenshot to the buttons.

```
on(release)                     on(release)
{                               {
  chatDisplay.scroll ++;          chatDisplay.scroll --;
}                               }
```

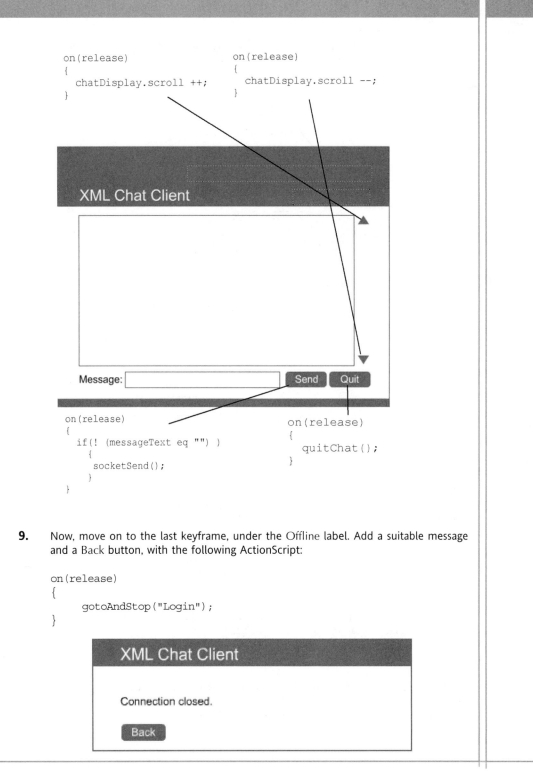

```
on(release)                     on(release)
{                               {
  if(! (messageText eq "") )        quitChat();
    {                           }
     socketSend();
    }
}
```

9. Now, move on to the last keyframe, under the Offline label. Add a suitable message and a Back button, with the following ActionScript:

```
on(release)
{
    gotoAndStop("Login");
}
```

To finish this section, use the remaining empty layer to place a `stop;` command on each of the frames that we've added content to (1, 10, 20, 30, 40).

The main script

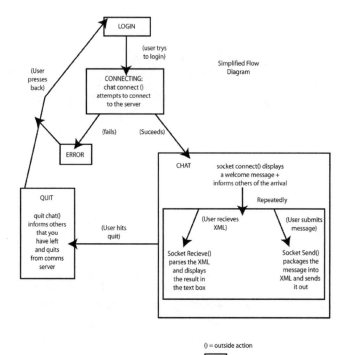

Simplified Flow Diagram

() = outside action

☐ = Frame

We now move on to the ActionScript that will control our movie, which you can see shown in diagram format above. Let's start by defining a couple of important variables in the first frame of the movie, on the "Actions" layer:

```
// Change the following variables to your chat server's URL
//and Port number
var serverAddress = "www.somewhere.com";
var serverPort = "1025";
```

Each of the following function definitions should be added to the same frame. We'll go through them all so that you can understand what's going on.

chatConnect

This function handles setting up the connection to the server, and sets up an XMLSocket object, which we use throughout the script. This is called when the user types in their user name into the box on the "Login" frame, and presses the "Okay" button.

```
function chatConnect()
{
  // Create a new XMLSocket object
  chatSocket = new XMLSocket();

  // Define its methods
  chatSocket.onConnect = socketConnect;
  chatSocket.onXML = socketReceive;
  chatSocket.onClose = socketClose;
```

Our XMLSocket module is going to be called "chatSocket" and here we set up the handlers for the onConnect, onXML and onClose events, as we discussed earlier in the chapter.

```
  // Go to the Connecting frame
  gotoAndStop("Connecting");
```

Once the XMLSocket is instantiated, and its event handlers have been set up, the user is redirected to the "Connecting" frame, and is shown the "connecting" message.

```
  // If there is an error connecting, redirect to the Error
➡ frame
  if (!chatSocket.connect(serverAddress, serverPort));
  {
    gotoAndStop("Error");
  }
}
```

A connection with the server is then attempted, as we have discussed previously, and if an error occurs, the user is redirected to the Error page.

socketConnect

This function is the handler for the onConnect event for the XMLSocket. This is very similarly structured to the handleConnect function that we saw earlier on in this chapter.

```
function socketConnect(success)
{
  if(success)
  {
    chatDisplay = "<p>Welcome to the chat room at " +
➡ serverAddress  + "</p>";
    gotoAndStop("Chat");
```

The serverAddress variable used here is defined in the first frame of our movie, and is the IP address or URL of the chat server.

When the user connects to the chat room successfully for the first time, it flags up a welcome message in the chat display area (the main text box), along with the server address. The user is then sent to the "Chat" frame.

```
                              userName = stripTags(userName);

                              newUserXML = new XML(userName);
                              newUserXML.nodeName = "NEWUSER";

                              // Send the XML object to the server through the
                          ➥ chatSocket object
                              chatSocket.send(stripTags(newUserXML));
```

You will notice that there is a function used here called `stripTags`, which removes any reserved HTML characters (such as the characters < and >) from `userName`. We'll explain why we need to do this in a moment.

We would also like the other users in the chat room to be made aware that a new user has connected, so this function sends an XML fragment to the server containing the `userName`, in the following format:

```
<NEWUSER>Joe Bloggs</NEWUSER>
```

This will cause a message to appear on all of the other users' screens, announcing Joe's arrival. The remainder of the function is fairly straightforward – if there is some kind of connection error, we send the user to the Error page.

```
       }
       else
       {
       // There was an error connecting to the server,
    //so go to the error page
         gotoAndStop("Error");
       }
    }
```

socketReceive

The `socketReceive` function is the handler for chatSocket's onXML events. Its purpose is to break up the different types of messages that it may receive, and to deal with them appropriately. The messages that we're going to be dealing with are:

- NUMCLIENTS – the CommServer sends out the number of clients currently connected to it whenever a client connects or disconnects in a single node.

- USER – when a message is sent to the server, the username of the sender is sent in a USER node.

- MESSAGE – when a message is sent from a client, it is sent in this node.

- NEWUSER – when a user joins the chat, the client sends this node, containing the user name.

- USERLEFT – this message is sent when a user disconnects from the server using the "Quit" button, and contains the user's name.

```
function socketReceive(messageXML)
{
  // Create an arbitrary container for the message
  var myMessage = new Object();

  // This is a container for the resulting new message
  var toDisplay = "";
```

The handler is called whenever the XMLSocket receives XML, so we need to establish what data has been received. As we've observed, the best way to do this is to loop through each child of the received XML, and act appropriately. Remember that this isn't the only option – with applications for which you can be absolutely certain of the structure of any messages received, you may prefer to search through the XML in a more structured way. For instance, you could set up your XML data to exactly match the object structure of your movie, because the node structure of an XML document is very similar to Flash's own object oriented structure.

Here, we're going to select the first node in the object and use its `nextSibling` property to loop through the top-level node structure:

```
// Obtain the first child node of the received XML
var childNode = messageXML.firstChild;

do
{
```

Then we check what type of node has been encountered, and act appropriately.

```
if(childNode.nodeName == "NUMCLIENTS")
{
  // NUMCLIENTS node found
  userDisplay = childNode.firstChild.nodeValue + " user(s)
  ➥online";
}
```

A NUMCLIENTS node has been encountered, so the program updates the `userDisplay` variable, to display the number of users currently online. This is displayed at the top right of the chat window.

The NUMCLIENTS node for 5 online users will look like this:

```
<NUMCLIENTS>5</NUMCLIENTS>
```

Flash parses XML in a way that at first may seem a little counter-intuitive. Remember that the number '5' is actually held inside a text node within the NUMCLIENTS node. You could imagine that there is an invisible 'TEXT' XML tag with '5' as its value. To Flash, this might look like the following:

```
<NUMCLIENTS><TEXT VALUE="5"></NUMCLIENTS>
```

In order to access the number 5, we therefore need to access `node.firstChild.nodeValue`.

```
else if(childNode.nodeName == "USER")
{
  // USER node found
  myMessage.user = childNode.firstChild.nodeValue;
}
```

If it wasn't a NUMCLIENTS node, we check to see if it's a USER node. If it is, its value is added to the empty `myMessage` object in a new property of that object called `user`.

The only reason we move this variable around like this is that we need some kind of temporary storage whilst looping through each child node of the original message.

```
else if(childNode.nodeName == "NEWUSER")
{
  // NEWUSER node found
  myMessage.message = childNode.firstChild.nodeValue + " has
  ➥joined the channel";
}
```

If the node wasn't a NUMCLIENTS node, we carry on and check for a NEWUSER node.

This node is sent whenever a user joins the server, and we assign Joe Bloggs has joined the channel to the message property of our temporary message object.

```
else if(childNode.nodeName == "MESSAGE")
{
  // MESSAGE node found
  myMessage.message = unescape
  ➥(childNode.firstChild.nodeValue);
}
```

Whenever we send a message to the chat server, we first run the `escape` function, which turns standard plain text into URL-ENCODED text. We made use of this function when dealing with `loadVariables` in previous chapters, and we use the reverse function `unescape` here to decode the received message.

All the messages that we send to the server are first encoded into URL-ENCODED format, so we need to decode it here so that the message is readable.

If it wasn't any of the above, it might be a MESSAGE node. If it is, we assign its value to the message property of the temporary message object.

```
else if(childNode.nodeName == "USERLEFT")
{
  // USERLEFT node found
  myMessage.message = childNode.firstChild.nodeValue + "
  ➥ has left the channel";
}
```

Finally, it might be a USERLEFT message, in which case we set the message to Joe Bloggs has left the channel.

```
        }
        while ( childNode = childNode.nextSibling )

        // Update the chat display area by putting the new message at
        // the top

        if(myMessage.message.length > 0)
        {
          toDisplay = "<p>";

          if(myMessage.user.length > 0)
          {
            toDisplay += "<b>" + myMessage.user + "</b> : ";
          }

          toDisplay += myMessage.message + "</p>";
          chatDisplay = toDisplay + chatDisplay;

          // Scroll the list back to the top
          chatDisplay.scroll = 0;
        }
        trace(chatDisplay);
      }
```

The final part of the function formats the output for display, appends it to the top of the message display window and sets its scroll back to zero if a new message has been posted. This is so that the user is always made aware that a new message has arrived.

socketClose

```
        function socketClose()
        {
          gotoAndStop("Offline");
        }
```

In comparison to the last function, this one seems almost too simple! All we do here is to send the user to the Offline frame, which alerts them to the fact that their chat session has been terminated.

socketSend

Besides receiving data, the other major function our chat room handles is sending a message to the server. This is handled by the socketSend function. We have already seen how to send a message to the server, and this is just a slightly more complex implementation of what we saw earlier.

```
function socketSend()
{
  // Create an empty XML object
  myXML = new XML();

  // Put the userName variable into an XML object and
  // let it be called "USER," so that the
  // resulting XML will look like <USER>Joe Bloggs</USER>

  userXML = new XML(userName);
  userXML.nodeName = "USER";

  // Place the message to be posted into an XML object:
  // Eg. <MESSAGE>A short message</MESSAGE>

  messageXML = new XML(escape(stripTags(messageText)));
  messageXML.nodeName = "MESSAGE";

  // Append the two XML objects to the main XML object as
➥ nodes
  myXML.appendChild(userXML);
  myXML.appendChild(messageXML);

  // Send the XML object to the server through the chatSocket
➥ object
  chatSocket.send(myXML);

  // Clear the message box
  messageText = "";
}
```

The function is run when something is typed into the message box on the chat page, and the Send button is pressed. The data sent to the server is in the following format:

```
<USER>Joe Bloggs</USER><MESSAGE>Hello World!</MESSAGE>
```

As we have done previously, we create two XML objects to hold the message information – the user name and the message, and then append them to a third container object. We then send this container object (myXML) to the server through the chatSocket object.

The only thing left to do is to empty the messageText text box by setting its contents to "" (the empty string).

quitChat

Our next function is used to handle closing the chat session, and gets called when the user presses the Quit button in the Chat frame:

```
function quitChat()
{
// Put the userName variable into an XML object
// and let it be called "USERLEFT," so that the
// resulting XML will look like <USERLEFT>Joe Bloggs</USERLEFT>
  closeXML = new XML(userName);
  closeXML.nodeName = "USERLEFT";

// Send the XML object to the server through the chatSocket
➡ object
  chatSocket.send(closeXML);
```

The first part of the function sends a USERLEFT fragment to the server, which alerts all other users on the server to the fact that the user has left the chat area. When an active client receives this, a message should appear on their screen, which tells them that the specified user has quit.

```
// Close the XMLSocket connection
chatSocket.close ();

// Redirect to the Offline frame
gotoAndStop("Offline");
}
```

We close the connection to the server using the close method and send the user to the Offline frame.

stripTags and strip

The last two functions work closely together, and fix a small problem in our otherwise trouble-free program! The problem I refer to stems from the fact that it's fairly easy to create XML objects whose data contains markup tags. You might want to add HTML tags to format your messages, and this is fine, so long as you get them right. If not, the resulting HTML may break the application when it's written to the chat display box, and make the chat room unusable. You could easily extend this program to filter out other kinds of characters or unacceptable language.

Let's take a quick look at an example:

```
<USER>Joe Bloggs</USER><MESSAGE>Check this out ---> www.mysite.com
<cool eh?) </MESSAGE>
```

Here, Joe has sent a message to the server that contains two reserved characters in HTML – the '>' and the '<' character. This means that when the resulting message is received, the following HTML will be added to the output screen:

```
<p><b>Joe Bloggs :</b> Check this out ---> www.mysite.com <cool
eh?</p>
```

This may not seem too important at first, but what happens is that Flash fails to parse the HTML correctly, and the results are unpredictable, but definitely not good! What we need to do is to replace the '<' and '>' symbols with their HTML equivalents.

In HTML, special characters are special identifiers – so '<' and '>' become '<' and '>' respectively. The functions stripTags and strip are what we use to replace all instances of these characters with their HTML equivalents.

```
function stripTags(theString)
{
  tempString = new String(theString);

  tempString = strip("<", "&lt;", tempString);
  tempString = strip(">", "&gt;", tempString);

  return( tempString );
}
```

The stripTags function just runs successive calls to strip, and accepts three arguments:

- theChar is the character to search for

- replaceChar is the character to replace theChar with

- theString is the string in which to search

First, we want to check to see if there is an occurrence of the character. If there is, we use the function String.split, with theChar specified as the character on which to split. What this means is that we divide the string up into shorter strings, wherever there is an occurrence of theChar. Here's the code:

```
function strip(theChar, replaceChar, theString)
{
  if(theString.indexOf(theChar)   != -1)
  {
    stringArray = theString.split(theChar);
```

Let's say we have the string "Check out my site > at > www.somewhere.com". Once the above code has been executed, the contents of the stringArray variable would be the following 3 items:

```
"Check out my site "
" at "
" www.somewhere.com"
```

```
    returnString = stringArray[0];

    for(x = 1; x < stringArray.length; x++)
    {
```

```
                returnString += replaceChar + stringArray[x];

        }
```

The function then loops through each item in the array, and appends it to a new string, with `replaceChar` in between each one:

```
        "Check out my site " + "&lt;" + " at " + "&lt;" + "
        www.somewhere.com"

          return (returnString);
        }
        else
        {
          return(theString);
        }
      }
```

We then return the result and the function ends.

Get chatting

Now that you've finished all of the ActionScript, just export your Flash movie, make sure that your socket server is up and running,and invite all your friends to join you for a friendly network chat! To test it out at the moment, you can run the application from two browser windows, or if you are on a local area network, from computer to computer.

If you want to install the chat application on a web server, you're going to have to give your friendly ISP a call first. Your ISP may or may not be willing to run commServer on its server because of security issues.

Security Issues

Security is one of the most important issues to consider when developing any kind of application, whether it is a database, a game, or an e-commerce system, and there are a number of things of which a programmer needs to be aware when working over the Internet or in any network situation.

I'm just going to run through a few of the main security issues that you will encounter when developing multi-user applications.

Domain Restriction

Flash has an in-built security feature known as "domain restriction," which only allows an SWF file in a particular domain to access server-side scripts and data from locations within that same domain. In practical terms, it means that we can only load in XML data from the same server that our SWF file is located on, and we cannot load in data from other servers.

Let's say that we had an SWF file located on our web server, which is located at www.mydomain.com/mymovie.swf and we want to load in some data from the file www.mydomain.com/data.txt using our old friend `loadVariables`.

The request is only allowed because the `data.txt` file is in the same domain as the `mymovie.swf` file – www.mydomain.com. If we were to attempt to load data from a file in another domain, such as www.anotherdomain.com/otherdata.txt, assuming that this file exists, no data would be loaded. Interestingly, Flash doesn't report an error when you attempt to do this, which can lead to a lot of frustration. One point to note is that it is also permitted to access files and scripts in a subdomain of the location of the SWF file, so it would be fine to load in data from mysubdomain.mydomain.com/data.txt.

This domain restriction applies to the XMLSocket object too, which means that when we make our multi-user applications, it is necessary for all of our SWFs to be in the same domain as the XML Socket Server.

Interestingly, the restrictions only apply to the Flash browser plug-in and ActiveX component. If we compile our movies into a projector for download, access to other servers is permitted.

There are two ways to get around the domain restriction security feature should the need arise for you to access data from a server in a different domain from your flash file.

The first is to set up what is known as a "Proxy script" - a very simple script that resides on the same domain as your SWF. All this does is to accept requests from the SWF, and pass them on to a different server. This second server returns some information or runs a script based on the information it receives from the proxy script. If any information is returned, it is received and passed back to the SWF.

This is a good method for accessing data on other servers, but it is quite CPU-intensive for the server that hosts the proxy script, especially if there are a large number of users or there is a lot of traffic.

The second method for bypassing the security restriction is to use "Domain Name System (DNS) aliasing" which entails setting up an "alias" for the required server, which acts as a pointer to the server. This requires knowledge about DNS and server administration, so it's best to talk to your system administrator about this.

Port Access

Any given web server is able to accept transmissions over a number of different protocols, the one that we use the most being HTTP – the web protocol. Others include FTP for file transfer, POP for mail and Telnet for interacting with UNIX-based servers.

Web servers accept communication via each protocol only through a specified 'TCP port' – there can be one or more for each protocol. You can think of a port as a doorway through which data can travel, but only certain forms of data are allowed through each door.

When a port is 'open' the server is in a state where it is accepting data via that port. If it is 'closed', no data can travel through it. Each port is given a unique number or ID, and some ports are associated with certain protocols. For instance, the HTTP port is generally 80, although this can differ in some circumstances.

In Flash, there is another security feature that limits the ports to which an XMLSocket object can connect. These ports are numbered from 1024 upwards. The reason for this is that most port numbers are below this value, and most of the powerful protocols are associated with these port numbers. By disallowing any connection with these ports, we reduce the possibility that a hacker could misuse an unsuspecting SWF file to take advantage of certain security holes that might be present in applications which accept data via those ports.

Don't worry if this all sounds quite intimidating. All you have to remember is that if you set up an XML Socket server, it is imperative that it runs on a port greater than or equal to 1024.

Data Security

Another major issue with using XMLSocket objects to transfer data to and from a server is that XML sent via an XMLSocket is just as secure as sending data with HTTP – in other words, not very secure at all!

When you use the Web to buy something, I think you would probably agree that you would not be happy ordering from a site that doesn't use what is known as a 'secure server.'

A secure server is one that uses the HTTPS protocol to transfer data, and it is this protocol that we use to send important information such as credit card details across the web. HTTPS uses extremely powerful encryption algorithms to ensure that the credit card number cannot be intercepted along its way from one computer to another.

Other protocols, such as HTTP can be intercepted in transit, and thus are not viable for transmitting information that may be highly important or private details such as credit card numbers. Unfortunately, the same holds true for data sent via an XML Socket, so it is not a good idea to rely on them to transmit important data.

Conclusion

Well done! You've just created your first real-time multiuser Flash application! Over the next few chapters you're going to build on the knowledge you've gained here, and you will be learning some more advanced techniques and technologies as we go on. You're now well on your way to being able to put together a multiuser environment where people can move around and interact in real-time.

Chapter 5

A Realtime
Application

Once you have a good idea of how to make your Flash movies talk to one another over the Internet – and you should do by now – you need to figure out *what* they should be saying to each other. The biggest problem we face in working with a real-time connection is that every little hiccup in the network, every little spate of Internet congestion can show up very obviously as a lag in the client response time. Consequently, it's very important to keep your messages as concise as possible – conveying the information you *need* to, and no more – so as to make the application work without eating up all the available bandwidth in the process.

Of course, we could take this to extremes, and work out how to code our messages in such a way as to use the smallest possible number of ones and zeroes. Along the way, we'd totally undermine all the advantages of XML – apart from anything else it would be a real nightmare to debug! No, we'll leave all that binary encoding to the hardcore programmers, and aim for a useful balance between efficiency and good old-fashioned ease-of-use. In the course of this chapter, we're going to take a look at three important ways in which we can reduce the load our applications put on the network:

- Identifying redundant information, and rationalizing the design of our messaging system

- Storing data on the server, so that application state information can be accessed centrally

- Sending messages to specific clients only, rather than broadcasting everything to everyone

In order to do the last two of these, we're going to need a more sophisticated server than the simple relay we looked at in the last chapter, and MultiServer fits the bill quite nicely - it's fairly simple compared to most servers you're likely to find being used in a production environment, but it's designed to be easily extensible, and should give you a very good idea of the possibilities that more complex servers open up to us.

Talking the same language

One of the most important aspects of building any multiuser application is determining the "language" that your system will use. In this respect, the freedom that XML affords you to structure your documents in any way you desire can even start to feel like a stumbling block. Where should I put my username? How do I structure my draw coordinates? You may even feel a sudden onset of paranoia – *"what if I make the wrong decision? I don't want to have to rewrite my parser again!"*

The danger is that your designs never actually get built because you can't come to a definitive conclusion about the data structure. Most of us, by now, have heard the jokes describing how to succeed as a middle manager in a large corporation: never make any decisions, that way you'll never make any mistakes. Hang around long enough, and they'll make you VP.

Unfortunately, this approach won't work in development (and it'll bury you as a project manager). As you gain experience with multiuser systems, you'll get better at forecasting the data model (what your XML messages look like). In the meantime, you'll spend at least an iteration or two trying one message format, writing a parser script to handle it, and then changing your mind and starting over. That's normal, and in the end, you'll get noticeably faster at writing those parser scripts. Practice, practice, practice.

The best advice is to keep your parsing modular. Don't try to pull all the XML data out and into your movie with one huge parsing function. Instead, organize your parser into separate functions. Try to let your functions mirror the structure of the document itself.

Now take a deep breath. Not because we're about to learn something difficult – but because we're *not*. You've already ingested everything you need to know about building multiuser environments in Flash. Breathe easy, and most of all, relax. We're not going to introduce any new objects or features. You've earned a break from all that.

Instead, we're going to take what we've learned so far and use it to build a more complex multiuser application; in this case, a virtual whiteboard.

Building a multiuser whiteboard

Just as everyone connected to our chat application in the last chapter received and displayed chat messages, participants in our whiteboard application will receive and display messages that describe where to draw on the screen. In the chat example, we parse the incoming XML file and pull out the text that describes the message and the sender's name. That data is then placed in textfields for display. The whiteboard will do the same. We'll parse the incoming XML file and pull out the data that describes what should be drawn on screen. Instead of displaying this data in textfields, we'll use Flash's attachMovie method to "draw" on the stage.

Building a single-user whiteboard

First, let's spend a few moments thinking about those parts of our system that don't involve server connections and XML. Essentially, we want to let users draw lines on the screen, letting them pick and choose from a range of different styles, weights, and colors. How do we do this?

In fact, we really just need to follow the mouse pointer around the screen and draw lines whenever the mouse button is clicked. The only slight problem is that Flash doesn't have its own draw method, so we'll need to build our own. One very effective (not to mention versatile) way to do this is to create a movie clip depicting a diagonal line. We copy the line (with duplicateMovieClip or attachMovie) to wherever the mouse happens to be, and scale it so that it connects seamlessly to the last-recorded mouse position. By simply manipulating the position and scale properties of each copy, we can plot lines that connect any two points on the screen.

To see an initial version of the whiteboard (single user), load up whiteboard.fla in the 6.1 folder of the code download. The resulting SWF will produce the following drawing environment.

There are a few limitations to this technique. First, if you move your mouse quickly, the pen doesn't draw between dots. This is because Flash runs its scripts based on the framerate. If the mouse moves 100 pixels between frames, the dots that our movie draws will be 100 pixels apart. Try raising and lowering the framerate of the example to see how this affects the drawing behavior. Unfortunately, even if we attempt to crank the framerate outside the bounds of reason (i.e. 40 fps), our movie will still leave gaps if we move the mouse fast enough.

We could mathematically calculate the distance between points and (using some linear algebra) place dots along the path. However, this exposes another problem. As the number of objects placed on screen goes up, the framerate of our movie goes down. Eventually, the movie becomes noticeably sluggish.

Before we look at a solution for this, let's examine the code that allows us to plot points.

The function to plot a point looks like this:

```
PlotPoint = function (x, y) {
    Var myDepth = attachDepth++
    This.attachMovie ("pt", "pt"+ myDepth, myDepth)

    Var myPointMc = this["pt"+ myDepth]

    //align the clip with the coordinates
    MyPointMc._x = x;
    MyPointMc._y = y;
}
```

What if we could simply draw lines between the points? Well, Flash doesn't have a "drawline" method either, but there is a handy little trick that will let us build one. This technique has been around since Flash 4, and it's remarkably simple. Instead of duplicating dots, we duplicate lines – diagonal lines to be precise. By manipulating the _xscale and _yscale of the line movie clip, we can easily draw a straight line between any two points.

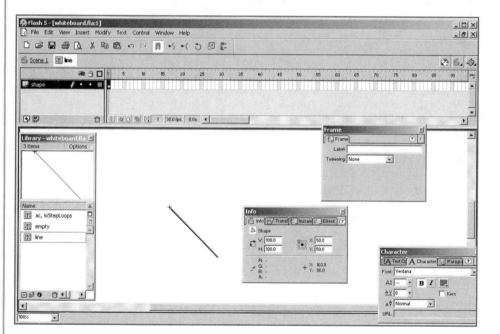

To accomplish this, we need to keep track of the last known position of the mouse. Our line movie clip is (conveniently) 100 pixels tall by 100 pixels wide.

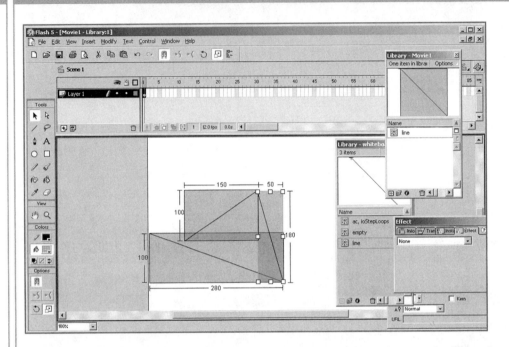

To draw a line between two points, we set the _x and _y coordinates of the movie clip to align with one point, and set the _xscale and _yscale so that the line stretches to meet the other point. We don't need triangles or Pythagoras (phew!). We simply find the distance between the x coordinates (which we use to set our _xscale) and the distance between the y coordinates (which we use to set our _yscale).

A function to draw a line between two points looks like this:

```
Drawline = function (x1, y1, x2, y2) {
    Var myDepth = attachDepth++
    This.attachMovie ("line", "line"+ myDepth, myDepth)

    Var myLineMc = this["line"+ myDepth]

    //align the clip with the first point
    MyLineMc._x = x1
    MyLineMc._y = y1

    //compute distances
    var dx = x2 - x1
    var dy = y2 - y1

    //assign scale values
    MyLineMc._xscale = dx
    MyLineMc._yscale = dy
}
```

Drawing lines is one step trickier than plotting points. You need to keep track of the current point being plotted as well as the last point plotted. Each new line connects to the previous line's endpoint (coordinates).

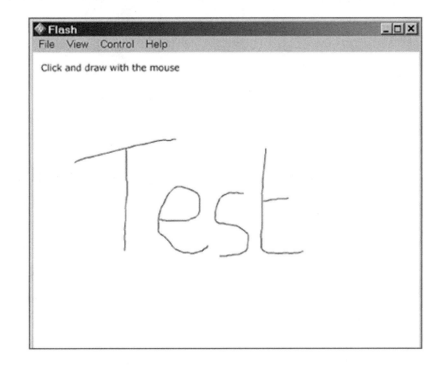

Checking for mouse movement before drawing

You might have noticed that our movie makes no attempt to determine whether the spot under the cursor has already been painted. So clicking and holding the mouse in one spot will cause our movie clips to pile up, slowing down our movie considerably over time, but accomplishing little insofar as changing the appearance of the stage.

Even though we're not there yet, remember that every interaction which results in a draw to the stage must be communicated to the other whiteboard participants. Increasing the efficiency of the draw routines at the outset will minimize the number of messages we have to send. Minimizing the number of messages we have to send will make our application faster and smoother.

In its current state, our whiteboard is a lot like a felt-tip pen. The ink continues to wick through the paper as long as you hold the pen against the paper, even if the pen isn't moving. If the pen stays in one spot for too long, you get a big mess. What we want to do is create the effect of a ball-point pen, where ink only flows onto the paper if the pen is moving.

To accomplish this, we compare the current mouse coordinates with the coordinates of the last paint command. If the distance between them is greater than a certain threshold, then the paint function is called again.

Thanks to our line drawing method, we're already storing the coordinates of the last endpoint. All we need is a function to determine the distance between two points:

```
function distance (x1, y1, x2, y2)
{
    var dx = x2 - x1;
    var dy = y2 - y1;

    return math.sqrt((dx*dx) + (dy*dy));
}
```

Instead of calling the paint function directly from our mouse handler, we'll instead call a new function called paintIfMoved.

```
paintIfMoved = function ()
{
    var dx =  lastPaintX - _root._xmouse;
    var dy = lastPaintY - _root._ymouse;

    var dist = Math.sqrt((dx*dx) + (dy*dy));

    if (dist > textureWidth)
    {
        var xscale = dx;
        var yscale = dy;
        paint (_root._xmouse, _root._ymouse, xscale, yscale);
    }
}
```

The variable textureWidth is set on the root level of the movie. This variable allows us to control the threshold sensitivity at which the system detects mouse movement. In our example we set textureWidth = 4.

Our paint function is responsible for remembering the last coordinates of the mouse:

```
paint = function (x, y, xscale, yscale)
{
    attachMovie (textureTemplate, attachDepth++, attachDepth)
    this[attachDepth-1]._x = x;
    this[attachDepth-1]._y = y;
    if (_xscale != null)
    {
        this[attachDepth-1]._xscale =_xscale
        this[attachDepth-1]._yscale = _yscale
    }
```

```
        else
        {
            this[attachDepth-1]._xscale = 1;
            this[attachDepth-1]._yscale = 1;
        }
        lastPaintX = x
        lastPaintY = y
    }
```

Setting up the MultiServer socket server

For this example, we're going to use MultiServer 2.0, which you can download from www.shovemedia.com.

Why this particular server? Well, I wrote it and I know that it will work nicely for us in this example. As you progress in your multiuser career, you might even decide to write your own XML parsing and routing server. It's not that hard, and MultiServer and other open-source examples can serve as a base from which to build.

Once more, you'll need the Java Runtime Environment installed, which you can get from java.sun.com if you don't have it installed already. The machine you're doing this on is the one that your Flash file will connect to using the "server" variable we talk about below.

Here's a list of the files that make up the server itself:

- **MultiServer.java** -- the class that gets everything running. It's responsible for putting the server into a "listen" state.

- **XmlHandler.java** -- an XmlHandler gets created for each client connection.

- **pinger.java** -- an object which sets up a heartbeat between the server and client. If the heartbeat cannot be detected, we kill the connection.

- **Logger.java** -- an object which logs messages to a file.

- **xml classes directory**-- xml parsing jar libraries.

- **xmlTest** -- sample & server test application.

The following files contain Java XML parsing/building libraries. Copy them from their place in the code download to the lib directory of your Java installation, and add them to your classpath.

```
xerces.jar
jdom.jar
```

You can set the classpath by typing this into the command prompt:

```
set
CLASSPATH=c:\jdk1.3.1\lib\xerces.jar;c:\jdk1.3.1\lib\jdom.jar;
```

If you don't understand the Java classpath and how to edit it, you'll find information on this in the readme files in your Java installation.

To run the server, copy all the `.class` files to your server. Add the JAR files referred to above to your classpath. Now open up a command prompt, navigate to the multiuser root directory and type:

```
java MultiServer 9000 logfile.log
```

This is assuming that you want to run the server application on port 9000. UNIX users will want to add an "&" to the end of this command so that it spawns a new process. You should now be able to connect to your MultiServer, so give it a whirl. The xmlTest directory contains a simple connection test SWF that you can use to verify that your installation was successful.

To use this, simply press the CONNECT button, then type in a message in the format shown and you should get the message shown in the lower box.

Making a connection

```
connect = function (ip, port)
{
    xsock = new XMLSocket();
    xsock.onConnect = sockConnect;
    xsock.onXML = processXML;

    xsock.connect (ip, port)
}
```

By now, connection functions like this should be looking pretty familiar. Once we've determined our connection state, call sockConnect. When we receive XML, it's sent to processXML.

```
sockConnect = function (bool)
{
    if (bool)
    {
        trace ("connected")
    }
    else
    {
        trace ("refused")
    }
}
```

sockConnect doesn't do anything at this stage, but this is where you would kick off a "The Server Is Down" error message. We'll come back and use this function later. Assuming that everything connected correctly, incoming XML will be passed to processXML.

First things first, we have to send *out* XML before we can read it *in*.

Instead of calling the painting on the stage directly, we're going to send a paint message to everyone connected to the server, including ourselves. It'll have all the necessary information that we would have sent to the paint function directly.

The paint function becomes:

```
paint = function (x, y, xscale, yscale)
{
    var paintObj = new Object();
    paintObj.type ="paint";
    paintObj.x = x;
    paintObj.y = y;

    if (xscale != null)
    {
        paintObj._xscale = xscale;
```

```
                paintObj._yscale = yscale;
        }

        lastPaintX = x;
        lastPaintY = y;

        var xmlDoc =Object.io.objToXML ("broadcast", paintObj)
        xsock.send (xmlDoc)
    }
```

First, we build an object called paintObj which contains:

```
paintObj
{
    Type = "paint"
    X = x
    Y = y
    _xscale = xscale
    _yscale = yscale
}
```

We then send that object to a convenience function which builds it into an XML document that looks like this:

```
<broadcast type="paint" x="231" y="123" _xscale="10" _yscale="15"
➡/>
```

The function that does this is pretty simple too:

```
Object.io.objToXml = function (ObjName, mc)
{
    var x = new XML();
    var xdata = x.createElement(ObjName);
    for (var i in mc )
    {
        xdata.attributes[i] = mc[i]
    }
    x.appendChild(xdata)

    return x
}
```

After creating a new node with the name passed in the ObjName argument, we add an attribute to the node for every variable in the data object. When the loop is finished, the resulting node is attached to the document object.

The last line:

```
xsock.send (xmlDoc)
```

takes the message we've built and sends it down the open socket connection. From here, we have to trust that the server will route it back to us (and everyone else). That's MultiServer's job, and it does it very well. As it happens, Multiserver has a rule that all documents with a top-level nodename of "broadcast" get routed to all connected recipients. This means that we can expect the message we just sent out to appear at our processXML function.

Receiving the plot coordinates

```
processXML = function (dataDoc)
{
    trace (dataDoc)

    var data = dataDoc.firstChild;
    var nodeName = data.nodeName;

    if (nodeName == "ping")
    {
        pong()
    }
    if (nodeName == "broadcast")
    {
        if (dataDoc.firstChild.attributes.type == "paint")
        {
            processPaint (data);
        }
    }
}
```

Did you follow that? When the data arrives, we check the nodeName of the main node of the document. If it's "ping", we call the pong function. If it's "broadcast", and the type attribute is set to "paint" we pass the data node to the process paint function.

These messages cause the pong function to execute:

```
<ping />

<ping time="500" />

<ping><test><test><test></ping>
```

The ping messages help ensure that a user's connection hasn't gone into limbo. If a MultiServer client stops responding to ping messages (we reply with <pong/>), the connection is assumed dead.

These messages cause the processPaint function to be called:

```
<broadcast type="paint" />
<broadcast x="123" y="456" type="paint" />
```

These messages do not:

```
<broadcast msg="fire"/>

<type type="broadcast"/>
```

The processPaint function:

```
processPaint = function (xmlDoc)
{
    trace ("processPaint");
    var paintObj = Object.io.xmlToObj (xmlDoc);

    attachMovie (paintObj.texture, attachDepth++, attachDepth);
    this[attachDepth-1]._x = Number(paintObj.x);
    this[attachDepth-1]._y = Number(paintObj.y);
    if (paintObj._xscale != null)
    {
        this[attachDepth-1]._xscale = Number(paintObj._xscale);
        this[attachDepth-1]._yscale = Number(paintObj._yscale);
    }
    else
    {
        this[attachDepth-1]._xscale = 1;
        this[attachDepth-1]._yscale = 1;
    }
}
```

That looks a whole lot like the old paint function. Instead of using data passed to the function as arguments, we're going to look inside the XML fragment for the data we need. In this example, I use a handy utility function that lets me map the attributes in a node to properties of an object:

```
Object.io.xmlToObj = function (doc)
{
    var returnObj = new Object ()

    for (var i in doc.attributes)
    {
        returnObj[i] =  doc.attributes[i]
    }

    return returnObj
}
```

Clearing the screen

Now that our whiteboard is capable of drawing lines, it'd be nice to be able to erase the screen. If one person erases the screen, it needs to be communicated to everyone else. So, we define a new message:

```
<clearScreen/>
```

When the user presses the clear button, we'll send this message to everyone.

When we receive a `clearScreen` message, the following code will remove all of the dynamically drawn lines from the stage.

```
processClearScreen = function (xmlDoc)
{
    trace ("clearScreen")

    for (var i=0;i<attachDepth ;i++ )
    {
        this[i].removeMovieClip()
    }

    attachDepth=0
}
```

There's only one problem. Our server doesn't know how to handle a `clearScreen` message. MultiServer by default only recognizes:

```
Broadcast
SendToId
SetId
SendToOthers
SetAppClass
Pong
```

We could change our message format to something like:

```
<broadcast type="clearScreen" />
```

That's what we've done with our paint messages so far. But what happens if we want to use MultiServer for something else that requires a `clearScreen` message? We don't want the users in one application to accidentally clear the screen in another.

Unfortunately, broadcast messages are sent to *all* connected users. So if we have two different applications that know how to respond to the message above, the cross-talk described is exactly what will happen.

The solution is two fold. First, we separate the server-side whiteboard logic. Second, we'll solve this hole in our server's vocabulary. We'll do both in the next section.

Making your whiteboard talk

We're going to move onto the whiteboard example in the 6.3 folder now. In order for the whiteboard to be able to connect to your MultiServer, it needs to know where it is. By default, the whiteboard will look for the server on the machine it itself is running on – the localhost. This has an IP address of 127.0.0.1. If you are running your whiteboard across a network, change the IP address to that of the computer that the MultiServer is running on.

```
#include "ioLib.as"
#include "whiteboard.as"

textureTemplate = "texture1"
textureWidth = 4

attachDepth=0

connect ("127.0.0.1", 9000)
```

Start a connection to the whiteboard and begin drawing. Now start a second window and begin drawing there. Compare the two windows. They aren't the same, are they? Why not?

When a new user connects to the whiteboard server, they become eligible to receive broadcast messages sent in the future. But they don't get sent messages that describe the state of the whiteboard as it was when they entered. The server isn't set up to "remember" the state of the board. If it was, we could automatically send new users all the messages they missed while they were absent.

Convincing the server to do this is fairly easy. Just a few lines of Java code will allow the server to keep a list of all the messages that have arrived. A few more will empty the list every time someone sends a clearScreen command. When new users connect, we loop through the list of messages and send them a copy of each.

Adding this functionality requires no changes to the client – well, almost. If the Flash client understands how to process the messages that will be sent to it when it connects (which ours does), it needs only to sit back and wait for the messages to start rolling in. Once it's finished processing them, it will effectively be caught up, and its screen should look like everyone else's.

However, adding this functionality does change the server. Depending on the server you decide to use, the login process might be more complex than simply connecting to a port and sending broadcast messages.

The MultiServer XML router includes the sample whiteboard code that will help us keep our Flash clients in synch. In order to use it, the Flash movie must send a special message telling the server which message handling class to use. To join the whiteboard application, we send:

```
<setAppClass classname="whiteboard"/>
```

MultiServer interprets this message as a command to load the file whiteboard.class as a message handler. The file must be located in the classpath in order to load successfully – that's why the "dot" or "current directory" path was added to our classpath example during the installation instructions.

Messages with nodenames other than "broadcast" (and a handful of other low-level messages – see the documentation for a complete list) are sent to the whiteboard class for processing. As you might have guessed, whiteboard.class will record incoming messages and update new users with the current list. It also recognizes a clearScreen message, and upon receiving it will purge the message list.

whiteboard.class defines its own handler for an addUser message type. A chatroom can have its own addUser handler; a racing game can have one as well.

So, to add ourselves to the list of whiteboard participants, we send:

```
<addUser id="someId"/>
```

The server will acknowledge us by replying with the current message list.

If you have a Java developer on hand, no doubt she will have her own login and initialization routines. You'll need to agree on the sequence of messages that ultimately result in the new user's screen being initialized with the state of the whiteboard.

For our initialization sequence, we'll add some named frames to our timeline.

Open whiteboard.fla in the 6.4 folder. There are now three labeled frames in our movie:

■   Connect

■   EnterName

■   Draw

We use the sections of the timeline to create different states that our movie can be in. The first state allows our application to attempt a connection to the server.

Frame 1 Code

```
#include "ioLib.as"
#include "whiteboard.as"

textureTemplate = "texture1"
textureWidth = 4

attachDepth=0

connect ("127.0.0.1", 9000)

stop()
```

We add a call to setAppClass to our socket callback.

```
sockConnect = function (bool)
{
    if (bool)
    {
        trace ("connected")
        setAppClass("whiteboard")
        getUserName()
    }
    else
    {
        trace ("refused")
    }
}
```

The `setAppClass()` function constructs and sends the necessary `setAppClass` message, and `getUserName` forwards the playhead to the next state.

```
setAppClass = function (classname)
{
    var xmlObj = new Object()
    xmlObj.classname = classname

    var xmlDoc = Object.io.objToXml ("setAppClass", xmlObj)
    xsock.send (xmlDoc)
}

getUserName = function ()
{
    gotoAndStop("enterName")
}
```

The next state allows the user to enter a unique name. This is the id sent to the server in the `addUser` message.

Frame 2 code

```
instructions = "Enter name"
stop()
```

Pressing the OK button sends the `addUser` message, and sends the movie to the third state, draw, via a `gotoAndStop` action.

The draw state simply offers a blank screen.

The beauty of the MultiServer application is that having a separate class for each routing function means that you can run many, many applications using the same server instance. To take advantage of this, it'd be a good idea to clean up our Flash client a bit.

Although sending messages with the nodename `broadcast` is convenient, it's inefficient; especially if we might use MultiServer for other applications. Instead, let's define a `paint` message:

```
<paint  user="myUsername"  texture="texture1"  x="50"  y="50"  _xscale="55"
➥_yscale="40" />
```

Our `paint` function becomes:

```
paint = function (x, y, xscale, yscale)
{
    var paintObj = new Object()
    paintObj.user = myId
    paintObj.texture = textureTemplate
    paintObj.x = x
    paintObj.y = y

    if (xscale != null)
    {
        paintObj._xscale = xscale
        paintObj._yscale = yscale
    }

    lastPaintX = x
    lastPaintY = y

    var xmlDoc = Object.io.objToXML ("paint", paintObj)
    xsock.send (xmlDoc)
}
```

`Whiteboard.class` knows to route paint messages only to those users who are members of the whiteboard application (i.e. only those users who need it). Its user list is built from all the clients who set their application class to `whiteboard` and then sent an `addUser` message.

Server-side stuff

Let's take a look at the Java code that supports our whiteboard's newly found memory:

```
public void process (XmlHandler owner, Document xmlDoc)
{
    this.owner = owner;

    String name = xmlDoc.getRootElement ().getName ();

    if (name.equals ("addUser"))
    {
        String id =xmlDoc.getRootElement ().getAttributeValue ("id");
        addUser (id);
    }
```

```
            if (name.equals("removeUser"))
            {
                String id =xmlDoc.getRootElement().getAttributeValue("id");
                removeUser(id);
            }

            if (name.equals("paint"))
            {
                paint(xmlDoc);
            }

            if (name.equals("clearScreen"))
            {
                clearScreen();
            }
        }
```

Custom application classes in MultiServer are expected to implement a process method. This receives two objects; owner, which provides access to routing functions, and xmlDoc, the document to be processed.

Just as in our ActionScript, the first step is to figure out what kind of message we're dealing with. We extract the nodename and compare it to the message types we know how to handle. The four message types used by whiteboard.class are:

- addUser

- removeUser

- paint

- clearScreen

Again, just as in ActionScript, we pass the message (or a portion of it) to a function meant to handle the specific message type.

Java uses an object called a Vector to hold all of the members of the whiteboard application. It's similar to an ActionScript Array object. Java has Array objects too, but you're required to specify how big they are when you create them. Vectors don't have this limitation.

At the top of the whiteboard class, we define two Vectors. One holds the id list, the other holds paint messages:

```
        protected static Vector idList = new Vector ();
        protected static Vector messageList = new Vector ();
```

If you're just getting started with Java, you might be wondering what protected and static are. In Flash, every object in the movie has access to every other object and variable in the movie. Not so in Java, which uses the keywords `private`, `public`, and `protected` to specify which classes have access to what members.

Static is one of the most poorly named identifiers in the entire Java language, so don't worry if it's initially hard to remember. Static objects are shared by all instances of a given class. What does that mean? If ten users connect to the whiteboard, ten instances of `whiteboard.class` are created – one for each user. You might think that Java would run the code in the whiteboard class ten times, and it does. However, only one `idList` and only one `messageList` are created and shared by all the instances because they are marked with the `static` keyword.

Now that we have our Vectors created, we can add and remove users from the id list:

```
public void addUser (String id)
{

    // check to make sure the user isn't already in the list
    if (!userExists(id))
    {
        synchronized (idList)
        {
            idList.insertElementAt (id, 0);
        }

        Document setIdDoc = new Document (new Element ("setId"));
        setIdDoc.getRootElement().addAttribute ("id", id);

        this.owner.setId (setIdDoc);

        getMessageList();
    }
}
```

Because the list is shared, we have to account for the fact that multiple requests might arrive simultaneously. We use the synchronized command `synchronized (idList)` to make sure that only one thread can write to the `idList` at a time.

After the user's id is added to `idList`, the `addUser` function sends a `setId` message to the connection owner. The end result is that the variable `this.owner.id` is set to the desired id. To understand why, take a look at the next function.

```
public void broadcastToWhiteboard (Document xmlDoc)
{
    String nextId;
    Object[] idListArray;

    synchronized (idList)
    {
        idListArray=idList.toArray();
    }
```

```
    for (int i=idListArray.length-1; i >= 0 ;i-- )
    {
        nextId = (String) idListArray[i];

        if (nextId != null)
        {
            this.owner.sendToId (xmlDoc, nextId, this.owner.id);
        }
    }
}
```

Defining a `broadcastToWhiteboard` function allows us to send our messages to everyone in idList. Multiserver's owner object (passed to our custom class automatically) defines the method `sendToId()`. It expects to be called with the syntax:

```
SendToId (xmlDocument, toId, fromId)
```

The underlying code checks to make sure that `fromId` matches the id used in `setId` (so that someone doesn't try to spoof a message from someone else). That's why the `addUser` function called `setId` with the current id.

The last statement in the `addUser` function is `getMessageList`. This function returns a copy of all the messages in the `messageList` Vector:

```
public void getMessageList ()
{

    // don't allow non-list members to get the list
    if (userExists (this.owner.id))
    {
        // for every message in the list, send it to the current
user

        Document replyDoc;
        Object[] messageListArray;

        synchronized (messageList)
        {
            messageListArray=messageList.toArray();
        }

        for (int i=messageListArray.length-1; i >= 0 ;i-- )
        {
            replyDoc = (Document) messageListArray[i];
            this.owner.reply (replyDoc);
        }
    }
}
```

Again, the underlying MultiServer code gives us access to a message routing function. This time we use `reply`. It sends an XML document to the current user.

You might have noticed that we check to see if the user's id exists. The `userExists` code allows us to make sure that the requested id isn't taken. You'll probably find yourself using this or something similar every time you create another multi-user project:

```java
public boolean userExists (String id)
{
    // look through the list for the given id.
    // return true if found, false otherwise

    String nextId;
    boolean found = false;
    Object[] idListArray;

    synchronized (idList)
    {
        idListArray=idList.toArray();
    }

    for (int i=idListArray.length-1; i >= 0 ;i-- )
    {
        nextId = (String) idListArray[i];

        if (nextId.equals (id))
        {
            found = true;
        }
    }

    if (found)
    {
        return true;
    }
    else
    {
        return false;
    }
}
```

Because this function is built to simply return true or false, we can use it everywhere that we wish to determine if a given user id is valid.

Paint messages are very simple to handle. We want to add the message to the `messageList` (so that new incoming users will receive a copy). Then we send the message to all whiteboard users:

```java
public void paint (Document xmlDoc)
{
```

```
        synchronized (messageList)
        {
            messageList.insertElementAt(xmlDoc, 0);
        }

        broadcastToWhiteboard (xmlDoc);
    }
```

Handling a `clearScreen` is easy too. Simply clear the message list, and route the message along:

```
    public void clearScreen (Document xmlDoc)
    {
        synchronized (messageList)
        {
            messageList.clear();
        }

        broadcastToWhiteboard (xmlDoc);
    }
```

The only task left is removing users from the `idList` when they disconnect. Since MultiServer is in charge of handling the actual connection, it will notify us with a `removeUser` message at the appropriate time. All we have to do is process it:

```
    public void removeUser (String id)
    {
        synchronized (idList)
        {
            idList.removeElement(id);
        }
    }
```

When users disconnect, they'll be removed from the `idList` so that the system doesn't try to send messages to users who are no longer connected. Simple, huh?

Once the server is capable of remembering the messages that have passed through it, the core whiteboard engine is complete. Now, we can start adding additional features, and this is where the real fun starts.

Color

The final version of the whiteboard also adds three slider objects to the stage. Each controls a variable on the main timeline. R, G, and B are then sent along with paint messages:

```
    paint = function (x, y, xscale, yscale)
    {
        var paintObj = new Object()
        paintObj.texture=textureTemplate
        paintObj.r = _root.R
```

```
paintObj.g = _root.G
paintObj.b = _root.B
paintObj.x = x
paintObj.y = y

if (xscale != null)
{
    paintObj._xscale = xscale
    paintObj._yscale = yscale
}

lastPaintX = x
lastPaintY = y

var xmlDoc =Object.io.objToXML ("paint", paintObj)
xsock.send (xmlDoc)
}
```

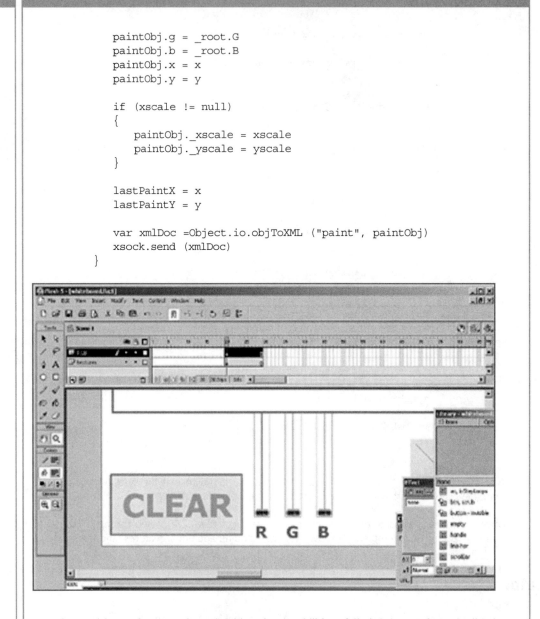

On the receiving end, we use the scriptable color capabilities of Flash 5 to transform the line into the correct color. Now that we've got other interface elements on the screen, let's add a stage movie clip and mask it. This will allow us to easily confine the boundaries of the whiteboard:

```
processPaint = function (xmlDoc)
{
    trace ("processPaint")
    var paintObj = Object.io.xmlToObj (xmlDoc)
```

```
        stage.attachMovie (paintObj.texture, attachDepth++,
➥ attachDepth)
        stage[attachDepth-1]._x = Number(paintObj.x)
        stage[attachDepth-1]._y = Number(paintObj.y)
        if (paintObj._xscale != null)
        {
            stage[attachDepth-1]._xscale = Number(paintObj._xscale)
            stage[attachDepth-1]._yscale = Number(paintObj._yscale)
        }
        else
        {
            stage[attachDepth-1]._xscale = 1
            stage[attachDepth-1]._yscale = 1
        }

        //colorize
        setRGB (stage[attachDepth-1], paintObj.r, paintObj.g,
➥ paintObj.b)
    }
```

The setRGB() utility function performs the actual color transform:

```
    setRGB = function (mc,r,g,b)
    {
        if (r!=null)
        {
            var myColor = new Color(mc)
            myColor.setRGB(r<<16|g<<8|b)
        }
        else
        {
            var myColor = new Color(mc)
            var myColorTransform = { ra: "100", rb: "0", ga: "100",
➥ gb: "0", ba: "100", bb: "0", aa: "100", ab: "0"}
            myColor.setTransform (myColorTransform)
        }
    }
```

Most of the work is done by the main if clause, but if we pass color values, the color transform is removed.

Conclusion

In this chapter we've had a look at how you can get Flash applications to talk to each other across a network. The whiteboard example shown is no Photoshop, but hopefully it'll provide a few hours of fun as you and your friends scrawl messages to each other's computers.

But it needn't end there. Feel free to adapt this in any way you choose. Why not expand its features? Try creating additional linked texture movie clips. Instead of a simple diagonal line, experiment with simple tweened shapes. Our final whiteboard example has five example textures to get you started (the wibbly one is great fun).

Chapter 6
Avatars in Flash

Our ability to learn is centered wholly around pattern recognition. Whether learning a new skill, language, technique, or fudge brownie recipe, the process is roughly the same. Our brains take input from our five senses and try to make sense of the new information by comparing it to what it has learned in the past. After seeing plenty of examples, our brains eventually "get" what they have in common and are thereafter capable of recognizing when new inputs match the patterns they've seen before.

Our ability to communicate new ideas hinges upon our ability to relate those ideas to old ideas. New patterns build on old patterns. You've now been exposed to a number of multiuser Flash techniques and examples, and should have a pretty good idea of what this involves. This chapter will finish off our section of Flash multiuser applications by taking you step-by-step through the process of building an avatar chat system.

You should recognize the programming techniques from previous chapters. Even if you don't feel like you quite "get it" yet, this chapter provides another example of the patterns involved. Compare it to what you've already seen and don't be afraid to experiment on your own. Chances are, you'll find you understand better than you're consciously aware. Learning is often like that.

You've probably already seen a half-dozen avatar chat applications on the Web. Features vary, of course, but most allow you to:

- Move around the screen

- Send messages to the room

- See the other visitors and their messages

- Communicate something about your mood or lifestyle through the appearance of your avatar

The main factor that sets a "good" avatar system apart from a "bad" one is often the level and quality of the interactions between the graphical representations of different users. Graphic avatar chat systems strive to improve upon the text chat pattern by offering a visual dimension of communication. For this chapter's example, I wanted to take advantage of that added dimension and more effectively approximate the sense of touch. I quickly dismissed the floating heads pat answer.

I decided to start with the simplest, most widely understood symbol of touch that came to mind – the handshake. Start with a simple pattern that more-or-less everyone understands, and build upon it. Thus, the highfive avatar chat system was born.

As you'll see, the secret to this system's success is not a complex XML syntax or an intricate routing algorithm. On the contrary, the XML "language" we use will consist of only a few short message types. We'll then use Flash to interpret those XML messages into visual movement and animation.

Planning

The very first thing to do on a project of this sort is determine the specification. Deciding ahead of time which features are in and which features are out is absolutely essential to maintaining your sanity. The larger your team, the more critical this step becomes.

Developers often complain about something called "scope creep". Scope creep begins the first time someone agrees to add to the feature list after the planning stage is already complete and (supposedly) agreed upon. After the first change, it gets easier and easier to justify more changes, and before long, the project is spiralling out of control. Even if you tend to work solo, you're still not immune. Self-inflicted scope creep is just as real and just as dangerous.

A specification document (even if it's a simple, bulleted feature list) keeps everyone – particularly yourself – on track, and provides the objective authority to just say "no" to scope creep. This strategy reduces the chances of anyone's feelings getting hurt – especially if you involve everyone who will be working with the plan to help write it.

Highfive chat feature overview

Each user in the highfive chat will be represented by a graphic of the human hand. Handshake states for the location of the user's hand graphic —"up-high", "down-low", and so on – will be selected in response to pre-determined keystrokes. When these keys are pressed, a user's avatar will attempt to shake hands with their nearest neighbor.

In order for a given handshake animation to successfully play, the user represented by the nearest neighbor must perform the same keystroke within a specified timeout. A text field at the bottom of the screen will allow users to submit short chat messages, displayed in a text bubble beside the user's avatar rather than in a common chat-text window.

Now that we have some sense of what we want our application to do, we should determine the functionality that our clients will need. In a larger project, these would be defined as use cases. Since we'll only have one such use case, a simple list will suffice.

Each user can:

- Choose a name
- Send a message
- Receive messages from other users
- Move their avatar around the screen
- Select a handshake state

Most of the list is fairly straightforward. The only item demanding more attention in the planning stage is the last one. What are the handshake states? The following diagram outlines the ten states an avatar can exist in. Remember, once we've finalized this list, changes and additions will have to wait until version two.

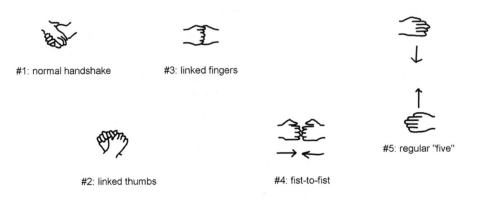

#1: normal handshake

#3: linked fingers

#5: regular "five"

#2: linked thumbs

#4: fist-to-fist

Designing

Before we spend a lot of time building illustrations of hands and animating them into handshakes, we need to plan how our illustrations will fit together. Each hand has to be a separate movie clip, because each hand represents a unique user, and each user can control the position of their hand. How do we make the animations line up? How can we structure our movie so that the animations are as easy as possible to produce?

The first thing to do is look back at our spec. What items in the feature list create dependencies upon our animations? Looking back we find:

- Move their avatar around the screen

- Select a handshake state

Moving an avatar around the screen is easy. We'll simply move the container movie clip. But since each avatar is separate, we'll have to align hands before performing the handshake animations. Otherwise, each hand will be shaking, but they will be shaking thin air, rather than each other.

After studying the diagram above, it also becomes apparent that for any given handshake, there are two animations—right hand and left hand. Once our system determines that two avatars should shake hands, it'll send one avatar timeline to a keyframe depicting the left hand and the other avatar to a different keyframe depicting the mirrored right-hand state. We'll use the timeline of each avatar movie clip to depict the left and right states for a handshake animation.

Speaking of states, there will be ten of them – one at rest, the other nine representing different handshake styles. So, it looks like we'll need nineteen states; rest (1), and left and right depictions of the nine handshakes (18).

By carefully centering the registration points for all of our animations across the origin (_x = 0, _y = 0) we'll guarantee that the left and right portions will line up as long as their container clips are located at the same coordinates.

To get started, we'll draw the handshakes as separate keyframe animations without worrying about complex movie clip nesting. Once everything looks right, we'll create new movie clips by copying and pasting keyframes into the new movie clip objects. If we're careful, everything should line up in the final version the same way it did in the original.

Server design

The server required to support this example is very simple because there aren't very many different message types. That doesn't mean we should avoid designing our message types in advance, though.

Once again, let's take a look at the functionality specified for our users. We'll map our message syntax directly from there. The functionality we want to offer a user is:

- Choose a name

- Send a message

- Receive messages from other users

- Move their avatar around the screen

- Select a handshake state

An addUser message will cover the first requirement, setting the user's name:

```
<addUser id="someId" />
```

Next, a chat message type to cover chat messages:

```
<chat fromId="myId" message="message here" />
```

Let's add a move message type to support moving an avatar around the screen:

```
<move id="myId" _x="123" _y="100" />
```

And, finally, a handshake type lets us communicate our handshake attempts to other users.

```
<handshake state="uphigh" />
```

Did we forget something? Well, our spec is covered, but there is one thing users can do which we overlooked. They can disconnect. That's not scope creep; that's reality, so let's add one more message type.

```
<removeUser id="removedId" />
```

The removeUser message is generated automatically by the MultiServer application. All we need to do is catch it in our Flash movie.

Making the connection

Let's start with the pieces we've seen before. Example Highfive 6.1 connects to MultiServer and asks for a name. An addUser message is routed to all connected users. Upon receipt of this message, Flash creates a new "avatar" clip using the attachMovie command. Each user can move his/her avatar by clicking on the stage.

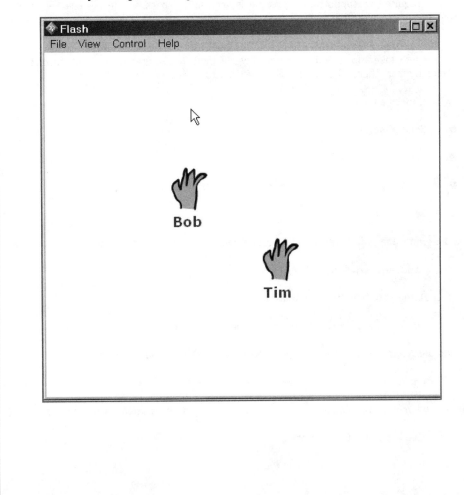

*Full instructions on how to get MultiServer up and running are in **Chapter 5**. Don't forget to set the classpath and to change the IP address of your server in `highfive.fla` if you're not running the server on your local machine.*

The connection logic is straight out of **Chapter 5**. We won't go over it again here, but let's take a look at the changes we've made.

```
sockConnect = function (bool) {
   if (bool) {
      trace ("connected")

      setAppClass("highfive")

      getUserName()

   }
   else {
      trace ("refused")
   }
}
```

The sockConnect function, as you'll remember, is called once we've determined the success of XmlSocket.connect. Instead of setting our application class to whiteboard as we did in **Chapter 5**, we set it to "highfive". The setAppClass Flash function is exactly the same, it builds a message that looks like:

```
<setAppClass class="myClassName" />
```

MultiServer interprets this message and loads highfive.class (which we'll examine in a moment):

```
processXML = function (data) {
   trace (data)

   var dataDoc = data.firstChild
   var nodeName = dataDoc.nodeName

   if (nodeName == "ping") {
      pong()
   }

   if (nodeName == "addUser") {
      processAddUser (dataDoc)
   }
```

continues overleaf

```
    if (nodeName == "removeUser") {
      processRemoveUser (dataDoc)
    }

    if (nodeName == "move") {
      processMove (dataDoc)
    }
  }
```

The `processXML` function is the callback for `XmlSocket.onXML`. This version is capable of handling four message types:

- ping
- addUser
- removeUser
- move

Those message types are handled by the following functions respectively:

- pong
- processAddUser
- processRemoveUser
- processMove

Let's take a look at each, one-by-one.

```
  pong = function () {
    myObj = new Object()
    myXml = Object.io.objToXml ("pong", myObj)
    xsock.send (myXml)

    pings++
  }
```

As noted in **Chapter 5**, MultiServer expects incoming ping messages to be replied to with `<pong/>` in order to keep the connection active.

Here's a reprint of `Object.io.objToXml` for your reference. We'll be using it extensively.

```
  Object.io.objToXml = function (ObjName, mc) {
    var x = new XML();
    var xdata = x.createElement(ObjName);
    for (var i in mc ) {
      xdata.attributes[i] = mc[i]
    }
    x.appendChild(xdata)

    return x
  }
```

In this case, mc is an empty object, so no attributes are created.

```
processAddUser = function (xmlDoc) {
  var userObj = Object.io.xmlToObj (xmlDoc)

  attachMovie ("avatar", "user"+userObj.id, attachDepth++)

  var userMc = this["user"+userObj.id]

  userMc._x = Number (userObj._x)
  userMc._y = Number (userObj._y)
  userMc.id = userObj.id
}
```

The processAddUser function creates a new avatar movie clip for the new user from the linked library item. It is named "user"+id, so if the user's id is "kat", the instance name of the avatar will be set to "userkat". We're using the xmlToObj utility function to pull XML attribute data into an object that we can access with dot syntax.

Here's that listing again:

```
Object.io.xmlToObj = function (doc) {
  var returnObj = new Object ()

  for (var i in doc.attributes) {
    returnObj[i] =  doc.attributes[i]
  }

  return returnObj
}
```

If the processAddUser function receives

```
<addUser id="Thomas" _x="123" _y="321" />
```

userObj has the following values:

```
userObj.id = "Thomas"
userObj._x = "123"
userObj._y = "321"
```

We convert the _x and _y values of userObj to Number objects, and use them to set the coordinates of our new avatar movie clip.

```
processRemoveUser = function(xmlDoc) {
  var userObj = Object.io.xmlToObj (xmlDoc)

  this["user"+userObj.id].removeMovieClip()
}
```

The `processRemoveUser` function uses the same technique. Instead of creating a movie clip, it removes one.

```
processMove = function (xmlDoc) {
  var userObj = Object.io.xmlToObj (xmlDoc)

  var userMc = this["user"+userObj.id]

  userMc._x = Number (userObj._x)
  userMc._y = Number (userObj._y)
}
```

Not much new here. Look at the id property, use it to figure out which avatar movie clip should be moved, and move it!

A look at the Java code

Now let's take a look at the server code (which you can find in `highfive.java`).

```
protected static Vector idList = new Vector ();
protected static HashMap userData = new HashMap ();
```

The `highfive` class defines two static objects. One is a Vector that holds the user id list for the highfive application. We did the same thing for the whiteboard.

A HashMap is another very useful Java utility Object. It allows you to create a list that maps unique keys to unique objects. Once we've stored an object and its key in the HashMap using the `put` method, we can retrieve it by passing the same key to the HashMap's `get` method.

The highfive application will store XML Documents that use the user's id as a key in the HashMap. We'll talk about this more in a moment.

```
public void process (XmlHandler owner, Document xmlDoc) {

  this.owner = owner;

  String name = xmlDoc.getRootElement ().getName ();

  if (name.equals ("addUser")) {
    addUser (xmlDoc);
  }

  if (name.equals ("removeUser")) {
    removeUser (xmlDoc);
  }

  if (name.equals ("move")) {
    move (xmlDoc);
  }
}
```

Once again, our custom application classes under MultiServer are expected to implement a process function to catch incoming XML messages. The highfive class can handle three different message types:

- AddUser

- RemoveUser

- Move

Each message type is passed to a separate handler function.

```
public void addUser (Document xmlDoc) {

    String id = xmlDoc.getRootElement().getAttributeValue("id");

    // check to make sure the user isn't already in the list

    if (!userExists(id))
    {
        // tell everyone else first so we don't get
        // 2 messages for ourself

        broadcastToHighFive (xmlDoc);

        synchronized (idList) {
            idList.insertElementAt(id, 0);
        }

        Document addIdDoc = new Document (new Element ("addUser"));
        addIdDoc.getRootElement().addAttribute ("id", id);

        synchronized (userData) {
            userData.put (id, addIdDoc);
        }

        Document setIdDoc = new Document (new Element ("setId"));
        setIdDoc.getRootElement().addAttribute ("id", id);

        this.owner.setId (setIdDoc);

        getUserList ();
    }
}
```

This function operates almost identically to the addUser function for **Chapter 5**'s whiteboard.

These lines are new:

```
Document addIdDoc = new Document (new Element ("addUser"));
addIdDoc.getRootElement().addAttribute ("id", id);

synchronized (userData) {
  userData.put(id, addIdDoc);
}
```

Once we've verified that the user's requested id is not already taken and added that id to the idList Vector, we need to create a userData document for the current user. This document will in turn be sent to newly arriving chat-room visitors and will contain information describing how to properly display the users who are already present.

At this point, the only information known about the new user is their id, so we create a document that looks like:

```
<addUser id="thisId" />
```

The document is stored in the userData HashMap for future reference.

MultiServer calls the removeUser function automatically when a user disconnects. We can use this fact to inform those users still present in the chat room to remove the old user's avatar.

```
public void removeUser (Document xmlDoc) {

  String id = xmlDoc.getRootElement().getAttributeValue("id");

  synchronized (idList) {
    idList.removeElement(id);
  }

  synchronized (userData) {
    userData.remove(id);
  }

  broadcastToHighFive (xmlDoc);
}
```

First, remove the disconnected user's id from the idList Vector, then remove their user data XML Document from the userData HashMap, and finally send a out message to remaining users. Here, we're simply forwarding on the message generated by MultiServer which has the format:

```
<removeUser id="disconnectedId" />
```

The move function is a bit more interesting. Because incoming users need to know where to place the other avatars on screen, the server needs to save this information somewhere any time an avatar is moved.

```
public void move (Document xmlDoc) {

    Document addIdDoc = new Document (new Element ("addUser"));
    addIdDoc.getRootElement().addAttribute ("id",
➥       xmlDoc.getRootElement().getAttributeValue("id"));
    addIdDoc.getRootElement().addAttribute ("_x",
➥       xmlDoc.getRootElement().getAttributeValue("_x"));
    addIdDoc.getRootElement().addAttribute ("_y",
➥       xmlDoc.getRootElement().getAttributeValue("_y"));

    synchronized (userData) {

userData.put(xmlDoc.getRootElement().getAttributeValue("id"),
➥   addIdDoc);
    }

  broadcastToHighFive (xmlDoc);
}
```

We create a new XML Document object and give it a nodename of "addUser". Newly arriving users will eventually be the recipients of these messages, so we just go ahead and build them as addUser messages to begin with. After creating a new Document object with a top-level element of "addUser", the function adds attributes for the user's id, _x, and _y values. This document is then stored in the userData HashMap using the id as a key.

```
public void getUserList () {

// don't allow non-list members to get the list
// because they won't be notified of changes

  if (userExists (this.owner.id)) {

    // For every user in the list, send userData to the current
    // user since we've pre-formatted these as "addUser"
    // messages, they're ready to go.

    Document replyDoc;
    Object[] idListArray;

    synchronized (idList) {
      idListArray=idList.toArray();
    }

    for (int i=idListArray.length-1; i >= 0 ;i -- )
    {
      replyDoc = (Document) userData.get( (String)
➥       idListArray[i] );
      this.owner.reply (replyDoc);
    }
  }
}
```

The end of the `addUser` function calls `getUserList`. This function is responsible for sending `addUser` messages from the `userData` HashMap to the user who has just connected. First, we create an array from the `idList` Vector. We loop through this array of ids, each time using the id to access the respective `userData` object. Since the objects stored in the `userData` HashMap are XML Documents, we can simply pass them to the `owner.reply` method. The document objects are thereby sent to the current user.

We've seen the `broadcastToHighFive` function several times now. It's similar to the `broadcastToWhiteboard` function from **Chapter 5**.

```
public void broadcastToHighFive (Document xmlDoc) {

  String nextId;
  Object[] idListArray;

  synchronized (idList) {
    idListArray=idList.toArray();
  }

  for (int i=idListArray.length-1; i >= 0 ;i -- )
  {
    nextId = (String) idListArray[i];

    if (nextId != null)
    {
        this.owner.sendToId (xmlDoc, nextId, this.owner.id);
    }
  }
}
```

Again, we form an array from the `idList` Vector, loop through each of the items, and use `owner.sendToId` to route the XML Document to the next id.

That covers the communications overhead (thank goodness!). Just a few short additions will allow us to send chat messages and trade secret handshakes.

Sending chat messages

Example Highfive 6.2 adds the ability to send chat messages. The chat text is displayed in a bubble beside the user's avatar.

Take a look at the code on the send button. When pressed, the contents of the chat textfield is passed to the `sendChat` function:

```
sendChat = function (msg) {
  var xmlObj = new Object
  xmlObj.id = myId
  xmlObj.message = msg

  var xmlDoc = Object.io.objToXml ("addUser", xmlObj)
  xsock.send (xmlDoc)
}
```

The following lines are added to the processXML function:

```
if (nodeName == "chat") {
  processChat (dataDoc)
}
```

We define the processChat function to handle it:

```
processChat = function (xmlDoc) {
  var userObj = Object.io.xmlToObj (xmlDoc)

  var userMc = this["user"+userObj.id]

  userMc.chat.value = userObj.message
  userMc.chat.gotoAndPlay(2)
}
```

Unfortunately, Flash doesn't allow us to detect the rendered height of a textfield. So, we have to do more than check a _height property in order to figure out where to draw the speech bubble. Take a look at the timeline for the chatBubble object in the library of Highfive 6.2

The first frame is empty. If the movie is on frame 1, no text is displayed. The processChat function kicks the timeline in motion with a gotoAndPlay(2) action after it sets the value textfield with the contents of the message.

You'll note that each successive frame in the timeline contains the same code:

```
if (value.maxscroll < 2) {
  stop()
}
else {
  play()
}
```

Because the textfield is set to multiline and wordwrap, the scroll property can be used to determine whether the textfield is too small to display the message text. If the maxscroll property is 1, then the textfield doesn't need to be any larger, and we can safely stop the progression of the timeline. Otherwise, we let the timeline move steadily forward until we find a frame in which the textfield is large enough.

The added bonus of this technique is that the message is slowly revealed as though a person were talking or typing in real-time, even though technically, the entire message text is already present.

These lines are added to the process function in `highfive.java`:

```
if (name.equals("chat")) {
  chat(xmlDoc);
}
```

As is the following method to handle it:

```
public void chat (Document xmlDoc) {
  broadcastToHighFive (xmlDoc);
}
```

The handshake is added in example Highfive 6.3

Can I have a shake with that?

Cool, now we can send messages. That was pretty easy, right? Well, there's one more function to add – the high five! That was the whole concept in the first place.

```
onClipEvent (keyDown) {

  var keycode = Key.getCode()

  //numeric keypad "5"

  if (keycode==101) {
_root.shake ("high")
       }
}
```

We'll use the numeric keypad to decide which handshake to attempt. Based on the key pressed, we'll send a different string to the shake function, which builds the shake message and sends it to the server. On the receiving end, this string will help us determine which frame to jump to in the avatar movie clip.

```
shake = function (state) {
  var xmlObj = new Object()
  xmlObj.id = myId
  xmlObj.state = state

  var xmlDoc = Object.io.objToXml ("shake", xmlObj)
  xsock.send (xmlDoc)
}
```

We'll use the `objToXml` utility function one more time. The shake function simply builds and sends a message in the format:

```
<shake id="currentId" state="handshakeState" />
```

The server will gladly relay this message to all highfive users after we add a handler to `highfive.class`.

These lines are added to the process function in `highfive.java`:

```
if (name.equals("shake")) {
  shake(xmlDoc);
}
```

As is the following method to handle it:

```
public void shake (Document xmlDoc) {
```

continues overleaf

```
                    broadcastToHighFive (xmlDoc);
            }
```

That's all we need for the server! Such is the power of object-oriented design.

Shake messages will be routed to all highfive users. We need to catch the messages in Flash and display the appropriate animations.

These lines are added to the client's process function:

```
        if (nodeName == "shake") {
          processShake (dataDoc)
        }
```

Any documents with "shake" as the top level nodename are sent to the processShake function.

```
        processShake = function (xmlDoc) {
          var shakeObj = Object.io.xmlToObj (xmlDoc)

          var userMc = this["user"+shakeObj.id]

          //add the state attribute contents to the shakeQ

          userMc.shakeQ[userMc.shakeQ.length] = shakeObj.state

          // Only process the queue if it was empty and the avatar
          // is at rest otherwise the queue should get processed
          // automatically by what's already going on

          if (userMc.shakeQ.length == 1 && userMc.state=="rest") {
            processShakeQ (userMc)
          }
        }
```

Now it gets interesting. First, we use the id attribute of the document to determine which user sent the message. With that information we can determine which avatar needs to receive the data.

Instead of doing anything with the state attribute directly, we'll add it to the avatar's queue for future use. The shakeQ is simply an array that holds the shake states in the order they were received. In the event that the queue was empty and the avatar is at rest, go ahead and process the queue.

If the queue isn't empty or the avatar is in a different state, then there's already a sequence in motion, and we should wait. processShakeQ will be called eventually.

First, we determine what the first handshake state sitting in the queue is. We don't remove it yet – that will be done later.

```
        processShakeQ = function (userMc) {
```

```
        if (userMc.shakeQ.length > 0) {
          var nextState = userMc.shakeQ[0]
        }
        else {
          var nextState = null
        }
```

Based on the state request, the avatar is either sent back to the rest position, or the function continues processing.

```
        if (nextState == null) {
          userMc.state = "rest"
          userMc.partner = null
          userMc.direction = ""

          userMc.gotoAndStop (userMc.state)
```

If the avatar already has a partner with whom the pair are exchanging a multi-step handshake, the function skips straight ahead to compare the two. If they're the same, we'll see an animation, if they're not, we won't.

```
          userMc._x = userMc.oldX
          userMc._y = userMc.oldY
        }
        else {

          userMc.state = nextState

          if (userMc.partner == null) {
```

If a partner hasn't been selected yet, we'll use the getClosest function to select one. The leftmost partner gets their direction flag set to "Left," the rightmost to "Right". We'll use this data to determine which frame the avatar should jump to.

```
            userMc.partner = getClosest (userMc)

            // and they partner with you

            userMc.partner.partner = userMc

            // Whoever's on the left, takes on the left animation
            // Whoever's on the right, takes on the right animation

            if (userMc._x < userMc.partner._x) {
              userMc.direction = "Left"
              userMc.partner.direction = "Right"
            }
            else {
              userMc.direction = "Right"
              userMc.partner.direction = "Left"
            }
```

Finally, we align the current avatar with their partner after storing our initial position. If we don't do this, our animation will play and once finished, both avatars will return to the rest state and lie on top of one another. This is because the rest states of each clip are the same, whereas the animation states for left and right partners are not.

```
            userMc.oldX = userMc._x
            userMc.oldY = userMc._y

            // Move the avatar movieClip so that it
            // aligns with its partner

            moveAvatarTo (userMc, userMc.partner._x,
                userMc.partner._y)
        }
      else {

            // If the avatar already has a partner, go ahead and
            // see if their states match

            compareStates (userMc, userMc.partner)
        }
      }
    }
```

The getClosest function looks in the avatars array (which we're populating with the avatar movie clips when they're created) and figures out the distance from the current avatar to each of the other avatars. A reference to the clip with the smallest distance is returned.

```
getClosest = function (mc) {

    // Loop through the list of avatar movieClips and
    // determine which one is closest to us

    var bestDist = 10000

    for (var i in avatars) {
      if (avatars[i] != mc) {
        var dx = mc._x - avatars[i]._x
        var dy = mc._y - avatars[i]._y
        var dist = Math.sqrt((dx*dx) + (dy*dy))

        if (dist < bestDist) {

            // The current distance is the best so far

            bestDist = dist
            var partner = avatars[i]
        }
      }
```

```
            }

        return partner
        }
```

A quick change to the `processAddUser` function is responsible for populating the array:

```
    processAddUser = function (xmlDoc) {
        var userObj = Object.io.xmlToObj (xmlDoc)

        attachMovie ("avatar", "user"+userObj.id, attachDepth++)

        var userMc = this["user"+userObj.id]

        avatars[userObj.id] = userMc

        userMc.shakeQ = new Array()
        userMc.state="rest"

        userMc._x = Number (userObj._x)
        userMc._y = Number (userObj._y)
        userMc.id = userObj.id
        }
```

and we can't forget to remove these movie clips during `processRemoveUser`:

```
    processRemoveUser = function(xmlDoc) {
        var userObj = Object.io.xmlToObj (xmlDoc)

        delete ( avatars[userObj.id] )

        this["user"+userObj.id].removeMovieClip()
        }
```

One way or another, all paths lead to `compareStates`. Either the `moveAvatarTo` function was used to align partner movie clips, or the clips were already aligned.

```
    compareStates = function (mc1, mc2) {

        // Remove the current states from their respective queues

        var mc1state = mc1.shakeQ.shift()
        var mc2state = mc2.shakeQ.shift()

        if (mc1state == mc2state) {

            // If they match, play the associated animation

            mc1.gotoAndPlay (mc1.state + mc1.direction)
```

continues overleaf

```
                    mc2.gotoAndPlay (mc2.state + mc2.direction)

                    //Break the setTimeout

                    mc1.interupted = true
                    mc2.interupted = true
                }
                else {

                    mc1.gotoAndStop (mc1.state + mc1.direction)

                    // Break the current timeout

                    mc1.interupted = true

                    // The other avatars have a set amount of time to respond
                    // to the current avatar's request for a high-five

                    setTimeout (mc1)
                }
            }
```

If the states of the two avatars match, we'll play the animation that's located on the frame label equal to the handshake state plus "Left" or "Right". This requires our avatar timeline to be built to match. We'll examine that in a moment.

If the states don't match, the current avatar's (the avatar whose processShakeQ function kicked off the compareStates call) handshake state is placed back in his/her queue. This allows the partner an opportunity to match handshakes within a specified timeout.

If we didn't do this, it'd be incredibly difficult to get a match. User A would send their request, only to be denied. Even if User B immediately responded with the same handshake, User A's request would have already been removed from the queue. Too late, denied. User A could re-send the same request, but User B's request would have been removed as well.

```
        setTimeout = function (mc) {

            // Call "wait" repeatedly until the frameloop ends.

            mc.timeLoop.reset()
            mc.timeLoop = new Object.io.frameloop()
            mc.timeLoop.addFrame (this, "wait", mc)

            // When the frameLoop ends, call this.getNextState (mc)

            mc.timeLoop.setDone (this, "getNextState", mc)

            mc.timeToWait = 150
            mc.interupted = false
        }
```

There are a number of ways to achieve a timeout in Flash. This is only one of them. It uses another utility function from ioLib, an open-source distribution of Flash behaviors you can download from http://www.shovemedia.com/ioLib

Here we tell Flash to keep running the wait function until the end method of our frameloop is called. The wait function, on the other hand, will eventually call end once the timer counts down to zero.

```
wait = function (mc) {
  if (mc.timeToWait-- == 0) {
    mc.timeLoop.end()
  }
}

getNextState = function (mc) {

  // getNextState will be called regardless of *how* the
  // frameLoop ended.
  // If the timeout wasn't interupted, keep going,
  // otherwise don't do anything

  if (!mc.interupted) {

    // We were left hanging!
    // Remove the current state from the queue

    mc.shakeQ.shift()

    // See if there's a new shake state sitting in the queue

    processShakeQ (mc)
  }
}
```

When the timeout ends, getNextState is called. As long as the timeout wasn't interrupted, it means that none of the other avatars responded to our request for a handshake. Nobody likes us. This avatar should remove the current handshake state from their queue and try processing the queue again.

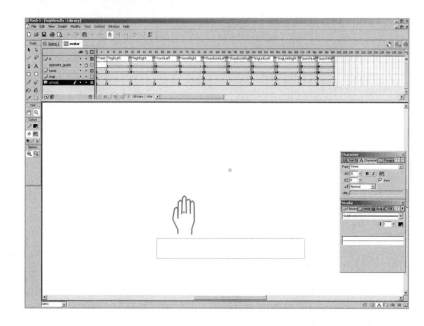

The end result of the above code is this: if two users whose avatars are closest together request the same handshake state within a certain amount of time, each avatar will play an animation. If the handshake states don't match, the avatar movie clip will be sent to the first frame of the animation as a cue to the other users (i.e. "Gimme Five!")

The timeline for our avatar clip is set up with right and left "states" for the handshakes. At the end of each animation, the clip calls:

```
_root.processShakeQ (this)
```

Conclusions

This chapter concludes our section on creating multiuser applications with Flash. Now that we've given you a little taste of what's possible, you should be beginning to see some of the untapped potential inherent in multiuser applications. Flash has a lot to offer this world, particularly when you consider what its core promise of download-friendly motion graphics can add to a multiuser application.

We're going to move on to take a look at Shockwave Director multiuser applications in the next section. You might be full of ideas, and you might not know very much about Director, but don't go away – you've only got half the picture of what's possible. Both packages have quite separate strengths whilst holding out the same magic potential for mould-breaking multiuser applications.

Director, for example, allows for both server-side and client-side scripting in Lingo, saving you the hassle of either messing around with some Java as we've done in this chapter, or finding someone to do it for you. If you don't have Director 8.5, download the trial version, have a look, and save yourself the annoyance of one day laboriously developing the concept from hell in Flash only to realize afterwards that you could have done it in a fraction of the time using Director.

The example in this chapter is just one very small example of what happens when you start to emulate common human interactive experiences. As the use of multiuser systems online increases, you'll be seeing more and more systems like this one. Imagine what could happen when a site starts slowly building up a library of gestures like this. Eventually, it may be possible to build engines that allow users to define their own avatars and their own message types. Perhaps you'll be the one to build it! You're certainly now capable of building your own avatar.

Always plan out what you want your avatar to be capable of, define the messages that control that behavior, and write code to read and write those messages. You'll find that every multiuser system is built following those steps, and they'll save you much pain.

By the time this book reaches your hands, the Web will be a different place than it was the day these words were written. Everyone who touches the Internet changes it slightly. With more and more content being driven by the users themselves, the exceptions may well become the rule – who can say?

The systems you've seen here are only the beginning of what's possible. Multiuser content inherently makes a site more about the people that vist it, and less about the corporation that built the site.

When you start to think about the technology from that perspective, it truly changes the value system of what is important and what isn't. Your telephone isn't about the telephone company; it's about your family and friends. Your electricity isn't about the electric company; it's about hot water, music, and lights. The Internet is slowly giving itself a voice to say what and whom it is about, and the answer will probably surprise us all.

Your guess, as a matter of fact, is as good as mine.

Chapter 7
Making connections and transferring data

The beauty of multiuser applications lies in their ability to facilitate communication. Multiuser applications mean that people are no longer just dealing with a server in an unknown location somewhere that doesn't care what kind of day they're having; they're interacting with other human beings. Those human beings may or may not care what type of day you're having, but it's a definite step forward.

We've said earlier that it is this sort of application that will shape the future of the Web, and this section of the book is going to be dealing with building these applications using Macromedia's sophisticated flagship Director software. Nowhere has the importance of multiuser technologies been made more apparent than with Macromedia's focus on the upgrade to Director's multiuser capabilities as one of the two major advances made with the release of version 8.5 of the software (the other advance being the 3D capabilities).

The first step in developing any multiuser application is to make a connection between one or more instances of the application so that they can then share and manipulate data, preferably over a network connection. This chapter will discuss the creation of connections between movies, which is accomplished in Director by using the Multiuser Xtra.

As we saw in the last section, there are two major questions to address when thinking about multiuser applications. Firstly, how do we make our application communicate with other users or, in other words, how do we make the connections? Secondly, once we've made the connection, how do we send the information, or, what format do we send the data we want to exchange in? Let's take a look at the options that we have before we make our first Director multiuser application.

What type of connection?

There are two considerations that we need to look at when considering how our individual movies should communicate with each other, and these are **peer-to-peer** and **client-server**. We first met these terms way back in the very first chapter, but there are some specific factors to bear in mind when considering Director implementations, so let's have quick re-cap.

Peer-to-peer refers to direct communication between movies without the use of the server application. In the simplest form, this involves two movies running simultaneously which can exchange information. This method of communicating is often used for online multiuser games to avoid the expense and delay of handling all the traffic at the server. While the server application is not necessary, one of the movies is designated to be the host or server movie, through which all communications are directed as shown in the diagram.

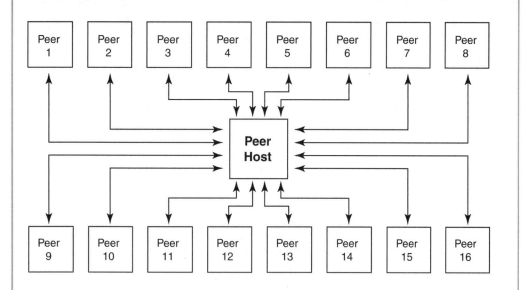

It is possible to communicate without the server, but this doesn't mean that peer-to-peer networks don't need to use the server at all. On the contrary, there are a number of valid reasons for the server to be used in peer-to-peer communication.

Firstly, and most importantly, peer-to-peer connections in Director require that each movie participating in the connection have a known IP (Internet Protocol) address. This isn't a big issue when developing for an intranet environment where the members of a particular group using the application would have known, fixed IP addresses. In the case of a public, open, or unknown environment, then it is impossible to establish connections directly using this mode as the IP addresses of the participants won't be known.

This would also be the case when users of the application attempt to connect on systems that have their IP addresses dynamically assigned, such as many intranets, cable, DSL, and dialup Internet connections. In those cases, the IP address for the given computer may change each time a new network connection is established.

Use of the server is also necessary if you wish to exceed 16 simultaneous connections, and if you need to use some of the more advanced features of the Multiuser Xtra, such as group, database, and administrative functions.

As you can probably see from the diagram shown, **client-server** applications – while more complicated to develop – offer a greater flexibility than their peer-to-peer cousins.

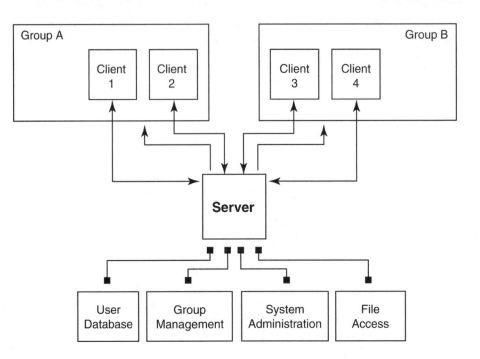

In client-server mode, the server acts as the go between for all information passed between instances of the Multiuser application. The server can determine a participant's network address, which overcomes the limitation of needing pre-established IP addresses for each user in the peer-to-peer model we talked about above.

In client server applications, the server itself can carry some of the processing burden of certain tasks, lessening the demands placed on the connection to the user's machine. In other words, the server can help lessen the bandwidth necessary to run your application.

The server allows for user databases, group management, and file serving to be handled at one finite location as shown in the diagram. The server can also act as a gathering spot for individual users who can then branch off into peer-to-peer communications later, lowering bandwidth and the processing burden on the server.

By now, you may be thinking that the client-server method of communication is the best solution, but there are still some disadvantages to this approach that need to be considered. The biggest problem is that, with all traffic flowing through a common system, applications involving high-use or large files place a significant load on the server. This can usually be overcome with good preplanning and design.

You'll probably have worked out by now that a peer-to-peer application is the simpler to create of the two choices, and that's what we're going to start our Director Multiuser career with in this chapter, before going on to look at client-server applications in later chapters.

Sending Information

Having decided how we want our Multiuser application to communicate with other instances of the application, we have two choices for the way in which we wish to send this information. The choice is whether to use TCP or UDP communication protocols. In order to resolve this decision, it's best to ask yourself a few questions.

Will users be accessing your application from behind a firewall?

If any users will be attempting to access your application from behind a firewall, then TCP is your only option. Firewalls rely on TCP formatted packets to determine which information is allowed into or out of the networks to which they are attached. Since UDP packets lack some of that critical information, they will be tossed out as garbage by the firewall handling that traffic.

How important is efficiency?

UDP has fewer overheads, so it's faster and can significantly reduce server load when multiplied over several users.

How large is the information that will be transferred?

As we've just said with reference to firewalls, UDP lacks the packet ordering information that is carried in a TCP packet. If the information you're sending is too large to fit in a single packet then it must be broken up into multiple ones. If that's the case then it is possible that the packets won't arrive at their destination in the same order that they were sent. This is possible since packets traveling over an IP network do not have to follow the same path to their destination.

For example, a message that must be broken down into three packets may leave the originating system in 1, 2, 3 order only to arrive at the destination system in 1, 3, 2 order. The packet ordering information found in TCP packets allows the receiving machine to cache and reorder packs (or re-request them if they don't arrive) allowing the message to be reconstructed into its original form.

UDP messaging doesn't contain this information, so in the scenario given, the message would be useless. UDP does have individual packet-error correction through a **checksum** scheme, so it is reliable to send information that will fit into a single packet. This information would typically be short pieces of text data, such as the coordinates for object placement in a 3D avatar program.

A checksum is the result of a mathematical calculation based on the actual data within the file. A checksum is considered unique to the data, and by calculating and comparing its value before and after the data transfer it can be determined whether the data arrived without error (i.e. without changing). Checksum calculations are beyond the scope of this discussion, but additional information on their use and mathematical implementation in standard network protocols can be seen at http://www.faqs.org/rfcs/rfc1071.html

It is worth bearing in mind that your application does not have to use UDP or TCP exclusively. For instance, in a multiuser 3D driving game, the positions of the cars can be transferred with UDP as the game plays. At the start of the game, users could select from a list of car models located on the server. The model that the player selects would probably be too large for UDP, and would therefore be better transferred to them over a TCP connection.

TCP connections can also be used as a redundancy for UDP. If an error or lost message occurs during a UDP transfer, the information can be re-requested over a TCP connection for greater reliability.

Making the connection

Once all the planning is complete, we can begin to build the code for our multiuser application. What we're going to do in this chapter can be achieved simply with the Xtra, and we don't need to connect to the multiuser server yet – we'll be doing that in the next chapter.

The Multiuser Xtra is part of the standard installation of Director 8.5. To determine if it has been installed, enter the following in the message window:

```
Showxlib
```

This should yield results similar to those shown.

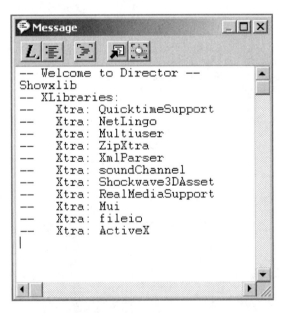

The line **Xtra: Multiuser** shows that the Xtra is installed and ready for use. If this line does not appear in the list, try re-installing Director using the default installation settings.

Creating an instance of the Multiuser Xtra

The first step in establishing a connection is to create a new instance of the Multiuser Xtra using some very simple Lingo.

1. Start by creating a new movie. Select the first cast member, and open a new movie script (go to Window > Script or use CTRL/CMD-0).

2. Name the script main. In the script, create an `on startmovie` handler like this:

```
on startmovie

end startmovie
```

3. Before we create our instance of the Multiuser Xtra, let's set a variable to assign it to. Enter this line before the handler:

```
global gmultiuserClient
```

4. Now that we have a variable to assign our instance to, we can create the instance. Add this line inside the handler:

```
gMultiuserClient=new(Xtra "multiuser")
```

5. Finally, let's add some Lingo to make sure that if an instance of the Multiuser Xtra already exists, it's replaced with the new one. Add this before the line you've just added:

```
--clear the instance if it exists so we can create a new one
if objectP(gMultiuserClient) then
gMultiuserClient=0
end if
```

Your completed code should now look like this:

```
global gmultiuserClient

on startmovie

  --clear the instance if it exists so we can create a new one
  if objectP(gMultiuserClient) then
  gMultiuserClient=0
  end if

  gMultiuserClient=new(Xtra "multiuser")

end startmovie
```

6. In the Property Inspector, click on the Script tab, and select Movie to make sure that our script is the correct type.

Each connection to a server needs an instance of the Xtra to be created. We still need to create an instance when dealing with peer-to-peer connections because, since one peer must act as the server, connecting to a peer is considered the same as connecting to a server.

We've only defined one global variable to store our Xtra instance, so our script is only efficient when making a single connection. If we wanted to make more than one connection – say, connect to a server for chatting, and another server for sending e-mail messages, then a different script would be necessary. We'll be looking at doing this later, but it basically involves using a parent script to create a connection object. The connection object then stores the parameters for a connection and allows the dynamic creation of multiple connections.

Event handling with the Multiuser Xtra

We now have our single Xtra instance stored in a global variable. In order to do anything beyond this point, we need to understand how the Multiuser Xtra handles events within Director. Once we've seen how this works, we can go on to set up some event handlers.

Synchronous and asynchronous operations

If you're familiar with other aspects of Director programming then you'll know that most aspects are synchronous in nature. In other words, handlers and events are processed in the order in which we call them. This is possible because everything is happening in our own little world, free from the influences of outside factors such as network traffic and server load.

It's a bit like what happens when you get up in the morning and make some coffee. Since you're entirely in control, these events will happen in that order every time you choose. If you go to the local diner to get your coffee instead, you will probably rely on someone else to get it for you. You put in your request for coffee and that person inevitably helps two other people, goes for a break, and gets a phone call before eventually showing up with your coffee.

If you were only capable of handling **synchronous** operations, you would have to wait for your coffee before doing something else, like reading the morning paper. Fortunately this is not the case in real life and neither is it the case for handling multiuser traffic in Director. The Multiuser Xtra handles things **asynchronously**, giving us the capability to easily send out messages and wait for responses while doing other things. It also allows us to "listen" for incoming traffic and to handle events that occur without knowing the sequence in which they'll occur in advance. This is accomplished by setting up **callbacks**.

For the sake of clarity, when we talk about "messages" in this chapter, we don't simply mean text messages that users can see on screen. Instead, we are referring to any information that we send from our application to another. This could be information that never gets displayed, such as coordinates, or it could be text.

Callbacks

A callback is established by adding a specific parameter to our instance of the Xtra, which we created above, in our `startMovie` handler. Once assigned to an instance of the Xtra, these parameters act as event monitors. We assign them with the event to which they respond, how to respond to that event, and what additional parameters to pass along in that response.

The first callback we'll encounter will be a message callback. This assigns a handler to be executed when your application receives an incoming message. There are two primary types of message callbacks, those that handle default messages, and others that handle specific messages. The default message callback is in the following form:

```
mycallback=gMultiuser.setNetMessageHandler
(#defaultmessageHandler, script "scriptname")
```

Here, `#defaultmessageHandler` is the name of the handler which should be executed when a default message is received and `"scriptname"` is the name of the cast member where `#defaultmessageHandler` resides. We're not specifying any additional parameters such as message subject or message sender to this callback, so it'll be executed when any message is received by our application.

That's good, but what if we want a bit more control over our messages? In that case, we have to set up a handler to deal with a specific type of message. We can use information such as the subject and the sender of a message to filter out specific messages.

Receiving a message of a specific type is just as easy as receiving a default message, but the callback that intercepts it will need to contain a few more parameters. Such parameters would allow the callback to identify the message's subject or sender, and then execute an appropriate handler.

In addition, we can flag the callback with a Boolean value, which allows us to decide whether to include the actual text of the message in the callback. In this case, the callback looks like:

```
mycallback=gMultiuserClient.setNetMessageHandler \
(#Handlername, script "scriptname", "subject", \
"senderID", boolean_includemessagetext)
```

Compared to our default handler above, the extra parameters here include:

- `subject` – the subject of the incoming message

- `SenderID` – the username of the sender

- `boolean_includemessagetext` – the Boolean value mentioned, indicating whether the message contents should be passed to the callback handler

If we ask for them, the contents of the message are identical to those returned by the following code from our earlier example:

```
mymessage=gMultiuser.getnetmessage()
```

By setting the Boolean flag to `true` in the callback routine, we can avoid having to explicitly request the message in the subsequent handler. The message is, instead, passed as the second argument to the handler.

This means that we've got the message information coming to us, so we'll need to write the handler that can deal with this. The key for doing this comes from examining the message itself. It is formatted as a property list such as:

```
[#errorcode:0, #recipients:["Username"], #senderID:"username",
#subject:"text", #content:"message_text", #timestamp:345738]
```

The message returned from the `getNetMessage` function is a property list. We'll be coming back to some of these, but let's run through the content of this property list so that we know what we're getting:

- #errorcode is an integer value. If the errorcode is 0, then this tells us that there's no error. (More on using this in the error checking section in a moment.)

- #recipients is a linear list of all the users who the message was sent to. As a linear list, it can be manipulated and searched with standard Lingo list functions.

- #senderID is a string value, which indicates the username of the sender.

- #subject is a string value which is defined by our movie. When writing the Lingo to send messages it will be necessary to specifically code a subject value for each message sent. In our message callback, specified above, we can use this subject to direct messages to specific handlers. Given this capability, the subject is typically viewed as routing information that is coded into the message so the message can be handled properly by the receiving application.

- #content is the actual message that was sent. It can contain any data type supported by Director including strings, integers, points, media of member, lists, etc.

- #timestamp is the time in milliseconds on the server, or the number of milliseconds the server has been in operation. By tracking this value it is possible to monitor server performance by sending messages to yourself. The time difference between returned messages indicates the time taken to process each request.

This is the format of our incoming message, and it's relatively simple to access the individual components using standard Lingo dot syntax. Following the call given above:

```
mymessage=gMultiuser.getnetmessage()
```

Each of the parameters contained in the message would be accessed in the following way:

```
myerrocode=mymessage.errorcode
myrecipients=mymessage.recipients
mysenderID=mymessage.senderID
mySubject=mymessage.subject
myContent=mymessage.content
mytimestamp=mymessage.timestamp
```

If UDP messaging is being utilized, there is one additional parameter that is available:

```
myUDP=mymessage.udp
```

If the message arrived via the UDP protocol then this parameter will be `true`, otherwise it is `false`.

Error checking

Error checking is a vital part of any application, but with a Multiuser project, the potential for things to go wrong is magnified by throwing network connections and server availability into the mix. Your application can run into serious trouble, seriously quickly. By carrying out thorough error checking, you can detect and resolve problems before they have had a chance to ruin the user's experience.

Many Multiuser commands are executed by setting a variable equal to a call such as:

```
mycallback=gMultiuserClient.setNetMessageHandler \
(#defaultmessageHandler, script "main")
```

The error code generated by the operation is returned in the variable. If the operation was successful then that code will be 0. Therefore the following code will return `0` in the message window if the operation was successful:

```
mycallback=gMultiuserClient.setNetMessageHandler \
(#defaultmessageHandler, script "main")
put mycallback
```

Any other number indicates an error occurred. Since there are over fifty possible error codes, those nice Macromedia people have provided a way of automatically translating these error codes into a text description of the error so that you don't have to go leafing through your handbook every time you get a string of indecipherable numbers returned. You can do this by using the `getNetErrorString` command as shown in the sample code above.

For those operations that do not allow direct access or return an immediate error result – receiving messages for example – an error code property is generally included in the message accessed by `myinstance.errorcode`. This returns the same numeric value, which can be translated to the text equivalent in the same manner as their more direct counterparts.

Connecting to a host

The last remaining element we need to get our application working is to add the code that connects it to a host system. This is not always necessary, considering a peer-to-peer application can function solely as the host system. However this is not a typical scenario, and in most cases, including both peer-to-peer and client-server applications, you will need to connect to a host system to enable message sending and receiving.

Security levels

The connection to a host application or server is made using the connectToNetServer function. This command can be issued in one of three formats depending on the level of security your connection requires. The basic connection lacks security features, but requires fewer parameters to establish and looks like this

```
newconnection=gMultiuser.connectToNetServer \
("serveraddress", serverportnumber, [#userID:"username", \
#password:"mypassword", #movieID:"mymovie"])
```

serveraddress is a string containing the server's domain name (www.myserver.com), or a complete IP address (127.0.0.1). serverportnumber is an integer value corresponding to the port number that the server is listening to. The standard is 1626, but that can be altered in the server configuration files (see the appendix on the multiuser.cfg file for details). It can also be set using the Waitfornetconnection command that would be issued in the host application of a peer-to-peer scenario.

The last parameter is passed as a property list and contains three user-defined items:

- userID is a unique arbitrary string value, which identifies the user by name. In a basic application like this, that string could be anything. In a more sophisticated setting that name would be an actual username, used with the password property for authentication against the server's database. In a peer-to-peer application, it would simply be a list of acceptable users.

- password is also a string value and, as mentioned above, is used in combination with the userID to authenticate a specific user. This can be accessed with getAttribute, or setAttribute, but only by users with an appropriate access level (we'll be taking a look at this in later chapters).

- movieID is the final string value. This is a name given by the author of the application to identify the movie as "friendly". Based on the name given here, the server or host application may accept or deny connection of that movie. If the connection is accepted, then further segregation can occur based on this name. For example, given the movieID of "demo", the server may limit certain features to that movie while a connecting movie with a movieID of "Goldmember" may get all the services.

The security possibilities here are generally sufficient for most applications intended for general public consumption. User access can be accepted, denied, or limited, based on the user name and password provided. Additionally, the movies connecting to a server can be limited in general by the movieID provided.

You won't really need the information that follows at this stage, but it will be very useful when you start looking at security issues later, and all it involves is some further modification of the basic connection format that we've just seen. If you're in a hurry to start building something, then move straight onto the "Our application" section.

Further security issues

Since the data being passed is generally not encrypted, it would be possible to steal it in transit. With that information, it would be possible to build an application that could fool the server into thinking it should have access. The second method of establishing a connection adds a couple of parameters to minimize that risk. That format looks like:

```
newconnection=gMultiuser.connectToNetServer("serveraddress",
serverportnumber, [#userID:"username", #password:"mypassword",
#movieID:"mymovie"], #mode, "encryptionkey")
```

The two additional parameters are mode and encryptionkey.

There are two possible modes: #smus is used to connect to a Shockwave Multiuser server, and #text creates a text only connection to a text based server such as an e-mail or IRC server.

> The text mode operation capability offers some interesting possibilities. IRC, SMTP mail servers, and NNTP net news servers are all controlled by simple text based commands. We're concentrating on the Multiuser Server for the moment, but there are some more details on this in Chapter 15.

encryptionkey is a string of text used to encode and decode messages sent to a Shockwave Multiuser server. The key contained here must also be present in the configuration file of the server you are connecting to. This parameter should not be included when operating in #text mode.

Using these extra parameters allows your messages to be encrypted while in transit to and from the server, making for an additional level of security over the standard connection format. In addition, when #smus is specified as the mode, the address of the sending machine is included in every message sent to the server in the format http://www.mysystem.com/directory/mymovie.dcr

The server's configuration files can then be modified to only allow movies with the proper path as detected in the encryption key to be allowed to connect, helping to prevent access to the server by unauthorized movies.

The third format for the `connectToNetServer` call is also available for use on multi-homed computers. While not a typical set-up, some computers (typically servers) have multiple IP addresses assigned to them. This last format allows the specification of the IP address of your local machine to use when creating a connection to a server. This format looks like:

```
newconnection=gMultiuser.connectToNetServer \
([#logoninfo: [#userID:"username", #password:"mypassword", \
#movieID:"mymovie"], remoteaddress:"serveraddress", \
remoteTCPport:serverportnumber, #localaddress: \
clientIPaddress, #encryptionkey: "encryptionkey"])
```

Finally, this last format is also used when establishing a connection using UDP with the following modifications:

```
newconnection=gMultiuser.connectToNetServer \
([#logoninfo: [#userID:"username", #password:"mypassword", \
#movieID:"mymovie"], remoteaddress:"serveraddress", \
remoteTCPport:serverportnumber, #localaddress: \
clientIPaddress, #localUDPPortnumber:UDPportnumber, \
#encryptionkey: "encryptionkey"])
```

The `localUDPportnumber` parameter is the UDP port number, which should be used on the client machine for messaging back and forth to the server. That port number should correspond to the UPD port number specified in the server configuration files.

Adding a connection, callbacks and error checking

Let's put all this knowledge into action. We need to place callbacks to send and receive messages, and a `connectToNetServer` command into our routine. We need to add a new text cast member, named `Output` to display the text taken from our message when we receive it. We'll also make sure that if an error occurs, it's displayed in the message window.

1. Begin by creating a new text object, and call it `Output`.

2. First of all, we set up a global variable to hold our instance of the multiuser Xtra. Then, we need to store a new instance of the multiuser Xtra in our variable, wiping any old instances that may already be there.

```
global gmultiuserClient

on startmovie

  --clear the instance if it exists so we can create a new one
  if objectP(gMultiuserClient) then
  gMultiuserClient=0
  end if

  gMultiuserClient=new(Xtra "multiuser")
```

3. Then the value for the IP address on our local machine is obtained, and can be shared with other users through the `getNetAddressCookie` command. Once we have the value, we can assign it to a variable and message it to other users' movies so that they have our address to make future connections.

```
--get our IP address

myaddress=gMultiuserClient.getNetAddressCookie()
```

4. After this, we can add our two callbacks:

```
mycallback=gMultiuserClient.setNetMessageHandler \
  (#defaultmessageHandler, script "main")

mycallback=gMultiuserClient.setNetMessageHandler \
  (#usermessageHandler, script "main", "Peer_test", "", 1)
```

5. We will now add a `connectToNetServer` command to our `startMovie` handler, and this will link up to our local machine by using the IP address we have set in the TCP/IP control panel. (We can connect to ourselves because we are creating a program that both listens and sends to the IP address on our computer.)

```
newconnection=gMultiuserClient.connectToNetServer \
  (myaddress, 1626, [#userID:"Admin", \
  #password:"mypass", #movieID:"peer_test"])

end startmovie
```

> When using this technique, it is best not to run more then one copy of the same program that acts as a host - if multiple hosts are available, then some confusing and unexpected results can occur!

6. In frame 2 add a frame script, to loop the playback head so that we're continually checking for messages:

```
on exitframe
    go to the frame
end
```

7. Even within the small confines of our application, we should define a default message handler to be executed when a message is received for which no other callback has been designated. For this example, we'll display the content of that message in the message window:

```
on defaultmessageHandler

  mymessage=gMultiuserClient.getnetmessage()
  --display the message content in the message window
  put string(mymessage)
```

8. If an error occurs, we also want to display that in the message window:

```
  --if the message contains an error then display that in the
  message window

  if mymessage.errorcode<>0 then
  put "The message contained an error"
  put gMultiuserClient.getNetErrorString(mymessage.errorcode)
  end if

end defaultmessageHandler
```

9. In our case the user message handler is called when the received message contains the subject "Peer_test". This is done like this:

```
on usermessageHandler me, message

  --put the message content in text member "output"
  member("output").text=message.content

  --if the message contains an error then display that in the
  message window
  if message.errorcode<>0 then
  put "The message contained an error"
  put gMultiuserClient.getNetErrorString(message.errorcode)
  end if

end usermessageHandler
```

10. Save your movie.

When we run this movie, it will create all the necessary objects to listen for incoming messages. Any default messages it receives will be written in the message window as text, while any text message with a subject of peer_test will be put into the new cast member, Output.

> As we're sending messages to ourselves, you might think that the messages are going nowhere and that this is all an illusion, but the networking protocols only require a properly formatted IP address to correctly deliver the message to the destination system and port. It will do this blindly – even though the IP in this case happens to be our own system, it is still treated by the computer as if it were not.

Sending information

A program that **listens** for connections and displays the results like we've just written does have some use; it could be used to allow submissions of files to a server in a service bureau. However, we're clearly limiting ourselves to less than half of the power and usefulness of a multiuser application. The other side of the equation comes in the form of **sending** information.

This is only slightly more complicated then receiving messages, and can be easily set up, based on the answer to a couple of primary questions: "who are we sending information to?" and "what information do we want to send?" By answering these two simple questions, we should be able to collect all the information we'll need to establish a connection and send data over it.

Our answers should include the following details:

- What type of connection are we creating – peer-to-peer or client-server?

- What is the specific address (IP address or domain name and port #) of the system we're connecting to?

- What is the size of the information we will be sending?

- What protocol will we be connecting with – TCP or UDP?

- What is the username or group that will receive the information?

More information is sometimes necessary for sophisticated applications, but this information will be a sub-set of the information above. For example, in an application that uses both TCP and UDP protocols, you'd need to specify which data used which protocol.

Sending a message is fairly straightforward. It is accomplished with the single command sendNetMessage. This is formatted like this:

```
newmessage=gMultiuser.sendNetMessage \
("username_or_group", "subject", "message")
```

This is the standard TCP version of the call, which will result in "message" being sent to "username_or_group" with a subject given in the string "subject". The message is sent to the server or peer host specified in the connectToNetServer command. In order to send a UDP message the format changes slightly as follows:

```
newmessage = gMultiuser.sendNetMessage([#errorCode: \
whichError, #recipients: "username_or_group" , \
#subject: "subject", #content: "message" , #udp: TRUE])
```

Sending a simple text message

We've just seen how to send a message, so let's add this into our application.

1. To send a simple text message, add the following handler to our Main script.

```
on sendmessage mymessage

 newmessage=gMultiuserClient.sendNetMessage \
("Admin", "Peer_test", string(mymessage))

 if newmessage<>0 then

 put gMultiuserclient.getNetErrorString(mymessagenewmessage)

 end if

end sendmessage
```

2. When our program is running, we can call this handler directly by typing into the message window:

```
sendmessage "Message to send"
```

In this case, the script will send the message to the userID of Admin with a subject of Peer_test. Since we connected to the server with that ID and we have a message callback specified for all messages with a subject of Peer_test, we're essentially sending the message to ourselves.

When the message comes back, it will be processed by the usermessageHandler, which will put the text into the text member output. We haven't built a host to connect to yet, so resist the temptation to try this now – we'll do that in a moment.

The sendNetMessage command may be easy to code and implement, but it is certainly not lacking in power or potential. Let's take a closer look.

What can we send in a message?

The simple answer to this question is "anything that Director can understand," including both text and binary data. That includes text, images of cast members, members' media, points, 3D vectors, lists, and other data.

In order to handle these items effectively, we need to know the maximum size of any item we intend to send before opening the connection to the server. For performance reasons, it's best to have the smallest discrepancy between the declared maximum size and the actual maximum message size as possible, but you should leave a safety margin in case of problems.

The setnetbufferlimits limit dictates the size of the internal buffers in Director. Any message that exceeds the limit will be truncated and unusable. This doesn't just affect single messages, but also limits the number of messages that the Xtra can queue in memory.

The syntax for setting the net buffer limits is:

```
newlimits=gMultiuser.setnetbufferlimits \
(readsize, maxsize, maxunreadmessages)
```

- readsize is the amount of data read at a time from the TCP/IP stream. The default value is 16k but it can be set higher when transferring larger files to increase performance.

- maxsize is the buffer size used when transferring or receiving messages. This buffer applies independently to all outgoing or incoming files, and the default value is 16k. If you are sending or receiving files that exceed this value, then the maxsize limit must be increased accordingly.

- maxunreadmessages is the maximum number of unread messages that the system will store in a queue. In a high traffic situation, messages can get backed up while they wait to be processed by the system. The default value for this is 100. You can test to see how many waiting there are by using the getNumberWaitingMessages command, and if this value reaches your maxunreadmessages limit then the limit should be increased to avoid problems.

If you don't know the maxsize value of your largest message, then it is possible to dynamically gather that information with some Lingo. If we knew that we were sending a shape member named "shape" to another user and that this was the largest object that we would be sending, we could use the size command to determine that member's size. That size could subsequently be used to adjust the maximum value for setnetbufferlimits. The Lingo would look like this:

```
set maxsize=member("shape").size
newlimits= gMultiuser.setnetbufferlimits((16*1024), \
maxsize, 100)
```

The value returned by the size command is in bytes, the necessary format for the setnetbufferlimits command. For the readsize value we use 16 x 1024 to convert 16 kilobytes to the bytes value of 16384. Using this format is easier to understand, implement, and debug then just using the bytes value straight up.

The ability to send data back and forth between users is the core capability of the sendnetmessage command but it doesn't stop there. Messages can also be sent to entire groups or to the system to execute specific system functions, and commands can be sent from one movie to another to initiate the direct execution of specific scripts or handlers. These capabilities are a little more advanced than our peer-to-peer application needs, though, so we'll save that discussion for later chapters.

Building a peer host

With the proper `setnetbufferlimits` set, our basic client application is complete. We should now be able to send and receive messages without any problems. In a client-server environment, this would be all you would need to do outside of configuring and adding scripts to the server. In a peer-to-peer environment, there are a couple more things we need to do to get everything up and running.

The first item of business is to add code, or build a separate application to act as the peer host. As we've mentioned before, Director does not allow direct connection of one peer to another, so all peers involved in peer-to-peer communication must be connected to a specific peer host. As we will see, the "host" may well be another instance of the Multiuser Xtra.

Once these connections are established, peers can communicate directly with one another, but the host still negotiates all the traffic between them. Even though the communications must go through the peer host, those that are directed to a specific peer are not made available to the host, allowing peer one to communicate with peer two without the host having the ability to access or display what was sent between them.

A peer host can be an application designed solely for this purpose, in which case a separate client would have to be written to allow communications to occur. If it's not done that way, then the functions of a peer host can be built into an application that also acts as a peer client. That client can then perform the dual role of initiating and participating in peer-to-peer communications.

The key difference between client and host coding in a peer-to-peer application is that the host has to wait for a connection to occur. This is accomplished using the `waitfornetconnection()` command in Lingo.

One of the key points made earlier in this chapter was that each instance of the Xtra we create could be used for only one connection to a host. With that limitation, we know that a special instance of the Xtra must be created for our peer host features. If our application is functioning as a peer host only, then the creation of one instance of the Xtra should be all that is necessary. However, we are building a dual-purpose peer host and client application, so at least two instances of the Xtra must be created.

You'll recognize this code as being very similar to the peer code that we looked at previously. Here, we're going to use it to create another instance of the Multiuser Xtra.

```
global gmultiuserClient, gMultiuserHost

on startmovie

  -- set host

  if objectP(gMultiuserHost) then
  gMultiuserHost=0
  end if
```

continues overleaf

```
gMultiuserHost=new(Xtra "multiuser")

myaddress=gMultiuserhost.getNetAddressCookie()

--set client

if objectP(gMultiuserClient) then
gMultiuserClient=0
end if

gMultiuserClient=new(Xtra "multiuser")

mycallback=gMultiuserClient.setNetMessageHandler \
(#defaultmessageHandler, script "main")

mycallback=gMultiuserClient.setNetMessageHandler \
(#usermessageHandler, script "main", "Peer_test", "", 1)

newconnection=gMultiuserClient.connectToNetServer \
(myaddress, 1626, [#userID:"Admin", \
#password:"mypass", #movieID:"peer_test"])

end startmovie
```

Once we've created a second instance of the Xtra with this code, we can develop each of the instances of the Xtra to have their own message callbacks. We have already covered the necessary callbacks for the peer side Xtra instance.

On the host side, things are slightly different. We still have to set up the message callbacks before calling `WaitForNetConnection` (the host analog of `connectTtoNnetSserver`), but a minimum of two message callbacks should be included as opposed to the one needed for the client. First, we need to include the `defaultmessagecallback`, which should be present regardless of the type of application you are developing.

Secondly, we need to include the logon callback. The host is responsible for negotiating the communications between clients, so it's clearly important that it can allow or disallow the connection of specific movies to that host application. The server has these features built in, but a special callback must be specifically written in a peer host to accomplish that same task. That callback would look like:

```
mycallback=gMultiuserHost.setNetMessageHandler \
(#logonmessageHandler, script "main", \
"WaitForNetConnection", "System", 1)
```

Essentially, the system sends itself a message containing the subject `WaitforNetConnection`, with a UserID of `System`. The only requirement of the logon callback handler is for it to be returned true (1) to allow that user to connect, or false (0) to disallow it.

```
on logonmessagehandler (me, message)

    return true

  end
```

This will allow anyone to logon, and is probably not the ideal way of handling logons. Fortunately, the message passed to this handler contains a list of valuable information, which can be used for determining if the connecting agent should be allowed to connect. The format of that message is:

```
[#userID: "connectinguserID", #password: "connectingpassword",
#movieID:"connectingmovieID"]
```

With this information, we have all we need to build a simple authentication routine:

```
on logonmessagehandler (me, message)

    myID=message.userID
    mypassword=message.password
    mymovieID=message.movieID

    set logonallowed=True

    if myID<>"Bob" then logonallowed=False
    if mypassword<>"letmein" then logonallowed=False
    if mymovieID<>"peer_test" then logonallowed=False

    return logonallowed

  end
```

In this case, if the username, password, or movieID are not what we expect then the logon is not allowed. Allowing multiple users with independent passwords or movies could be accomplished by checking information against compound property lists like:

```
["Bob":["password","movieID"]]
```

Here, each username has an associated password and movieID. Standard list manipulations would allow the host to quickly verify and authenticate any incoming connection requests.

Once the message callbacks are established, we can tell the system to WaitForNetConnection. This command can be formatted in two ways:

```
waitforconnection=gMultiuserHost.WaitForNetConnection \
("userID", portNumber, maxConnections, "encryptionkey")
```

This allows for listening for a basic TCP connection. The parameters have the same descriptions as the corresponding ones for connectToNetServer, with the additional parameter of maxConnections, a number between 1 and 16 that sets the number of movies that can connect to the peer host.

The second format allows for UDP messaging and the specification of a listening IP address on multi-homed machines.

```
waitforconnection=gMultiuserHost.waitfornetconnection \
([#userID: "userID", #maxConnections: maxConnections, \
#localAddress: localIPAddress, #localTCPPort: TCPPortNumber, \
#localUDPPort: UDPPortNumber, #encryptionKey:"encryptionKey"])
```

Final code

All this means that our final code will look like this, so enter the changes into your script if you haven't already.

```
global gmultiuserClient, gMultiuserHost

on startmovie

  -- set host

  if objectP(gMultiuserHost) then
  gMultiuserHost=0
  end if

  gMultiuserHost=new(Xtra "multiuser")

  myaddress=gMultiuserhost.getNetAddressCookie()

  mycallback=gMultiuserHost.setNetMessageHandler \
(#defaultHostHandler, script "main")

  mycallback=gMultiuserHost.setNetMessageHandler \
(#logonmessageHandler, script "main", \
"WaitForNetConnection", "System", 1)

  waitforconnection=gMultiuserHost.waitfornetconnection \
([#userID:"Host", #maxconnections:16, \
#localaddress:myaddress,#localTCPport:1626])

  if waitforconnection<>0 then
  put "Host Error:"
&gMultiuserHost.getNetErrorString(waitforconnection)
  end if

  --set client

  if objectP(gMultiuserClient) then
```

```
        gMultiuserClient=0
        end if

        gMultiuserClient=new(Xtra "multiuser")

        mycallback=gMultiuserClient.setNetMessageHandler \
      (#defaultmessageHandler, script "main")

        mycallback=gMultiuserClient.setNetMessageHandler \
      (#usermessageHandler, script "main", "Peer_test", "", 1)

        newconnection=gMultiuserClient.connectToNetServer \
      (myaddress, 1626, [#userID:"Admin", \
      #password:"mypass", #movieID:"peer_test"])


      end startmovie

      on defaultmessageHandler

        mymessage=gMultiuserClient.getnetmessage()
        --display the message content in the message window
        put string(mymessage)

        --if the message contains an error then display that
        --in the message window
        if mymessage.errorcode<>0 then put \
      "The message contained an error"

        put gMultiuserClient.getNetErrorString(mymessage.errorcode)

      end defaultmessageHandler

      on usermessageHandler me, message

        --put the message content in a new member after member 3
        member("output").text=message.content

        --if the message contains an error then display that
        --in the message window
        if message.errorcode<>0 then
        put "The message contained an error"
        put gMultiuserClient.getNetErrorString(message.errorcode)
        end if


      end usermessageHandler
      on defaultHostHandler

        mymessage=gMultiuserHost.getnetmessage()
```

continues overleaf

```
--display the message content in the message window
put string(mymessage)

--if the message contains an error then display
--that in the message window
if mymessage.errorcode<>0 then put "The message contained an
error"

put gMultiuserHost.getNetErrorString(mymessage.errorcode)
end defaultHostHandler


on logonmessagehandler (me, message)

  put "Host Logon: " &message

  return True

end

on sendmessage mymessage

  newmessage=gMultiuserClient.sendNetMessage("Admin", "Peer_test",
string(mymessage))

  if newmessage<>0 then

  put gMultiuserclient.getNetErrorString(mymessagemymessage)

  end if

end sendmessage
```

We can now run our movie and the text member Output will change to reflect whatever you type into the message window - as long as you precede the message with the Sendmessage command.

Congratulations! - you've just created your first Director multiuser application. This might feel good, but stay with us, because we've got some improvements to make to our application that will make things much better...

Managing connections on the peer host

The host application of the peer group has a couple of additional commands available that can help in some basic administrative capacities. These functions allow the movie to monitor who is connected at any given time, as well as to force the disconnection of any connected member.

The `getPeerConnectionlist` command returns a list of the userIDs of peer users currently attached to the host movie. This is a linear list, which will be empty when no users are connected. From this list we can do three things:

- Write routines that provide us with the number of currently connected users

- Test to see if a particular user is connected

- Display all those who are in an onscreen window

The syntax to display the number of users currently connected would be:

```
usercount=count(gMultiuserHost.getPeerConnectionlist())
```

If you wanted to know if a user named Bob were logged on, then you could use:

```
userconnected= findpos \
(gMultiuserHost.getPeerConnectionlist(), "Bob" )
```

This will return 1 if Bob is logged on and 0 if he's not.

To break a connection with a logged on user the `breakconnection` function is used. To break the connection made with `WaitForNetConnection` and established by user `"userID"` you could use:

```
err=gMultiuserHost.breakConnection("userID")
```

We can take this a little further. For example, say that you wanted to check to see if Bob was logged on and, upon remembering what an utter pain Bob is, you decided that you wanted to break the connection with him. Well, you could use the following routine to quickly dispatch with Bob and his irritating reminiscences of times past:

```
on bootuser
    userconnected = findpos \
(gMultiuserHost.getPeerConnectionlist(), "Bob" )
    if userconnected<>0 then
            err=gMultiuserHost.breakConnection("Bob")
    end if
end bootuser
```

So far, we've created an application that allows us to send and receive messages, but it's a little unsatisfying communicating through the message window. It would be nice to communicate with the outside world rather than just talking to ourselves, don't you think?

In order to do this, we're going to build on what we've learnt so far to create a simple peer chat application that will allow a system to connect to it and send messages. If it is saved as a projector or Shockwave movie then multiple instances of it can be launched, allowing several users to communicate with each other in peer mode.

As with all the examples in the book, the completed version of this application can be downloaded from the friends of ED web site. We'll start by taking a look at the visual structure of the application, which we'll leave you to create as you wish (or copy ours!), and then proceed to take you through the code that sits behind the collection of buttons and text boxes step-by-step.

Cast structure

There are two casts associated with the movie. The first is the internal cast, which is used for interface and graphical elements. The second cast is called Scripts and, unsurprisingly, holds all the scripts. The scripts cast consists of 2 movie scripts and 7 behavior scripts, all of which will be covered in detail in a moment.

Name	#	*	Script	Type	Modified
username_entry	6			Field	11/03/01 11:31 PM
Send	1			Button	11/03/01 11:22 PM
password_entry	7			Field	11/03/01 11:31 PM
message_text	5			Text	11/03/01 11:31 PM
Logon	2			Button	11/02/01 11:11 PM
Logoff	3			Button	11/02/01 11:11 PM
ip_address_entry	8			Field	11/03/01 11:31 PM
Chat_text	4			Text	11/03/01 11:31 PM
14	14			Bitmap	11/03/01 11:31 PM
13	13			Vector Sha...	11/03/01 11:31 PM
12	12			Shape	11/03/01 11:31 PM
11	11			Shape	11/03/01 11:31 PM
10	10			Shape	11/03/01 11:31 PM
9	9			Text	11/03/01 11:31 PM

Of the cast members located in the internal cast, only members 1 through 8 are important to the program's function. 9 through 14 are graphical elements (onscreen labels and such) that can be left out. The essential items in order are as follows:

1. Send: button to initiate the sending of the message
2. Logoff: button used to logoff the host system
3. Logon: button used to logon to the host system
4. Chat_text: text member used to display the messages passed through the host
5. Message_text: text member used as the input for the message outgoing message
6. username_entry: field for entering the username at logon
7. password_entry: field for entering the password at logon
8. IP_address_entry: field for entering the host IP address at logon

We'll be covering the scripts added to each of these cast members later – all you need to do at this stage is make sure that your design includes the above cast members in the locations specified by the next section. As you can see from the screenshots, my application is fairly plain, so this is your chance to add some creative visual sparkle to your application!

Score layout and basic design

The basic design of the application is as a two-mode program. You are either waiting to connect (start/logon screen) or you are connected (connected screen) and chatting. The score can therefore be setup with two groups of frames as shown in the screenshot. The first image shows the "Start" or logon screen.

The elements on this screen consist of the text fields username_entry, password_entry, and ip_address_entry. The logon button is also located here. The sprites for these span the first 5 frames. There are also two frame scripts that we'll cover later, one on the first and another on the fifth frame. The first frame script clears the fields for the logon so that they appear blank at runtime, while the script on frame 5 loops the playback while we wait for the logon button to be clicked. Finally, there's a "Start" marker designating the start of the section.

The second screen starts at the "connected" marker. This section spans two frames, with a loop script on the second frame to keep us on that frame while we chat (we'll cover the script later, don't worry). The elements located on this screen include the text fields chat_text and message_text to allow users to enter outgoing messages and view messages received. Also located here are the Send and Logoff buttons.

The scripts

The scripts are slightly modified versions of our earlier peer-to-peer example. The main difference is that the bulk of the code has been separated into two main movie scripts. One script contains the handlers that are host specific, and this is called host_scripts. The other script is used for client-specific handlers, and is called client_scripts. General program functions such as clearing fields and other housekeeping tasks are located in the host_scripts member. These scripts are starting to get big and look scary, so let's go through them slowly.

Creating the host_scripts movie script

1. Create a new script member, name it host_scripts, and change its type to movie.

2. With the newly created host_scripts member open, the first item of business is to declare the global variables that we will use. Add the following code to your script:

   ```
   global gmultiuserClient, gMultiuserHost
   ```

   These variables will hold the Xtra instances for the client and host portions of the program. One Xtra instance is needed for each connection to a server, so we need separate instances in order to run a host and client at the same time.

3. Our first handler will be on startMovie so that it executes at startup. This will initialize the host portion of the movie and send us to the frame Start:

   ```
   on startmovie

     -- set host

     if objectP(gMultiuserHost) then
     gMultiuserHost=0
     end if

     gMultiuserHost=new(xtra "multiuser")
   ```

4. The host will be running from our local machine so we can get our IP address using getNetAddressCookie and use that value to setup our WaitForNetConnection. (We could also store myAddress as a global to send to other users later on, but we're keeping this as simple as possible, so we won't do that this time.)

   ```
   myaddress=gMultiuserhost.getNetAddressCookie()
   ```

5. Our next step is to setup our callbacks to handle events that we can monitor and respond to as the host functions. As before, we're setting up a handler for default messages to capture anything unexpected and another for logon messages to let us keep track of the users connecting.

```
mycallback=gMultiuserHost.setNetMessageHandler \
(#defaultHostHandler, script "Host_scripts")

mycallback=gMultiuserHost.setNetMessageHandler \
(#logonmessageHandler, script "Host_scripts", \
"WaitForNetConnection", "System", 1)
```

6. After setting up the callbacks, we can begin listening for people to connect. Again, we are going to listen on our local IP address at the standard TCP port.

```
waitforconnection=gMultiuserHost.waitfornetconnection \
([#userID:"Host", #maxconnections:16, \
#localaddress:myaddress,#localTCPport:1626])
```

7. If any problems have occurred then we need to alert the user of the error:

```
if waitforconnection<>0 then
alert "A Host error has occured: "& \
getMyHostError(waitforconnection)
end if

go to frame "start"

end startmovie
```

8. The `clearfields` handler is then called from the `startMovie` script to set the entry fields for the various text display and entry cast members to blank:

```
on clearfields

member("username_entry").text=""
member("password_entry").text=""
member("message_text").text=""
member("chat_text").text=""

end clearfields
```

9. The `defaultHostHandler` is executed when the host gets a message that is not otherwise designated. In our case, that will consist of all messages other then the logon message. Keep in mind that this is specific to the host instance of the Xtra (`gMultiuserHost`) and should not be confused with the messages received by the client side of the application. The two instances are now completely separate and should be kept that way. The messages that this handler receives are displayed in the message window along with any error codes or messages that come with them:

```
on defaultHostHandler

mymessage=gMultiuserHost.getnetmessage()

--display the message content in the message window
```

```
put string(mymessage)

--if the message contains an error then display that
--in the message window
if mymessage.errorcode<>0 then
put "The message contained an error: " &
gMultiuserHost.getNetErrorString(mymessage.errorcode)
end if

end defaultHostHandler
```

10   The `logonMessageHandler` is necessary to authenticate a user when they connect to the system through a peer-to-peer connection. If we wanted to add a verification scheme to limit access by username, password, or IP address, then this is where we would put it. Here, we're just writing the login request to the message window and returning `True` to indicate that the requesting user should be allowed to connect.

```
on logonmessagehandler (me, message)

 put "Host Logon: " &message

 return True

end
```

11.   The `stopMovie` handler cleans up when the movie quits. Here, we check if the user is logged on by checking for the existence of `gMultiuserClient`. If that exists, then we log them off the system, close the callbacks for the host, and set `gMultiuserHost` to `0` to close down our host.

```
on stopmovie

 if objectp(gMultiuserClient) then
 logoff
 end if

 mycallback=gMultiuserHost.setNetMessageHandler \
(0, script "Host_Scripts")

 mycallback=gMultiuserHost.setNetMessageHandler \
(0, script "Host_Scripts", "WaitForNetConnection", "System", 1)

 gMultiuserHost=0

 clearglobals

end stopmovie
```

Creating the client_scripts script

The next script cast member is named client_scripts and it contains the handlers that run the client side of the application. This includes connecting to the host, and sending and receiving messages.

1. As with the host_scripts script, our first order of business is to declare our global variables.

```
global gMultiuserClient, gMultiuserHost
```

2. The first handler is the logon script, called by clicking on the logon button on the start screen. This handler does several things. First, it checks to see if there is already an instance of the Xtra, and if there is already an instance, then it clears it:

```
on logonscript

  --set client

  if objectP(gMultiuserClient) then
  gMultiuserClient=0
  end if
```

Then it gets the username, password and IP address information from the corresponding text entry members:

```
--The following lines collect the username, password and
--IP address info the user has entered.

  connectIP=member("IP_address_entry").text
  connectUser=member("username_entry").text
  connectPass=member("password_entry").text
```

If their contents are OK, the handler creates an instance of the Xtra, sets up the callbacks, and finally connects to the host:

```
--If any of the essential user information is blank then we
--alert that we are missing information and exit, otherwise,
--we can proceed with making the connection.

  if (connectIP="" or connectUser="" or connectPass="") then
  alert "A Username, Password, and Host IP address must be
provided to make a connection"

  else
```

3. Here, a new instance of the Xtra is created and assigned to our global variable `gMultiUserClient`:

```
gMultiuserClient=new(xtra "multiuser")
```

4. The Xtra instance is completely independent of the `gMultiuserHost` instance and therefore needs its own callbacks. In this case, we'll assign 3 callbacks. The first is the `defaultMessageHandler`, which handles all non-specific traffic not assigned to another callback. While not essential, it should still be included to catch all the unexpected messages that would be missed by the other callbacks.

```
mycallback=gMultiuserClient.setNetMessageHandler \
(#defaultMessageHandler, script "client_scripts")
```

5. Next, the `userMessageHandler` handles all messages of subject "Peer_test". All the messages that the client sends, that are to be shared and displayed on other client systems, will have this as their subject. Therefore, this is the general message-handling callback for content sent between the users logged onto the host.

```
mycallback=gMultiuserClient.setNetMessageHandler \
(#userMessageHandler, script "client_scripts", "Peer_test", "", 1)
```

6. The last callback is the `connectionSuccess` callback, which is called when the host responds to the connection request. This allows us to verify that we successfully connect to the host system and display the appropriate message on our screen.

```
mycallback=gMultiuserClient.setNetMessageHandler
(#connectionSuccess, script "client_scripts",
"ConnectToNetServer", "", 1)

 newconnection=gMultiuserClient.connectToNetServer \
(connectIP, 1626, [#userID:connectUser, \
#password:connectPass, #movieID:"peer_test"])

 if newconnection<>0 then
  alert "An error has occured: "& getMyClientError(newconnection)
 else
  go to frame "connected"
 end if


 end if

end logonscript
```

7. The following two handlers are functions that return the text version of any errors that occur. There is one handler for the client and one for the host instances of the Xtra.

```
on getMyClientError errorvalue

  return gMultiuserClient.getNetErrorString(errorvalue)

end getMyClientError


on getMyHostError errorvalue

  return gMultiuserHost.getNetErrorString(errorvalue)

end getmyHostError
```

--The connectionSuccess handler is executed when we connect to the server. We evaluate the errorcode in the message and if no error occurred then we display the logon success information in the "Chat_text" cast member. If the message containts an error then we execute the logoff script to clean up before going back to the start screen.

```
on connectionSuccess me, message

  if message.errorcode=0 then

  member("chat_text").text=""
  member("chat_text").text="Connection Successful at " \
& the long time&return

  member("chat_text").line[1].fontstyle=[#bold]

  else

  logoff

  end if

end connectionSuccess
```

8. The logoff script is executed as part of the clean-up operation when any user disconnects from the server. This can be triggered in several ways when an error occurs at logon, when the user stops the movie, or when the user clicks the logoff button on the interface. The objective here is to release all the callbacks and Xtra instances from memory before going back to the Start screen. To clear the callbacks, we simply set the callback message handler name to 0 for each callback that was initialized in the logon script above like this:

```
on logoff

  mycallback=gMultiuserClient.setNetMessageHandler \
(0, script "client_scripts")
```

continues overleaf

```
mycallback=gMultiuserClient.setNetMessageHandler \
(0, script "client_scripts", "Peer_test", "", 1)
mycallback=gMultiuserClient.setNetMessageHandler \
(0, script "client_scripts", "ConnectToNetServer", "", 1)

gMultiuserClient=0

go to frame "start"

end logoff
```

9. The primary goal of this exercise is to be able to send text messages from one user to another. This is achieved through the sendMessage handler. This handler gets the text message to be sent from the Message_text text member, which is an editable text member is visible when the user is connected. Along with the message to be sent, we also need the username of the sender, gleaned from the username_entry field that was filled in (and not yet cleared out again) when the user logged in.

```
on sendmessage

mymessage=member("message_text").text
myUsername=the text of field "username_entry"
```

10. We send the message using sendNetMessage, passing the username, the subject "Peer_test", and the message text as arguments. Remember, using the subject "Peer_test" here guarantees that this message will be handled by the UserMessageHandler callback to be described later:

```
newmessage=gMultiuserClient.sendNetMessage
(myUsername, "Peer_test", string(mymessage))

if newmessage<>0 then

put gMultiuserclient.getNetErrorString(mymessage)

end if

--clear the text box out after the message is sent

member("message_text").text=""

end sendmessage
```

11. The default message handler is rather different to the host handler that we've already discussed. Again, it traps all messages not handled by other callbacks, and displays them in the message window.

```
on defaultmessageHandler

mymessage=gMultiuserClient.getnetmessage()
```

```
--display the message content in the message window
put string(mymessage)

--if the message contains an error then display that in
--the message window
if mymessage.errorcode<>0 then

put "The message contained an error: " &
gMultiuserClient.getNetErrorString(mymessage.errorcode)

end if

end defaultmessageHandler
```

12. The last message callback is the `UserMessageHandler`. This handler takes care of incoming messages sent by other users by taking the content of the message and formatting it for display in the `Chat_text` cast member.

```
on usermessageHandler me, message

myDisplayLine=message.senderID &": "&message.content

--put the message content in a new member after member 3
member("chat_text").rtf=member ("chat_text").rtf&myDisplayLine&return

lastline=(member("chat_text").line.count)
lineWordnum=string(mydisplayline).word.count

member("chat_text").line[lastline].word[1].fontstyle=[#bold]
member("chat_text").line[lastline].word[1].forecolor=8
member("chat_text").line[lastline].word[2..linewordnum]
     .fontstyle=[#plain]
member("chat_text").line[lastline].word[2..linewordnum] \
     .forecolor=255

updatestage
```

13. If the message contains an error, then the error string is displayed as an alert:

```
--if the message contains an error then display that
--in the message window
if message.errorcode<>0 then
alert "An error has occured: "&
getMyClientError(message.errorcode)
 end if

end usermessageHandler
```

Creating the other scripts

The remaining scripts are behaviors that control interface elements or playback control by calling on the handlers that we've just carefully crafted.

1. The frame script in frame 1 calls the `clearfields` handler when the movie starts or the user logs off:

```
on prepareFrame me
 clearfields
end
```

2. The logon button on the Start screen has a behavior that calls the logon script:

```
on mouseUp me
 logonscript
end
```

3. As you'll remember, there's a frame script for looping at the last frame of each section:

```
on exitFrame me
 go to the frame
end
```

4. Attached to the `IP_Address_entry` sprite on the startup screen is a script that allows a default IP address to be specified as a property. Naturally you will need to specify your own address to set it as default. To find your IP address check the status on the multiuser server. That default is then displayed automatically each time we go to the Start screen.

```
property pMyIP

on beginsprite me

  member(sprite(me.spritenum).member).text=string(pMyIP)

end

on getPropertyDescriptionList
 set description = [:]
 addProp description, #pMyIP, [#default: "127.0.0.1",
     #format:#string, #comment: "Default IP address:"]
     return description

end
```

5. The Send button sprite on the Connected screen has a script that checks to make sure the text message entry member isn't empty. If it does contain something, it calls `sendmessage`.

```
on mouseUp me

  if member("message_text").text<>"" then
  sendmessage
  end if

end
```

6. Attached to the message_text sprite on the connected screen is a script that allows the message to be sent when RETURN is pressed on the keyboard. Like the last script, it checks to see if the text member is empty and calls sendmessage if it isn't.

```
on keydown me

  if the key=return then
  if member(sprite(me.spritenum).member).text<>"" then
   sendmessage
  end if
  else
  pass
  end if

end
```

7. Finally, the logoff button on the Connected screen calls the logoff handler when clicked:

```
on mouseUp me
  logoff
end
```

Welcome to the world of interactive Director multiuser applications! You've now created a functioning peer-to-peer chat application. The basics that we've covered in this chapter – establishing a peer-to-peer network connection and passing a text message along – can be built on to create applications that dynamically make connections as well as create, send, and handle any data available in a Director movie. You should be beginning to see the exciting potential of multiuser Director applications.

In the next chapter, we'll begin working with the Multiuser Server to manage messaging to groups and movies created for client-server environments. You probably want to take a quick break after this chapter, but don't go too far away – you've now done a lot of the hard work, and things only become more fun from here on in.

Chapter 8

Groups

In the last chapter, we saw how to create a basic peer-to-peer communication program and sent a text message to ourselves. That program used Lingo to initiate an instance of the Multiuser Xtra, set up a message callback, and connect to a host application. We also created the code necessary to create a simple host script.

As we know, while peer-to-peer networking often provides an adequate solution, there are certain limitations attached to it. These limitations include needing a known host IP address and the restrictive limit of 16 simultaneous users. Many projects will have requirements outside these parameters, and will require the more significant power of multiuser programming in Director; found in the **Multiuser Server** application that we'll be looking at in this and subsequent chapters.

In this chapter, we'll deal first of all with a few issues that could get in the way of using the Multiuser Server and create a connection to the server. Once you move beyond 16 users in your chat application, then you need to start managing where users are and what they're doing. To do this, we're going to look at groups – a key part of the Multiuser Server and a key part of the fully featured chat application that we'll have built by **Chapter 10**.

In this chapter, we're going to look at how to create, join, and leave groups. In the next chapter, we'll carry on to take a look at obtaining information about groups and manipulating it.

Configuring the Multiuser Server

The Multiuser Server is a standalone application that forms a part of the standard installation of Director 8.5. If you navigate to the folder that contains the Director 8.5 application, you should find a subfolder called Shockwave Multiuser Server 3.0. You'll see that this directory not only contains the Multiuser Server application itself, but a few other files and folders besides.

We'll run through the important ones now, just to satisfy your curiosity, but it is only the last two files – the configuration files – that we'll need to know about for the purpose of this chapter:

■ **DBObjectFiles**: This folder contains files related to user databases. These files include the actual database files and support files needed for the server to access the data files. We'll be covering databases in more detail in **Chapter 14**.

■ **Xtras**: This holds the Server Xtras that allow the server to perform tasks over and above those that are directly built-in. These Xtras serve essentially the same purpose as normal Xtras in Director, but aren't interchangeable with those.

■ **Scripts**: A folder that contains server-level scripts. There are several default scripts located in here – Displacher.ls, Globalscripts.ls, and Scriptmap.ls – which you may choose to adapt when configuring and developing your server-based application. These will be covered in depth in **Chapter 15**. At this point though, the key fact to take on board is that custom scripts can be written specifically for the movies that attach to the server.

■ **Movie.cfg**: This file can be modified to allow for movie-specific configuration. It's used to set parameters for groups and users which are specific to a movie that is attaching to the server. To apply a (possibly modified) copy of this file to a specific movie, it must be saved with the same name as the movieID used in the movie it is to control.

■ **Multiuser.cfg**: The main configuration file for the server application, which contains all the base default values used to launch the server. It also contains the registration information and 'maximum connections' value used to initialize the server.

If you open up either of these last two files, you'll notice that there are a lot of options in them. We'll be looking in detail at these options in the next chapter, but for now we need to change a couple of settings to allow us to carry on with our example. If you can't wait for some extra explanation, there's also an appendix that deals with the multiuser.cfg file.

Specifically, we need to license our version of the server by entering our serial number. We also need to make sure that those of you using systems that have more than one IP address, dynamically assigned IP addresses, or no connection at all know what this involves.

Versions and licensing

If you have a full license for Director 8.5, you're entitled to use the Multiuser Server with up to 2000 simultaneous users. In order to activate this capability you must modify the server configuration file multiuser.cfg by adding a valid Director 8.5 serial number.

Either a Mac or a Windows serial number will work universally, regardless of the platform on which the server is installed. In other words, Director for Windows will only run on a Windows system, but there is nothing to stop you from using the server application on a Mac.

Multi-homed systems

If you're using a machine that has more then one IP address assigned to its network adapter or if your system has multiple adapters, known as a multi-homed system, (sometimes referred to as a virtual hosts server) you'll find you need to modify the `Multiuser.cfg` file before starting your server and continuing with this chapter. If you're not using more than one IP address, you're free to skip the next paragraph.

We're going to look at these modifications now, so before we go any further it would be a wise move to copy the original `Multiuser.cfg` file into another folder, so you don't lose the original settings. Then open it up in a text editor like Notepad or Bbedit, and take a look at the section shown here – it's not very far down the file.

```
#================================================================
# General server configuration information.
#================================================================
# The default ServerPort value is 1626
# ServerPort = 1626
# Server IP address. This is optional, but must be specified if
# the server runs on a multihomed system or if listening on
  multiple
# ports. Specify the IP address plus a colon and the port number.
# If listening on multiple addresses, specify them each here.
```

Immediately following these comments, add a line specifying the IP address you would like the server to listen on, followed by a colon and the relevant port number – it should look like this:

```
ServerIPAddress = 127.0.0.1:1626
```

Finally, save the file.

Dynamically assigned IP addresses

If your system uses a dynamically assigned IP address, the Multiuser Server will connect to whatever secondary system is responsible for assigning it. Systems with dynamically assigned addresses include those using a dial-up connection; and some that use DSL, cable modems, or network connections via a DHCP (Dynamic Host Configuration Protocol) server.

The server begins listening on a particular IP address on a specific port at startup. If you're not connected to whatever system you're using when you start the Multiuser Server up, the server won't be able to work out what your IP address is, and won't work. Equally, if your connection fails after the Multiuser Server starts, then the IP address it uses when it makes a new connection won't work as the server won't know what it is. In both cases, you'll need to stop the server, reconnect to the host IP server, and restart the server before your multiuser scripts will work again.

Using the Multiuser Server without a connection

You can alter the Multiuser.cfg file as described above to listen on the 'local machine' IP address of 127.0.0.1:1626. This is useful when testing applications on a system that has no assigned IP address, so isn't connected to a network or to the Internet. It can also be used on systems that have lost their connection to a dynamically assigned IP address.

The ability to connect to yourself like this gives you the opportunity to work on and test projects in trying circumstances, but should not be considered a substitute for testing on a real network. Bandwidth and other network issues such as firewalls cannot be simulated on a local system, so always test your applications in a real-world environment before deployment. When using this, remember to use 127.0.0.1 as the IP address you are connecting to in the connectToNetServer commands in your scripts.

Launching the Multiuser Server

Once you've modified the configuration files as necessary, double-click on the server application to launch it. You should see something like the message shown in the screenshot:

The last entry but one indicates the number of connections allocated – just 50 in this case. Now that the server is up and running, we're all set to start making connections to it.

Making a connection

In order to make connections to this server, we will use a slightly modified version of the peer-to-peer script we created in the last chapter. We'll be using the message window to drive this application in the same way as we did in the peer-to-peer exercise. As with all exercises, if things go wrong, then compare your file with the finished version available for download from the friends of ED web site.

1. Open a new movie, click CTRL+0 to create a new movie script, and name the script Main.

2. Add the following code, which should be familiar from the last chapter. We're going to add a startMovie handler to create an instance of the Multiuser Xtra and assign it to the variable gMultiuserClient.

```
global gMultiuserClient, gMultiuserHost

on startmovie
 --clear existing instance so we can create a new one
  if objectP(gMultiuserClient) then
  gMultiuserClient=0
  end if
 --set client
 gMultiuserClient=new(xtra "multiuser")
```

```
myaddress=gMultiuserclient.getNetaddresscookie()

-- comment out the line above and substitute the line below with
-- the
-- proper address for your system if you have modified the IP
-- address
-- in the Multiuser.cfg file
-- This is necessary when the server is running on a different
-- system or different IP address then
-- The movie connecting to it,
-- myaddress="127.0.0.1"
```

3. Once the instance is established, we can set up two callbacks. We'll need one callback to deal with all incoming messages that are not assigned to another callback:

```
mycallback=gMultiuserClient.setNetMessageHandler \
        (#defaultmessageHandler, script "main")
```

4. We can now set up another callback – userMessageHandle – to deal with a specific type of message. In this case, that's a message with a subject of Client_test and no specified username specified. This means that all messages received by the client with a subject of "Client_test" will be routed to this handler regardless of the sender.

```
mycallback=gMultiuserClient.setNetMessageHandler \
        (#usermessageHandler, script "main", "Client_test", "", 1)
```

5. Finally, we connect to the server using the address stored in the myAddress variable on port 1626 using the username of "admin", a password of "mypass" and a movieID of "Client_test".

```
newconnection=gMultiuserClient.connectToNetServer \
        (string(myaddress), 1626, [#userID:"Admin", \
         #password:"mypass", #movieID:"Client_test"])
end startmovie
```

6. The defaultmessageHandler routine displays the incoming message in the message window. If the message contains an error, then this is also displayed.

```
on defaultmessageHandler
 mymessage=gMultiuserClient.getnetmessage()
 --display the message content in the message window
 put string(mymessage)
 --if the message contains an error, indicate in the message
 --window
  if mymessage.errorcode<>0 then
   put "The message contained an error"
   put gMultiuserClient.getNetErrorString(mymessage.errorcode)
  end if
end defaultmessageHandler
```

7. Remember how we created a text member called Output in the last chapter? Well, we're going to do that again now, and it'll perform the same role as a place for incoming messages to be displayed. Create a new text member, name it Output, and drag an instance of the text member onto the stage.

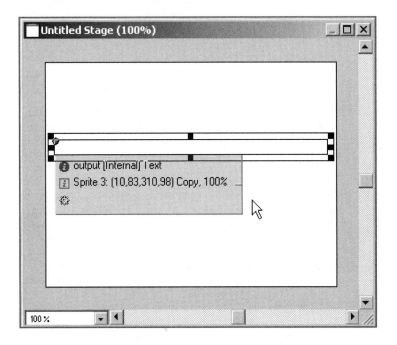

8. Now add the following code to our existing Main script:

```
on usermessageHandler me, message
  --put the message content in a new member after member 3
  member("output").text=message.content
  --if the message contains an error, indicate in the message
  --window
  if message.errorcode<>0 then
   put "The message contained an error"
   put gMultiuserClient.getNetErrorString(message.errorcode)
  end if
end usermessageHandler
```

The sendMessage handler takes the contents of the mymessage argument and sends it to the server. The destination user is "Admin" on the movie "Client_test". You may have noticed that this is the username and movieID we used to connect to the server, so we are, in effect, sending this message to ourselves.

```
on sendmessage mymessage
 newmessage=gMultiuserClient.sendNetMessage \
      ("Admin", "Client_test", string(mymessage))
 if newmessage<>0 then
  put gMultiuserclient.getNetErrorString(newmessage)
 end if
end sendmessage
```

9. We can now use this movie to connect the movie to the server – just run the movie, and you should see a few lines appear in the server window, indicating that the movie has connected to the server:

Now that we have established a connection, we're ready to get going. To do this, we need to introduce a key feature of the Multiuser Server that we'll be taking advantage of almost immediately: groups.

Multiuser groups

By defining groups complete with group-specific attributes, we can allow individual users to participate as a unit with their own special properties.

For example, a 3-D racing game might allow up to 16 cars (or players) on the track at any one time. A group could then consist of up to 16 players – perhaps the group attribute maxPlayers=16 defines this maximum, while playerNum represents the current number of players attached. If a new player connects and `playerNum` is equal to `maxPlayers`, then a new group can be created to which the new player is automatically assigned.

From here, things get interesting. Individual players in a particular group can message each other - or even the group as a whole – from their respective client applications. What's more, server-side scripts can be used to message players directly (perhaps with their finishing place when the game ends) or as a group (to pass the other cars' positions, so that their displays can be updated to reflect the current positions).

You should be able to start to appreciate the power we now have at our fingertips. So how can we make use of it?

Managing multiuser groups

Group functions are managed by the server application itself. So the key to group management is the ability to send function control messages directly from our client application to the server.

As you may recall from the last chapter, we can use the `sendNetmessage` command to send content from one movie to another. Fortunately for us, it can also send commands to the host system, so we'll be using it to perform all our group management function calls. First, let's make a few changes so that we can see what our groups are doing.

Showing group-related messages

The messages displayed in the server window can be modified to include messages that are displayed when groups are created and joined by users. Since this will give a good visual representation of what is going on as we explore the various group tools, it's a good idea to make the necessary modifications in the `Multiuser.cfg` file to activate that display.

1. Close down the server and open the `Multiuser.cfg` file in a text editor. Scroll down a couple pages (or use the Find option), and find the section that looks like this:

    ```
    #==============================================================
    # These flags control what messages the server will display at
    # startup. A "0" flag turns off messages.
    #==============================================================

    ShowLogonMessages = 1
    ShowCreateMovieMessages = 1
    ShowScantimeMessages = 0
    ShowCreateGroupMessages = 0
    ShowJoinGroupMessages = 0
    ```

2. Simply change the values of `ShowCreateGroupMessages` and `ShowJoinGroupMessages` from 0 to 1 to activate the message display.

```
Multiuser - Notepad                                          _ □ X
File  Edit  Format  Help
#================================================================
# These flags control what messages the server will display at
# startup.  A "0" flag turns off messages.
#================================================================

ShowLogonMessages = 1
ShowCreateMovieMessages = 1
ShowScantimeMessages = 0
ShowCreateGroupMessages = 1
ShowJoinGroupMessages = 0
```

3.   Save the file. When you restart the server, it will display messages whenever we create a group or add a user to an existing one.

Joining a group

Now that we've got that sorted out, let's start at the beginning, and look at how to join a group. The syntax for this is as follows:

```
joingroup=gMultiuserClient.sendNetmessage \
("system.group.join", "subject", "@groupname")
```

On the surface, this looks identical to the sendNetmessage commands we issued when sending content messages between users. However, if we break down the contents of the message we see the important distinctions that make this message different.

Message recipient
The recipient of the message is system.group.join, denoting the group function join on the currently connected system (our Multiuser Server). We pass this function the subject and content of the message.

Message subject
You're likely to have a lot of messages zinging around your application by the time you're finished, so how do you tell the Multiuser Server to tell them apart? The answer to this is to give your messages a subject. You can then develop a message callback for messages with certain subjects, so that the server can respond differently to different messages.

Every time a group system function is called, the server will respond to the requesting user with a list of data similar to this:

```
#errorCode: 0
#recipients: ["Admin"]
#senderID: "system.group.join"
#subject: "subject"
#content: "@groupname"
#timeStamp: 4208895
```

As we saw when developing our first `messagecallback` handlers in the last chapter, the standard reply format is simply a Lingo list containing this data. We can use the information in this reply to verify whether or not the operation was performed successfully, and on that basis we can carry on or respond to any errors that may have occurred.

Message content
The standard group name of the Multiuser Server indicates that all group names contain the @ prefix, so the content of our message is "@groupname". Assuming a group already exists with this name, we're simply added to that group. If not, the group gets created automatically.

By adding the following handler to our `main` movie script, we can demonstrate how easy it is to join a group:

```
on joingroup groupname
 newmessage=gMultiuserClient.sendNetMessage("system.group.join",\
"", string("@" & groupname))
 if newmessage<>0 then
  put gMultiuserclient.getNetErrorString(newmessage)
 end if
end joingroup
```

Add this script and run the movie (with MUS running as well), and the movie should connect to the server and display the messages in the server window shown in the screenshot.

MultiuserServer

File View Status Help

Shockwave Multiuser Server.

Reading the Multiuser.cfg file.

* RuntimeAttributes xtra has been loaded.

* DatabaseObjects xtra has been loaded.

* LingoVM xtra has been loaded.

Allocating connections.
....
Allocated 50 connections.
2000/10/21 20:29:32 Waiting for incoming connections.
+ 2000/10/21 20:29:37 Created movie Client_test.
+ 2000/10/21 20:29:37 Created group @AllUsers in movie Client_test.
+ 2000/10/21 20:29:37 Admin (192.168.10.1) connected to movie Client_test.
+ 2000/10/21 20:29:37 User Admin joined group @AllUsers.

There are a couple of things to note here that will prove useful a little further down the road. Firstly, when our movie Client_test attaches to the server, it's automatically assigned to a group called @AllUsers. Secondly, the user Admin (which we use to log on with) is added automatically to the group @AllUsers.

Everyone belongs somewhere

@AllUsers is the default group to which all users belong. **Everyone has to belong to at least one group**: it's impossible to belong to no groups at all. You can't leave @Allusers (as you can with other groups) without disconnecting from the server.

On the other hand, there's nothing to stop us joining another group. With your connection to the server still open, try typing the following command into Director's message window to call the joingroup handler we coded earlier:

```
joingroup "mygroup"
```

The server display window should now show something like the one pictured.

```
MultiuserServer                                          _ □ ×
File  View  Status  Help
+ 2000/10/21 22:00:28 Created movie Client_test.
+ 2000/10/21 22:00:28 Created group @AllUsers in movie Client_test.
+ 2000/10/21 22:00:28 Admin (192.168.10.1) connected to movie Client_test.
+ 2000/10/21 22:00:28 User Admin joined group @AllUsers.
+ 2000/10/21 22:01:49 Created group @mygroup in movie Client_test.
+ 2000/10/21 22:01:49 User Admin joined group @mygroup.
```

The user Admin has now intentionally joined the group @mygroup, and by doing so, Admin now belongs to the groups @AllUsers and @mygroup.

Joining multiple groups

If we want to join more than one group at once, we can just specify a list of all the groups as part of the group join message, so the message should now read:

```
joingroup"mygroup"joingroup=gMultiuserClient.sendNetmessage\
("system.group.join","subject", ["@groupname1", "@groupname2",\
"@groupname3"])
```

In the sendNetmessage statement of our original example we left the subject as "", allowing the usermessagehandler callback to write the server's response to Director's message window. As you may recall, the message subject is integral to determining which message callback is used when it's received by our application. The result should be something like:

```
#errorCode: 0
#recipients: ["Admin"]
#senderID: "system.group.join"
#subject: "subject"
#content: "@myGroup"
#timeStamp: 4208895
```

This verifies that we have successfully joined the group myGroup.

Quitting a group

Once we've joined a group, we may at some point want to leave it. This can be accomplished in a similar fashion to joining. The only difference is that we send the message to the leave function in system.group:

```
leavegroup=gMultiuserClient.sendNetmessage \
        ("system.group.leave", "subject", "@groupname")
```

Again, we can write a quick handler and add it to our main movie script:

```
on leavegroup groupname
 newmessage=gMultiuserClient.sendNetMessage \
        ("system.group.leave", "", string("@" & groupname))
 if newmessage<>0 then
  put gMultiuserclient.getNetErrorString(newmessage)
 end if
end leavegroup
```

With this addition, type the following commands into the message window to see the effect on the Multiuser Server:

```
joingroup "myGroup"
leavegroup "myGroup"
```

Remember to run the movie again (if you don't, your network connection may well have ceased due to a lack of activity, and you'll get an error message telling you that there is no current connection), and the following should appear in the server message window:

As you can see, the group @myGroup was automatically created for our movie, and user Admin has joined it. Admin then leaves @myGroup, and since there are no users left in the group, it's deleted automatically.

Generating group names automatically

There may be times when you want the server to decide your group name for you. If you had a multiuser game of checkers where the game starts once the two players are put into their own room then it would be best if the server determined the room's unique name. If the players were forced to choose a name for the room for themselves, then this could detract from the game experience.

Fortunately, the server has a built-in function createUniqueName, which creates group names that are unique to the movie requesting them. It is used as follows:

```
uniquegroup=gMultiuserClient.sendNetmessage \
("system.group.createUniqueName", "subject")
```

When executed, the server responds with a list of the following data:

```
#errorCode: 0
#recipients: ["Admin"]
#senderID: "system.group.createUniqueName"
#subject: ""
#content: "@RndGroup0"
#timeStamp: 5622497
```

An error code of zero indicates a successful operation, and the content of the message contains the unique group name that the server created – in this case, @RndGroup0. The user requesting the group name does not automatically join that group; instead a routine must be created to extract it, and explicitly ask the server to add the user to that group.

Creating unique groups

Let's create that routine to find out the name of a unique group and join a user up to it. How would a user join up to a group in a multiuser application? By clicking on a button maybe? There's one other decision to make before we dive in, and that's whether we want the user to stay in their old group as well as joining a new one. I think it's a bit rude not to say goodbye when you move across a room to greet a new group of people, so let's make sure that our user is logged out of their former group when they join our new group.

1. Open a new movie, and add a button cast member. Attach the word Create to the button.

2. Drag-and-drop that button onto the stage in sprite channel 1 and set it to span frame 1 and 2.

3. Create a text field by going to Insert > Control > Field. Name this text field output.

4. Go to the Property Inspector, and click on the Field tab. Make the text field scrolling and non-editable, as shown in the screenshot.

5. Add a frame script in frame 2 to "`go to the frame`" on exit frame so the movie holds and loops there during playback.

6. Add a behavior to the cast with the following script:

```
on mouseup
 createuniquegroup
end mouseup
```

7. Name it `join_random_group` in the Cast window and attach it to the button on the screen.

8. Create a new movie script, and name it `main`.

Scripting our unique groups

In the movie script `main` that we've just created, we need to add the following handlers. We'll use two global variables here: gMultiuserClient is our Xtra instance, and gGroupname is the group we currently belong to.

```
global gmultiuserClient, gGroupname
on startmovie
 --set client
 gGroupname=""
 member("output").text=""
 if objectP(gMultiuserClient) then
```

continues overleaf

```
      gMultiuserClient=0
    end if
     gMultiuserClient=new(xtra "multiuser")
     --myaddress=gMultiuserclient.getNetaddresscookie()
```

The act of creating and joining a unique group is a two step process, and the fact we are forcing the user to leave a group before joining a new one adds a third step. Each step requires a call to the server, and we expect a response for each call.

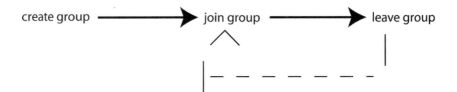

We therefore set up four callbacks. One of these is for defaultmessages, which is always present; and the other three are for each of the three steps we would like to perform: creating a unique group, joining that group, and leaving that group. As you will see, the process of each is to use one handler to issue the call to the server, and then use a callback to handle the server's response.

```
    mycallback=gMultiuserClient.setNetMessageHandler \
    (#defaultmessageHandler, script "main")

     mycallback=gMultiuserClient.setNetMessageHandler \
    (#createuniqueHandler, script "main", "create_unique", "", 1)

    mycallback=gMultiuserClient.setNetMessageHandler \
    (#joinuniqueHandler, script "main", "join_unique", "", 1)

    mycallback=gMultiuserClient.setNetMessageHandler \
    (#leaveuniqueHandler, script "main", "leave_unique", "", 1)

    newconnection=gMultiuserClient.connectToNetServer \
    (string(myaddress), 1626, /
    [#userID:"Admin", #password:"mypass", #movieID:"Client_test"])

    end startmovie
```

As ever, we need a handler to catch all the messages without a predefined callback handler:

```
    on defaultmessageHandler

    mymessage=gMultiuserClient.getnetmessage()
    --display the message content in the message window
    put string(mymessage)

    --if the message contains an error then display that
```

```
--in the message window
if mymessage.errorcode<>0 then put "The message contained an\
error"
put gMultiuserClient.getNetErrorString(mymessage.errorcode)
end defaultmessageHandler
```

This handler takes the groupname passed from the createuniqueHandler and tells the server we would like to join it. We use the subject "join_unique" to tag this message and differentiate the response in our callbacks above.

```
on joingroup groupname
 newmessage=gMultiuserClient.sendNetMessage \
("system.group.join", "join_unique", string(groupname))
 if newmessage<>0 then
  put gMultiuserclient.getNetErrorString(newmessage)
 end if
end joingroup
```

If we already belong to a group when we ask to join a new one, this handler is called to force us to leave the current group first. Again, the subject heading differentiates the response in our callbacks above.

```
on leavegroup groupname
 newmessage=gMultiuserClient.sendNetMessage \
("system.group.leave", "leave_unique", string(groupname))
 if newmessage<>0 then
  put gMultiuserclient.getNetErrorString(newmessage)
 end if
end leavegroup
```

We need a handler to be called when we click the button in the interface, and this is it. It first checks to see if we are currently in a group. If we are, it calls for us to leave that group. It then asks the server to create a new unique group for us. The subject of the message we are sending is "create_unique". We assigned the callback handler "createuniquehandler" to process the response from the server to this request. That response will contain the name of the new unique group.

```
on createuniquegroup
  if gGroupname<>"" then leavegroup gGroupname
 newmessage=gMultiuserClient.sendNetMessage \
("system.group.createUniqueName", "create_unique")
  if newmessage<>0 then
   put gMultiuserclient.getNetErrorString(newmessage)
  end if
end createuniquegroup
```

This handler is automatically executed when the server sends the response from the createuniquegroup handler. It gets the new groupname, assigns it to our global variable and writes it out as part of a message in the Output window. It then calls the joingroup handler so we can request to join the group.

```
on createuniquehandler me, message
 if message.errorcode=0 then
  gGroupname=message.content
  member("output").text=member("output").text& \
"You have created group "&gGroupname&return
  joingroup gGroupname
 else
  put gMultiuserclient.getNetErrorString(message.errocode)
 end if
end createuniquehandler
```

This handler is automatically executed when the server sends the response from the `joingroup` handler. If the operation was successful then it writes out a message in the Output window, letting us know that we joined the group successfully.

```
on joinuniquehandler me, message
 if message.errorcode=0 then
  member("output").text=member("output").text& \
"You have joined group "&gGroupname&return
 else
  put gMultiuserclient.getNetErrorString(message.errocode)
 end if
end joinuniquehandler
```

Similarly; this handler is executed when the server responds to the `leavegroup` handler. A message will be written in the Output window to let us know that we left the group successfully. It then sets the `gGroupname` variable to "" since we have left the group.

```
on leaveuniquehandler me, message
 if message.errorcode=0 then
  member("output").text=member("output").text& \
"You have left group "&gGroupname&return
  gGroupname=""
 else
  put gMultiuserclient.getNetErrorString(message.errocode)
 end if
end leaveuniquehandler
```

Once you've entered all this code, run the movie, and click on the Create button. You'll automatically create and then join a unique group. If we click the Create button a second time, we'll leave the first group, and create and join another group.

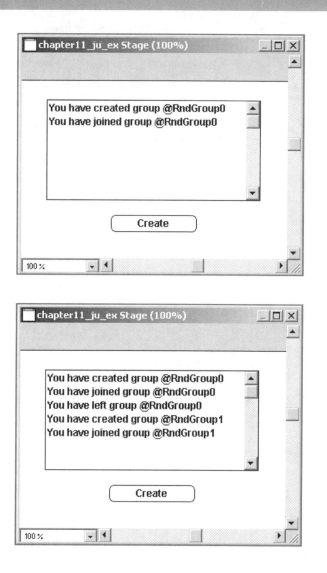

Conclusion

In this chapter, we've established how to go about creating, joining, and leaving groups, which are either specified explicitly, or created automatically by the server. This is a big step along the way to our fully functional chat application, which you'll have achieved in a mere two chapters time.

The next step is to learn how we can get information about groups and other users who are attached to the server, and this is exactly what the next chapter covers.

Chapter 9

Administration

The Shockwave Multiuser Server application comes with a set of configuration files that can be used to enable certain server features and limit access to a number of server commands. Multiuser Server configuration is carried out by modifying these configuration files before the server starts. The main server configuration file is named `Multiuser.cfg`.

In this chapter, we'll be having a look at how to go about editing this file to change user level settings. If you take a look at the file when we do this, then you'll see a variety of other changes that you can make. As making each change follows the same method, and the other changes are not so important, the full details of all other parts of this file are covered in the `Multiuser.cfg` appendix.

It's also possible to configure a small subset of properties at the movie level. This is done with a copy of the `Movie.cfg` file, also installed in the server application folder. Each movie connected to the server can have its own set of values for some configuration options. If no configuration file is found that matches a particular movie, then the server default values will be used.

After the Multiuser Server is running, it's possible to use server administration commands to display information about movies running on the server, including connected users and groups. There are also commands to enable and disable movies and to delete unwanted users from your server. This will build on what we learnt about users and groups in the last chapter.

We'll be using the `MUSAdministrator` movie (which can be downloaded from the friends of ED web site as usual) to help show us how these commands work, in order to save us from having to write repetitive handlers over and over again.

Editing the default server configuration

Locate the `Multiuser.cfg` file in the folder where the Multiuser Server is installed and open it with Notepad, SimpleText, or a plain text editor of your choice. You will see that the `.cfg` file is pretty much self-explanatory, showing the default options for most commands and explaining how to modify most settings.

As a matter of course, you may find that modifying this is unnecessary, as most of the default settings are adequate for most multiuser applications. As we said above, you'll find a reference for all the settings contained within the `Multiuser.cfg` file, with my additional comments on how and when to modify them, as an appendix. For now, let's take a quick look at the settings we need to modify before continuing.

User level settings

Perhaps the most important issue to consider when setting up multiuser applications is security. There are various ways in which you can configure the server to provide the desired level of security, but there is a basic level provided by the default settings that will probably be adequate for most multiuser applications. For example, new users are assigned a user level of 20.

For most functions that provide a security risk, such as deleting movies, or getting the IP addresses of other users, a user level of at least 80 is required by default. It makes sense that while you, as the administrator, might need the power to delete users or user groups that were getting out of line; you don't want your users to have this power.

Setting user levels

The default levels for users are OK, but we want to make ourselves into an all-powerful administrator. To do this, we just need to add one line to the `Multiuser.cfg` file.

1. Open the `Multiuser.cfg` file in Notepad, SimpleText or any other text editor. Save a copy of this somewhere else so that you can revert to the original file if problems arise.

2. Scroll down and locate the section of the configuration file that deals with `XtraCommands` and `Createuser` commands. The line you need to enter is:

```
XtraCommand = "CreateUser admin pass 100"
```

You can see this line added about halfway down the screenshot on the left. This line can actually be entered at any location of the `XtraCommands` section in your `Multiuser.cfg` file, but it's a good idea to group related configuration items so you can locate them quickly in the future.

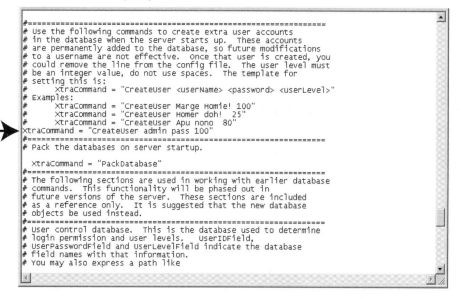

```
#===============================================================
# Use the following commands to create extra user accounts
# in the database when the server starts up.  These accounts
# are permanently added to the database, so future modifications
# to a username are not effective.  Once that user is created, you
# could remove the line from the config file.  The user level must
# be an integer value, do not use spaces.  The template for
# setting this is:
#       XtraCommand = "CreateUser <userName> <password> <userLevel>"
# Examples:
#       XtraCommand = "CreateUser Marge Homie! 100"
#       XtraCommand = "CreateUser Homer doh! 25"
#       XtraCommand = "CreateUser Apu nono  80"
XtraCommand = "CreateUser admin pass 100"
#===============================================================
# Pack the databases on server startup.

  XtraCommand = "PackDatabase"
#===============================================================
# The following sections are used in working with earlier database
# commands.  This functionality will be phased out in
# future versions of the server.  These sections are included
# as a reference only.  It is suggested that the new database
# objects be used instead.
#===============================================================
# User control database.  This is the database used to determine
# login permission and user levels.   UserIDField,
# UserPasswordField and UserLevelField indicate the database
# field names with that information.
# You may also express a path like
```

3. Make sure the line doesn't start with a # symbol – lines starting with a # are considered comments, and are ignored by the Multiuser Server application until they are removed.

What this line does is to instruct the server to create a new user in the database the next time the server is started. The user name is `admin`, the user's password is `pass` and the user level is 100, which grants this user the authorization to use all database functions on this server. You can use a different password or username for your system, of course.

We've just uncommented and slightly modified a line in `Multiuser.cfg`, and it's the same procedure for altering any of the other settings in the file. Just make sure that you save the file and restart the server after making the changes in order to make sure that the changes are applied (creating a copy of the file before making changes is never a bad idea, either).

Administering the server remotely

The Multiuser Server offers several server commands that a developer can use to monitor active movies and connected users. We're now going to use a Director movie that we've put together to allow you to administer a Multiuser Server remotely. It's called `MUSAdministrator.dir` and you can find it on the friends of ED website in the usual place.

For this to work properly, you'll need to have made the above changes to your `Multiuser.cfg` file, and entered your IP address as we did a couple of chapters ago.

Once you've loaded this into Director, and started it, you'll need to enter a username, password, and server address. You can put in the username and password that you've just entered into your `Multiuser.cfg` file, and enter your IP address under the server address column.

Multiuser Server Administrator

```
        userid: admin
      password: pass
        server: server
                              Connect
```

Displaying server properties

After the administrator user has logged onto the server you'll be able to use the `system.server` commands, as listed on the left of your screen. To issue a command, just click on the command name. The last command issued to the server and all server responses will be always displayed in the text areas located at the bottom of the screen.

getVersion
Try clicking on the `system.server.getVersion` command. This will produce Lingo with the syntax:

```
sendNetMessage("system.server.getVersion","subject", void)
```

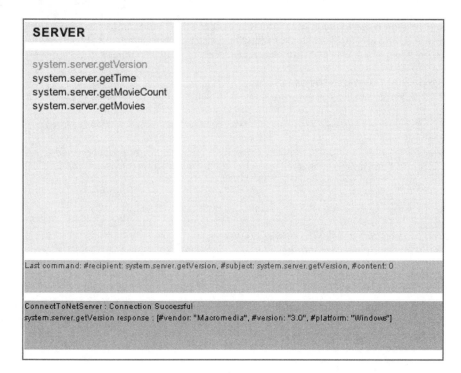

As you can see from the screenshot, the server response is a property list in the following format:

```
[#vendor: vendorname, #version: versionstring, #platform:
platformname]
```

This isn't possibly the most useful command, but it demonstrates the way things work nicely. To be fair, the #version property is actually quite useful for people who have used previous versions of the Multiuser Server. UDP traffic, for example, is only available in version 3, so you could use this command to run a check on the server version before trying to send UDP traffic.

You can also use this command to identify the platform and version for 3rd party servers that are compatible with SMUS. Tabuleiro Nebulae MUS Server, for example (more on that in the final chapter), returns the following info when running on a Solaris server:

```
[#vendor: "Tabuleiro", #version: "1.0", #platform: "Sun"]
```

getTime

The system.server.getTime command sends the following:

```
sendNetMessage("system.server.getTime","subject", void)
```

This retrieves the current server date and time as a string, for example:

```
"2001/11/11 13:55:12"
```

This information is useful if you want a human readable date and hour format – to include at the bottom of a message, for example. For message synchronization, it's generally better to examine the #timeStamp field provided with all server replies.

getMovieCount and getMovies

The next server command retrieves the number of active movies connected to the server, using:

```
sendNetMessage("system.server.getMovieCount","subject", void)
```

This returns an integer value. While this is useful, in most cases you probably need to know not only how many movies are connected, but also the names of those movies. A different command is used for this:

```
sendNetMessage("system.server.getMovies","subject", void)
```

This returns a list of names of the movies connected to the server. When this command is issued in the MUSAdministrator tool, the interface is updated to show the list of movies that are running. You can select a movie by clicking on it to enable the server.movie commands menu, as shown in the next picture.

Obviously, at the moment, you'll probably only be running DBAdministrator, but try running another multiuser application, and you'll be able to run the same commands on that as well. This application works for all multiuser applications, so it will be of value to you long after you've finished reading this chapter.

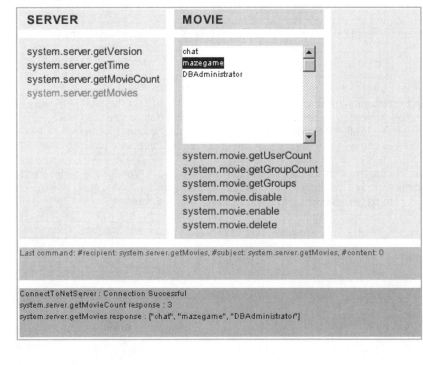

Working with server movie commands

Claiming that this application will be of use to you long after you've read this chapter would be a bit of an exaggeration if we only let you find out the names and number of movies running, along with the time and version details of those movies. With this in mind, if you leave server.server.getMovies selected in the left hand column, we'll have a look at the properties you can manipulate within your individual movies.

To prevent a possibly unwelcome shock, we should say that you will notice that one of these properties allows you to delete a movie. If you have the DBAdministrator movie selected, then you're going to shut down the movie you're working in by selecting that option, and will be presented with the (possibly irritating) need to restart the application.

getUserCount

The first server movie command available retrieves the number of users connected to any given movie, sending a command with the syntax:

```
sendNetMessage("system.movie.getUserCount","subject", \
"MazeGame")
```

The server will return a property list with values for #movieID and #numberMembers, for example:

```
[#movieID:"MazeGame", #numberMembers:15]
```

getGroupCount

A similar command is provided to retrieve the number of groups that exist inside a server movie:

```
sendNetMessage("system.movie.getGroupCount", \
"subject", "MazeGame")
```

This returns a property list with values for #movieID and #numberGroups, for example:

```
[#movieID:"MazeGame", #numberGroups:4]
```

All movies have at least one group, @AllUsers.

getGroups

In most cases you will also need to know not only the number of groups but the group names as well. The system.server.getGroups command is provided for this:

```
sendNetMessage("system.movie.getGroups","subject", "MazeGame")
```

This returns a property list with values for #movieID and #groups, for example:

```
[#movieID:"MazeGame", #groups:["@AllUsers","@RedTeam"]]
```

Try this command in the MUSAdministrator tool. The tool interface will change automatically to display the list of groups for a given movie. Selecting a group will enable the system.group commands menu, as shown in the next screenshot. We will cover server.group commands in a moment but there are three server movie commands remaining to be examined first.

SERVER	MOVIE	GROUP
system.server.getVersion system.server.getTime system.server.getMovieCount system.server.getMovies	chat **mazegame** DBAdministrator	**@AllUsers** **@redplayers**
	system.movie.getUserCount system.movie.getGroupCount system.movie.getGroups system.movie.delete system.movie.disable system.movie.enable	system.group.getUserCount system.group.getUsers system.group.delete system.group.disable system.group.enable

Last command: #recipient: system.movie.getGroups, #subject: system.movie.getGroups, #content: mazegame

system.server.getMovies response : ["chat", "mazegame", "DBAdministrator"]
system.movie.getGroups response : [#movieID: "mazegame", #groups: ["@AllUsers"]]
system.movie.getGroups response : [#movieID: "mazegame", #groups: ["@AllUsers", "@redplayers"]]

delete, disable, and enable
These commands can be used to delete a movie from the server or to prevent users from connecting to a movie in the future, so they can only be issued by users connected with administrative user access level.

The system.movie.delete command sends the Lingo syntax:

```
sendNetMessage("system.movie.delete","subject", "MazeGame")
```

This command automatically deletes the specified movie from the server and disconnects all users connected to the movie. It returns the name of the movie deleted, for example "MazeGame". Future connections to the movie are still allowed, unless the movie has been disabled.

The system.movie.disable command sends the Lingo syntax:

```
sendNetMessage("system.movie.disable","subject", "MazeGame")
```

This prevents new users from connecting to a specified movie, but it does not disconnect the users currently connected and does not destroy the movie. It returns the name of the movie deleted.

Disabled movies can be enabled with the `system.movie.enable` command:

```
sendNetMessage("system.movie.enable","subject", "MazeGame")
```

Working with server group commands

Server group commands are enabled in the `MUSAdministrator` tool when a group name is selected in the groups list. You'll notice that a quite a few of these are in exactly the same format as the movie commands we've just looked at. Don't worry — you're not suffering from a strange case of déjà vu, we're just targeting individual groups rather than the whole movie this time around.

getUserCount
Let's have a look at the first group command, `system.group.getUserCount`:

```
sendNetMessage("system.group.getUserCount", \
"subject", "@AllUsers")
```

This returns a property list with values for #groupName and #numberMembers, for example:

```
[#groupName:"@AllUsers", #numberMembers:8]
```

A small clarification is needed before we continue. If you test this command using the administrator movie you will notice that there are additional server responses being generated on the server output text field at the bottom of the `MUSAdministrator` screen. Why?

This happens because the `MUSAdministrator` tool will automatically send messages to change the administrator user to the movie that contains the target group. This is necessary to satisfy the Multiuser Server checking of the user access level permissions. Switching a user to a different movie without disconnection from the server is a new feature in the Multiuser Server included with Director 8.5, made possible by the `system.user.changeMovie` command. We will cover this command syntax later in the user commands section of this chapter.

getUsers
The `system.group.getUsers` command is sent by the Lingo syntax:

```
sendNetMessage("system.group.getUsers","subject", "@AllUsers")
```

The server response to the `system.group.getUsers` command in the `MUSAdministrator` tool will bring up the list of users connected to a given group on the server, for example:

```
[#groupName:"@AllUsers",#groupMembers:["player1","player2"]]
```

The list of the members who belong to that group may be quite long, so it is important that the setNetBufferlimits for both the server and the client are set high enough to accommodate the entire message. A rough estimate for the netbufferlimits can be established by multiplying the maximum number of users in a group by the maximum number of characters in their usernames.

So, if you expect 1000 people in a given group with a username maximum length of 8 characters, we will need 8000 bytes or 8K as the minimum for setNetBufferlimits to store the names. Each name is encompassed by quotation marks and separated by a comma, so this adds an additional three characters, bringing the total for our group of 1000 to 11,000 bytes or 11k.

You need to be aware and careful of setNetBufferlimits whenever thinking about requesting long lists, as with system.user.getGroups, which we'll be looking at in a moment.

Selecting a user on the list enables user commands to be given to the server.

delete, disable, and enable

Groups can also be deleted, disabled and enabled in the server. The syntax is similar to the movie commands:

```
sendNetMessage("system.group.delete","subject", "@redPlayers")
```

This function deletes the specified group from the server but doesn't disconnect current users of that group. For this reason, don't delete the default @AllUsers group – this will generate an internal server error, as the Multiuser Server keeps this as a default group to return people to if necessary.

```
sendNetMessage("system.group.disable","subject", "@redPlayers")
```

Disable prevents new users from joining a group. This command does not disconnect current users, and can be reversed with the system.group.enable command:

```
sendNetMessage("system.group.enable","subject", "@redPlayers")
```

createUniqueName

There is one additional server.group function that is not used in the MUSADministrator tool, system.group.createUniqueName. The syntax for this is:

```
sendNetMessage("system.group.createUniqueName","subject", void)
```

The response is a string representing a group name that has not been used by the current movie in the server, for example "Rnd767". This name can be used to create a unique group without the risk of having it duplicated by other users.

Working with server user commands

The last batch of server commands is related to user-specific properties. These are enabled when a user name is selected in the connected users list for a specific group, as shown in the screenshot. Again, you'll notice some similarities with other commands that we've looked at here. We've now moved as far down the structure as we can – from the movie level to the group level, and now, finally, to the individual user level.

getGroupCount
The command system.user.getGroupCount sends this syntax:

```
sendNetMessage("system.user.getGroupCount","subject", ["player1"])
```

It returns a property list with values for #userID and #numberGroups – the number of groups the specified user is a member of.

getGroups
There is also an option to retrieve a list containing the group names, system.user.getGroups. This sends the Lingo command:

```
sendNetMessage("system.user.getGroups","subject", ["player1"])
```

This returns a property list with values for #userID and #groups, for example:

```
[#userID:"player1", #groups:["@AllUsers","@redPlayers"]]
```

Every user is at least a member of the "@AllUsers" group.

getAddress

For peer-to-peer connections or connection logging you may want to retrieve the IP address used by the machine of any user currently connected to the server. The function `system.user.getAddress` can be used for this purpose (only by a user with an administrative user level, for security reasons):

```
sendNetMessage("system.user.getAddress","subject", ["player1"])
```

This returns a property list with values for `#userID` and `#ipAddress`, for example:

```
[#userID:"player1", #ipAddress:"192.168.0.7"]
```

delete

Administrative user level is also required to delete a user from the server. This is done with the `system.user.delete` command.

```
sendNetMessage("system.group.delete","subject", "player1")
```

The selected user is automatically disconnected.

There is one remaining user command, introduced with version 3 of the Multiuser Server. This can be used to change the movie a user is connected to, without actually dropping the connection to the multiuser server. The `server.user.changeMovie` command is used internally by the `MUSAdministrator` tool to log the administrator user to different movies, as we mentioned before. This command is virtually undocumented and a reference to it can only be found in the file `Release Notes` installed with the Multiuser Server, but it is very useful. Its syntax is:

```
sendNetMessage("system.user.changeMovie","subject", \
"anothermoviename")
```

"anothermoviename" represents the destination movie name, and is repeated in the server response. This command can only be used to change the user that sends the message – you cannot force another connected user to change movies.

This brings us to the end of our coverage of server administrative commands. A lot of the commands that we've seen aren't only useful for administration. Most are necessary when designing your multiuser applications – to retrieve a list of groups or users connected to a given movie in a lobby application, for example. The `MUSAdministrator` - tool is provided in source file format, with commented Lingo scripts, so take a look then and alter the source code for your particular purposes.

Working with group attributes

Now that we've seen a whole range of group admin features, we can move on to take a look at adding extra information to groups by way of setting group attributes. This is not something that really comes under the remit of administration, so these functions aren't included in the MUSAdministrator tool. We'll be illustrating them by adding some handlers into a movie script and using the Message window to pass values to these handlers as we have in previous chapters.

To illustrate the use of group attributes, let's consider a multiuser game for kids that allows them to work together to color a picture. In this application, there are five pictures to choose from and ten crayon colors. The group could have an attribute to store which of the five pictures the children selected to work on. The ten crayon colors could also be stored as attributes, allowing different colors to be associated with different groups or drawings.

Attributes are stored in server RAM so using them to store every little nugget of information that passes through the server would not be a good move – use them sparingly to store only essential groupwide information.

setAttribute
The process of assigning attributes to a group is very straightforward:

```
setmyattr=gMultiuserClient.sendnetmessage          \
     ("system.group.setAttribute", "subject",      \
            [#group:"@group",                       \
        #attribute:[#attributename1:"value",        \
                    #attributename2:"value",        \
                 #lastupdatetime:"date time:ms"]    \
     ]                                              \
     )
```

Here, we send the setAttribute function of the server's group routines a list of attributes to be associated with a particular group. The attribute property is a property list containing all the attributes to which values should be assigned.

The setAttribute call can be used to create or assign new attributes, or to change values of existing attributes. The lastupdatetime property is optional, but can be important when updating the changing values of a given attribute – say that, for example, several users in a group all have the ability to change that group's attributes. Before a 'change' request is posted, it's important to be able to establish whether someone else has already changed the relevant attribute.

That is to say that if one of our kids changed the crayon color, it would be important that all of those connected could see the change before opting to change it again. If two children tried to change the crayon color at the same time, then child B be able to see that child A has already done this, so that they can go and have a look and see what they think of child A's choice. Otherwise, child B could change the color before child A has a chance to experiment with their new color.

In cases such as this, the process of changing the attribute should proceed in a specific way. Firstly, when the attributes are created, the lastupdatetime property returned by the server should be captured and stored in a global variable or property object. Users who join the group after the attribute has been initially set can obtain the value from the getAttribute command.

Secondly, you need to include that value in your setAttribute command. The server will compare it to the current value of lastupdatetime for the given property and determine if they are the same. If they are not, then an update has occurred since the client movie last stored the update time. The server will return an error in response with the value for lastupdatetime, and the attribute value will not be changed at this point. The user can then be notified by an alert that an update has occurred since they last changed it and be given them the option to retry or cancel.

In our imaginary coloring application, this could mean a chain of events like this:

9.27 Child A changes the drawing color to blue.

9.32 Child B decides that blue is a boring color, and wants to change it. They click on a button to request orange crayons, the server checks to see that the last server update was 9.27, and grants the request for orange crayons.

9.33 Child C also decides that blue is boring, and decides to request pink crayons. The server checks to see that the last sever update was 9.32, discovers that it was 9.27 and child C has missed the color change. It tells child C that the color has already changed, child C goes back to the application and is introduced to the wonders of the color orange.

We'll be returning to the problems of concurrent data access when we look at databases in **Chapter 13**, for obvious reasons.

Setting an attribute will result in a response from the server such as:

```
#errorCode: 0
#recipients: ["Admin"]
#senderID: "system.group.setattribute"
#subject: "subject"
#content: ["@groupname":
        [#lastupdatetime: "2001/10/14 12:45:37.179000000"]
        ]
#timeStamp: 11704195]
```

This content of the message contains the group the attribute was added to and the lastupdatetime set for that attribute. It does not return the attribute that was set, or the value to which it was set. We'll be returning to the problems of concurrent data access when we look at databases in **Chapter 13**.

The following is an example handler for setting an attribute. The arguments of groupname and value for the attribute are passed to the handler. In this case, the attribute "Topic" is set for the group. Open up the version of last chapter's Director file available for download in this chapter, and add the following handler at the bottom of the Main movie script:

```
on setThisAttribute mygroup, myvalue
  newmessage=gMultiuserClient.sendnetmessage \
("system.group.setattribute", "", [#group: string \
("@" & myGroup), #attribute:[#topic:string(myvalue)]])

 if newmessage<>0 then
  put gMultiuserclient.getNetErrorString(newmessage)
 end if

end setThisAttribute
```

Now call this handler from our test movie's message window with the following command:

```
setthisattribute "AllUsers", "Welcome"
```

It should return a response from the system like this:

```
#errorCode: 0
#recipients: ["Admin"]
#senderID: "system.group.setattribute"
#subject: ""
#content: ["@allusers":
       [#lastupdatetime: "2001/10/14 12:45:37.179000000"]
       ]
#timeStamp: 11704195]
```

getAttributeNames
We've set some attributes, so how do we recover them? To obtain a list of attributes for a given group, you need to use the getAttributeNames command. A simple handler to execute this command would look like:

```
on getMYattnames mygroup
 newmessage=gMultiuserClient.sendnetmessage \
      ("system.group.getAttributeNames", "", \
      [#group: string("@" & myGroup)])

 if newmessage<>0 then
  put gMultiuserclient.getNetErrorString(newmessage)
 end if

end getMYattnames
```

If you then passed this handler our group name "AllUsers" after executing the setThisAttribute handler discussed above, it would return a response from the server that contains a linear list of attribute names in the content portion of the message as follows:

```
#errorCode: 0
#recipients: ["Admin"]
#senderID: "system.group.getattributenames"
#subject: ""
#content: ["@AllUSers": [#lastupdatetime, #topic]]
#timeStamp: 11715349
```

To obtain the value for any specific or group of attributes then the getAttribute command is used.

```
getAttvalues=gMultiuserClient.sendnetmessage          \
    ("system.group.getAttribute", "",               \
    [#group:"@group", #attribute:[#att1, #att2]])
```

This can be applied in our test movie with the following handler, so enter this at the bottom of your Main movie script:

```
on getMyattribute mygroup
 newmessage=gMultiuserClient.sendnetmessage \
    ("system.group.getAttribute", "", \
    [#group: string("@" & myGroup), #attribute:[#Topic]])

 if newmessage<>0 then
  put gMultiuserclient.getNetErrorString(newmessage)
 end if

end getMyattribute
```

We can then pass this handler the group "AllUsers" by entering the following in the message window:

```
getMyattribute "AllUsers", "Welcome"
```

This should return the following results:

```
#errorCode: 0
#recipients: ["Admin"]
#senderID: "system.group.getAttribute"
#subject: "subject"
#content: ["@AllUsers":[#Topic: "Welcome", #lastupdatetime:
"2001/10/14 12:45:37.179000000"]
      ]
#timeStamp: 11704195
```

The content of the message contains the group for which the request was made, a property list of the attributes, and the corresponding requested values.

deleteAttribute

Finally, when an attribute is no longer needed, it can be deleted using the `deleteattribute` command. This command can be applied to a single attribute in a single group, or to multiple attributes over multiple groups.

If you add the following handler to our test movie, then it will delete our "Welcome" attribute from the group @Allusers.

```
on deleteMyAttribute

newmessage=gMultiuserClient.sendnetmessage \
("system.group.deleteAttribute", "", \
[#group:"@Allusers", #attribute:#welcome])

 if newmessage<>0 then
  put gMultiuserclient.getNetErrorString(newmessage)
 end if

end deletemyattribute
```

You can test this by typing `deleteMyAttribute` into the message window. The server should respond in the following way:

```
#errorCode: 0
#recipients: ["username"]
#senderID: "system.group.deleteAttribute"
#subject: ""
#content: [:]
#timeStamp: 37705753
```

To delete single or multiple attributes from multiple groups or single groups, you can simply pass the target groups and/or multiple attributes in linear lists like this:

```
delmyAttr=gMultiuserClient.sendnetmessage        \
        ("system.group.deleteAttribute", "subject", \
        [#group:["@group1", "@group2",        \
        #attribute:[#attribute1, #attribute2]])
```

The result returned from the server is identical to that returned for a single group or attribute. Multiple responses or additional lists are not returned, so a single error-free response indicates a successful deletion.

Going from client-server to peer-to-peer

If we wanted, we now have enough knowledge to plan out an application that will connect to a server, join groups, and eventually have those groups branch off into a peer-to-peer networking scheme to conserve server resources.

From **Chapter 7**, we know that peer-to-peer networking doesn't require users to be connected through the server application, but it does require that a host with a known IP address be assigned to channel communications from user to user. Having groups of people meet on the server allows them to gather the necessary IP information to form a peer-to-peer group, since their IP address can be shared through the server. Once that information is established, then the group can establish peer-to-peer communications.

This has two major advantages. First, it saves server resources since all the traffic being generated by that group is now being passed through the peer host instead of the server. Second, it circumvents the user limitations of the server. When operating in peer-to-peer mode, those users are no longer attached to the server, freeing up their space for their users. The standard 2000 user limit allowed with a Director 8.5 license sounds like a lot, but it can be quickly used up on a busy server. The use of peer branching effectively makes the license nearly unlimited.

The process would be as follows:

First, a user connects to the server, and creates, and joins a new group. A group creation script then assigns three attributes:

- `#userlimit` is set to 16, the maximum number of users supported by peer-to-peer networking.

- `#hostuser` is assigned with the user's ID, since they created it.

- `#hostIP` is assigned with the user's IP address for the same reason.

As you will recall from **Chapter 7**, the host IP in a peer-to-peer scheme must be known explicitly. In order to pass the new user's IP to set the server attribute, we use the `getnetaddresscookie` command, as described in **Chapter 7**. Any new members joining the group would then be passed these attributes.

At any time, the current host can designate a new host if it is deemed necessary – if, for example, someone with a faster, more reliable connection than the current host joined the group.

At some point, the individual users would make a peer-to-peer connection to the designated host user IP as set by the person who initiated the group. At this point, the users may or may not log off the server system. Maintaining a server connection would continue to usurp server resources for the storage of connection, group, and attribute information in RAM. However, traffic handling and bandwidth usage would stop, as the users would communicate in peer-to-peer mode.

The advantage of maintaining such a connection would be that it would be easier to monitor for and recover from a user disconnect. The group could remain intact at the server level so a new host could be designated by the server in the case of a disconnect, and peer-to-peer communication could be resumed fairly quickly while the original host reconnects to the system. In a peer-to-peer only scenario, additional coding would have to be included which "pings" the other users of the group every couple seconds to check that they are still connected.

If a user's application did not respond to the ping message, then it would be assumed they have disconnected. If that user were the designated host, the remaining applications would connect to a predetermined secondary host. This would require an additional property or attribute like "Host Priority" to be assigned prior to the peer group formation from the server.

Each member of the group would then have a unique number (1 – 16) assigned to them. As needed, they would become the host application in the peer-to-peer scheme starting with priority #1, working down the list as host disconnect events occurred. Most network connections are good enough that the idea of needing all 16 hosts in a single session is a bit extreme, but you might as well code for the worst-case scenario.

Conclusion

Groups and group management are powerful features of the Multiuser Server. Much of the hard work involved in managing these entities is handled automatically by the server, thus limiting the amount of programming required to use them effectively.

A small set of simple techniques allows us to create, join, leave, and manipulate individual groups and their attributes. This ultimately lets us create dynamic multiuser environments in which users can move about freely, while maintaining a simple methodology for transferring information to and fro, regardless of their location within the system.

We now have all the information that we need to forge ahead and create a fully-functioning chat application, so that's exactly what we're going to do in the next chapter!

Chapter 10

A Simple Application

Now that we've looked at some commands and procedures that we can use to create a multiuser application with Director and the Multiuser Server, we're going to look at how we can apply them to a real-world task. So, in the course of this chapter, we're going to develop a simple chat application.

We're going to have a look at how to handle connections, messages, and groups in such a way as to let clients send text data to one another. Let's start off by setting out exactly what we want our application to do – an essential phase in the planning of any project.

Functionality

If I start at the beginning, and think through what I want a user to be able to do when they log on to my application, I come up with a list of features like this. Users should be able to:

- Log onto the server

- Determine what groups are currently available to join

- Create and/or join a specific group

- Determine which other users are members of that group

- Send text messages to those users

- Receive and display messages sent to them from other users

- Track the entry and departure of users to and from the group they're in

- Track the creation and deletion of groups

- Log off the server

Now, let's run through each of the components we'll be using to make all this possible. We'll start by looking at the various cast members we'll need, and then see how those cast members should be arranged in the score. We'll then take a look at the scripts that we must add in order to bring the application to life.

We recommend that you download the complete application simplechat5.dir from the friends of ED web site to look at as a reference as you build your application.

Building the interface

Before we get our fingers messy with the scripting that we'll need to provide this functionality, let's take a look at our interface. The interface is fairly plain for our purposes here, but this means that there's plenty of potential for you to customize the appearance to meet your own design needs.

The interface is going to consist of four main screens. The logon screen will – surprisingly enough allow users to logon to the system. The groups/message screen will allow users to send messages, create groups, join groups, display users and groups, and log off the system.

The logon screen

Frame 1 has a marker of Start, and the logon screen is defined from frame 1 to frame 5 of the score. On-screen elements include two editable text fields into which the user can enter a username (field username_entry) and password (field password_entry).

A logon button (member Logon) is also present to allow the user to submit these details to the server and attempt to log on. The program loops on frame 5 until this button is pressed. You can see what my version looks like in the screenshot.

```
simplechat5 Stage (100%)                              _ □ ×

Welcome to
SimpleChat

                  Username: [                    ]
                  Password: [                    ]
                           (    Logon    )



100%   ▼ ◄                                          ►
```

The Groups screen

When the logon requirements are fulfilled, the program will jump to the Groups marker. The dominant feature of this screen is the text member chat_text, which is where incoming messages are displayed. To the right of the screen is a scrollable text field group_display, which lists all the groups that are currently visible to the user.

```
simplechat5 Score                                   _ □ ×
 ◄  ◄  ►   ▽ Groups
        ▤   9:Hide dialog           8:Loop
Member ▼
       1  ◇ 10:chat_text
       2  ◇ 28
       3  ◇ 28
       4  ◇ 11:message_text
       5  ◇ 12:group_display
       6  ◇ 5:Join_Group
       7  ◇ 6:Send_Message
       8  ◇ 21:u
       9  ◇ 14:g.a
      10  ◇ 4:Logoff
      11
      12
      13
      14
      15
      16
      17
      18
      19
      20  ◇ 22
      21  ◇ 9:new_group_name
      22  ◇ 1:Create
      23  ◇ 2:Cancel
      24
```

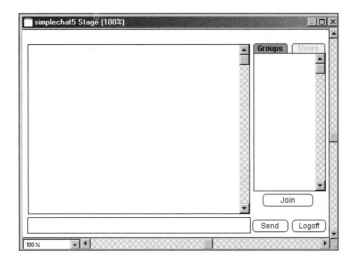

Just above the `group_display` field, you'll see a pair of buttons: one is shaded and labeled Groups, while the other is labeled Users. The second of these will be linked to a script that jumps us forward to the Users screen, which we'll look at in a moment.

Other elements on the Groups screen include the editable text box `message_text` on the bottom of the display, which is for entering new text messages to be sent. There's also a Send button to send the message, and a Logoff button to exit the system. The Join button allows the user to join whichever group has been selected in the `group_display` window. If New Group is selected (as it is by default) then a dialog appears into which we can enter a name for the new group we'd like to create.

This new group dialog is defined in sprites 20 – 23. The prepareframe handler in frame 20 sets the visibility of these to false when we enter the frame so they are not seen at first (don't worry, we'll be coming to the handler in the script section in a moment). When activated, there is a background box graphic containing the editable entry field new_group_name and two buttons Create and Cancel. When clicked, those buttons will either create the new group named in the text field or cancel the operation, as indicated by their respective names.

The Users screen

The Users screen is almost identical to the Groups screen, with just two exceptions. Firstly, it features the text field user_display on the right (in place of group_display), which contains the names of users in the current group (rather than the groups associated with the current movie). Secondly, since there are no groups here to join, the Join button is dropped, as are the new group dialog elements defined in sprites 20 – 23.

Once the user interface is set up, we can begin to develop the code that will make it sing and dance.

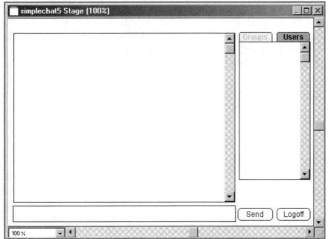

Interface cast members

Just in case you're keeping a watchful eye on the finished file for our application, the interface is responsible for all of the members of the internal cast in my file (the other cast holds the scripts, which is what we'll look at next). This contains 28 members, the first 21 of which are important for program functionality:

- **Members 1– 6** are buttons, which link to scripts that allow the user to create groups, cancel dialogs, log on and log off the system, join groups and send messages.

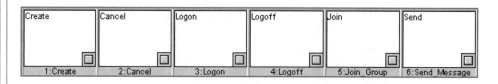

- **Members 7 – 9** are single line fields, used for entering username and password during login, as well as for entering a new group name within the new group dialog.

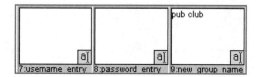

- **Members 10 and 11** are both text members: chat_text will be used to display incoming messages and must therefore be set to allow scrolling; message_text will let users enter any text they wish to send out as a message. In this case, we're going to limit this text to a single line, though it could quite easily be altered to allow for more.

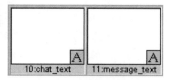

We're using text members rather than fields here so that we'll be able to format the text more easily. In the case of incoming messages, we shall be using type styles and color to differentiate the sender ID from the actual text of the message. No special formatting routines are present for the new message we are creating, but it would not take a lot of Lingo to add those later if we wanted.

- **Members 12 and 13** are both scrolling fields, which we'll use to display current lists of visible users and groups. In this case, we should see any groups that are available to the movie, and all the users that are in the current group.

12:group_display   13:user_display

■ **Members 14 – 21** are graphics that we'll use to define the buttons that allow the user to switch between a 'group list' view and a 'user list' view. You can't see it so well in the monochrome glory of this book, but each of the sets (four "Groups" graphics, and four "Users" graphics) are a different shade or color.

14:g.a   15:g.roll   16:g.down   17:g   18:u.a   19:u.roll   20:u.down   21:u

■ **Members 22 – 28** are various other elements that we'll use to make things look nice and tidy.

22   23   24   25   26   27   28

Writing the scripts

I've assigned all on-screen elements such as those that we've just created for our interface to the main Cast. For the sake of clarity, I've then assigned all scripts to a second cast, cunningly titled Scripts. The members of Scripts fall into three groups:

■ **Movie Scripts** handle general housekeeping functions, as well as those functions specifically related to users, groups, and the movie functions of the program.

■ **Parent Script** handles the creation and management of our connection to the server. All routines dealing with its creation and the manipulation of the properties it uses will be located here.

■ **Behaviors** control interface function, and serve as a bridge between the interface and the handlers contained within the movie and parent scripts.

The handlers within the movie scripts have been segregated into different scripts according to function, but this is only for organizational purposes. In principle, the first four cast members could be combined into one main movie script without any problems. Well, they could as long as all associated callback routines were updated to look for their respective handlers in the correct script location.

By contrast, handlers defined in the parent script connection should always reside there. While this isn't required by Lingo, it is simply good OOP practice to keep any routines that deal directly with an object together with the scripts that will have created that object.

The vast majority of the scripts in this application are designed to use, manage and manipulate a connection to the Multiuser Server application. The central importance of that connection means that we'll take a look at the connection script first. Following that, we'll examine the remaining movie scripts, and finish off by looking at the behaviors that manage the remaining movie and interface functions.

The 'connection' parent script

Inside the parent script connection, we're going to define all the handlers we need to assign and manipulate important data within our application. This should include all the program properties, message callbacks, and Xtra instances that we may need. By building the program in this way, any information relating to a particular connection will be wrapped up within that particular instance. This greatly simplifies the management and manipulation of any given connection while the program is running.

We'll be defining eighteen handlers within this script, which will serve a variety of purposes:

- Creating and initializing an instance of the Xtra (new, initialize, createinstance)

- Assigning and releasing callback handlers (initcallbacks, endcallbacks)

- Managing the connection (makeConnection, endconnection)

- Managing user lists (getusers, adduser, deleteuser, buildUserlist, getUserlist)

- Managing group lists (getGroups, buildGrouplist, getGrouplist, getmyGroup, setGroup)

- Sending text messages (sendNewMessage)

The server connection

The first order of business will be to connect to the server, and in most respects, the server setup we used in the previous chapter should work just fine. However, we're not going to assign the Xtra instance directly to a global variable as we did then.

While that approach is ideal for the purpose of making a single connection to a single server in a single program, it's just a little inflexible for our purposes. Ideally, we want code that can easily be used to create multiple connections, whilst being portable enough to be used in other applications. To accomplish this, we'll use the parent script to create our connection object.

Preparing to connect

1. Create a parent script called connection if you haven't already, and call up its script dialog.

2. Now add the properties that we'll need to track during our connection:

```
property pUserID -- userID we log in as
property pPassword -- userPassword we log in with
property pGroup -- the group we currently belong to
property pMovieID -- the name of our movie
property pUserList -- list of users in our group
property pGroupList -- list of groups in our movie
property pServerIP -- the IP address of the server
property pPort -- the port number the server is listening to
property pConnect -- the multiuser Xtra instance
```

If there are other properties that you need to include with your connection, then this is where you would add them. Other properties that you could use would be the Encryption key used for your connection, a UDP server address, a UDP port, and the value used to set the netBufferlimits if you expect to exceed the default values. In this case, none of these properties will be used so they have been left out.

3. Now we need to create a handler that allows for the creation of a new object, so add the following:

```
on new(me)
  me.initialize()
  return me
end
```

This simply calls the initialize handler, and returns the resultant object to the calling routine.

4. The initialize handler is where the properties we have defined are assigned their starting values. Since the instance of the Xtra and the message callbacks must be associated with this object, we call for them here as well.

```
on initialize(me)
  me.pUserID=empty        -- empty now, will assign when we connect
  me.pPassword=empty      -- empty now, will assign when we connect
  me.pGroup=empty         -- empty now, will assign when we connect
  me.pMovieID="SimpleChat" -- the name of our movie
  me.pUserlist=[]     -- no users yet, but will be stored as
linear list
  me.pGrouplist=[]    -- no groups yet, but will be stored as
linear list
  me.pServerIP="127.0.0.1" -- login to the local machine
  me.pPort=1626             -- using the standard port
  me.pConnect=0             -- no instance yet

  me.createinstance()       --call routine to create Multiuser Xtra
instance
  me.initcallbacks()        -- set up the message callback routines
end initialize
```

5. The code for the handler that actually creates the Xtra instance is a simple one-liner:

```
on createInstance(me)
  me.pConnect=new(Xtra "multiuser")
end createInstance
```

In this particular case, we could easily move this up into the initialize handler; in a more complex program though, there may be a lot more to do. By leaving it in a separate handler, we make it a lot easier to expand on this code at a later date without having to modify (and clutter up) the initialize handler itself. For similar reasons, we'll define a separate handler to take care of setting up callbacks.

Message callbacks

One vital aspect of program design involves establishing the specific types of message that we'll use to pass information between users. The needs of our program ultimately dictate what those messages will be, and in this case, they fall quite easily into three basic categories:

- Program status information being sent from user to user. We give these messages a subject that's indicative of the operation or event that has occurred – such as group_join or group_leave. As we'll demonstrate later on, these messages are sent to all the users who need them, and contain all the information required to keep those users' information up to date.

- Response messages generated by the server. These will either have a sender line that indicates they have come from "system.something", or use the subject "ConnectToNetServer" or "ConnectionProblem". They will get routed to connectionSuccess, connectionFailure, getGroupsHandler, or getUsershandler.

- The actual content of the messages being sent from one user to another. These ultimately need to be displayed on each user's screen, and are handled by the textmsgHandler callback. They are differentiated from other messages by use of the subject "text_msg".

Assigning message callback handlers

A handler called initcallbacks, as shown below, assigns our message callbacks. Add the following code to the connection script

```
on initcallbacks(me)
  if not me.pconnect=0 then    -- testing for a Multiuser instance

    -- default message handler
    me.pconnect.setNetMessageHandler(#defaultmessageHandler, \
                              script "main_scripts")

    -- execute when someone joins a group
    me.pconnect.setNetMessageHandler(#groupJoinHandler,      \
```

continues overleaf

```
                                        script "group_scripts", \
                                        "group_join", "", 1)

        -- execute when someone leaves a group
        me.pconnect.setNetMessageHandler(#groupLeaveHandler,      \
                                        script "group_scripts", \
                                        "group_leave", "", 1)

        -- execute when someone sends a text message to a group
        me.pconnect.setNetMessageHandler(#textmsgHandler,         \
                                        script "user_scripts",  \
                                        "text_msg", "", 1)

        -- execute when server returns a successful connection response
        me.pconnect.setNetMessageHandler(#connectionSuccess,      \
                                        script "movie_scripts", \
                                        "ConnectToNetServer", "", 1)

        -- execute when server returns a failed connection response
        me.pconnect.setNetMessageHandler(#connectionFailure,      \
                                        script "movie_scripts", \
                                        "ConnectionProblem", "", 1)

        -- execute on receipt of successful response to a getusers request
        me.pconnect.setNetMessageHandler(#getusersHandler,        \
                                        script "user_scripts", "",\
                                        "system.group.getusers", 1)

        -- execute on receipt of successful response to a getgroups request
        me.pconnect.setNetMessageHandler(#getGroupsHandler, \
                                        script "group_scripts","",\
                                        "system.movie.getgroups", 1)
    end if
end initcallbacks
```

One important point to observe is that the majority of messages sent and received by this program are for the sole purpose of maintaining the proper status of variables within it. The primary focus for the end user will be the messages that come up on the screen. Those messages, and the programming code to send, receive, and display them are actually a relatively small part of the overall program.

Since we assign these callbacks on initializing a connection object, we need to release them all before releasing that object. The endcallbacks handler is used when logging off the system to clear all the objects from memory. To release a callback, we set the handler property to 0 for each one we had previously initialized. We define this handler as shown below

```
on endCallbacks(me)
    if not me.pConnect=0 then    -- testing for a Multiuser instance

    -- zero all initialized message callbacks as part of cleanup process
```

```
me.pConnect.setNetMessageHandler(0, script "main_scripts")
me.pConnect.setNetMessageHandler(0, script "group_scripts", \
                                    "group_join", "", 1)
me.pConnect.setNetMessageHandler(0, script "group_scripts", \
                                    "group_leave", "", 1)
me.pConnect.setNetMessageHandler(0, script "user_scripts", \
                                    "text_msg", "", 1)
me.pConnect.setNetMessageHandler(0, script "movie_scripts", \
                                    "ConnectToNetServer", "", 1)
me.pConnect.setNetMessageHandler(0, script "movie_scripts", \
                                    "ConnectionProblem", "", 1)
me.pConnect.setNetMessageHandler(0, script "user_scripts","", \
                                    "system.group.getusers", 1)
me.pConnect.setNetMessageHandler(0, script "movie_scripts","", \
                                    "system.movie.getgroups", 1)
    end if
end endcallbacks
```

We must now define handlers that will actually create, manage, and destroy our connection to the server. We can identify three distinct groups of handlers: those specifically concerned with managing a connection to the server, those involved with managing users, and those involved with managing groups. Many of the following handlers are simply designed to read or manipulate properties of whatever connection object has been used to call them.

Managing the connection

To manage our connection, we first define a handler called makeConnection, which users will be able to call from the interface by simply clicking on the Logon button. Code attached to this button should pass it a username and password, as specified in the relevant text fields on the interface. We use these values (along with properties such as pServerIP, pPort, and pMovieID) to make a ConnectToNetServer call on the pConnect object, and thus attempt to connect to the server. If UPD and/or encryption keys were to be used in the connection, they would be added to this call as we discussed in previous chapters.

```
on makeConnection(me, myID, myPass)
    -- send the ConnectToNetServer message using our object
    -- properties and the username/password from the interface
    myerror=me.pConnect.ConnectToNetServer(me.pServerIP, me.pPort, \
            [#userID:myID, #password:myPass,#movieID:me.pMovieID])
    if not myError then     -- on successful connection, set up ID
variables
        me.pUserID=myID
        me.pPassword=myPass
        return myError
    else                    -- otherwise alert that an error occurred
        alert "An error occurred: " &
me.pConnect.getNetErrorString(myError)
        return myError
```

continues overleaf

```
        end if
    end makeConnection
```

If the connection is successful, the object properties for `userID` and `Password` are set to the values passed by the calling routine. If the connection fails then there's no point in setting these values as the connection will be cleared and additional calls to this routine will be necessary to make the connection.

If the connection does fail (or we disconnect intentionally) we can use the `endconnection` handler as part of the cleanup operation that releases our Xtra instance and clears it from memory. We accomplish this by simply setting the `pConnect` property of our connection object to `0`.

```
    on endconnection(me)
        me.pConnect=0
    end endconnection
```

The `getusers` handler is called when an update to the `userlist` is required. It asks the server to return a list of users for the current group on the current connection (as stored in the object property `me.pGroup`)

```
    on getusers(me)
        myError=me.pConnect.sendNetMessage("system.group.getusers", "", \
                                        string(me.pGroup))
        if myError<>0 then
            put me.pConnect.getNetErrorString(myError)
        end if
    end getusers
```

Like many of the following handlers, the `adduser` handler is simply designed to let us manipulate one of the properties of a specified connection object. In this case, we append a user name to the list of users associated with our connection.

```
    on adduser(me, userID)
        append me.pUserList, userID
    end adduser
```

Since we are keeping a local list of users, we must also be able delete a user should they log off the system. The `deleteuser` handler simply uses the `deleteAt` command to remove an entry from our list of current users, using a specified username to establish which entry should be deleted.

```
    on deleteuser(me, userID)
        deleteAt(me.pUserList, getpos(me.pUserList, userID))
    end deleteuser
```

We use the `pUserList` property to hold a list of all the users who are currently registered within the same group as us. On joining a new group, we must rebuild that list from scratch, in order to reflect the change. We'll be looking at the mechanics of retrieving that user list shortly; the buildUserList handler is simply responsible for duplicating its contents (accessed via the myList argument) and storing them in pUserList:

```
on buildUserList(me, myList)
  me.pUserList=duplicate(myList)
end buildUserList
```

The duplicate command here is very important. If we assigned myList directly to the pUserList property, then pUserList would simply end up referencing the original list (specified as a parameter in the calling code). Since this list is defined separately from the connection object, it can easily be modified (or even destroyed), and this would effectively change (or erase) the contents of pUserList. By using the duplicate command, we create a new copy of the user list in memory, completely separate from the original, and therefore avoid this problem.

The getUserlist handler simply returns the current contents of the calling object's user list (as held by its pUserList property):

```
on getUserlist(me)
  return me.pUserList
end getUserlist
```

Managing groups

The getGroups handler asks the server to return a list of groups for the current connection, so we'll call it whenever an update to the groupList is required.

```
on getGroups(me)
  myError=me.pConnect.sendNetMessage("system.movie.getgroups", "")
  if myError<>0 then
    put me.pConnect.getNetErrorString(myError)
  end if
end getGroups
```

The buildGroupList handler works in much the same way as buildUserlist (as discussed above). In this case, we populate the connection object's pGroupList property with a duplicate of a specified list of groups.

```
on buildGroupList(me, myList)
  me.pGroupList=duplicate(myList)
end buildGroupList
```

We define getGroupList to return the contents of pGroupList to the calling routine.

```
on getGroupList(me)
  return me.pGroupList
end getGroupList
```

getMyGroup returns the current groupname stored in the pGroup property of the connection object:

```
on getmyGroup(me)
   return me.pGroup
end getmyGroup
```

SetGroup simply sets the property pGroup to a new value contained in myGroup (as specified by the calling code).

```
on setGroup(me, myGroup)
   me.pGroup=myGroup
end setGroup
```

The property pGroup is the local storage bin for the name of our current group. By calling this handler, and sending it a new group name, all subsequent routines accessing that data will return the new group name. Storage of the groupname on a local level decreases network traffic by limiting the need to request the groupname from the server. It does, however, require that we are diligent and careful about making calls to this routine. Changing the name here essentially changes it for the whole program, and this could cause problems if not maintained properly.

Sending messages

The sendNewMessage handler is directly responsible for sending text messages between users, and is therefore very important to the application. It's fairly simple though, using our current group name (me.pGroup) and a subject of "text_msg" to call the server function sendNetMessage() and relay the specified message to all appropriate users:

```
on sendNewMessage(me, message)
   myError=me.pConnect.sendNetMessage(me.pGroup, "text_msg",
string(message))
      if myError<>0 then
      put me.pConnect.getNetErrorString(myError)
   end if
end sendNewMessage
```

The movie scripts

We've now defined all the basic functionality we'll need to make and control a connection to the server. We must now define the rest of the handlers we're going to need, and we'll do so in the following movie scripts:

- Main_scripts sets up the program (startmovie) and houses the default message handler (defaultMessageHandler)

- group_scripts deals with all group-specific tasks (JoinThisGroup, groupJoinHandler, groupLeaveHandler, getGroupsHandler, joinGroup, leaveGroup, updateGroupDisplay, newGroupDialog, killClicks, cancelNewGroup, group_create)

- **user_scripts** deals with all user-specific tasks (sendMessage, textmsgHandler, getUsersHandler, updateUserDisplay)

- **movie_scripts** contains functions that put the connection parent script to use (logon, logoff, connectionSuccess, connectionFailure)

The last of these defines the vital handler login, which sets up an instance of the connection script that we looked at earlier, and assigns it to the variable gMyConnection. Each of our new handlers will use this object to access the functionality we've already seen, and pass information back and forth through the server connection it creates. We therefore need to declare gMyConnection as a global variable within each of our movie scripts, so that all the other handlers can access it.

Setting up the program

If you haven't already, set up a movie script called main_scripts, and add the following code:

```
global gMyConnection

on startmovie
  member("username_entry").text=""
  member("password_entry").text=""
  member("Group_display").text=""
  member("User_display").text=""

  member("chat_text").text=""
  member("message_text").text=""
  --set client
end startmovie
```

The purpose of this handler is to clear the text and field input members before the user sees them. This ensures that these fields are blank at startup, as you would expect them to be.

The defaultMessageHandler receives all the messages that do not have a specific handler to deal with them. This handler is not essential to the project, but it should always be included to catch all the messages that were not planned for. In this case, if such a message is received its contents are simply written out to the message window. If it contained an error, then that error is also written out to the message window.

```
on defaultMessageHandler
 myMessage=gMyConnection.pConnect.getNetMessage()
 --display the message content in the message window
 put myMessage
 --if the message contains an error then display that in the \
message window
 if myMessage.errorCode<>0 then
  put "The message contained an error: " \
```

continues overleaf

```
&gMyConnection.pConnect.getNetErrorString(myMessage.errorCode)
  end if
end defaultMessageHandler
```

Handling groups – the 'group_scripts' movie script

As we saw in the last chapter, the basic mechanics of joining a group are actually very simple – it's really only a matter of mastering one simple command. Unfortunately, this proves to be just one small piece in a much bigger puzzle when it comes to dealing with multiple users. The process then becomes complicated by the fact that each individual user needs to keep an up-to-date copy of all the groups that currently exist for the given movie.

In theory, we could achieve this by having each movie repeatedly query the server for a current list of groups. However, since users can move from group to group at any time, creating or deleting groups as they go, we'd need to request updates very frequently to keep the information accurate. Even with just a few users, this would inevitably generate a huge quantity of network traffic, and put a fairly significant load on the server.

A far more efficient mechanism involves defining an event-based protocol that issues explicit update commands. In order to design such a protocol, we must first determine what events could result in a change to the list of groups that are currently associated with our movie.

As we know from previous chapters, the Multiuser Server will automatically create a new group for us if we attempt to join one that doesn't already exist. Likewise, it will automatically delete a group when the last user leaves it. It therefore makes sense to let everyone know whenever someone joins or leaves a group. When other users receive the message, they can automatically request an update for the list of available groups, keeping traffic to a minimum whilst keeping everyone up to date.

Joining a group

For the sake of flexibility, we're going to separate the group joining process into a number of different handlers.

The first of these handlers is JoinThisGroup. This extracts the name of the group we'd like to join from the interface, and then passes it to JoinGroup, which is going to look after the mechanics of messaging the server with a system.group.join call. By defining these separately, we leave ourselves the option of calling JoinGroup directly, just in case we want to specify the group name from some other source.

If you haven't already, set up a movie script called group_scripts, and add the following code:

```
global gMyConnection, gGroupLine

on JoinThisGroup
  if gGroupline<>0 then
    myText=field("Group_Display").line[gGroupLine]

    if myText="New Group" then
```

```
                newGroupDialog
          else
             --    joinGroup string(char 2 to myText.char.count of myText)
             joinGroup string(myText.char [2 mytext.char.count])
          end if
       else
          alert "Please Select a Group to Join"
       end if
    end JoinThisGroup
```

The `joinGroup` handler makes a `system.group.join` function call to the server, using the specified `groupname` to implement the actual group joining transaction.

```
    on joinGroup groupname
       -- check to see if we currently belong to a group
       currGroup=gMyConnection.getMyGroup()
       --if we do belong to a group, then leave it first.

       if currGroup<>Empty then
          leaveGroup CurrGroup
       end if

       myError=gMyConnection.pConnect.     \
                     sendNetMessage("system.group.join", \
                                    "group_join", string("@" & groupname))
       if myError<>0 then
          put gMyConnection.pConnect.getNetErrorString(myError)
       end if
    end joinGroup
```

Part of this process involves calling `gMyConnection.getMyGroup()` and retrieving the group to which our connection object is current assigned. From our earlier look at the `connection` script, we know this returns the property `pGroup` from the calling connection object – in this case, `gMyConnection`. Before joining another group, we ensure that we've left the current one.

This lets us fulfill our program's requirement that any user only belongs to one group at a time. This requirement is dictated by the design of our program, and not by the capabilities of the Xtra itself, which permits users to belong to several different groups at once.

Of course, if we had just logged in, `pGroup` would be `empty` so there'd be no need for us to leave any groups before joining the new one. The process of leaving a group requires as many messages as joining one, so this tactic helps to keep network traffic down – we'll look at the 'group leave' handlers shortly.

When we use the `joinGroup` handler, it makes a server function call with the subject `"group_join"`. If the server successfully executes the function, it will send us a response using the same subject, along with the senderID `"system.group.join"`. We've already set `groupJoinHandler` as the message callback handler for `"group_join"` messages, and now it's time to define its functionality.

Add the following code to the `group_scripts` movie script. The first section tests whether the specified message was sent in response to a `system.group.join` call.

```
on groupJoinHandler me, message
  -- check if this message is the response to a 'join' request
  if message.senderID="system.group.join" then
    -- message tells us we've successfully joined a group
    myDisplayLine="You have joined group: "&message.content
    -- notify all users that we've joined the group
    myError=gMyConnection.pConnect.sendNetMessage("@AllUsers",   \
                      "group_join", [#userID:gMyConnection.pUserID, \
                                    #myGroup:message.content])
    if myError<>0 then
      put gMyConnection.pConnect.getNetErrorString(myError)
    end if

    gMyConnection.setGroup(message.content)
    gMyConnection.getUsers()
```

If the message is sent the join was successful, so we display a message indicating that fact. We also send out a `"group_join"` message to `AllUsers`, whose contents consist of a property list that contains our `userID` and the name of the group we joined.

If the message isn't sent, then we must be receiving one of the public notification messages that we just set up – in other words, someone has joined one of the groups. We find out whether they joined our current group, and make sure that the public notification actually came from someone else. All being well, we go ahead and update our user list:

```
  else
    -- message tells us that someone has joined a group
    myGroup=gMyConnection.getMyGroup()
    senderID=value(message.content).userID
    senderGroup=value(message.content).myGroup

    -- check if the other user has joined our current group
    if senderGroup=myGroup then
      if message.senderID<>gMyConnection.pUserID then
        myDisplayLine=message.senderID&" has joined the group"
        gMyConnection.addUser(message.senderID)
        updateUserDisplay
      end if
    end if
  end if
```

So, our handler gets called twice when we join a new group, and just once when someone else does. If the message affects us for either reason, then we update our interface to reflect the change.

```
    -- check if the sender joined our group, or we are joining the group
    if (senderGroup=myGroup or message.senderID="system.group.join") then

        -- update the interface to reflect the change
        oldDelimiter=the itemDelimiter
        the itemDelimiter=":"

        --put the message content in a new member after member 3
member("chat_text").rtf=member("chat_text").rtf&myDisplayLine&return
        lastLine=member("chat_text").line.count
        set
member("chat_text").line[lastLine].item[1].fontStyle=[#bold]

        --if message contains an error, display that in the message window
        if message.errorCode<>0 then
            put "The message contained an error"
            put
gMyConnection.pConnect.getNetErrorString(message.errorCode)
        end if

        the itemDelimiter=oldDelimiter
    end if

    gMyConnection.getGroups()
end groupJoinHandler
```

Leaving a group

The process of leaving a group is essentially the same as joining one. For the most part, these handlers are direct copies with the messages altered to reflect a leave event (system.group.leave) as opposed to a join event (system.group.join). All we need to do, then, is add the following handlers to the group_scripts movie script.

The leaveGroup handler is always passed to the group name that we are leaving. The handler then issues a group leave message to the server with the subject of group_leave. The following message callback handler is assigned to messages with that subject:

```
on leaveGroup groupname
    myError=gMyConnection.pConnect.sendNetMessage("system.group.leave", \
                                        "group_leave", groupname)
    if myError<>0 then
        put gMyConnection.pConnect.getNetErrorString(myError)
    end if
end leaveGroup
```

The primary difference between this and the corresponding joinGroup routine is that a user who is leaving the group will not need to update any variables. A leave message will always be followed by either a join or logoff: in the former case, the join command will handle any necessary updates, while in the latter case, you aren't going to need any!

In spite of this, all other users in the leaver's group will need to delete the leaver from their user list; so the groupLeaveHandler (which is very similar to the groupJoinHandler that we saw earlier) is very important:

```
on groupLeaveHandler me, message
  if message.senderID="system.group.leave" then
    --the message is the response to our leave request
    myDisplayLine="You have left group: "&message.content
    myError=gMyConnection.pConnect.sendNetMessage("@AllUsers",  \
                "group_leave", [#userID:gMyConnection.pUserID, \
                                #myGroup:message.content])
    if myError<>0 then
      put gMyConnection.pConnect.getNetErrorString(myError)
    end if

  else
    --the message is a notification that someone left a group
    myGroup=gMyConnection.getMyGroup()
    senderID=value(message.content).userID
    senderGroup=value(message.content).myGroup

    if senderGroup=myGroup then
      --they left our current group, so update userlist
      if message.senderID<>gMyConnection.pUserID then
        myDisplayLine=message.senderID&" has left the group"
        gMyConnection.deleteUser(message.senderID)
        updateUserDisplay
      end if
    end if
  end if

  -- if the sender left our group, or if we are leaving
  if (senderGroup=myGroup or
message.senderID="system.group.leave") then
    -- update our interface to reflect the changes
    oldDelimiter=the itemDelimiter
    the itemDelimiter=":"
    --put the message content in a new member after member 3

member("chat_text").rtf=member("chat_text").rtf&myDisplayLine&return
    lastLine=member("chat_text").line.count
    member("chat_text").line[lastLine].item[1].fontStyle=[#bold]
    --if message contains an error
    if message.errorCode<>0 then
      --display error in the message window
      put "The message contained an error"
```

```
                put
    gMyConnection.pConnect.getNetErrorString(message.errorCode)
        end if
        the itemDelimiter=oldDelimiter
      end if

      gMyConnection.getGroups()
  end groupLeaveHandler
```

Managing groups and group lists

As users create, join, and leave groups, it's necessary for each user to update their group display list. This list should contain all the groups available to the current movie at any given time. We accomplish this (still in the group_scripts movie script) by calling the updateGroupDisplay handler each time a user joins or leaves a group:

```
on updateGroupDisplay
   myGroup=gMyConnection.getMyGroup()
   myList=gMyConnection.getGroupList()

   member("Group_Display").text="New Group"
   myText="New Group"

   repeat with counter=1 to count(myList)
     if (getat(myList, counter)<>myGroup and \
         getat(myList,  counter)<>"@AllUsers") then
       myText=myText&return&getat(myList, counter)
     end if
   end repeat

   member("Group_Display").text=myText
end updateGroupDisplay
```

This acquires the current group and the list of available groups by calling their respective functions in the connection script. Using a repeat loop, the current group list is added to the display field after New Group, which always appears at the top of the list. The current group was obtained early so we could filter it out of the list. We do not want to list the group we are currently in as a choice of groups available to us to join, since we're already members there.

If we receive a message from the server with the senderID "sender.movie.getgroups", its contents should comprise a list of all the groups currently available to our movie, and will automatically invoke the getGroupsHandler callback:

```
on getGroupsHandler me, Message
   if message.errorCode=0 then
     myList=value(value(Message.content).groups)
     gMyConnection.buildGroupList(myList)
     updateGroupDisplay
```

continues overleaf

```
       else
          put "The message contained an error"
          put
gMyConnection.pConnect.getNetErrorString(message.errorCode)
       end if
   end getGroupsHandler
```

We pass the list of groups to the `connection` object's `buildGrouplist` method, and call the `updateGroupDisplay` handler to update the group display.

The `newGroupDialog` handler is called when the Join button is pressed on the groups screen and New Group is selected in the group list window. This handler clears the text field used to enter the new group name, and sets the dialog sprite properties to visible. Finally, it sets the `mouseDownScript` to call the `killClicks` handler. This allows us to control how `mouseDown` events are handled while the dialog box is visible:

```
   on newGroupDialog
      member("new_group_name").text=""
      repeat with counter=20 to 25
         sprite(counter).visible=true
      end repeat
      the mouseDownScript="killClicks"
   end newGroupDialog
```

The following handler, `killClicks` is called when a `mouseDown` event occurs while the New Group dialog box is active. This handler prevents `mouseDown` events outside the dialog box from registering normally – instead they simply result in a system beep occurring:

```
   on killClicks
      if rollover()<20 then
         beep
         stopevent
      else
         pass
      end if
   end killClicks
```

`CancelNewGroup` is called whenever the dialog box is no longer needed. This can occur when the user clicks either the Cancel or the Create button. The handler hides the dialog box sprites by setting their visibility to `false`. It also sets the `mouseDownScript` to "", allowing the user to interact normally with the interface again:

```
   on cancelNewGroup
      repeat with counter=20 to 25
         sprite(counter).visible=false
      end repeat
      set the mouseDownScript to ""
   end cancelNewGroup
```

The group_create handler is called when the user clicks the Create button in the new group dialog box on the Groups screen. This handler sets the variable myName to the text content of member new_group_name and passes it to the joinGroup handler. This initiates the whole messaging process described above, which ultimately leads to our creating a new group, joining it, and leaving our current group. The last call, cancelNewGroup, calls the necessary handlers to close and hide the new group dialog, sending us back to the interface to message in our new group:

```
on group_create
  myName=member("new_group_name").text
  joinGroup myName
  cancelNewGroup
end group_create
```

Handling users – the 'user_scripts' movie script

You'll be glad to hear that managing users and user lists within our application is a fairly straightforward task. In fact, compared to our last set of code, it should seem like a walk in the park! We'll be defining four handlers here (getUsersHandler, updateUserDisplay, sendMessage, textmsgHandler), the last two of which actually serve to let the user send and receive text messages.

Once we've ensured that the global variable gMyConnection is available to our user scripts, we must define getUsersHandler. This is the callback routine initiated upon receipt of the server's response to a system.getusers request, which in turn is initiated by the getUsers handler in the connection script.

Provided no error is present in the message, this routine uses the content of the message (which we know from the previous chapters contains a linear list of users in the requested group) and passes them to the buildUserList routine of the connection object gMyConnection. It then calls the updateUserList handler that handles the actual process of displaying the usernames in the interface.

Once again, if you haven't already created it, make a user_scripts movie script, and add this code:

```
global gMyConnection

on getUsersHandler me, Message
    if message.errorCode=0 then
      myList=value(value(Message.content).groupMembers)
      gMyConnection.buildUserList(myList)
      updateUserDisplay
    else
      put "The message contained an error"
      put
gMyConnection.pConnect.getNetErrorString(message.errorCode)
    end if
  end getUsersHandler
```

Just as we need an `updateGroupDisplay` handler to refresh the displayed group list whenever a group is created or destroyed, we require a similar one to refresh our user list whenever a user (whether it's us or someone else) joins or quits our group. Basically, this list should always contain the username of every single user currently in the same group as us, and we need some code to ensure that this is so.

Our `updateUserDisplay` handler simply acquires the current user list (using the `getUserList` method defined on our connection object) and loops through each entry, adding each one to the `"User_Display"` field:

```
on updateUserDisplay
  myList=gMyConnection.getUserList()
  member("User_Display").text=""
  repeat with counter=1 to count(myList)
    member("User_Display").line[counter]=getat(myList, counter)
  end repeat
end updateUserDisplay
```

Extracting and displaying message text

Sending messages is accomplished with two simple handlers: one for extracting and sending the message text, the other for handling and presenting the received messages. We must therefore start by defining a handler to extract our text from the interface and pass it on to the sending routine that we defined for our all-purpose connection object:

```
on sendMessage
  myMessage=member("message_text").text
  gMyConnection.sendNewMessage(myMessage)
  member("message_text").text=""
end sendMessage
```

This handler will be called directly from the interface; it collects the message text from the assigned text field and passes it the `sendNewMessage` handler for `gMyConnection`. That then transmits the message to the server, using our current group name and a subject of `"text_msg"`.

As we observed in the last chapter, messages can be addressed to groups rather then users, in which case all users in the specified group (including ourselves) will receive the message. This is what we are doing here. The fact that the sender also receives the message means that if we assign a callback routine to the subject `"text_msg"`, we can use it to format and display the sent message in our chat message window. In this case, the routine is a handler called `textmsgHandler`, and is defined as follows:

```
on textmsgHandler me, message
  myDisplayLine=message.senderID &": "&message.content
  --put the message content in a new member after member 3

member("chat_text").rtf=member("chat_text").rtf&myDisplayLine&return
  lastLine=(member("chat_text").line.count)
  lineWordNum=string(myDisplayLine).word.count
```

```
member("chat_text").line[lastLine].word[1].fontStyle=[#bold]
member("chat_text").line[lastLine].word[1].foreColor=8

member("chat_text").line[lastLine].word[2..lineWordNum].fontStyle=[#plain]

member("chat_text").line[lastLine].word[2..lineWordNum].foreColor=255

    updateStage

    --if the message contains an error then display that in the message window
    if message.errorCode<>0 then
      put "The message contained an error"
      put
gMyConnection.pConnect.getNetErrorString(message.errorCode)
    end if
end textmsgHandler
```

This handler simply receives the message and formats it in the text display window.

Connecting the movie – the 'movie_scripts' movie script

Our last few functions are among the most important in the entire application. They are responsible for taking the name and password data that we entered on the start screen, and using them (along with an instance of our generic connection object, the now-familiar gMyConnection) to establish a connection with the server.

Making and breaking the connection

The successful execution of the following logon script will result in a returned message from the server with the subject "ConnectToNetServer" and an errorcode of zero:

```
global gMyConnection

on logon
    -- get the username and password values from the fields
    myName=member("username_entry").text
    myPass=member("Password_entry").text
    -- if either are blank then alert and exit
    if (myName="" or myPass="") then
      alert "A Username and Password must be provided"
    else
      --login
      gMyConnection=new(script "Connection")
      myError=gMyConnection.makeConnection(myName, myPass)
      if not myError then
        --logged in successfully
        go to frame "Groups"
      else
```

continues overleaf

```
          --login failed, clean up and try again
        gMyConnection.endCallbacks()
        gMyConnection.endConnection()
      end if
    end if
  end logon
```

In our `messageCallback` setup routine we have directed these messages to the handler `connectionSuccess` which is also located in the movie script `movie_scripts`:

```
on connectionSuccess me, message
  if message.errorCode=0 then
    member("chat_text").text=""
    member("chat_text").text= \
              "Connection Successful at " & the long time&return
    set member("chat_text").line[1].fontStyle=[#bold]
    joinGroup "Lobby"
    gMyConnection.getGroups()
  else
    --if message contains an error, display it in the message window
    alert "An Error Occurred: " & \

gMyConnection.pConnect.getNetErrorString(message.errorCode)
    gMyConnection.endCallbacks()
    gMyConnection.endConnection()
    go to frame "Start"
  end if
end connectionSuccess
```

In this handler, we verify that the `errorCode` was 0. If it was, we acknowledge the successful login by updating the text message screen text cast member (called `chat_text`) in the interface. Immediately afterwards, we call the `joinGroup` routine, passing the group name `"Lobby"` as an argument, which forces us to join a group called 'Lobby'.

We know from previous chapters that on connecting to the server we're automatically associated to the AllUsers group, and this is still the case. However, since our messaging routine is strictly group-based, any message sent by a user who is exclusively a member of the AllUsers group would be relayed to every other user who was currently connected, regardless of what group they were in at the time.

This is clearly not what we want here. We'll continue to use the AllUsers group in our maintenance routines to update the group display, but for the purpose of messaging content between users, we must ensure that all users belong to another group as well.

Of course, we must first handle the possibility that the logon script fails to connect properly:

```
on connectionFailure me, message
  alert "An Error Occurred: " &            \
  gMyConnection.pConnect.getNetErrorString(message.errorCode)
  gMyConnection.endCallbacks()
```

```
        gMyConnection.endConnection()
        go to frame "Start"
    end connectionFailure
```

When we click the Logoff button, the following handler is called. The handler follows a systematic process of disconnecting from the server and sending the user back to the login screen of the application:

```
    on logoff
      currGroup=gMyConnection.getMyGroup()
      leaveGroup CurrGroup
      myError=gMyConnection.pConnect.sendNetMessage("@AllUsers", \
          "group_leave", [#userID:gMyConnection.pUserID, #myGroup:currGroup])
      if myError<>0 then
        put gMyConnection.pConnect.getNetErrorString(myError)
      end if
      gMyConnection.endCallbacks()
      gMyConnection.endConnection()
      go to frame "Start"
    end logoff
```

The process starts by getting the user's current group. We then leave that group by calling the leaveGroup handler, and passing it our current group. Through our callbacks described above, we know that will initiate a series of events that will result in our leaving the specified group. Unfortunately, since we are disconnecting from the system the leaveThisGroup callback handler will not be executed correctly.

If you recall, one of the functions of this handler was to notify the remaining users of our departure with a "group_leave" message sent to @AllUsers. Since this function is essential for the others to stay up-to-date we need to get around this. That is accomplished by including the message to @AllUsers as part of the logoff process in this handler. After sending that message we clean up by calling endCallbacks and endConnection before going back to the logon screen at frame Start.

Our application is now nearly complete. We have only to wire up the interface, and we should be ready to chat to our hearts' content!

Behaviors – Interfacing it all together

All the remaining handlers (numbers 6-18 in my scripts cast) are behaviors that serve to connect our interface to the underlying application code we've just been defining. Most of the Lingo for these handlers takes a very basic on event form – we won't comment on it here unless it contains something unusual in addition to this.

global gGroupline on mouseUp me 6:Hilite field line	global gMyconnection on mouseUp m logon 7:Logon	on exitFrame me go to the frame end 8:Loop	Global gGroupline on prepareframe me 9:Hide dialog	on mouseenter me set myname = member(sprite(me. spritenum).member).name 10:button_behavior	on mouseUp go to frame "Users" end 11:jump_to_users

on mouseUp go to frame "Groups" end 12:jump_to_groups	on mouseUp me if member(sprite(me. spritenum).mem).text <> "" then 13:sendmessage	on keydown me if the key=return then if member(sprite(14:sendmessage or	on mouseUp me JoinThisGroup end 15:join group	on mouseUp me cancelnewGroup end 16:cancel button	on mouseUp me group_create end 17:create group but	on mouseUp me logoff end 18:logoff

Starting with member 6 of the scripts cast we have the following:

- **6:Hilite field line** – Attached to the group_display member in the groups section of the program. This script highlights the line we click on to show which group we wish to join. The index of the selected line is then stored in the global variable gGroupLine for later use by the group joining routines:

```
global gGroupLine

on mouseUp me
   member(sprite(me.spriteNum).member).line[the mouseLine].hilite()
   gGroupLine=the mouseLine
end
```

- **7:Logon** – attached to the logon button, this simply calls the logon handler in response to a mouseUp event.

- **8:Loop** – used as a frame script, containing "go to the frame" in an on exitFrame handler

- **9:Hide dialog** – a frame script for the first frame of the group section; this hides the dialog box and deselects all lines in the group_display member:

```
global gGroupLine

on prepareframe me
  repeat with counter=20 to 25
    sprite(counter).visible=false
```

```
      end repeat
      member("Group_display"). line[member(("Group_display") \
      .line.count)+1].hilite()
      gGroupLine=0
   end
```

- **10:button_behavior** – a three-state button behavior that is attached to the groups and users tabs in the interface

- **11:jump_to_users** – a behavior that is attached to the Users tab in the interface. This script contains an on mouseDown handler, which sends us to frame users

- **12:jump_to_groups** – attached to the Groups tab in the interface, this script contains an on mouseDown handler that sends us to frame groups

- **13:sendmessage** – this behavior is attached to the send button of the interface. It checks to make sure the message_text cast member is not empty. If it is not, it calls the sendMessage handler as described above

```
on mouseUp me
   if member(sprite(me.spriteNum).member).text<>"" then
      sendMessage
   end if
end
```

- **14:sendmessage on return** – attached to the editable text member message_text in the interface, this handler allows the RETURN or ENTER key to be used to send a message. On keyDown it checks to see if the key in question is RETURN. If it is, and the member is not empty, the sendMessage handler is called. Otherwise, the event is passed and the typed character appears in the box.

```
on keyDown me
   if the key=return then
      if member(sprite(me.spriteNum).member).text<>"" then
         sendMessage
      end if
   else
      pass
   end if
end
```

- **15:join this group** – calls JoinThisGroup from a mouseUp script and is attached to the Join button in the interface.

- **16:cancel button** – calls the cancelNewGroup routine on mouseUp to exit the create group dialog without creating a new group. It is attached to the cancel button on the create new group dialog box.

- **17:create group button** – this behavior is attached to the Create button on the create new group dialog. It calls group_create from a mouseUp handler.

■   **18:logoff** – this handler calls the `logoff` routines from a `mouseUp` handler. It is attached to the `logoff` button on the interface.

Once you've done all this, your application is ready to go. Congratulations, you've now got a fully usable and customizable chat application. (Read on to the next chapter to see one possible customization.)

Conclusion

The application outlined in this chapter illustrates the basic principles behind a simple multiuser chat application. While not overly sophisticated, and lacking in server-side scripting, it provides a useful basis for understanding how messages and message handling can be used effectively to monitor and control program state. The use of a connection object in the form of a parent script should also help you to develop applications that are more portable, more powerful, and easier to debug.

Chapter 11

Scripting the Server

In **Chapters 7** to **10**, we showed you how to create multiuser applications using both peer-to-peer and client-server techniques. Those applications relied solely on the clients to manage connections and other communications, using the server or peer host merely as a traffic distributor. This taught us some useful information about the way that multiuser applications are built in Director.

Prior to the release of Multiuser Server 3.0 with Director 8.5, those techniques were the only ones available, but the improved Multiuser Server has changed all that. Along with additional elements such as multithreading, and server–side file access, it includes **Server–Side Scripting**, or the ability to write Lingo scripts that are executed by the server at run time.

In this chapter we will look at how server–side scripting can streamline multiuser application development and how specific scripts are assigned to movies attached to the server. We'll examine the process of writing these scripts, and discover the Lingo that can be used. We'll also take a look into server specific Lingo features, such as server–side file handling, multithreading, and – perhaps most importantly – how to debug server–side scripts.

Streamlining production

As we saw with **Chapters 7** to **10**, multiuser applications can be built in Director with no server–side scripting at all. This begs the question: Why bother? The short answer to that is: to achieve simplicity.

If you remember, the client program in those chapters was designed to handle all aspects of the connection involved in the multiuser environment. Even for a simple application like our chat example this entailed a large number of different elements. Consider all the general interface functions: sending, receiving, and displaying text messages. Then remember all the additional functions, including those governing group management, and those that sent out and responded to messages that relayed program state to other users.

We needed to write scripts for all of these functions, despite the fact that many were common to all users. Surely there could be a way of avoiding the additional scripting? Well, there is! The server is centrally located and this is where we can see the usefulness of server–side scripting. Essentially, it allows us to write a single script to handle common housekeeping and other centralized tasks at the server.

A single script centrally located on the server has other distinct advantages. First, a single script tends to be easier to debug. In some cases, updates and changes can be applied to the server application without having to reissue the client application, making minor updates and bug fixes much easier to apply.

Creating server – side scripts

The creation of server side scripts is a fairly simple process. Essentially, a server–side script is a set of Lingo handlers saved as a text file with an `.ls` extension. They can therefore be created using any standard text editor, but the best tool for creating server–side scripts is Director itself.

Using Director, we can create a script cast member that is saved to a file with the `.ls` extension, but retains the familiar Lingo environment of color-coding, help screens, and command lists (some debugging will also be available.) We do this like so:

1. Create a new script cast member, and then click the info button to the right of the member name entry box to bring up the script property inspector.

2. Set the type to movie and click the link script as button.

3. Through the standard file dialog box that appears next, you can save your script member as an external file with an `.ls` extension.

Don't expect to be able to run this movie in Director authoring mode for testing. The server has some very specific commands to which Director may not respond – any test should be carried out using the server itself.

Now that we know how to make scripts, the next step is getting the server to recognize them.

Assigning scripts to movies

In order for server–side scripting to be functional on a given server, three files are required:

- `LingoVM.x32`

- `Dispatcher.ls`

- `Scriptmap.ls`

Of these three files, only one is not user–editable and that is the **LingoVM.x32 Xtra**, which must be present in the Xtras subfolder of the Multiuser Server folder. The other two are located in the scripts subfolder and they are both user–editable.

Dispatcher.ls
When the server is launched, the server object reference is passed to `dispatcher.ls`. The purpose of this script is to control the messaging between the server and Lingo scripts. It acts as the bridge between the server object and the underlying script objects that are assigned to the server. Opening this script in a text editor will reveal a fairly long script containing a large number of handlers, many of which are commented out by default to prevent their execution.

The only required handlers within this script are `on initialize`, `on configCommand`, `on serverEvent`, and `on incomingMessage`. The remaining handlers can be used for such tasks as debugging and system monitoring during testing, but should be omitted on a production server for security reasons. We will look at those handlers later in the chapter.

Scriptmap.ls
The server uses this file to assign scripts and script files, which fall into three categories: general movie scripts, global scripts, and script objects. Individual script files are assigned to each category through their respective handlers.

The most commonly modified handler is the on scriptmap handler, which is used to assign specific script files to movies or groups within a movie. Let's take a look at the default script for this handler.

```
on scriptMap

  theMap = []

  -- Example of a script mapped to a movie:
  -- theMap.append([ #movieID: "BlackJack*", #scriptFileName:
  -- "BlackJack.ls" ] )


  -- Example of a script mapped to a movie and group:
  -- theMap.append( [ #movieID: "Debuq", \
                      #groupID:"@DebugGroup", #scriptFileName:
  "Debug.ls" ] )

  return theMap

end
```

The variable theMap is used to store a property list, which contains at least the movieID and the file name of the script to be associated with that name. For example, if we wanted to associate the script scorekeeper.ls (which is found with other custom scripts in the Multiuser Server's Scripts subfolder) with the movie "myGame" then we would modify this script in the following way:

```
on scriptMap

  theMap = []

  -- Example of a script mapped to a movie:
  theMap.append( [ #movieID: "myGame",#scriptFileName:"scorekeep-
  er.ls" ] )

  return theMap

end
```

If we then placed the file scorekeeper.ls into the scripts folder for the server and restarted it, that script would be loaded, compiled and made available to all movies connecting the server with a movieID of "myGame".

Scripts can also be made exclusively available to specific groups within a movie. If we wanted to make the script mix_fuel.ls available only to the group "top_fuel" of the movie "dragRacing" then we would modify the script as follows:

```
on scriptMap

  theMap = []

  -- Example of a script mapped to a movie:
  theMap.append( [ #movieID: "dragRacing", \#groupID:"@top_fuel",
  #scriptFileName:"mix_fuel.ls" ] )

  return theMap

end
```

In addition to assigning scripts to specific movies or groups, we can also assign scripts to be accessible to all the movies attached to the server. These are referred to as global scripts and they are assigned in the on globalScriptList handler. The default version of this handler looks like:

```
on globalScriptList

  theList = [ "GlobalScripts.ls" ]

  -- Add the names of any scripts that you want to load
  -- as global scripts
  -- theList.Append( "MyGlobalScripts.ls" )

  return theList

end
```

GlobalScripts.ls

This file is loaded by default when the server is started, and is located in the Scripts subfolder of the standard Multiuser Server 3.0 installation. This file is not essential to the operation of the server and, by default, contains no handlers. This means that modifying or removing it is not necessary if no global handlers are desired for your movie. If global handlers are to be added (a handler that would allow all users to message the system operator, for example), then that handler could be added to the globalsScripts.ls file.

Adding that handler to globalscripts.ls wouldn't involve any modifications to the scriptmap.ls file. Modifications to the scriptmap.ls file would be necessary if you created additional script files to house your global handlers – say you wanted to be ultra organized and separate specific handlers into different script files.

If we saved that handler (or a series of handlers) for communicating with the system manager in a file called message_sys_op.ls, then we would modify the globalScriptList handler as follows:

```
on globalScriptList

 theList = ["GlobalScripts.ls"]

 theList.Append("message_sys_op.ls")

 return theList

end
```

> *The global script list is linear, as the scripts are available to all movies and are not assigned to specific movies or groups.*

The final handler in the scriptmap.ls file is the on scriptObjectList. Any scripts that should function on the server as parent scripts should be listed in this handler. For example, you could have a parent script used primarily to generate a countdown timer, but which could also be called on to generate a timer object for a number of different groups. If this script were called timer.ls, you would add this parent script in the following way:

```
on scriptObjectList

 theList = []

 -- Add names of scripts that you want to load as script objects
 theList.Append( "timer.ls" )

 return theList

end
```

It is important to note that the server only reads .ls files at startup. This is true whether they are required by the server (dispatcher.ls and scriptmap.ls), or not (globalsScripts.ls or any custom scripts you develop). You need to restart the server after making changes to these files so that the server will recognize the amendments. There is one way around this that can be utilized during development. In dispacher.ls, the script handler on incomingMessage has the following section commented out:

```
-- case subject of
--  "System.Script.Admin.Reload":
--   put "LingoVM: reloading all scripts."
--    tlist = thread().list
--    repeat with t in tlist
--     t.forget()
--    end repeat
--   the timeoutList = []
--   me.loadScriptMap()
```

```
--    exit
--    "System.Script.Admin.Ping":
--       sender.sendMessage(subject, msg)
--       exit
--    "System.Script.Admin.ShowState":
--       showServerState()
--       exit
-- end case
```

Un-commenting this section and restarting the system will allow you to send a message to the server with the subject `"System.Script.Admin.Reload"`. The system will respond to that message by reloading the scripts that are assigned to the server. This feature should be turned off on a production server, as it would be fairly simple for a malicious individual to reload your scripts.

Server–side Lingo

One of the great things about server–side Lingo is that it's written using the same syntax and structure as client–side or Director Authoring Mode Lingo. The structure is the same, but there are several keyword additions specific to the server, and several that are unavailable to the server. While the differences in keywords are too numerous to enumerate here, and fairly well documented in the manuals which ship with Director 8.5, they can be summed up fairly easily by the functions they perform.

- **Unavailable Lingo commands** are those that deal with the stage, sprites, cast members, casts, movies, frames, and some system commands (such as `restart`, the `desktoprectlist`, color depth, and so on).

- **Available commands** deal with program flow, variable manipulation, lists, properties, and other data structures.

- **Server–side only Lingo commands** include those for server–side file access, server–side multithreading and server–side debugging.

The structure of a server – side script is an event-based system in which the server responds to specific events generated by a movie. The server passes each event to the script that has been assigned to the event-generating movie.

This structure is analogous to the Lingo events such as `on mousedown` and `on exitframe` that we have all grown to know so well. These events may be easier to mentally conceptualize then the events recognized by the server, but events are coded and handled in exactly the same way within the server script files.

The events are as follows:

- on movieCreate
- on movieDelete
- on userLogOn
- on userLogOff
- on groupCreate
- on groupDelete
- on groupJoin
- on groupLeave
- on incomingMessage
- on serverShutDown

The server needs to pass information to each handler in the form of arguments, so that there'll be enough information about the origin of the event to be able to write code to process it. The format for this is typically:

```
on moviecreate (me, movie, group, user)

end moviecreate
```

These standard events can then be coupled with additional custom handlers by calling those custom handlers from within the main event handler.

The on incomingMessage handler is similar to the message callback handler in client–side scripts. It is invoked when any incoming message arrives at the server. Through the use of a **case statement** within this handler, we can sort messages by subject and pass the contents of that message to specific handlers within the server-side script. This is accomplished by sending a message from the client to "system.script":

```
mymessage=gMultiuserClient.sendnetmessage \
            ([#recipients:"system.script", \
            #subject:"checkforfile", #content:"newgraphic.gif"])
```

This message would then be received by the server, and processed by the on incomingMessage handler:

```
on incomingMessage (me, movie, group, user, fullMsg)

mysubject=fullMsg.subject
mycontent=fullMsg.content

case mysubject of
  "checkforfile":
      me.checkforfile(user, mycontent)
end case

end incomingMessage
```

The handler is passed the full compliment of information necessary to process the request as a series of arguments. Among those is the `fullMsg` argument, which contains the equivalent of the `getNetmessage` results gathered in a client movie. From that, we're able to get the subject of the message and the content. The subject is used in the case statement to differentiate the message from others and to call the appropriate handler.

In this case, the content is the file name. We pass the file name and user who sent the message to the `checkForFile` handler. This handler looks in the root directory of the hard drive (in this case c:\) for the specified file. We then message the requesting user back the results of the search for the file.

```
on checkforfile (me, user, filename)

    fileandpath="c:\" & filename

    myfile=file(fileandpath).exists

  if myfile then
   returnMessage = "File is present"
  Else
   returnMessage = "File is not present"
  end if

  user.sendmessage("system.script.CheckForFile", \
   string(returnMessage))

  end checkForFile
```

Messaging users, groups, and movies

The file handling routines will be covered at greater depth later in this chapter. I will, however, delve into the messaging portion of this script now, as it demonstrates an important principle for general server scripting since it's slightly different to that used in client–side scripting.

Server–side message sending uses the `sendmessage` command, which of course is analogous to the `sendNetmessage` command in client–side scripting. The major difference is that we do not have an Xtra instance to assign the message to. Instead we send the message as a function of a movie, a group, or a user attached to the server.

Messaging a particular user is the easiest method to implement. The syntax is:

```
user.sendMessage("system.script.subject", "message")
```

The user is passed to the calling handler as an argument – as shown above in the `on incomingMessage` handler. The subject as shown is `"system.script.subject"`. The term "subject" can be replaced with an appropriate subject but the prefix `"system.script"` must be present to ensure that return messages are properly received. If your desired subject were `getfile` then `"system.script.getfile"` would be the appropriate subject to use.

Since we are directly targeting the user from which the request originated, there is no recipient specified in the parenthetical body of the message. This is not the case when we message a particular **group**:

```
group.sendMessage("recipient", "system.script.subject", \
                                        "message")
```

Or a particular **movie**:

```
movie.sendMessage("recipient", "system.script.subject", \
                                        "message")
```

For these calls, "`recipient`" should be replaced with a username, or a linear list of user names that the message should be sent to. The values of the group and the movie are retrieved from arguments passed to the handler just as the value for user is above.

Multithreading

In **chapter 10**, we introduced the concept of asynchronous operations – operations that allow one process to occur while waiting for another to complete. As we discussed then, we normally think of Director programming as occurring in a synchronous fashion. Event A occurs and we do something; when that's finished, we wait for event B to happen, and so on in a linear fashion.

In multiuser programming from the client–side we learned that events could occur asynchronously. Event A occurs, we respond, but while waiting for the results of that response, we can go forward and receive events B, C, or D, and respond in kind to those. This allowed us great flexibility in processing multiple chains of events that occurred in different orders without having to worry about that order.

Multithreading adds another level of complexity to the mix. The concept of a thread can be a difficult one to grasp, so try picturing a single lane road. Traffic moves in a single direction down that road, generally keeping to a linear fashion. Along the way, we may have stop lights and signals holding traffic up while waiting for certain events to occur; a child crossing the road, the lights turning back to green.

The cars are like instructions in Director, moving down the instruction stack in a linear fashion, and stopping when an event is needed to proceed. This is the normal process in a single threaded application such as Director. It is perfect for the single or low user environment for which Director was originally intended – after all, a single user can only generate a single linear set of events. But the multiuser environment has changed our simple road, and we need a new method to control the traffic.

When hundreds or thousands of users occupy the single thread, it becomes backed up with requests, since they can only be processed one at a time. Our road is grid-locked. Now, imagine if it were possible for each driver on the road to generate his or her own lane on demand. (I've a feeling you may like this idea, but it may take some time before we see it on our freeways.)

That lane would have its own stoplights that worked independently from the other lanes, and the flow of traffic in that lane would be unaffected by the other lanes. Therefore traffic might come to a grinding halt in one lane if a pothole appeared, while traffic still moved freely in other lanes. Of course, flying over in a helicopter, we can still see what each lane is doing, and someone in a car in lane 1 could use his cell phone to call someone in lane 10 to find out how fast he's going.

This is exactly what threads do for you in a multithreaded application.

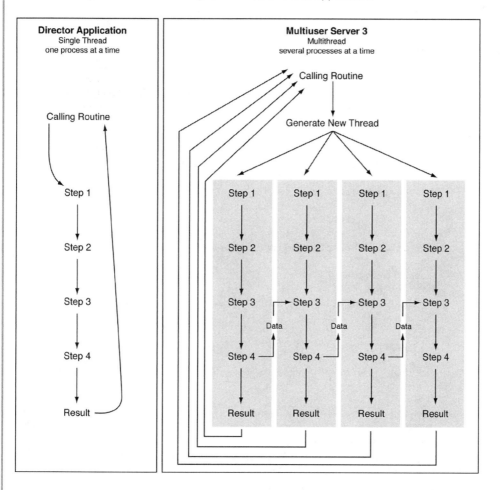

We can start a process in its own thread, where it has its own set of variables and values. As that thread progresses, it is isolated from other threads so that bugs and errors that occur in that thread do not throw off the values in other threads. We can request and set variable values from one thread to another, and the threads can all be processed and move along independently of each other.

This is accomplished through cooperative multitasking in which each thread is spawned into its own memory space independent of other threads. These "mini-programs" then share the processor to accomplish their mission. Of course, the program is now much more efficient in handling asynchronous traffic and allows applications that have a much higher usage load to be developed.

Unfortunately, it's not all plain sailing. Multithreading can result in increased complexity and difficulty in debugging. We all know how daunting it can be to debug a single–threaded application like a standard Director movie, but we take a deep breath, and by following the program along through its linear execution pattern we can usually find bugs and correct them. This is much like listening to another person in a one on one conversation. As that person speaks, if we are paying attention, we can usually pick out words that do not fit into the conversation at hand. Now if we were to try and do the same thing in a crowded room with everyone talking at the same time you can image the difficulty that we would be faced with. Especially if one wrong word spoken in the room could alter or mess up the conversations that others were having.

Threads have to be created using the `thread().new()` command. Once a thread is created, individual handlers or whole scripts can be assigned to execute within that handler. If we wanted to open our welcome message file using a new thread, we would alter our code to look as follows:

```
on incomingMessage (me, movie, group, user, fullMsg)

  mysubject=fullMsg.subject
  mycontent=fullMsg.content
  fileThread=thread().new("myFileThread")

  case mysubject of
   "checkforfile":
     filethread.call(#checkforfile, me, user, mycontent)
  end case

end incomingMessage
```

This creates a single new thread named `"myFileThread"`using the new command. This command has the following syntax:

```
myThread=thread().new(threadname, stacksize)
```

The `stacksize` is the amount of RAM in bytes dedicated to the thread. Since each thread is operating independently of the other threads, each will require its own separate block of RAM in which to function. The actual amount of RAM used by a particular thread is dynamically allocated, so specifying it here is optional.

If the amount of RAM is specified and the system requires more RAM to complete the operation, then problems arise. Since this is the case, the stack size should only be set when doing very basic tasks in a thread. In such cases, we can specify a small amount of RAM for the process to run in, instead of allowing the system to allocate a default amount.

Connecting threads

Running independently of other threads, each thread functions within its own block of RAM. Within that sphere is space for an independent set of all the variables necessary for the thread to complete its tasks. In some cases, a thread can be executed to completion without any contact with other threads within the program. Independent threads of this type are the easiest to develop because we avoid any potential complexities that can arise during data–sharing.

Threads are, however, mainly used for repetitive or very complex tasks – the nature of such tasks dictates that it's very likely that the results they generate will need to be shared with other threads at some point. Fortunately, server–side Lingo contains several commands that allow this to happen. Basic communication between two threads is illustrated in the following example, which employs two possible repetitive tasks that may be found in a multiuser environment: alphabetizing a list of users, and selecting a user from within that list.

To do this, make a quick test message handler and attach it to a standard button in our test movie. The message sends a list of names to the script engine of the server with the subject of "getname".

```
global gMultiuserClient

on mouseUp me

 myname=member("filename").text

 newmessage=gMultiuserClient.sendnetmessage \
     ([#recipients:"system.script", #subject:"getname", \
     #content:["Tom", "Bob", "Kevin", "Carl", "Alice"]])

 if newmessage<>0 then

  put gMultiuserclient.getNetErrorString(newmessage)

 end if
 end
```

In our server script, we modify the incomingMessage handler to react to messages with the subject "getname", as used above. In this case, we create two new threads (alphathread and getnamethread).

To these we assign handlers for alphabetizing the list we sent (#alphanames) and get a specific name from that list (#nthname) respectively.

```
on incomingMessage (me, movie, group, user, fullMsg)

mysubject=fullMsg.subject
mycontent=fullMsg.content

fileThread=thread().new("myFileThread")

case mysubject of

  "checkforfile":
   --me.checkforfile(user, mycontent)
   filethread.call(#checkforfile, me, user, mycontent)
  "getname":
   alphathread=thread().new("myalphaThread")
   getnamethread-thread().new("myNameThread")

   alphathread.call(#alphanames, me, user, mycontent)

   getnamethread.call(#nthname, me, user)

 end case

end incomingMessage
```

The alphanames handler takes the message content, sorts it, and then uses produceValue to make that list available to other threads. When the produceValue command is issued, the thread will stop and wait for the next thread to retrieve the value.

```
on alphanames me, user, content

  --extract the list from the message

  alphalist=value(content)

  --sort the list alphabetically

  sort(alphalist)

  --make the list available to other threads

  produceValue(alphalist)

end alphanames
```

The nthname handler locates the appropriate thread by name and assigns its reference to the local variable alphathread. It then issues an awaitvalue command to that thread to retrieve the ordered list. When this command is issued, the execution of the thread is halted until the value it is requesting is made available. Once it is available, execution resumes and in this case, the second name on the list is written out to the server message window.

```
on nthname me, user

 alphathread=thread("myalphaThread")

 --wait for the sorted list from the alphathread

 mylist=alphathread.awaitvalue()

 --display the name in position 2 of that list

 put getat(mylist,2)

end nthname
```

This type of data–sharing between threads is fairly basic since we are only sharing between individual threads. More complex possibilities exist in the form of multithread data–sharing.

An example of such a process would be a score–keeping routine. If there were several threads running in a game, and they all required an accurate score for proper function, then the score generation thread would have to make the score value available to all threads. Of equal importance in such a scenario is the possibility of data corruption.

Anyone familiar with database programming has probably been introduced to the possible pitfalls associated with multiuser environments where common data is simultaneously available to multiple users or processes. The common scenario spelled out in most database tutorials is an inventory database. If we have 50 units of Product X and someone adds one to his shopping basket at the same Time as someone else, then the final result should be that the inventory is reduced to 48. If timed correctly, both users could receive a current value of 50, both subtract one from 50, and the net result is that there are 49 left.

In the case of our score–keeping routine, if all the users have a correct total score of 250 and person A scores 25, then the score would be updated to 275 and sent out to all other users. If person B scores 15 points after person A, but before they receive the updated value of 275 from the server, then it would be possible that 265 (250 + 15) would be the score total issued to all users rather then the proper score of 275.

Why is this? Because two users altered a value before the appropriate updates were made by the server, resulting in only the last update being properly registered. Multiuser Server 3.0 has several built–in Lingo commands for handling data between multiple threads simultaneously, including some that prevent this kind of data corruption.

Before exploring the commands and process necessary for multithread data sharing, it is important to note what can be shared using these methods. Unlike single thread sharing where we can share data in the form of strings, lists, integers, and so on, multithread data–sharing is limited to lists. Linear and property lists are both supported.

Locking data

In the thread producing and manipulating the data, we need to lock the list using the `lock` command:

```
lock(myData)
```

Locking the data prevents other threads from directly manipulating the specified list. When locked, only the locking thread has the proper authority to change or unlock the data. The changes can only come in the form of additions, deletions, and direct changes to the list data itself.

By restricting our activity to these actions, the pointer to the location of the list stored in RAM does not change, meaning we continue to look at and manipulate the same set of list data in RAM – which has been locked. If we set the value of our list using the = then we will assign a completely new list to our reference variable. The pointer in RAM will change and data will no longer be locked.

The threads that require the data from the main manipulation thread need to contain a `wait` statement. That statement should contain a reference to the list that it is waiting for such as:

```
wait(myData)
```

The execution of the thread will pause when this command is executed and will not resume again until the data is made available from the data providing thread with the `notifyAll` command:

```
notifyAll(myData)
```

After the `notifyAll` command, the locked list can be unlocked using the `unlock` command:

```
unlock(myData)
```

Unlocking it frees the list to be manipulated by any calling routine; care must be taken when shared variables are unlocked to prevent data corruption from occurring.

Orphaned objects

Another important multithreading feature is the `sweep` command. As we manipulate and alter data shared between multiple threads, it is possible to generate an "orphaned" object. This occurs when two objects reference each other, and either object is deleted. Since the reference still exists, then the data will remain in RAM even though the main object that created it is gone.

Orphaned objects waste valuable system resources, and should be checked for periodically. You need to use the sweep command with the status parameter to check the issuing thread for orphans.

```
orphanlist=sweep().status()
```

will return a list of orphaned objects. If `orphanlist<>[]` then the `sweep().free()` command can be issued to delete those orphans from RAM.

Server–side file operations

One of the unique features of server–side scripting is the ability to access files located on the server. This file access allows several operations, including:

- Testing for the presence of a specified file
- Reading partial or full files
- Creating and writing files
- Moving files
- Gathering file information (such as size and creator)
- Creating and deleting folders
- Deleting files
- Renaming files
- Reading and setting the file type

The first issue when dealing with files on a server is the designator for folders. On a Mac, the character used in paths to designate folder separators is a :, while on Windows operating systems it is a \. Clearly, this is a problem when writing server–side code for a multiplatform environment.

To create cross–platform server–side scripts, it would be useful to include a handler that would assign the separator character to a property, or global variable. This can be accomplished using the `FolderChar` command:

```
global myChar

on getFolderChar me
 myChar=file().folderchar
end getFolderChar
```

Finding files

The ability to access files on the server has many uses: you can share files among groups of users, distribute files to coworkers, and clients can submit files. We have already examined a couple of these operations, including how to determine whether a file exists on the server or not. The Lingo for that operation looks like:

```
file("filepathname").exists()
```

In addition to having the ability to determine if a specific file exists, we can also get a list of the files in a particular directory. Using the `getat` command (not to be confused with the `getat` list command) we can write a quick routine to list all the files and folder in the root of our "c" drive:

```
counter=1
myfileprops="empty"

repeat while myfileprops<>void
 myfileprops=file("c:").getat(counter)
 put myfileprops&return
 counter=counter+1
end repeat
```

This routine will print out the properties for each file in the c: root directory in the output window of the server. Each call returns a property list such as:

```
[#name: "c:\AUTOEXEC.BAT", #folder: 0, #visible: 1]
```

The #name property contains the full file and pathname for the file located. The #folder property is a Boolean value indicating whether the file is a folder or not, and the #visible property is a Boolean value that indicates whether the file is hidden or not. A hidden folder would look like this:

```
[#name: "c:\RECYCLED", #folder: 1, #visible: 0]
```

The routine above works by passing a counter value starting at 1 as an argument for the getat command. Position 1 is the first file in the folder. We continue to cycle through the files, adding 1 position to the counter value until getat(x) returns a void value, indicating that there is no file at that position. All files will be returned with no gaps, so a void value indicates that we have hit the end of the list.

Reading and writing files

In addition to locating and listing the files on the server, we can also read files from the server:

```
myvalue=file("filepathname").read()
```

is used when reading text files. If we need to read a binary file, we replace the read command with readvalue as follows:

```
myvalue=file("filepathname").readvalue()
```

Both the commands above read the entire file when called. With a slight modification to the call, we also have the ability to read specific portions of files. This can be important when quickly extracting small portions of useful information buried within large files, and is more efficient in both time and memory usage then reading the entire file into RAM and trying to sort through it.

The number of bytes we wish to read in determines the portion of the file that we read. That number is simply used as an argument in the read and readvalue commands. To read the first 100 bytes of a text file, the command would look like:

```
myvalue=file("filepathname").read(100)
```

The ability to read files from the server is a significant feature, which opens may doors for the distribution of files through a multiuser application. The server does not stop there – it also allows file writing and creation through server–side scripting. The basic file writing calls are very similar to the calls for reading files we discussed above. To write a text file, we replace the `read` call with a `write` call:

```
myvalue=file("filepathname").write(textDataToWrite)
```

The value of `myfile` will be returned as 0 if the operation is successful and 1 if it fails. If the file already exists and is not locked, it will replace the contents of the existing file with `textDataToWrite`. If the file does not exist, then it will be automatically created. This call works only with text data. If we wish to write binary data then we need to use `writevalue`:

```
myvalue=file("filepathname").writevalue(binaryDataToWrite)
```

Using this call, we can write any binary data that Director supports – including SW3D files, images, sounds, and so on. The functionality and returned values are the same as those for `write`.

Replacing and maintaining data

When the `write` and `writevalue` commands are called, they replace the data in the opened file. If the data is written to an existing file, then the existing data will be replaced with the data that's just been written.

If you need to maintain the data in the original file when the new data is written, then there are two options. You can read the contents of the entire file into RAM, perform the necessary manipulations in RAM, and resave the entire file. Again, this method should only be used for very small or rarely used files.

The more efficient approach would be to position the file pointer within the file where we want to start writing. This is accomplished using the `position` command:

```
file("filepathname").position=filePosition
```

`filePostion` is an integer value representing the position of the next byte to be written or read within a file. The allowable values for `filePosition` range from 0 (the first position) to the last byte within the file. The last byte position can be obtained using the size command:

```
myFileSize=file("filepathname").size
```

This will return the size of the file in bytes. Since position and size both work in bytes, then the value returned by the size command not only tells us how big the file is, but also the position of the last byte in the file. This is important as it allows us to append data to the end of a file without having the read the contents of the entire file into RAM. A simple routine will move the file pointer to the end of the file and allow the next set of data to be appended to the file:

```
file("filepathname").position=file("filepathname").size
```

The position function is also valuable for reading files as we can set the file pointer to a position within the file in combination with the `read` or `readvalue` commands. Finally, the position command can also be tested:

```
myPosition= file("filepathname").position
```

An example of a valuable use for this would be adding a name to an alphabetical list in a text file. In a typical multiuser environment, such a file would be altered frequently. As the file expands with new names, or contracts with deletions, the actual position of any given name can change.

To work with this, we could write a routine that reads through the file and compares each name to the name we want to add. When we find the one that should come AFTER our test name, we read the file position with the position command. We then read from that point to the end of the file, append the contents of that operation to our name to be added, set the file pointer back to where we originally found our insertion point and write the data back out.

Creating unique filenames

A common problem associated with allowing file writing to a server is developing a method to allow unique filenames to be assigned to incoming files. We could write a custom routine using the `getat` command described above to list all the files in a given directory and assign those names to a list. We could then generate random names based on random numbers, and compare them to the `getat` list to make sure the name does not already exist, so we can use that name.

This is an arduous way of doing things, and in a directory with a lot of files, it may take some time to process. Any processing delays on a busy server could ultimately lead to the same name being assigned to two files before either file was written. This is especially true if the file creation process is multithreaded.

Fortunately, there is a safer and more direct way to create unique filenames built into the server. The `getTempPath` command allows the creation of unique filenames in a given directory. The syntax is:

```
newfile=file("pathname").getTempPath([#extension:".ext", \
#create: TrueOrFalse])
```

The name of this call is a little confusing, as it really has nothing to do with the temporary folder, or indeed any system–defined folder at all. The "pathname" provided can be any valid path on the system and it may be provided as an absolute path or a path relative to the server application location.

The `#extension` provided will be the extension used in the new filename and should include the "." in the designation. The `#create` property is a Boolean value designating whether the file should be created or not. The function will return the file and pathname when called, or an error code of 1 if the operation was unsuccessful.

Other file operations

Files can also be deleted, renamed, and exchanged with simple and straightforward commands such as:

```
deleteAfile=file("FilePathName").delete()

renameAfile=file("FilePathNameToChange").exchange("newFileName")
```

In this case, a full path must be designated for the original filename, but the path is left off on the new filename. This is due to the fact that we need to find the file, but once we've found it, we can only change the filename and not the path. If the path needs to be altered then we need to use the copyTo command in association with a delete command.

The copyTo command copies the entire contents of a file from one location to another. The syntax is:

```
copyAfile=file("FilePathNameToCopy").copyTo("newFilePathName")

exchangeAfile=file("FilePathName1").exchange("FilePathName2")
```

Each of these commands returns a non-zero error code if the operation fails.

In addition to the multitude of file commands, there is a command used specifically for creating folders, and one for deleting folders:

```
file("pathname").createfolder()

file("pathname").deletefolder()
```

Their application is as simple and straightforward as it looks.

> A note of caution when using file Lingo in server–side scripting. The server is operating on your system with administrator level privileges: when someone tells it to do something, it has the authority to do it. Given this fact, it's important to write your scripts carefully so that a malicious user cannot hack scripts together in a way that may harm your system.

Server–side script debugging

As much as we would like everyone to believe that we write perfect code every time we park ourselves in front of the Lingo script window and start typing, the fact remains that while the goal may be perfection, we are imperfect beings.

Since problems and unforeseen circumstances inevitably rear their ugly heads, we are always strapped with the problem of working bugs out of our code.

Director 8.5 does have some excellent built-in debugging tools, but, unfortunately, they are not also built into the Multiuser Server. The aim of this section is to show how good debugging principles can be applied to debugging server–side scripts.

There are three basic types of bugs that occur in programming. There are **compile time errors**, **run time** errors, and **logic** errors. In writing Lingo in Director we have all experienced each of these types, but there are differences in the ways they become evident to the programmer. We will look at each of the types, and how we handle them separately.

Compilation errors

Compilation errors occur when there is an obvious problem – an undeclared variable, for instance – that prevents the application from compiling the source code into a final runtime script object. In Director, these errors will show up as a dialog box with the line number of the script error.

Check out the following default message handler:

```
global gMultiuserClient

on defaultmessageHandler

 mymessage=gMultiuserClient.getnetmessage()
 --display the message content in the message window
 put string(mymessage)

 --if the message contains an error then display that in the
 --message window
 if mymessage.errorcode<>0 then put \
    "The message contained an error"

 put gMultiuserClients.getNetErrorString(mymessage.errorcode)

 end defaultmessageHandler
```

This handler would make Director issue the dialog box pictured.

Did you spot the mistake? Of course you did!

We mistyped the variable name gMultiuserclient by adding an extra 's' on the end. The variable gMultiuserclients is previously undeclared, so the script cannot compile. The Multiuser Server does not display dialog boxes to warn of similar compilation errors. Instead, at start-up, each script is read in and a script object is generated in RAM from the specified script text file. This is the equivalent of recompiling the scripts in Director and it normally only occurs at start-up.

We can demonstrate how the server handles these errors by introducing an error into our previous on logon script, which was used to load the welcome message from a file as follows:

```
on userLogOn (me, movie, group, user)

  myfile=file("c:\welcome.txt").exists

  if myfil then
   myMessage=file("c:\welcome.txt").read
  Else
   mymessage="No Messages"
  end if

  user.sendmessage("system.script.Welcome", string(mymessage))

end userLogOn
```

In this case, we've got a common typo mistake in line 5: "if myfil then" instead of the original "if myFile then". When we restart the server the following appears in the server output window alerting us to the compilation error:

```
MultiuserServer

File   View   Status   Help

Shockwave Multiuser Server.

Reading the Multiuser.cfg file.

* RuntimeAttributes xtra has been loaded.

* DatabaseObjects xtra has been loaded.

* LingoVM xtra has been loaded.

* Lingo Script Error: Variable used before assigned a value
*    Error in Lingo code:
 if myfil then?

-- "LingoVM problems compiling script file  ch16a.ls"




# Allocating connections.
.....................................
.....................................
.....................................
.....................................
.....................................
.....................................
.....................................
.....................................
.....................................
.....................................
.....................................

# Allocated 2000 connections.
# 2001/11/29 10:50:52 Waiting for incoming connections.
```

As shown, the server simply alerts us to the fact that the offending script did not compile, and provides a brief description of what the problem was and where it occurred. It then proceeds to allocate connections and make itself available for use. Since it did not compile, this script will not be available for use by the movie it was assigned to. If other scripts are assigned to other movies and no errors or warnings were specifically issued for those scripts, then those scripts would be available to their respective movies. In short, only those that do not compile will not be available.

In such a situation, you need to reopen the script in a text editor, make the appropriate corrections, resave the file, and restart the server.

Runtime errors

The next type of error is the runtime error. These occur when the code compiles but contains errors that prevent proper execution. One such example is the Property not found error (see the screenshot) that results from a request for the property of a variable that does not exist.

This message callback script is used to display whether a file is present on the client–side, and line 3 has been altered to read put message **contents**, rather than put message **content**.

```
on checkfilehandler me, message

  put message.contents
  --put the message content in a new member after member 3
  member("output").text=message.content

  --if the message contains an error then display that in the
message window
  if message.errorcode<>0 then
   put "The message contained an error"
   put gMultiuserClient.getNetErrorString(message.errorcode)
  end if


  end checkfileHandler
```

This provokes the run time dialog box pictured, which states that the property put message.contents is not available.

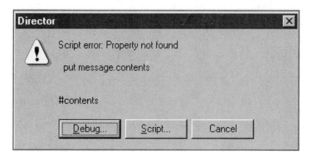

If we make a similar modification to server scripts, the result is slightly different. The following modification is again made to the on logon script:

```
on userLogOn (me, movie, group, user)
myfile=file("c:\welcome.txt").exists

  if myfile then
   myMessage=file("c:\welcome.txt").read
  Else
   mymessage="No Messages"
  end if

  user.sendmessag("system.script.Welcome", string(mymessage))

  end userLogOn
```

In this case, look at line 11: user.sendmessage has been changed to **user.sendmessag**. When the server loads the script at startup, no compilation errors occur, as this is perfectly legal in Lingo terms. But, when we run our connecting movie an error will occur since **sendmessag** is not a viable handler or property for the object user. An error is then displayed in the server output window to alert the operator to the error.

Errors of this type result in the termination of the operation being performed, but the script will remain available for other calls.

The remedy for this is the same as earlier – open the original script in a text editor, make the appropriate corrections, resave the file, and restart the server.

MultiuserServer

File   View   Status   Help

Shockwave Multiuser Server.

Reading the Multiuser.cfg file.

* RuntimeAttributes xtra has been loaded.

* DatabaseObjects xtra has been loaded.

* LingoVM xtra has been loaded.

\# Allocating connections.

\# Allocated 2000 connections.
\# 2001/11/29 11:56:31 Waiting for incoming connections.
+ 2001/11/29 11:57:23 Created movie Client_test.
+ 2001/11/29 11:57:23 Admin (192.168.1.29) connected to movie Client_test.
* Lingo Script Error: Handler not found in object
*   Error in Lingo code:
 user.sendmessag("system.script.Welcome", string(mymessage))

Logic errors

This last type of error is the most difficult to correct. Logic errors occur when scripts compile and run as expected, but return results that were not expected. Logic errors can also result in run time errors, which appear in the output windows.

Those who have used earlier versions Director without the integrated debugging features may use an old favorite debugging technique: the use of `put` commands, built into the server code at strategic locations. Using `put` in a server–side script displays the results in the server's output window much the same as it displays the results in the message window within Director.

I am sorry to have to break the news that this technique is flawed. Firstly, it only gives a picture of the specified variable's state at the point of execution where we insert the `put` statement. Secondly, it does not allow for the monitoring of threads, and so is not efficient when solving complex debugging problems.

Running the server – side script debugger

Rather than use the `put` commands, we need to turn to a more sophisticated solution. Fortunately, a debugger movie is included on the Director 8.5 installation CD-ROM. This includes all the features of the standard Director debugger, plus a few added twists specific to server–side scripts.

1. First, copy the debugger movie folder (located in the `Multiuser Examples` folder on the Director 8.5 Installation CD) to your Director 8.5 Xtras folder. This will allow us to launch the debugger movie as a Movie in a Window by selecting it from the Xtras menu. In order for the movie to function, it should be running at the same time as our client application (it could also be run from a projector or from Director on an other system).

2. Go to the Multiuser Server 3.0 folder and then into the Scripts subfolder. Make a backup copy of your `dispatcher.ls` file in a safe place – you'll need to copy this back when you're done debugging.

3. In the Multiuser Server > Scripts subfolder of the Debugger folder that you copied into the Director 8.5 Xtras folder, there's a copy of `dispatcher.ls` and `debugger.ls`. Copy both of those to the Multiuser Server > Scripts folder. These files allow the debugger movie to connect to the server and monitor the events taking place as the target script executes.

4. In the Multiuser Server 3.0 folder, open the `multiuser.cfg` file and uncomment (remove the # from) the following two lines. This allows the debugger scripts to be executed correctly by the Xtra:

```
# XtraConfigCommands for LingoVM
# XtraCommand = "DebugScript Debugger.ls"
```

5.   Now save the amended `multiuser.cfg` file, and launch the server.

6.   Launch Director 8.5 and open the Debugger movie in the Debugger > Client folder. Open the cast window and select the Serversidescripts cast library.

7.   Import the server-side script you would like to debug using the Import Link to External File option, and be sure to select the actual file in the Multiuser Server > Scripts folder that you plan to debug. Save the movie and close Director 8.5

8.   Open your client application in Director 8.5 and select Xtras > Client > Debugger from the menu. This will then open the Debugger movie in a Movie in a Window.

Xtras	Window	Help

Update Movies...

Filter Bitmap...
Auto Filter...
Auto Distort...

Client	▶	ServerSideScripts
WindXtra	▶	Debugger
NCI	▶	Director --

mui-gui ▶
DirectMedia ▶
ShapeShifter3D
3DPI
Convert WAV to SWA...
Import PowerPoint File...
Convert 3D Files...
Buddy API Help

When the window appears, click the Local IP button if the server is running on the local machine. If not, enter the server information in the Server text field at the top of the window. Enter any User Name or Password, as required.

In the middle left of the window, select the script you want to debug from the drop–down Script Name: field. The chosen script should appear in the scrolling field below. Click the Log In button to connect the debugger to the server.

Using the debugger

A breakpoint halts a script and allows you to execute the rest of the script one line at a time. With the debugger running, you can add breakpoints to your scripts much as you would with the standard Director debugger.

To insert a breakpoint on a line, simply click on the line in the script display window, and that line number will appear in the Line: window next to the red stop sign button. When you run your client movie and the scripts hit that line, execution will be halted. The Handler, Variables, and Thread Status boxes will display the relevant current information for these elements.

Director itself does not support multithreading, so the one major difference between this debugger and the one that is built into Director is the thread status feature.

Once a breakpoint inserted in a thread is called, the thread will stop responding to events sent to it by the server. This is not the case for breakpoints within other event driven handlers such as timeout scripts.

Clicking the green buttons allows execution of the thread to continue. From left to right, the first button steps through the scripts ignoring calls to outside handlers. The middle button steps through the scripts including outside handlers and the far right button resumes normal executions (Exit Stepmode).

To turn off the breakpoint, select the same line again and click the Breakpoint (red stop sign) button again. The display at the bottom will register that it was clicked on again, but it is in fact turned off.

If you want to track the value of a specific variable, enter the name of that variable in the field to the left hand side of Examine button, then click the button. The name of the variable will appear in the Variables window, followed by its value and finally its type. Types can be helpful in determining the relevance of a variable value to the rest of the program, and include `param` for parameter, `local` for a local variable, and `global` for a global variable.

The debugger movie described was authored in Director using commands that are specifically designed for complicated debugging tasks. These commands can also be used outside the debugger application within your program during the development cycle. This allows the potential for custom debugging operations, which can include:

- The customized insertions of breakpoints

- The determination of variable types and values

- The determination of the amount of RAM allocated for a given process

- The determination of currently running script objects, threads and handlers

- The determination of the order and position of the currently running script objects, threads and handlers within the structure of the compiled script

Conclusion

Server–side scripting may seem to be a somewhat daunting proposition, as its centralized nature and distance from the core Director application lead to a widely different development experience. But remember, server–side scripting offers many powerful features that will allow for faster development of more complex and interesting multiuser applications. The results will be well worth the effort.

Chapter 1

Chapter 2

Chapter 3

Chapter 4

Chapter 5

Chapter 6

Chapter 7

Chapter 8

Chapter 9

Chapter 10

Chapter 11

Chapter 12

Chapter 13

Chapter 14

Chapter 15

Chapter 12

Creating avatars

In this chapter, we'll look at extending the sort of chat programs you've seen so far by adding some form of visual representation to our users. Any type of visual representation of a user is known as an **avatar**. In this case, our avatars are going to use some facial gestures, but an avatar can be anything up to and including a complete physical representation of a user.

We'll give our users the chance to assign some visual characteristics to their online personae, and convey emotional overtones alongside their text messages by manipulating the characteristics they've chosen. OK, we're going to let our users pull faces at each other.

We'll start by discussing the motivation behind this sort of system, and present the brief for our project. Then we'll look at the detail of how we might design a 'face design' module, applying the idea to a variety of faces. After that, it's time to get creating in Director.

Gestures

So, why should we want to add all the extra complication of showing faces in our chat applications – after all, don't smileys do the job? Well, to a certain extent they do. Text-based communication is enhanced by the huge variety of possible shapes one can construct from ASCII text. Consider the difference between these two statements:

Justy: Oh yeah, it was a great movie!!

Justy: Oh yeah, it was a great movie!! :oP

There's obviously a measure of sarcasm in the second statement. The use of 'emoticons' adds an extra dimension, but they are what you could call public domain gestures. In other words, they convey the same meaning irrespective of who uses them. Wouldn't it be great to be able to project your personality?

So, what sorts of gestures can we show in a Director application? Perhaps we could take photos of ourselves in various gestures and use those? There are two difficulties with this approach: firstly, not everyone has access to a digital camera. Secondly, what if you suddenly discover that you want to convey an expression that you didn't take a photo of?

It's far better to construct a facial gesture based on **components**. We'll define a 'face schema' to describe various types of eyebrows, eyes, and mouths, and then allow the user to throw together a suitable combination for themselves. If you take a look at the Director file for this chapter in the download, you'll see that we've provided 150 different types of head to choose from.

If we multiply this by the number of eyebrows, eyes, and mouths available, then we'll get the total possible faces. So 150 x 12 x 12 x 12 = 259,200. Try taking that many photos! Of course, as a Director developer, you're perfectly capable of defining your own components, which opens up the possibility for even more expressions.

The FaceChat application

Storyboarding an idea is a great way to bring it into reality without having to go through the process of actually building it. Here are a series of shots depicting the fairly simple flow through the program. We start with the Welcome screen, which should always give the user at least a rough idea of what's in store for them:

The user must now choose a head and hairstyle for their avatar and connect to the server. This could be a fixed IP address for some applications, but for our purposes, it's convenient to be able to specify that ourselves. On a more trivial note, this screen will randomly show gestures, via a simple behavior attached to each facial component. Here's the Choose Face screen:

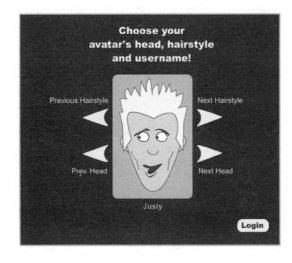

Then it's login time! Pity there's nobody else there yet. Justy shows his disappointment by making a face. In our simple example, there is only one group: 'Room Of Faces', and the user joins it by default. The greeting that the user receives is that of a standard chat room – we see this on the Face Chat screen:

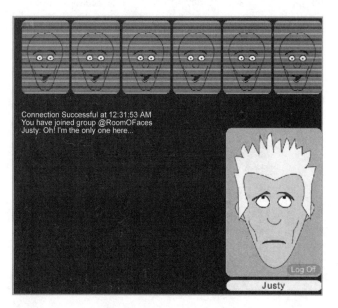

The challenge that now faces us is how users can change their expressions easily. We can't have a mess of controls there – it would quickly get in the way – so our interface must be simplicity itself. My solution to this is to allow the user to click the face component they wish to change, and move their mouse left or right to scroll through a list of possible facial components.

In case the features are too small to making clicking on them easy, we'll add three sets of buttons to do the job. When the user rolls their mouse over the avatar, they see a set of gesture-controlling arrows:

Clicking on these arrows changes the appropriate facial component. For example, clicking one of the white arrows changes the 'eyes' component.

Eventually, some pals arrive. Each has their own avatar, lovingly hand picked from the 150 available. Whenever any of these participants send some text, their gesture is sent along with it.

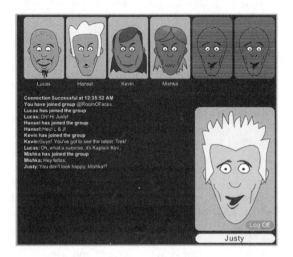

If at any time the connection to the server is interrupted, we see the Chattus Interruptus screen, shown below.

Design and development

The project presented in this chapter is not perfect – we've concentrated on showing you how to set up avatars, and there are improvements that could be made. We'll be taking a look at some of these at the end of the chapter.

You'll notice the graphics for FaceChat are fairly large in terms of file size. If this was going to function as a downloadable chat program, then these would need to be reduced for a final product either by optimizing the graphics, reducing the number of options, or by avoiding loading them in all at once. We'll look at that last solution at the end of the chapter.

The chat client we'll use is based largely on the material we covered back in **chapter 10**, and there's nothing essentially new to what we're doing. Its responsibilities are to:

- Log the user in to the server, providing their name and selected head.

- Log the user out of the server, providing their name.

- Notify the server of any text sent by the client.

- Notify the server of any gesture change sent by the client.

Likewise, the server-side code we're going to use will basically listen for connections and messages from clients. With the help of a few custom handlers, it will keep track of the various client avatars, and notify the connected clients of:

- Newly connected clients (providing their name and selected head).

- Newly disconnected clients (providing their name).

- Any chat text sent by a particular client.

- Any gestures sent by a particular client.

One very important consideration here is how we can make our gesture handling code **reusable**. Further down the track, we may wish to build this into some other application, and it could be very difficult to untangle and reapply our code unless it's written in a way that anticipates this requirement. For that reason, we're going to build all this code in a self-contained module – like the Connection module we've used in earlier chapters, it will effectively operate as a standalone application.

What needs to go into a face-handling module?

Let's start thinking about how we define the possible faces we can 'manufacture'. We could take a very flexible approach (think of 3-eyed aliens) but for simplicity's sake let's keep things relatively human, and say that a face is composed of:

- A basic head with nose and hair

- Two eyes

- Two eyebrows

- A mouth

We shall restrict the complexity of these elements so that we have a predefined member for crossed eyes, another for shifty eyes, and so on. To make a face, the user just needs to select the appropriate combination of elements and hit Send.

What we now require is a module that can accept parameters for these variables, and use them to display the correct face. We also need to consider the fact that we'll be dealing with multiple faces, and the system we're going to build can cope with up to six other connected users' faces.

As for the face that belongs to a particular user, we need the idea of a selection within a selection – that is, the user chooses what type of face they want for their avatar, and then in the context of a session, chooses what gestures that face will make.

Organizing FaceChat

Let's look in turn at each of our FaceChat client's cast libraries:

- Internal holds the basic graphics from which we'll build our client interface:

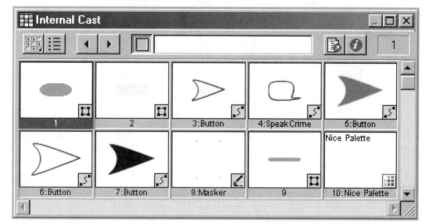

- Scripts contains all our movie scripts, parent scripts, behaviors, and essentially just about anything that has any code attached to it:

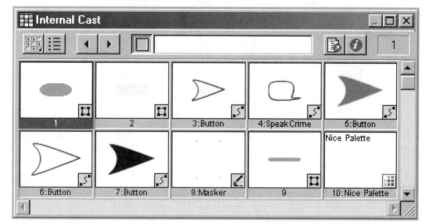

Don't worry if you can't read all the details on the screenshot – we'll be spending a fair bit of time going through all of these very shortly.

◼ Text defines all the text and field members we'll need:

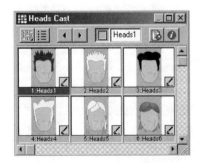

◼ Heads, Eyes, Eyebrows, and Mouths casts define graphic components for large face images, while sHeads, sEyes, sEyeBrows, and sMouths contain smaller copies of these components:

● Faces defines two default faces – one (User Head) will be used as the default face whilst picking an avatar, while the other (NoFace) will indicate an unoccupied space in the 'chat room':

Exploring the Scripts cast

As usual, the meat of our client application can be found in the Scripts cast, and the four movie scripts that sit in positions one through four should be particularly familiar to you. They're essentially the same scripts that we used in **Chapter 10**:

● main_scripts – for general housekeeping

● group_scripts – for group management

● user_scripts – for user management

● movie_scripts – for connection management

This cast also contains two parent scripts – Comm Module and Face Module – the former of which is largely based on Chapter 10's Connection module, with just a little additional server-side functionality. By contrast, Face Module will need to be implemented from the ground up. As far as possible, we'll use these modules to encapsulate all the functionality we need for multiuser communication and avatar management respectively.

Over the next few pages, we'll run quickly through the changes required to update our Chapter 10 scripts for use in the FaceChat application. We'll then move on to look at the Face Module and the server-side scripts that we'll use to make the whole thing dance.

Updating the main_scripts movie script

This movie script takes care of initializing our application and provides a variety of public handlers for use by buttons and the like. We'll use it to define handlers for interfacing with the Face Module, as well as a handful more that hook it up to the Comm Module.

Initialization
We start by initializing the variables and modules:

```
global gFaceMod
global gCommMod

on startMovie
  clearglobals
end
```

When the user clicks the face on the Welcome screen, an attached behavior calls FaceChat_Init, which creates our two modules and sends the user on to the Choose Face screen:

```
- Master init for the FACECHAT program.
on FaceChat_Init
  set gFaceMod = new(script"Face Module")
  gFaceMod.Init()
  set gCommMod = new(script"Comm Module")
  go "Choose Face"
end
```

Having chosen a face and username, the user clicks Login; this results in a call to FaceChat_Login, which takes them to the Face Chat screen:

```
on FaceChat_Login
  - Log the User in
  set theResult = gCommMod.Init(member("User Name").text)
  if theResult = #ok then go "Face Chat"
end
```

Public face handlers
The next few handlers are public wrappers for functions that we're going to define in the Face module. They effectively 'wrap up' specific method calls on the gFaceMod object as simple event handlers, and even throw in a little error handling for safety's sake. If we take a quick look at one of them, you should get the general idea:

```
on SelectNextHead
  if voidP(gFaceMod) then exit
  gFaceMod.SelectNextHd()
end
```

The first few (SelectNextHead, SelectPrevHead, FaceMod_SelectNextHair, FaceMod_SelectPrevHair) are the handlers we'll wire up to our Choose Face arrows, enabling us to access the gFaceMod object methods – SelectNextHd, SelectPrevHd, SelectPrevHr, SelectPrevHr – with which to scroll through the various heads and hairstyles that are available.

In each case, if gFaceMod doesn't exist, we exit right away and do nothing. This effectively provides a 'safety wrapper' around each of these functions, serving as an intermediary between the object and anything that needs to interact with it – the interface, for example.

Next, we define public handlers for adding (FaceMod_AddUser) and deleting (FaceMod_DelUser) users from the list of those who are currently logged on, as well as updating this list (FaceMod_UpdateUsers). The first two take a similar form to our previous code:

```
on FaceMod_AddUser pUserSpec
  if voidP(gFaceMod) then exit
  gFaceMod.AddUser(pUserSpec)
end
on FaceMod_DelUser pUser
  if voidP(gFaceMod) then exit
  gFaceMod.DelUser(pUser)
end
```

The UpdateUsers code is the only handler of any complexity, looping through each of the entries in the provided list rUserList and adding all but our own avatar to the list. As usual, we exit quickly if the gFaceMod doesn't exist:

```
on FaceMod_UpdateUsers rUserList
  if voidP(gFaceMod) then exit
  repeat with i = 1 to count(rUserList)
    set theUser = getPropAt(rUserList,i)
    set theHead = getAProp(rUserList,theUser)
    — No need to process *this* user
    if theUser <> gCommMod.pUserID then
      gFaceMod.AddUser([#name:theUser,#head:theHead])
    end if
  end repeat
end
```

We define FaceMod_MyHead, FaceMod_MyFace, and FaceMod_ConnectedUsers to let us retrieve various properties from the gFaceMod object:

```
on FaceMod_MyHead
  if voidP(gFaceMod) then
    return #noFaceMod
  else
    return gFaceMod.MyHead()
  end if
end
```

continues overleaf

```
on FaceMod_MyFace
  if voidP(gFaceMod) then
    return #noFaceMod
  else
    return gFaceMod.MyFace()
  end if
end

on FaceMod_ConnectedUsers
  if voidP(gFaceMod) then
    return #noFaceMod
  else
    return gFaceMod.pConnectedUsers
  end if
end
```

The next few handlers all deal with gesture changes. Here's the first, which modifies our current 'eye' selection to the previous one in the list:

```
on FaceMod_PrevEye
  if voidP(gFaceMod) then exit
  gFaceMod.ChangeUserFeature(1,-1)
end
```

For our purposes, eyes are feature 1, brows are feature 2, and mouth feature 3. Using the appropriate value in our call to ChangeUserFeature(), we specify which feature we'd like to modify and what step to apply to the list entry we're using. In this case, we call ChangeUserFeature(1,-1), which takes our eye selection one step back in the list. Subsequent handlers follow a similar pattern:

Handler name	Object method call
FaceMod_PrevEye	gFaceMod ChangeUserFeature(1, -1)
FaceMod_NextEye	gFaceMod.ChangeUserFeature(1, 1)
FaceMod_PrevBrow	gFaceMod.ChangeUserFeature(2, -1)
FaceMod_NextBrow	gFaceMod.ChangeUserFeature(2, 1)
FaceMod_PrevMouth	gFaceMod.ChangeUserFeature(3, -1)
FaceMod_NextMouth	gFaceMod.ChangeUserFeature(3, 1)

Public communication handlers

Before we finish with our main Movie Script, we need to provide some handlers for use with our messaging system. This first pair of handlers deals with sending gestures with a call to the SendGesture method on gCommMod. It also deals with sending chat text with a call to our old friend sendmessage, which is defined in the movie script user_scripts as usual:

```
on FaceMod_SendGesture
  if voidP(gFaceMod) then exit
  gCommMod.SendGesture()
end
```

```
on SendChatText
  sendmessage()
end
```

The equally familiar `defaultmessageHandler` is used to catch any messages from the server:

```
on defaultmessageHandler
  mymessage=gCommMod.pConnect.getnetmessage()
  if mymessage.errorcode<>0 then
    put "The message contained an error " & \
        gCommMod.pConnect.getNetErrorString(mymessage.errorcode)
  end if
end defaultmessageHandler
```

Updating the group_scripts movie script

Apart from updating old references to `gMyConnection`, there isn't much we need to tweak in this script. We begin by globalizing the usual suspects:

global gCommMod, gFaceMod, gGroupline
....

The only other changes we need to make are within the `groupJoinHandler` handler. When someone joins a group, it's either us (in which case we request a list of user names from the server) or someone else (in which case we extract their details from the message); and we then update our local user list accordingly.

```
on groupJoinHandler me, message
  if message.senderID="system.group.join" then
    —the message is the response to our join request
    ....
  else
    —the message is a notification that someone joined a group
    mygroup=gCommMod.getmyGroup()
    senderID = message.senderID
    senderGroup=value(message.content).mygroup

    — FACECHAT: Update the Small Face displays
    if senderID=gCommMod.pUserID then
      — We joined the group, so check for others in that group
      myError=gCommMod.pConnect.sendNetMessage("@allusers", \
                                        "GetUserNames", "", 1)
      if myError<>0 then
        put gCommMod.pConnect.getNetErrorString(myError)
      end if
    else
      set theUser = getAProp(message,#senderID)
      set theContent = getAProp(message,#content)
      set theHead = getAProp(theContent,#myHead)
      put "Adding a user:" && [#name:theUser,#head:theHead]
      FaceMod_AddUser [#name:theUser,#head:theHead]
```
continues overleaf

347

```
      — gFaceMod.SendGestureHandler([#name:senderID, \
                            #head:43,#gesture:[2,6,3]])
    end if
    ....  end if

  — if the sender joined our group, or if we are the \
      joining person then
  — update our interface to reflect the changes
    ....
    gCommMod.getgroups()
end groupJoinHandler
....
```

Updating the user_scripts movie script

This script doesn't need much modification at all. Since I've used a few slightly different naming conventions, you need to replace the global declaration by substituting gCommMod for gMyConnection, and make sure the member names you use match up to those on the stage:

```
global gCommMod, gFaceMod

on getUsersHandler me, Message
  ....
end getUsersHandler

on updateUserDisplay
  mylist=gCommMod.getUserList()
  member("Current Users").text=""
  repeat with counter=1 to count(myList)
    member("Current Users").line[counter]=getat(mylist, counter)
  end repeat
end updateUserDisplay

on sendmessage
  myMessage=member("User Chat").text
  gCommMod.sendNewMessage(myMessage)
  member("User Chat").text=""
end sendmessage
```

As well as making these superficial changes, we need to add a little extra functionality to the textMsgHandler handler. If our chat text starts to overflow beyond 16 lines, we chop off the topmost one:

```
on textMsgHandler me, message
  myDisplayLine=message.senderID &": "&message.content

  —put the message content in a new member after member 3
  member("Chat Text").rtf=member("Chat \
   Text").rtf&myDisplayLine&return
  lastline=(member("Chat Text").line.count)
```

```
    lineWordnum=string(mydisplayline).word.count

member("Chat Text").line[lastline].word[1].fontstyle=[#bold]
member("Chat Text").line[lastline].word[1].forecolor=8
member("Chat Text").line[lastline].word[2..linewordnum]\
                                    .fontstyle=[#plain]
member("Chat Text").line[lastline].word[2..linewordnum]\
                                    .forecolor=255
— FACECHAT: Check for text overflow
if lastline > 16 then
  — remove the top line
  set theText = member("Chat Text").text
  delete line 1 of theText
  set member("Chat Text").text = theText
end if

updatestage
—if message contains an error, display it in message window
if message.errorcode<>0 then
  put "The message contained an error"
  put gCommMod.pConnect.getNetErrorString(message.errorcode)
end if
end textMsgHandler
```

Updating the movie_scripts movie script

For this application, we're going to wrap all our connection functionality into the Comm Module, so we don't actually need the logon and logoff handlers previously defined in this script. Otherwise, the changes we need to make are once again fairly superficial.

```
global gCommMod
....
on connectionSuccess me, message
  if message.errorcode=0 then
    member("Chat Text").text=""
    member("Chat Text").text="Connection Successful at " \
                                    & the long time&return
    member("Chat Text").line[1].fontstyle=[#bold]
    joingroup "RoomOFaces"
    gCommMod.getgroups()
  else
    —if message contains an error, display it in message window
    alert "An Error Occured: " & \
          gCommMod.pConnect.getNetErrorString(message.errorcode)
    gCommMod.endcallbacks()
    gCommMod.endconnection()
    go to frame "Chattus Interruptus"
  end if
end connectionSuccess
```

continues overleaf

```
on connectionFailure me, message
  alert "An Error Occured: " &
gCommMod.pConnect.getNetErrorString(message.errorcode)
  gCommMod.endcallbacks()
  gCommMod.endconnection()
  go to frame "Chattus Interruptus"
end connectionFailure
```

Coding the Communications module

In case you hadn't seen this coming, our system should ultimately operate as follows:

1. The user alters their face to produce the desired gesture (handled by the Face Module)

2. At some point, either when chat text is sent, or at their own initiation, the user sends the gesture to all other connected users (handled by the Comm Module)

3. The server receives requests from the Comm Module, and relays messages to any other FaceChat clients

Let's take a careful look at how we need to upgrade our earlier Connection module to handle these requirements. Most of the initial changes we need to make here should be fairly self-explanatory. We add a global declaration for our instance gFaceMod of the Face Module, and tweak the initialization settings for the Comm Module properties so that pMovieID reflects our current application. pServerIP is defined in terms of the user-specified text field "Server IP":

```
- Communications module
global gFaceMod
....
on initialize(me)
  ....
  me.pGroup=empty - No groups; same reason
  me.pMovieID="FaceChat" - That's us
  me.pUserlist=[] - no users yet, but will be stored as linear list
  me.pGrouplist=[] - no groups yet, but will be stored as linear list
  me.pServerIP=member("Server IP").text - login to the specified \
    machine
  me.pPort=1626 - using the standard port
  ....
end initialize
```

We now add a brand new function Init, which verifies the user name we entered, attempts to connect to the server with a call to makeConnection, and prepares the 'User Chat' text interface for us:

```
on Init(me,pUser)
  -Check the username for validity
  if the number of words in pUser > 1 then
```

```
            alert "Sorry, I require a single word user name!"
            return #invalidLogin
            exit
        end if
        set pUserID = pUser
        set the text of member "User Name noedit" = pUser
        makeConnection(me, pUser, "", 10)
        member("User Chat").text="Type your text here!"
        return #ok
    end Init
```

The next changes occur when we initialize our callbacks. We need to define a few more – our three new callback handlers (GetUserNames, RegisterHead, and send_gesture) will be used to keep our list of other users bang up to date, and make sure we get to see any gestures they throw our way...

```
        on initcallbacks(me)
            if not me.pconnect=0 then
                ....
                me.pconnect.setNetMessageHandler(#getGroupsHandler, \
                    script "group_scripts", "", "system.movie.getgroups", 1)
                — NEW FACECHAT HANDLERS
                me.pConnect.setNetMessageHandler(#mGetUserNames_Response, \
                                                me, "GetUserNames", EMPTY, 1)
                me.pConnect.setNetMessageHandler(#mRegisterHead_Response, \
                                                me, "RegisterHead", EMPTY, 1)
                — execute when someone sends a gesture
                me.pconnect.setNetMessageHandler(#SendGestureHandler, \
                                                me, "send_gesture", "", 1)
            end if
        end initcallbacks
```

It goes without saying that we also need to add a few lines within the endcallbacks handler, just to tidy things up once we're finished:

```
        on endcallbacks(me)
            — zero all initialized message callbacks as part of cleanup
            if not me.pconnect=0 then
                ....
                me.pconnect.setNetMessageHandler(0, script "group_scripts", \
                                                "", "system.movie.getgroups", 1)
                — END FACECHAT CALLBACKS
                me.pconnect.setNetMessageHandler(0, me, "GetUserNames")
                me.pconnect.setNetMessageHandler(0, me, "RegisterHead")
                me.pconnect.setNetMessageHandler(0, script "Face Module", \
                                                "send_gesture", "", 1)
            end if
        end endcallbacks
```

On successfully establishing a connection, we want to let the server know what head we're using, so one of the first things we do is make a call to mRegisterHead:

```
— ===============
on makeConnection(me, myID, myPass)
  — send the connectToNetServer message using our object
  — properties and the username/password collected from the
interface
  myerror=me.pConnect.connectToNetServer(me.pServerIP, me.pPort, \
              [#userID:myID, #password:myPass,
#movieID:me.pMovieID])

  — if we connect sucessfully then set up our ID variables
  if not myError then
    me.pUserID=myID
    me.pPassword=myPass
    — Broadcast the FACECHAT head
    me.mRegisterHead()
    return myError
  else  — otherwise alert that an error occured
    ....
  end if
end makeconnection
....
on sendNewMessage(me, message)
  ...
end sendNewMessage
```

After a whole bunch of familiar management functions, we get to the end of the original Connection module, where we need to add some more new functions to complete the new Comm Module module.

The first few deal with maintaining a list of current users on the server. mGetUserNames simply messages the server with the subject "GetUserNames" (we'll program a response to this that lists all connected users in a moment).

```
on mGetUserNames(me)
  me.pConnect.sendNetMessage([#recipients:"system.script", \
                                #subject:"GetUserNames"])
end
```

The next handler deals with the response we just mentioned. If we weren't already registered on the server as a current user, it should return a non-zero error code. This prompts us to register our head on the server:

```
on mGetUserNames_Response(me,vMsg)
  if vMsg.errorCode <> 0 then me.mRegisterHead()
end
```

Here's how we register a head – the public handler FaceMod_MyHead() exposes the relevant property of the gFaceMod object, which we embed in the body of a new "RegisterHead" message to the server:

```
on mRegisterHead(me)
  - Send a message to the server, registering our head.
  set theHead = FaceMod_MyHead()
  me.pConnect.sendNetMessage([#recipients:"system.script", \
                              #subject:"RegisterHead",      \
                              #content:theHead])
```

While we're at it, we call SendGesture to ensure that the correct facial gesture is assigned:

```
  - Also, let the Server know our current gesture
  SendGesture(me)
end
```

If someone else registers a head, the server will message us with the information, and the callback handler mRegisterHead_Response will pick up the pieces for us, updating the gFaceMod object via the public handler FaceMod_UpdateUsers:

```
on mRegisterHead_Response(me,vMsg)
  - Receive message from server, notifying us of another user's head
  set theHeads = getAProp(vMsg,#content)
  FaceMod_UpdateUsers(theHeads)
end
```

This simply messages the server with a user name and gesture, under the subject send_gesture:

```
on SendGesture(me)
  - Broadcast our Gesture
  myError=pConnect.sendNetMessage(pGroup, "send_gesture", \
              [#name:pUserID,#gesture:the pUserFace of gFaceMod])
  if myError<>0 then
    put pConnect.getNetErrorString(myError)
  end if
end
```

On receiving a send_gesture message from the server, the callback handler SendGestureHandler swings into action. It pulls out details of the gesture from the message body, and then loops through the list of users stored in gFaceMod, updating facial features as required:

```
on SendGestureHandler(me, message)
  set theContent = getAProp(message,#content)
  - Check for Gestures from another User
  set theName = getAProp(theContent, #name)
  if theName <> pUserID then
    - Process the external gesture
```

continues overleaf

```
            set theUsers = FaceMod_ConnectedUsers()
            set theNum=-1
            repeat with i = 1 to count(theUsers)
              set theUser = getAt(theUsers,i)
              if getAProp(theUser,#name) = theName then
                set theNum = i
                exit repeat
              end if
            end repeat

            — Retrieve the gesture
            set theGesture = getAProp(theContent, #gesture)

            — iterate through small eyes, eyebrows, and mouths.
            repeat with g = 1 to 3
              set theFeatureName =
  getAt(["sEyes","sEyeBrows","sMouths"],g)
              set the member of sprite 20 + 5*(theNum-1) + g = \
                    member getAt(theGesture,g) of castLib
  theFeatureName
            end repeat
          else
            — Ignore any gesture messages from ourselves
          end if
        end
```

And with that, the client-side connection logic is just about done. We now have a framework in place with which to send facial gesture information to and fro alongside our text messages. We're just lacking the means to define those gestures and actually view them! No problem: it's time to build ourselves a Face Module.

Coding the Face Module

The role of the Face Module is to manage the avatars that are presented on screen – both the user's avatar, and any connected users' avatars.

This module is where just about all our face-related action occurs, and it provides handlers that allow us to select the avatar's head and gestures. It also keeps track of other users' faces by providing methods to allow the addition and subtraction of those users.

As we've established, each avatar is composed of a single head, a pair of eyebrows, a pair of eyes, and a mouth. The head will always remain fixed, although the avatar may be instructed to change its facial elements. We therefore need the following general properties:

```
        property pNumHeads
        property pNumHairTypes

        property pNumEyes
        property pNumBrows
        property pNumMouths
```

We also need properties for the main user's avatar:

```
property pUserHair
property pUserHead
property pUserFace
```

As well as one to refer to other connected users:

```
property pConnectedUsers
```

We declare the gCommMod as a global variable (so that we can use it later on) and add a standard instantiation handler, which simply passes the buck of initialization onto the Init function:

```
global gCommMod

on new(me)
  me.Init()
  return me
end
```

Initialize variables
Here, we specify the number of heads and hair types from which users can choose:

```
on Init(me)
  set pNumHeads = the number of members of castLib "Heads"
  set pNumHairTypes = 10
```

The media in this Director file's Heads and sHeads (small heads) cast libraries are created in such a way that we in essence have two dimensions to iterate through: hair and heads.

First, count the facial media. Doing it this way ensures it's OK to add further gesture components.

```
set pNumEyes = the number of members of castLib "Eyes"
set pNumBrows = the number of members of castLib "EyeBrows"
set pNumMouths = the number of members of castLib "Mouths"
```

Here, `pUserHead` is a number from 1 to `pNumHeads`, which indexes the user's selected head. The following snapshot of the 'Heads' cast library illustrates the fact that each block of ten consecutive heads has the same face shape, whereas every tenth head has the same hairstyle:

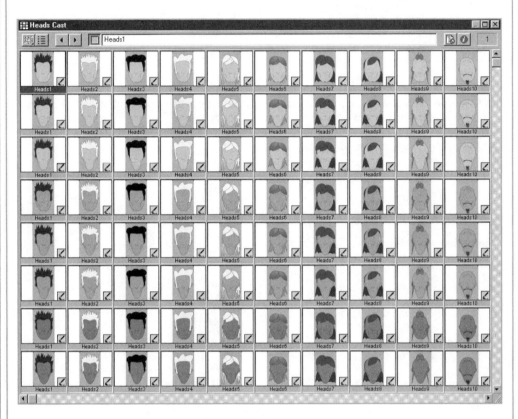

So, if we want to select the next head type and keep the same hair type, we just need to increment `pUserHead` by 10. We also increment `pUserHair`.

```
set pUserHead = 1
set pUserHair = 1
```

This tiny little list is the storehouse of the user's chosen gesture that is displayed on their screen.

```
set pUserFace = [1,1,1]
```

This list is managed so that it keeps track of any other users who have connected to this machine. It is a linear list of proplists to allow us to keep track of the position that a particular user occupies.

```
set pConnectedUsers = []
```

Then, we initialize our various display fields and prep the connected users list:

```
repeat with f = 1 to 6
  setAt pConnectedUsers, f, []
  set theMember = "User#" & string(f)
  set the text of member theMember =" "
end repeat

set the text of member "Chat Text" = " "
set the picture of member "User Head" = the picture of \
                                    member pUserHead of
castLib "Heads"

end
```

Public interface methods

These are public interface methods designed to improve the level of encapsulation of this script. In other words, we 'ask' the object to do something for us (such as reporting the value of its variables) instead of just peeking inside and helping ourselves!

```
on MyHead(me)
   return pUserHead
end

on MyFace(me)
   return pUserFace
end
```

User Head and Face Selection Handlers

The following handler is called whenever there is a need to display the main user's head:

```
on DrawHead(me)
   set the picture of member "User Head" = the picture of member \
                                    pUserHead of
castLib "Heads"
end
```

Here are the handlers we called in the main section for clicking through the various hair and heads for use:

```
on SelectNextHr(me)
  set pUserHead = pUserHead + 1
  set pUserHair = pUserHair + 1

  if pUserHair > pNumHairTypes then
    set pUserHair = 1
    set pUserHead = pUserHead - pNumHairTypes
  end if
```

continues overleaf

```
      if pUserHead < 1 then
         set pUserHead = pNumHeads + pUserHead
      end if

      DrawHead(me)
   end

   on SelectPrevHr(me)
      set pUserHead = pUserHead - 1
      set pUserHair = pUserHair - 1
      if pUserHair < 1 then
         set pUserHair = pNumHairTypes
         set  pUserHead = pUserHead + pNumHairTypes
      end if

      if pUserHead > pNumHeads then
         set pUserHead = pNumHeads - pUserHead
      end if

      DrawHead(me)
   end

   on SelectNextHd(me)
      set pUserHead
      if pUserHead > pNumHeads then
         set pUserHead = pUserHead - pNumHeads
      end if

      DrawHead(me)
   end

   on SelectPrevHd(me)
      set pUserHead = pUserHead - pNumHairTypes
      if pUserHead < 1 then
         set pUserHead = pNumHeads + pUserHead
      end if

      DrawHead(me)
   end
```

User features

In order for this handler to work equally well for all gesture components, we simply provide a list here:

```
   on ChangeUserFeature(me, pFeature, pDir)
      set theFeatureName =
   getAt(["Eyes","EyeBrows","Mouths"],pFeature)
```

... grab the value of the feature from the face list:

```
set theCurrentFeature = getAt(pUserFace, pFeature)
```

... change the feature:

```
set theCurrentFeature = theCurrentFeature + pDir
```

... wrap around to the top if it's less than one:

```
if theCurrentFeature < 1 then
    set theCurrentFeature = the number of members of castLib
theFeatureName
    end if
```

... send it back to the beginning if it's greater than the maximum:

```
if theCurrentFeature > the number of members of castLib
theFeatureName then
    set theCurrentFeature = 1
    end if
```

... and update the list of features:

```
setAt pUserFace, pFeature, theCurrentFeature
set the member of sprite (pFeature+2) = member
theCurrentFeature of castLib theFeatureName

end
```

Connected users display

This part deals with the display of the other users' faces. The first handler adds users. A `UserSpec` is all the information required to display the user's head and name. The first thing we do here is pick up the name and head specifications:

```
on AddUser(me, rUserSpec)
    set theName = getAProp(rUserSpec,#name)
    set theHead = getAProp(rUserSpec,#head)
```

Find a free spot in the slots allocated to others:

```
set theFreeSpot = -1
repeat with i = 1 to count(pConnectedUsers)
    set theUser = getAt(pConnectedUsers,i)
```

And check for the possibility of a duplicate user name:

```
if theUser = [] then
    set theFreeSpot = i
```

continues overleaf

```
            exit repeat
        else
          if theUser = rUserSpec then
            put ("Duplicate User" && theUser)
            exit
          end if
        end if
      end repeat
```

If all's clear, we can exit this bit:

```
      if theFreeSpot = -1 then
        — Gracefully exit  (well, silently, anyway!)
        exit
      end if
```

Then add the user to our list of connected users in its spot:

```
      setAt pConnectedUsers, theFreeSpot, rUserSpec
```

Display the appropriate name:

```
      set theTextDisplay = "User#" & string(theFreeSpot)
      set the text of member theTextDisplay = string(theName)
```

Show their head. Note that we've hardwired a sprite number here (in terms of writing flexible code, this isn't exactly great practice, but it isn't the end of the world):

```
      set s = 20 + 5 * (theFreeSpot-1)
      set the member of sprite s = member theHead of castLib "sHeads"
    end
```

We also need to remove departing friends. This begins by finding the entry:

```
    on DelUser(me, rUserName)
      set theEntry = -1
      repeat with i = 1 to count(pConnectedUsers)
        set theUser = getAt(pConnectedUsers,i)
        if getAProp(theUser,#name) = rUserName then
          set theEntry = i
          exit repeat
        end if
      end repeat
```

If that name doesn't exist, we need to generate a runtime alert:

```
      if theEntry = -1 then
        —alert "Development error- no such user name" && rUserName
        exit
      end if
```

Otherwise we can remove the appropriate name:

```
set theTextDisplay = "User#" & string(theEntry)
set the text of member theTextDisplay = " "
```

And show a blank head:

```
set s = 20 + 5 * (theEntry-1)
set the member of sprite s = member "NoFace"
— FInally, remove the entry from pConnectedUsers
setAt pConnectedUsers, theEntry, []
end
```

Programming the server

As we learned in the last chapter, it's often sensible to offload certain tasks onto the server. Here, we'll use server-side scripts to implement:

- Group management functions

- Functions for sending out and responding to messages that relay program state between users

- Any other tasks that are common to all users and can therefore be centrally located

The server-side code for this particular project isn't too complicated. We're going to define just one new script called FaceChat.ls, in which we'll define a grand total of six properties, three standard handlers and eight custom handlers.

- The properties pMovie, pUserNames, pHeadList, pFaceList, pChatLog, and pChatLogLength will be used to store lists of the names, heads, and faces associated with each of the users who are currently connected, as well as storing recent chat messages, and a reference to the movie itself.

- The standard handler movieCreate is called when the first user of the movie logs onto the server. We use this to call mInitRoom and mInitChat, which will initialize all the properties we defined.

- userLogOn is called whenever a user logs on to the movie, and we'll use this to call mAddUser, which adds the specified user to our list of names. Along with mDeleteUser, these handlers help the server maintain an up-to-date list of all the users who are currently logged onto the movie.

- incomingMessage is called when a message is sent to the server, and we'll use it to route incoming messages to one of four custom handlers (mGetUserNames, mRegisterHead, mChat, and mGetChatLog) according to its subject.

Let's go through the code we need to put into our FaceChat.ls file.

Creating the FaceChat server script

We start by declaring all the properties we're going to need:

```
property pMovie

property pUserNames
property pHeadList
property pFaceList

property pChatLog
property pChatLogLength
```

Then add some handlers to deal with initializing a new movie:

```
on movieCreate(me, movie, group, user, fullMsg)
  — Save the movie reference
  me.pMovie = movie
  — Initialize the ROOM, and CHAT properties.
  me.mInitRoom()
  me.mInitChat()
end movieCreate

on mInitRoom(me)
  me.pUserNames = []
  me.pHeadList = [:]
  me.pFaceList = [:]
end mInitRoom

on mInitChat(me)
  me.pChatLog = []
  me.pChatLogLength = 10
end mInitChat
```

When a user logs onto the movie, we add their name to its pUserNames property, and call sendmessage to tell everyone about it:

```
on userLogOn(me, movie, group, user, fullMsg)
  me.mAddUser(movie, group, user, fullMsg)
end userLogOn

on mAddUser( me, movie, group, user, fullMsg )
  — Add the user to our user names list.
  (me.pUserNames).add(user.name)
  — Tell everyone that this new user joined
  movie.sendMessage(me.pUserNames, "AddUser", user.name)
end mAddUser
```

```
on mDeleteUser( me, movie, group, user, fullMsg )
   - Delete the user from our user names list.
   (me.pUserNames).deleteOne( user.name )
   - Tell everyone that this user left.
   movie.sendMessage( me.pUserNames, "DeleteUser", user.name )
end mDeleteUser
```

On receiving a message from one of the clients, we check to see what the subject is, and take an appropriate course of action:

```
on incomingMessage(me, movie, group, user, fullMsg)
   case fullMsg.subject of
      "GetUserNames": me.mGetUserNames( movie, group, user, fullMsg )
      "RegisterHead": setAProp me.pHeadList, user.name, fullMsg.content
                         me.mRegisterHead( movie, group, user, fullMsg)
      "Chat":          me.mChat( movie, group, user, fullMsg )
      "GetChatLog":    me.mGetChatLog( movie, group, user, fullMsg )
   end case
end incomingMessage
```

If the subject reads GetUserNames, we send back a list of user names (as held in the pUserNames property):

```
on mGetUserNames( me, movie, group, user, fullMsg )
   user.sendMessage( fullMsg.subject, me.pUserNames )
end mGetUserNames
```

If the subject reads Register Head, we use set AProp to modify (or create) an entry in the pHeadList list, and call the mRegisterHead routine to notify other users of who is logged in:

```
on mRegisterHead( me, movie, group, user, fullMsg )
   user.sendMessage( fullMsg.subject, me.pHeadList)
end mRegisterHead

on mChat(me, movie, group, user, fullMsg )
   - Chop off the first message if the log is full.
   if (me.pChatLog).count() >= me.pChatLogLength \
                      then (me.pChatLog).deleteAt(1)
   - Append the incoming chat to the end of the log.
   (me.pChatLog).append( user.name & ":" && fullMsg.content )
   - Send the last message from the log to all users.
   movie.sendMessage( me.pUserNames, fullMsg.subject, me.pChatLog\
[ (me.pChatLog).count() ] )
end mChat

on mGetChatLog( me, movie, group, user, fullMsg )
   movie.sendMessage(user.name, "GetChatLog", me.pChatLog )
end mGetChatLog
```

Assigning the FaceChat server script to our movie

Of course, before we can use our new script, we need to tell ScriptMap.ls to make it available to our movie. Find the Scripts subfolder in your MUS application directory, and open up the ScriptMap.ls file. We just need to add one line to it, telling the server to assign the FaceChat.ls script to any movie whose name begins with the string "FaceChat":

```
on scriptMap
  theMap = []
  theMap.append([#movieID "FaceChat*", #scriptFileName
"FaceChat.ls"])
  return theMap
end
```

This allows for the fact that you may get through several different versions of the project in the course of development. As long as you always save them with names like FaceChat01.dir or FaceChat144.dir, you should have no need to modify the server script map settings.

Taking things forward

We'll conclude this chapter by discussing what we could do to improve on the application we've developed. As it stands, our movie is lacking some of the attributes you might expect in a finished product. The four most obvious ways to improve our movie are probably:

- User-definable graphics

- Unlimited connections

- Animated gestures

- Positional morphing gestures

User-definable graphics

One attribute of the current system that has both good and bad points is the shared facial libraries (the heads, eyes, eyebrows, and mouths that we index for each user). This approach is good in that when we select a particular gesture, we know that other connected users will be able to see that gesture – identical components are available on their own FaceChat client. It's also bad, because it means we end up with a bulky client, whose size is almost entirely attributable to our exhaustive list of graphical components.

We could make our system much more elegant by taking advantage of the fact that Director can source its media from pretty much anywhere. How could this be achieved practically? Let's talk about metafiles – files that describe other files. Picture the following scenario:

You're already logged into @RoomOfFaces. Somebody else decides to do the same. Your FaceChat client is sent the user's name, and a URL. Their user name is placed under a blank face, and the

URL specifies a text file, so the client quickly downloads that. This text metafile is examined, and is determined to contain four lines. The first is another URL, this time it points to a 'head' graphic; obviously this graphic is in a format that Director can load. The next three lines are also URLs; this time they point to three directories – can you guess what they are? That's right, they're directories containing graphics of eyes, eyebrows, and mouths.

This system could be expanded, and abstracted to the point where any type of facial component could turn up and be used. Think of weird avatars, like huge gelatinous blobs, and things that barely qualify for the term 'face'.

For the sake of speed, the system could firstly download the head, then one each of the facial components, so we could at least see what the other user looks like while we wait for the rest of the graphics to load. A system of this sort would of course create a pressure to create avatars which make efficient use of media; one would expect the number of facial components to be fewer than they are in our current system.

Unlimited connections

Allowing six connections is hardly miserly, but by the same token it's never a good idea to place a hard limit on anything in the computer world.

The solution to this is entirely graphical: there's actually nothing in the code itself that limits us to only six users, except for the check that we use to prevent an error. The problem is entirely one of screen real estate. Our system is simple in that it provides six fixed spots for connected users; what is required is an open system that allows us to, for example, scroll the faces as we desire, or perhaps even move them around the screen, like playing cards.

Whenever we need to allocate sprites on the fly in Director, we can build a sprite manager. This has only two jobs: the giving and receiving of sprites. Thus, when we need to render a head, we simply ask the sprite manager for four contiguous sprites, that is, four sprites in a row, and assign our media to those sprites. The only other task is that of mapping a particular user name to a particular run of sprites. A property list like the following can achieve this:

```
["Justy"[1,2,3,4],"Marjee"[5,6,7,8],"Stang"[9,10,11,12]]
```

Animated gestures

Ah! This is a fun one, and so very easy. Well, easy if you use filmloops (or linked Flash movies, of course). Just lay out some animations of facial components in your Score, make a filmloop of them, and use them as animated components. The easiest thing to do would be to animate eye pupils; that way you can make some very sly looks indeed! An animation in which only the element's position is animated is great from a low file size point of view.

Positional morphing gestures

Related to animated gestures is the idea of morphing between gestures. Realistically, the only way to do this is to make use of positional, rotational, skewed, and scaled gestures. These would work best with our eyebrow and eye components; although it would also work nicely for some mouth shapes. Here's an example of the kind of gesture you could achieve in this way:

The idea would be to store a face component's gesture as a list of information relating to its position, rotation, scaling, etc. Then as an entire gesture is changed, the system needs only to morph between the last and next set of positions, rotations, and so on.

Let's say we want to morph between position p1 and position p2, described as (x1,y1) and (x2,y2). The Lingo might look like this:

```
— Return the point that lies between two points
— t lies in the range 0.0 - 1.0, where 0.0 corresponds
— to the first point, and 1.0 corresponds to the
— second point.
on MorphPoint rX1, rY1, rX2, rY2, rT

    set xD = rX2 - rX1
    set yD = rY2 - rY1

    set mX = rX1 + rT * xD
    set mY = rY1 + rT * yD

    return point(mX,mY)

end MorphPoint
```

This strategy applies easily to any scalar property – scale, rotation, ... You'd have to decide on how many frames of morphing were acceptable, and provide values of t for each frame. You might end up with something like this:

```
set x1 = 100.0 — Obtain these from the component
set y1 = 50.0  — positions
set x2 = 175.0
set y2 = 120.0
repeat with f = 0 to numFrames
  set t = f/numFrames
  set theMorphedPoint = MorphPoint(x1,y1,x2,y2,t)
  put theMorphedPoint
end repeat
```

Conclusion

We've only just scratched the surface of what could be done to jazz up the FaceChat application. Hopefully this chapter has inspired you to take things further. You can now extend chat applications with some avatars that can make faces at each other! In the next chapter we'll learn how to store data in this multiuser environment. This means, for instance, that you could set up this system to remember what Justy looks like when he logs back into the chat room. It also means you can do a lot more besides, so keep reading.

Chapter 13

Databases

In this chapter, we're going to look at various ways in which we can ensure that information on users and movies persists from one user session to the next. We will focus on the advantages of using a database, and the possibilities that Lingo offers for your applications to interact with the server to create and access this stored information.

We will be using a specially developed tool, DBAdministrator, to demonstrate how this access is possible. This tool automates a lot of the tasks involved in creating a database, and you may even find it very useful in helping you set up your own databases later on.

Building a community

The goal of most multiuser applications is to foster the development of an online community. Visitors are encouraged to interact with other members of the community, share data, improve their status according to their actions, and generally earn respect from their peers. In the course of participation on a multiuser application a user can also acquire goods (clothes, furniture, points), and customize their appearance.

It's only to be expected that these achievements will be preserved between user sessions – what happens if you lose your Internet connection, or simply decide to take a break for dinner and return to the multiuser world later on in the day? The answer is simple: the multiuser application must record and preserve the current state of each user on the server, and let you retrieve your own user state as required.

This is only possible if the application can recognize users when they return to the community. It must also keep a record of each user's distinctive characteristics, as well as the personal information they submitted when they joined. What is the user's name? How many points have they scored? Are they carrying anything? It is impossible to build up an online community without keeping a record of its users most important characteristics.

Let's consider the basic requirements for a user record:

- It must persist between user sections, even if the server crashes or goes offline.

- Access to the information must be fast but secure, so that only authorized users have access to it.

Storing information on the server

The most obvious place to keep these records is on the same machine as the Multiuser Server is running. All client movies need to access this machine anyway, and the physical proximity should help to keep data access times very low. The next question is: how do we store this information?

Using text files

One option for simple, persistent data storage is to use a text file on the server. This file can be accessed using server-side Lingo scripting. Some developers use this approach to record a log of player actions, or to retrieve chunks of static information to be passed to the player using a server side script.

For most multiuser applications, however, this option is not the best solution. Accessing text data with server-side Lingo is usually a very slow process, especially as many situations will require this code to parse the record file to extract or add information to it, and there are also problems when different users need concurrent access to the text file.

Most developers agree that the flat text file approach is simply not flexible enough for more sophisticated applications. There are better ways to access information in a hierarchical and secure way, and this is the reason that databases were created.

Using a database

Databases are ideal tools for storing structured data. They allow data to be searched, indexed, retrieved and updated quickly and in a reliable way. They have other advantages too, as all the information is stored in one place rather than stored in several places, which means that the information being gathered can be utilized in a useful way (for marketing or troubleshooting purposes, for example).

A typical database is composed of **tables** and **records** (also known as **rows**). The following diagram shows a simple database table filled with records for four different users:

ID	LASTNAME	FIRSTNAME	NICKNAME	PASSWORD
1	Smith	John	johns	9x2ui
2	Cooper	Mary	mary22	bb789
3	Johnson	Be	ben-j	a342
4	Pereira	William	billp	mjio2

Most databases can hold multiple tables as well – for example, you might create one table to hold user data and another for billing information. Each **field** (or **column**) can hold one pre-defined type of data. In our example above, the ID column stores integers, whereas the LASTNAME column can only store strings of characters.

The actual task of creating a database for your application can be rather complex. Before you do anything else, you must choose a database engine, the program that's going to handle the creation and maintenance of your database files. Widely used database engines include Microsoft Access, Microsoft SQL Server, FileMaker Pro, MySQL, PostgreSQL, and Oracle.

Each engine has its own distinct characteristics in terms of speed, capacity, price, and the platforms it supports. Some can even be used in a client-server configuration, where the database engine is installed on one machine and can serve data to applications running on other computers.

The application simply directs queries to the database engine, which extracts the requested information from any relevant tables in the specified database. This might simply be a matter of extracting a specific set of records from one table, or it may involve collating data from several different records, which may even be in different tables.

Nowadays, most popular databases allow us to make use of the relationships between records in different tables – for example, comparing this table with the one on the previous page, we can deduce that Ben Johnson (whose user ID is 3) has an avatar with medium length black hair, and has earned 180 points so far:

ID	HAIRLENGTH	HAIRCOLOR	POINTS
1	Long	White	100
2	Short	Brown	50
3	Medium	Black	180
4	Short	Blonde	260

So, depending on the database engine you're using, you may be able to use complex queries that retrieve data from different rows and more than one table at a time. Fortunately, there's a fairly standard way to construct these queries, using **Structured Query Language** (or **SQL**).

Different database engines have different limitations on the type and size of data that can be stored in each column, so it is not easy to move sets of data between different servers. Some database engines also need additional configuration before they can be used. This includes setting permissions for different users, and setting the location of database storage files. So, while a generic database engine is a great tool in your arsenal, it also introduces you to a whole new set of problems, and requires a new set of technical skills. If only there was a way to use databases without mastering this whole new world of SQL queries and database programming...

Setting up the database

Luckily, when the software engineers at Macromedia designed the Shockwave Multiuser Server, they tackled this problem for us! Instead of providing a generic connection to external database engines, the Multiuser Server includes its own database engine, complete with a very flexible database structure and all the commands you might need to build, use, and expand your data store. In fact, databases are created automatically the very first time you run Multiuser Server, so you can start storing data right away! Let's have a look at the Multiuser Server Database Objects (DBObjects) and how to use them.

Creating a database

Creating a Multiuser Server database is very easy: just start the server and the database files will be created automatically for you. That's it! You can find these files stored under the main installation directory in a sub-directory called DBObjectFiles. These files hold the tables, indexes, and binary files that store your database data in a format derived from the popular Dbase IV file format.

This format is still used in applications like Microsoft Visual FoxPro and there are several utilities available to view and edit the data in the DBF files directly if you want to do so. However, editing the DBF files directly is probably not a good idea for a number of reasons:

- These database files are specifically designed for use with the Multiuser Server, and certain data elements are stored in a format that won't be meaningful to any of the other applications you might use to view DBF files.

- Most data is stored as Lingo values in binary format, and this data can be lost if you open the database tables with another application.

- The Multiuser Server maintains a strong relationship between database tables, and any attempts to add data manually may break indexes and corrupt the whole database.

All in all, it is much safer to use the Multiuser Server (and the commands it offers) to manipulate the data files.

In most cases, you shouldn't need direct access to the database files at all – however, there are just a couple of exceptions to this rule. While it's not a good idea to edit individual files in the DBObjectFiles folder, you can quite safely duplicate the database by copying the **entire folder** from one server to another.

It is a good idea to make a backup copy of your database from time to time in a similar fashion. In either case, you'll need to make sure that the Multiuser Server isn't running when you attempt to copy these files. You can also reset your database to an empty state by simply deleting all the files with the DBObjectFiles folder. A new, empty database will then be created the very next time the Multiuser Server starts up.

Administering the database

By default, some database operations (such as creating users or changing a user's password) can only be performed by users who have a userlevel of 80 or more. This is a security measure to ensure that only authenticated users can modify or query the database files. We've already done this, when we altered the Multiuser.cfg file and set ourselves up with a username of admin, the password pass, and a userlevel of 100.

If you skimmed over that section, you simply need to add the following line to the XtraCommands / CreateUser section in the Multiuser.cfg file (you'll spot it by virtue of the none-too-subtle references to 'The Simpsons'):

```
XtraCommand = "CreateUser admin pass 100"
```

Using MUS Database functions

Database operations are executed internally by the Multiuser Server in response to messages that have been issued by connected users. A user will never manipulate the database objects directly, but with regular messages (directed to special recipients) issued from your Director movie.

For example, a message with the recipient `system.DBAdmin.createUser` will instruct the server to create a new user in the database, according to parameters supplied in the content portion of the message. The Multiuser Server will carry out the instruction and reply to the user (using the same subject) with any error codes that may have prevented the operation from completing.

In order to help you visualize this process and understand the role of each of the commands and their associated parameters, we've included a tool called `DBAdministrator` in the download files for this book. Now would be a good time to locate the `DBAdministrator.dir` file and load it into Director.

Introducing the DBAdministrator tool

Once you've opened the `DBAdministrator.dir` file, start up the Multiuser Server and play the movie. The first screen you'll see is the login interface, where you must enter a userid and password with which to access the server specified in the bottom input field:

Multiuser Server Database API Example

userid: admin
password: pass
server: mus.yourcompany.com

[Connect]

Use the database administrator account we created earlier and specify either your server machine's IP address (192.168.0.1 for example) or a fully qualified domain name (such as multiuser.yourcompany.com) through which it can be reached. If you are running the Multiuser Server on a local machine without a connection for testing purposes, then you can use the testing IP address of 127.0.0.1.

After you click the Connect button, the movie will attempt to connect to the server and you will be taken to the command screen. Check the server output field at the bottom of the screen for any error messages returned by the server. If the connection is established you will receive the following message:

```
ConnectToNetServer : Connection successful
```

If you don't get this message, make sure that you have launched the Multiuser Server, check that your IP address is specified correctly, and try again.

You are now ready to send database commands to the server. Before we do that though, let's quickly run through the different types of database objects that are available on the server.

Introduction to DBObjects

There are four types of DBObjects you can interact with:

- DBUser objects are used for storing any items of user-specific information (such as e-mail addresses) that have nothing to do with any particular movie.

- DBApplication objects are used to store movie-specific information (such as the highest score ever achieved in a particular game).

- DBPlayer objects are used to store user-specific information that is relevant to a particular movie (such as a user's current high score in a game). Any one user may be using a number of different multiuser movies on our server. While they would only ever have one DBUser object assigned to them, they might have many DBPlayer objects.

- DBAdmin is the database administrator object. There is only one DBAdmin in each database, and this is an internal database object that handles administrative tasks. DBAdmin functions are typically used to create and delete users (DBUser) and applications (DBApplication) from your database, and also to declare new types of data that can be stored in the database (attributes). For security reasons, most DBAdmin functions can only be performed by a user connected with an administrative userlevel of 80 or more.

Let's start by looking at how to use DBAdmin commands to create new attributes and DBUsers in the database.

Attributes and DBAdmin

All of these DBObject types make use of attributes to store information. Once an attribute has been declared, it becomes globally available within the database, and can be used by all DBObject types (DBUser, DBApplication, and DBPlayer) to store data.

The database engine used within the Multiuser Server gives you a lot more freedom and flexibility than most. You can determine the organization of your database dynamically, and each attribute can hold any type of Lingo value, including strings, numbers, rects, points, lists – even media and vector types. This would not be possible with a more conventional approach to data storage, where the data types usually need to be declared when each specific field is created.

Before we can use an attribute to store data, we need to declare it in the database with the DBAdmin object's declareAttribute command. The Lingo command syntax for which is:

```
sendNetMessage ("system.DBAdmin.declareAttribute", \
                "subject",[#attribute:#shoeSize])
```

To test this command in the DBAdministrator tool, simply select the DBAdmin item on the menu bar at the top of the screen, and pick the declareAttribute command from the list of commands down the left-hand side. Enter the name of an attribute you'd like to declare in the attribute field – and be sure not to include the # sign, as it should be declared as a string rather than a symbol – and click the Execute command button. You can use the text fields at the bottom of the interface to examine the command that was sent to the server along with the server response, including any error messages that may have been generated.

> *All the database commands we present in this chapter can be tested in a similar fashion using the DBAdministrator tool. For example, the screenshot shows the result of executing the declareAttribute command.*

DBAdmin | DBUser | DBApplication | DBPlayer | Logout

DBAdmin
createUser
deleteUser
getUserCount
getUserNames
createApplication
deleteApplication
declareAttribute
deleteAttribute
createApplicationData
deleteApplicationData

declareAttribute
attribute: shoeSize

[Execute command]

Last command: system.DBAdmin.declareAttribute - content: [#attribute: #shoeSize]

ConnectToNetServer : Connection Successful
system.DBAdmin.declareAttribute response : [#attribute: #shoeSize]

Go ahead and create a number of attributes on the server. We shall need them to test some of the other database functions. Create the attributes #shoeSize, #hairColor, #hairStyle, #age and #highScore.

DBUser objects

A `DBUser` object stores information about a particular user registered on your server. You can create a `DBUser` object using the `DBAdmin.createUser` function. The Lingo syntax for this is:

```
sendNetMessage("system.DBAdmin.createUser","subject", \
        [#userid:"Dana", #password:"redBoat", #userlevel: 20])
```

The `#userlevel` property here is optional: if you do specify a value, it should be an integer between 1 and 100; if you don't, the new user will be created with the default userlevel value (as specified in the server configuration files, usually 20). Try using the `DBAdministrator` tool to create the `DBUsers` "Dana" and "Daisy". We will use them in our examples shortly.

A `DBUsers` object can be removed from the database using the following command:

```
sendNetMessage("system.DBAdmin.deleteUser","subject", \
        [#userid:"Dana"])
```

There are also two commands that let you examine the database to retrieve the number of `DBUsers` registered, along with their names. These commands require no parameters:

```
sendNetMessage("system.DBAdmin.getUserCount","subject",void)
sendNetMessage("system.DBAdmin.getUserNames","subject",void)
```

The server reply to the first will be an integer that indicates the number of users currently registered on the database. The reply to the second will be a Lingo list containing all the user names. Try out both commands using the `DBAdministrator` tool and check the return values in the server output field.

DBApplication objects

Now that we have some `DBUsers` registered in the database, it's about time we added a few `DBApplication` objects as well. As we've already learned, these can be used to store movie-specific information on the database – typical examples include a tally of the number of visitors a movie has received, or the current high score from all user sessions. `DBApplications` objects are also created using a `DBAdmin` function:

```
sendNetMessage("system.DBAdmin.createApplication","subject", \
        [#application:"MazeGame",#description:"Our chat example"])
```

`DBApplications` can also be removed from the server using the following command:

```
sendNetMessage("system.DBAdmin.createApplication","subject", \
        [#application:"MazeGame"])
```

Create two `DBApplication` objects called "MazeGame" and "SeaBattle". You can make up your own descriptions for them.

Storing and retrieving attributes

Let's use the objects and attributes that we've created so far to actually store some data.

DBUser

The command you should use to store an attribute for a DBUser is:

```
sendNetMessage("system.DBUser.setAttribute", "subject", \
[#userid:"Dana", #attribute:[#shoeSize:8 , #hairStyle:"short"]])
```

It's possible to set multiple attributes in a single command, as long as each one is specified as a different entry in the #attribute property list. Of course, the command will only work if the specified user exists in the database and the attribute being set has already been declared. Use the DBAdministrator tool to create new attribute values for DBUsers Dana and Daisy, with these values for Dana:

```
#shoeSize = 8
#hairStyle = "short"
#hairColor = rgb(10,40,255)
#age = 28
```

...and these for Daisy:

```
#shoeSize = 7.5
#hairStyle = "curly"
#hairColor = rgb(0,0,0)
#age = 32
```

Take a look at the screenshot to see the DBUser.setAttribute page after the #hairStyle attribute is set for the user Dana.

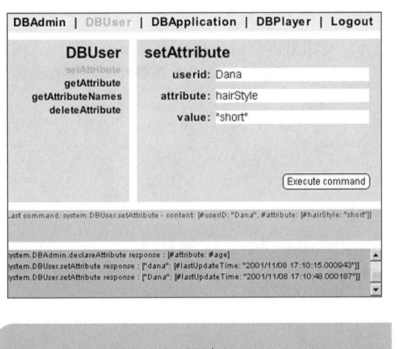

On some occasions it may be necessary to determine whether a given attribute is already set for a user before you attempt to retrieve its value. This is where the DBUser.getAttributeNames function is used:

```
sendNetMessage("system.DBUser.getAttributeNames", \
              "subject", [#userid:"Dana"])
```

Try this command in the DBAdministrator tool, using the username "Dana". You should find the server response very interesting:

```
DBAdmin  |  DBUser  |  DBApplication  |  DBPlayer  |  Logout

        DBUser            getAttributeNames
      setAttribute           userid: Dana
      getAttribute
   getAttributeNames
     deleteAttribute


                                                    Execute command

Last command: system.DBUser.getAttributeNames - content : [#userID: "Dana"]

system.DBUser.setAttribute response : ["Daisy": [#lastUpdateTime: "2001/11/08 17:13:55.000009"]]
system.DBUser.getAttributeNames response : ["Dana": [#status, #userlevel, #password,
#lastUpdateTime, #LASTLOGINTIME, #shoeSize, #hairColor, #hairStyle, #age]]
```

Check the response field at the bottom of the screen – it should list the following attributes:

> #status, #userlevel, #lastUpdateTime, #lastLoginTime,
> #shoeSize, #hairStyle, #hairColor, #age

Well, we know about the #shoeSize, #hairStyle, #hairColor and #age attributes; after all, we set them ourselves. But where do the other attributes come from?

Every DBUser created on the database has a small set of default attributes created automatically by the server:

- The #userlevel attribute and the hidden #password attribute are specified when you create the DBUser.

- The server also sets a default #status attribute when you create the DBUser. This is a generic attribute you can use to store any information about this user. It has no special function other than being always present for all users and the fact that it does not need to be declared.

- The #lastLoginTime attribute is updated automatically and indicates the last time the user has connected to the server.

- This is also the case with the #lastUpdateTime attribute: it reflects the last time any attribute of this DBUser has been altered.

Retrieving the value of a DBUser attribute is a simple operation. The syntax of this command is:

```
sendNetMessage("system.DBUser.getAttribute","subject", \
        [#userid:"Dana",#attribute:[#shoeSize , #hairStyle]])
```

Again, it's possible to retrieve multiple attributes in a single command, just as long as each attribute is specified as a different entry within the #attribute list. Try getting values for some of the attributes on the DBUser Daisy – you can retrieve those you set yourself, built-in attribute values like #status and #userlevel, and even the invisible #password attribute if you have adequate rights. (By default, only users who are registered with a userlevel of 100 can retrieve and set the #password attribute for other users.)

If you examine the server response on getting an attribute, you will see that it consists of a list containing the user name and values for the attributes you requested. The message also contains the #lastUpdateTime attribute value for this DBUser, which we'll be looking at later.

The remaining DBUser function is used to delete a user attribute, or attributes, from the database:

```
sendNetMessage("system.DBUser.deleteAttribute","subject", \
        [#userid:"Dana",#attribute:[#shoeSize , #hairStyle]])
```

DBApplication

All DBUser functions can be used to set and get attribute values for a DBApplication object, although this requires a slightly different syntax:

```
sendNetMessage("system.DBApplication.getAttributeNames", \
                "subject",[#application:"MazeGame"])
```

Try using the DBAdministrator tool to get the attribute names for the DBApplication object "MazeGame". Click the DBApplication menu item at the top, and select getAttributeNames from the command list. Enter "MazeGame" as the application name, and click the Execute Command button. The following list of default attributes should be returned:

```
#description, #lastUpdateTime
```

The server creates these attributes automatically. The #description attribute is initialized to the value you have used in the DBAdmin.createApplication function, and the #lastUpdateTime attribute holds the date of the last modification for this DBApplication object, just like its DBUser counterpart.

The list of attributes will also return any attributes you have set for this particular DBApplication data, using the setAttribute command:

```
sendNetMessage("system.DBApplication.setAttribute","subject", \
        [#application:"MazeGame",#attribute:[#highScore:1000]])
```

Now use the DBAdministrator tool to set different values for the #highScore attribute in each of the DBApplication objects MazeGame and SeaBattle. You can then retrieve the updated values using the getAttribute command:

```
sendNetMessage("system.DBApplication.getAttribute","subject", \
              [#application:"MazeGame",#attribute:[#highScore]])
```

Of course, we are also provided with a way to delete attributes that have previously been set on a DBApplication object:

```
sendNetMessage("system.DBApplication.deleteAttribute", \
    "subject", [#application:"MazeGame",#attribute:[#highScore]])
```

There is one additional DBApplication object function, getApplicationData. We will cover it later in this chapter when we explain ApplicationData attribute sets and how to use them.

DBPlayer

As noted earlier, DBPlayer objects let us store any information pertaining to a particular DBUser and their connection to a particular DBApplication. Let's say you want to store Dana's #highScore attribute for each of the two applications SeaBattle and MazeGame. You can't store this information in either of the DBApplication objects, since each of these will already hold the current #highScore for all players.

You could conceivably create additional attributes (#highScoreSeaBattle and #highScoreMazeGame) for Dana's DBUser object, but she only has to start playing a few more different games, and the long-term impracticality of this solution becomes painfully apparent.

The perfect situation is to create a couple of DBPlayer objects: one to represent the user Dana playing application SeaBattle, and another to represent Dana playing the MazeGame. Each object can have its own #highScore attribute, and each one can hold different values.

As it happens, there are no DBAdmin functions for creating DBPlayer objects. Instead, they are created automatically when the movie first uses a DBPlayer.setAttribute command, and they survive in the database for as long as their parent DBUser and DBApplication objects continue to exist. If you delete a DBUser object, the server will automatically remove any related DBPlayer objects, and a similar thing happens when you delete a DBApplication.

DBPlayer commands are very similar to DBUser and DBApplication commands, but note that you must always specify both the userid and the application:

```
sendNetMessage("system.DBPlayer.setAttribute","subject", \
        [#userid:"Dana", #application:"MazeGame", \
        #attribute:[#highScore:1000 ,
                       #highScoreTime:"15 hours 10 minutes"]])
```

Once a DBPlayer attribute is set, you can retrieve its value using the DBPlayer.getAttribute function:

```
sendNetMessage("system.DBPlayer.getAttribute", \
        "subject", [#userid:"Dana",
                       #application:"MazeGame",
                       #attribute:[#highScore]])
```

DBPlayer objects also support the getAttributeNames command. For example:

```
sendNetMessage("system.DBPlayer.getAttributeNames", \
            "subject",[#userid:"Dana", \
                        #application:"MazeGame"])
```

If you try using the DBPlayer.getAttributeNames command in the DBAdministrator tool, you will discover that DBPlayer objects have two attributes that are created by default and maintained by the server. The first of these is #lastUpdateTime, which serves just the same purpose as it did for the DBUser and DBApplication objects, and the other is #creationTime. This attribute represents the moment at which the object was created on the server, which corresponds to the time its first attribute was set.

Finally, the DBPlayer object offers a deleteAttribute command with which to remove a player attribute from the database. The usage is similar to its DBUser and DBApplication counterparts:

```
sendNetMessage("system.DBPlayer.deleteAttribute", \
            "subject", [#userid:"Dana", \
                        #application:"MazeGame", \
                        #attribute:[#highScore]])
```

Altering user access

Now that we've seen how to create and manipulate users and their attributes, it's probably worth commenting on one of the other configuration settings that we might like to tweak. Once we start using the database to store information about the users who are logging on to the server, we might like to start restricting access to our file, based on that information.

By default, the authentication level specified in the multiuser.cfg configuration file is "UserRecordOptional". Basically, this means that the only time you'll ever get refused a connection is if you submit the wrong password along with a registered userID. Now that we actually have some users recorded in our database, we can afford to get a little more picky.

Open up the mulituser.cfg file, and locate the section shown below:

```
#=================================================================
# Set the authentication level that determines who can log on
# to the server.  Possible values are:
#     None - anyone may log in with any name and password
#                (as long as another user has not already connected
#                to the movie using the same name)
#     UserRecordRequired - users may only log in if they
#                have a DBUser record in the database
#     UserRecordOptional - if a DBUser record exists for the
#                the given name, then the correct password is
#                required.  If there is no record, then the
#                connection is allowed.  (user level set to the
#                value of "db_default_userlevel")
```

continues overleaf

```
#================================================================
XtraCommand = "Authentication UserRecordOptional"
```

The code and comments are fairly self-explanatory: you can see that the default setting here is UserRecordOptional, which effectively allows anybody to log into your application, regardless of whether or not they have a DBUser record in the database. In order to limit access to users with an existing account, simply change the final line to read as follows:

```
XtraCommand = "Authentication UserRecordRequired"
```

You may also wish to update the opening echo statement to reflect this change. Scroll to the top of the file and find this section:

```
#================================================================
# Echo statements get displayed in the server window. Add an
# echo to the beginning of a line to verify that it has been
# read by the server.
echo Reading the Multiuser.cfg file.
```

Replace the echo command with the following lines of code:

```
echo Reading the modified Multiuser.cfg file.
echo Note: Users require an account to log on.
```

Save the file and relaunch the server. You should see the new message appear at the top of the server window, indicating that the server is reading the correct file at startup and executing your configuration. Your new security settings have taken effect, and only users with a DBUser record will now be able to log in.

Preventing concurrent data access

We mentioned the #lastUpdateTime attribute returned in all getAttribute commands earlier, but promised to come back to it later so let's take a look at this now. This is an optional feature to use when setting attributes and may not be required for all applications, but it can be very useful. Consider the following scenario:

- User A gets the value of the #highScore attribute for the DBApplication MazeGame, which currently stands at 1,000 points. He compares this value to his score in the game – now 1,200 – and decides that the #highScore attribute needs to be updated.

- User B is playing the same game, and also decides that his score (of 1100) is higher than the current #highscore and that he should update the #highScore attribute.

Given this situation, it's quite possible that both users will try to update the #highScore attribute at the same time. If A were to update the property just a split second before B, then the final result would be 1,100 since the update from user B will overwrite any changes made by user A. How can we avoid allowing multiple users the chance to modify DBUser attributes at the same time?

This is where the `#lastUpdateTime` proves very useful. When a user requests an attribute with `getAttribute`, the server always returns the `#lastUpdateTime` property, as we have already seen. The user can store this value and send it back to the server in a special format of the `DBUser.setAttribute` command:

```
sendNetMessage("system.DBUser.setAttribute","subject",  \
    [#userid:"Dana",#attribute:[#shoeSize:8],            \
                    #lastUpdateTime:"2001/11/08 17:13:55.003456"])
```

This command is just the same as the original `setAttribute` command, but with the additional specification of the `#lastUpdateTime` property. When the server receives a command that contains this property it will check to see if the `#lastUpdateTime` property is still valid. This indicates that no user has updated the `DBApplication` object since the original `getAttribute` command was issued, and that it is safe to update the attribute value.

The server will only update the value if this condition is true: if the `lastUpdateTime` property values do not match then the server will not update the property and will reply to the user with a Data concurrency error message error code. So, in this case, User B would be faced with the depressing but true realization that he still wasn't quite good enough to be the best.

This variation on the basic command can also be used with `setAttribute` functions for objects of type `DBUser` and `DBPlayer`.

Working with ApplicationData attribute sets

There are three more functions that we've skipped over so far, which are used to work with `ApplicationData` attribute sets. These are sets of related attributes created by the database administrator object that cannot be modified by the user. They are:

- `DBAdmin.createApplicationData`

- `DBAdmin.deleteApplicationData`

- `DBApplication.getApplicationData`

It's probably easiest to understand them by examining a practical example. Suppose you have a chat application, the lobby for which presents different scenarios to the user depending on the time of the year. Each scenario is determined by a set of properties such as `#backgroundPicture`, `#ambientMusic`, `#numOfUsers`, and `#waiterName`. Let's say you have three different possible scenarios determined by the following set of properties:

	Scenario 1	Scenario 2	Scenario 3
#backgroundPicture	"greenRoom"	"redRoom"	"blueRoom"
#ambientMusic	"rock"	"jazz"	"salsa"
#numOfUsers	5	10	15
#waiterName	"robert"	"anthony"	"diane"

You can store each scenario as one ApplicationData set. Additional sets can be created in the database at any time and your movies will retrieve the updated data directly from the server, so no modification to your Shockwave movies is necessary.

Let's create some ApplicationData sets on our database. First, you need to declare the new attributes. Use the DBAdministrator tool and the DBAdmin.declareAttribute command to declare #backgroundPicture and #numOfUsers. For this example we don't need to actually declare large sets of data, and the DBAdministrator tool is prepared to declare ApplicationData sets consisting of two attributes. If you use your own Lingo scripts, you can of course specify more attributes.

After the two new attributes are declared, use DBAdmin.createApplication to create a new application called "CustomLobby". When the database is prepared, we can create ApplicationData sets using the DBAdmin.createApplicationData command:

```
sendNetMessage("system.DBAdmin.createApplicationData",    \
                "subject",[#application:"CustomLobby",     \
   #attribute:[#backgroundPicture:"greenRoom" , #numOfUsers:5]])
```

Each ApplicationData set is a property list of related attributes, and can have any number of elements. These elements cannot, however, be modified by the user.

Use this function three times in the DatabaseAdministrator tool to create three ApplicationData sets with the following values:

```
ApplicationData set #1
application: CustomLobby
attribute1: backgroundPicture
attribute1value: "greenRoom"
attribute2: numOfUsers
attribute2value: 5

ApplicationData set #2
application: CustomLobby
attribute1: backgroundPicture
attribute1value: "redRoom"
attribute2: numOfUsers
attribute2value: 10

ApplicationData set #3
application: CustomLobby
attribute1: backgroundPicture
attribute1value: "blueRoom"
attribute2: numOfUsers
attribute2value: 15
```

The following screenshot is of the DBAdministrator interface after executing one createDBApplicationCommand, showing the command parameters and the server response:

```
DBAdmin | DBUser | DBApplication | DBPlayer | Logout

        DBAdmin          createApplicationData

        createUser       application: CustomLobby
        deleteUser
        getUserCount      attribute1: backgroundPicture
        getUserNames
        createApplication     value1: "greenRoom"
        deleteApplication
        declareAttribute   attribute2: numOfUsers
        deleteAttribute
        createApplicationData    value2: 5
        deleteApplicationData
                                        [ Execute command ]

Last command: system.DBAdmin.createApplicationData - content: [#application: "CustomLobby",
#attribute: [#backgroundPicture: "greenRoom", #numOfUsers: 5]]

system.DBAdmin.declareAttribute response : [#attribute: #backgroundPicture]
system.DBAdmin.declareAttribute response : [#attribute: #numOfUsers]
system.DBAdmin.createApplicationData response : [#application: "CustomLobby"]
```

That's it. The ApplicationData sets have been created on your database, and you can retrieve them using the DBApplication.getApplicationData command. This is used to query the database and retrieve all ApplicationData sets that match a given criteria. Let's start with the format that uses #text values to look for attributes:

```
sendNetMessage("system.DBApplication.getApplicationData", \
            "subject",[#application:"CustomLobby", \
                        #attribute:#backgroundPicture, \
                        #text:"blueRoom"])
```

Test this command using the DBAdministrator tool. Enter CustomLobby as the application name, backgroundPicture as the attribute to be searched, and blueRoom as the text to be matched. The server will reply with a list containing the ApplicationData set that matches these criteria. The screenshot shows the result of this operation.

You can also use different forms of this command to search for data using a number. Try the same command selecting the number format in the DBAdministrator tool, and check the server output:

```
sendNetMessage("system.DBApplication.getApplicationData", \
            "subject",[#application:"CustomLobby",          \
                        #attribute:#numOfUsers, #number:5])
```

Finally, we can use the third format for the getApplicationData command to match a range of numbers:

```
sendNetMessage("system.DBApplication.getApplicationData", \
            "subject",[#application:"CustomLobby",          \
                        #attribute:#numOfUsers,              \
                        #lowNum:7, #highNum: 15])
```

Try this format of the command using the DBAdministrator tool to query for ApplicationData sets with the #lowNum value of 7 and #highNum value of 15. Check the server output to confirm that two different ApplicationData sets will be returned, since both match the criteria specified in the command.

ApplicationData sets can be deleted with the DBAdmin.deleteApplicationData command. This command also has three formats to match attributes by: #text, #number, and #range. These are exactly equal to the DBApplication.getApplicationData formats, with a different recipient id. The syntax for these commands is reproduced below:

```
sendNetMessage("system.DBAdmin.deleteApplicationData",    \
               "subject",[#application:"CustomLobby",      \
                          #attribute:#backgroundPicture, \
                          #text:"blueRoom"])

sendNetMessage("system.DBAdmin.deleteApplicationData",    \
               "subject",[#application:"CustomLobby",      \
                          #attribute:#numOfUsers, #number:5])

sendNetMessage("system.DBAdmin.deleteApplicationData",    \
               "subject",[#application:"CustomLobby",      \
                          #attribute:#numOfUsers,          \
                          #lowNum:7, #highNum: 15])
```

Most multiuser developers prefer to store different sets of read-only grouped attributes directly in the Shockwave files rather than on the server, so few movies actually use ApplicationData objects. They may still be useful for your particular application, especially if you need to add more sets of read-only data (questions for a trivia game, for example) and don't want to force your users to download a new copy of your Shockwave movie when you do this.

Limitations of the Multiuser Server internal database

The database within Multiuser Server is a very powerful piece of software, and its capabilities should easily be enough for most of your day-to-day database needs. However, a few developers complain about the fact that the data is stored in a proprietary format, and there is no easy way to use this data with other external tools.

Another common complaint is the lack of connectivity with enterprise-level database backends running on a different machine, and the inability for multiple servers to share the same database. Not many developers require these capabilities, but it would be great to be able to use external databases if the need arose, especially if you could do it without altering any of your Lingo.

Extending the Multiuser Server

Fortunately the Multiuser Server can be extended using Xtras, and there are a couple of Database Xtras available on the market that can help to work around these limitations. At the time of writing, we were able to evaluate late beta versions of MUDBOX (MultiUser DataBase Object Xtra) and MUSTARD (MultiUser Server That Accesses Relational Databases), both produced by SmartPants Media Inc. You can find the full documentation for these Xtras and evaluation versions available to download at the company's web site http://www.smartpants.com/xtras

Using the same database for multiple servers

A key feature of the MUDBOX and MUSTARD Xtras is the ability to connect to an external database source that does not need to reside on the same machine as the server. You can use a MySQL database server running on a Linux machine, for example. This opens the possibility of using one database for multiple SMUS machines, and it is one of the main reasons you should consider evaluating these Xtras. If your application needs to support multiple multiuser servers accessing the same set of data, there is really no other way to go. External databases can also provide advantages in terms of speed, flexibility, and scalability.

Considering the move to an external database engine

Before you hurry down this route, remember that – as powerful as external database engines can be – you will be introducing new elements in your server environment. You have to consider the bandwidth taken by the Xtra to query an external database located on another machine, and the costs and knowledge involved in setting up and maintaining this external database source.

Depending on the Xtra solution you choose, this can be as simple as setting up an ODBC (Open Database Connectivity – an open standard application programming interface for accessing a database) data source on the same Windows 2000 server, or as complicated as setting up tables and permissions on an enterprise-level Oracle database.

In my experience, the vast majority of multiuser applications have no need for an external database engine, but applications that have hundreds of users submitting simultaneous database commands to one or more servers may benefit from this approach.

Supporting the DBObjects command set

One key element you should consider when evaluating database solutions is their support for the `DBObjects` commands. MUDBOX is a replacement for the built-in database support, so it supports all the commands and the object model we have described in this chapter. By contrast, MUSTARD is quite a different tool, providing a bridge between a Multiuser Server and an ODBC database using pre-defined SQL commands. Let's examine the basic characteristics of each solution.

MUDBOX

This is a multiuser Xtra that allows developers to seamlessly use an external database for all of the `DBObject` functions. Essentially, MUDBOX replaces Macromedia's `DBObject` Xtra, but implements all of its methods seamlessly. It allows the flexibility to use whichever database you wish, and the power to expand the utility of the Multiuser Server.

This means that you can use an enterprise-level external database engine without having to learn any new languages. You can also use it to configure multiple instances of the Multiuser Server so that they access the same database. This allows you to exceed the limitations of a single multiuser server instance, while still keeping your data consolidated.

The process of installing MUDBOX is a simple one, consisting of replacing the DBObjects Xtra with MUDBOX and adding a few lines to the multiuser.cfg file. MUDBOX will automatically connect to the database source indicated in the multiuser.cfg file and create all the tables it needs on the first run.

Once it's installed and configured you can pretty much forget all about MUDBOX. It is a great solution if you need your data available externally whilst maintaining your application's compatibility with the internal DBObject commands.

MUSTARD

This is a powerful Xtra that allows Director applications to easily perform database queries and updates through the Multiuser Server. The purpose of this Xtra is to allow developers to run predefined SQL commands from a remote Director application using the Multiuser Server.

Rather than having your application specify SQL queries, you can create special "MUSTARD Handlers" – essentially predefined SQL commands. To perform a particular query, you then simply call a MUSTARD handler, and pass in the appropriate data in the form of a property list. Data is immediately returned as a list of property lists, where each "row" in the database is represented by a property list, and each property represents a particular column in the database.

One great advantage of this strategy is that you do not need to distribute a specialized Xtra with your Director applications, as all queries are performed through the server. MUSTARD will work with any ODBC-compliant database, and data can be stored and returned in any Director format (including property lists, media, integers, and strings).

The goal of MUSTARD is to allow developers the flexibility of a true relational database model, and free developers from any perceived limitations of the DBObjects model. Developers can create any database structure that may be required by their application, and can easily share this data with other non-Director applications if necessary.

Of course, all this power comes with a price: since MUSTARD does not support the DBObjects commands, it's necessary to learn SQL and design your own database structure. It is a powerful solution for extending the Multiuser Server, but it will be overkill unless your project genuinely needs it. It's not the kind of solution that you want to be looking at using on your first Multiuser Server application.

Nebulae MUS Database Support

At the time of this writing, there is one additional database solution available for multiuser applications written in Shockwave. Tabuleiro Nebulae MUS is a Java-based multiuser server that runs on Linux, MacOSX, Solaris, FreeBSD, and other Unix-like systems. This server is not an extension of the Shockwave Multiuser Server but a complete replacement for it; you may find that it proves a good solution should you need to host your multiuser server on an ISP that does not support Windows.

This server comes with its own internal database engine and also supports some popular Unix database engines like MySQL and PostgreSQL. It also supports all `DBObject` commands transparently, and the internal database structure is created automatically the first time the server is run, much like MUDBOX. If you need to run your multiuser servers and keep your database files on a Unix-based system it may be a good idea to have a look at this product – further details on this and other alternatives to the Multiuser Server are discussed in **Chapter 15**.

Conclusion

The ability to store and recall data as and when you want it is a key part of a successful multiuser application. Now that we've covered this, you're fully equipped to and create some really impressive multiuser applications, and this is exactly what we're going to do in the next chapter.

Chapter 14

An
Advanced
Application

Now that we've looked at each of the key components involved in writing multiuser applications (server–side scripting, chat, controlling avatars, and groups), it's time to have some serious fun with all that knowledge! So, in the course of this chapter, we're going to walk through the processes involved in making a professional standard multiuser online game.

The specific example we'll be using to demonstrate this process is a three-dimensional car game. A lot of what we talk about is generic, and even the finer points involved here can easily be adapted to many other applications, so please don't disappear if your sphere of interest happens to lie elsewhere.

Why 3D?

The inclusion of the Shockwave3D Xtra in Director 8.5 has really raised the creative bar for working with 3D on the Web. Although the introduction of quads in Director 7 made it possible to work with simple 3D environments and applications, the new Xtra takes 3D in Director to a totally new level. While 3D is fairly peripheral to the multiuser technologies explored in this book, 3D and multiuser applications are natural bedfellows, and nowhere is this more obvious than with a game.

At a fundamental level, all multiuser applications are designed to let two or more people interact in a common environment. It's always important to present this environment effectively, if only to stop users getting confused and losing interest. You'll almost certainly want to make use of familiar visual cues to make the user interaction as intuitive as possible.

Of course, the most familiar (and therefore the most intuitive) interface most people have is with the real world, and what better way to start simulating the real world on a flat screen than by using a trick that we know all too well from the movies: a perspective-based simulation of a three-dimensional world.

There are various other ways to represent three dimensions in a medium that only allows us two (using plans/elevations, for example) but it's no surprise that the most natural representation corresponds to the way our eyes see the world – in perspective.

The games industry has developed in such a way that the vast majority of console games are now developed as 3D applications, and the multiuser aspects of the latest generation of consoles are emphatically apparent.

The game

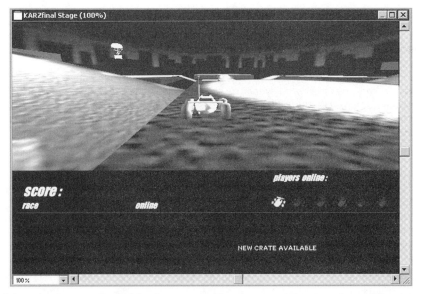

"Karz" is a simple game in which players can drive cars around an empty, multilevel car park, which happens to be suspended in the middle of a void. The objective of the game is to drive around grabbing crates of contraband as they fall from the sky and to do so before anyone else gets them. All that without falling into the void, of course. Your aim is to amass as much stash as possible. You can take a look at the finished game out by downloading it from the friendsofED.com site in the usual way.

To start, we'll take a look at the concepts behind the game, and the ways in which we've answered some of the questions all multiuser applications have to deal with. Those questions are usually best dealt with as early as possible in the development cycle, so it seems appropriate to look at these now. We'll look at:

- The interactive components of the game

- How player performance is rated

- The kind of models we'll use

- How players will log into the game

- How groups will be organized

- How the beginning, middle, and end of a multiuser game can be defined

- Considerations about lag and collision detection in multiuser games

Interactivity

A key part of the design of this type of game, and fundamental in determining whether people like it or not, is how the car reacts to a player's input. This is the **interactive design** of the game, and here, this comprises the four arrow keys that control his car, as this is the only realtime input a player has.

Car games are a classic genre with their own special kind of attraction. Cars are an ideal subject for interactive movement using a keyboard – more complex systems like the human body might jump or walk sideways, creating a highly complex system to simulate, whereas cars can only turn left and right, accelerate and reverse. This kind of game does not even need a literal simulation of gravity, friction, momentum and so on, a simple system with an intuitive 'feel' is all that is required.

What makes these cars a little different to your average racing game is the fact that if you're driving fast and turn quickly, you'll skid sideways, and the fact that you'll fly if you drive off the edge. The flying has an almost "Crouching Tiger, Hidden Dragon" feel to it, lending the game a slightly surreal air. It also adds an interesting skill component, as with a bit of practice it's possible to jump across floors and connecting roads, gaining valuable seconds on your opponents.

This is very much a casual game, so we aimed at providing instant gratification: there's no waiting around for groups to be allocated, no registration process, and it's immediately obvious how to drive your car.

Scoring

Scoring is a measure of a player's success, and also a challenge: "well, that was OK, but you could do better". High scores tables increase the feeling of competition – it's important that there's no limit (or at least a practically impossible limit) to the scoring system for two reasons. Firstly, if you have reached the maximum score, there's no point in playing any further. More importantly, a high score table where everyone has the same score is – at best – a depressing sight.

The scoring system for this game is in its infancy: you score a point plus the number of people you're competing with for each crate that you hit. Permutations on this could include placing a time limit on a round (at the moment, the person who hangs around the longest wins), averaging score over time (giving the score a higher skill component), and awarding more points for crates caught in mid-air or soon after landing.

Models

Low polygon 3D design is a fairly advanced art form in its own right – arcade games have been using 3D since the late 80s, and volumes have been written on what constitutes good 3D design.

Polygon count is the critical factor: each polygon needs to be there for a reason, as each one takes its toll on the performance of the game. In the case of designing for Shockwave 3D, a rough rule of thumb is that if you are aiming for as wide an audience as possible, keep the polygon count per scene below 8-12,000. Go above this, and you are expecting players to have a top end machine and video card by today's standards (this will rapidly change, no doubt).

Performance can also be affected by other factors, including the screen size, the number of effects (such as particle emitters), the calculations that need to be performed for each frame, the extent of the visibility of the objects, and so on.

In this game, each car is made up of about 1000 polygons:

and the world itself is about 5000:

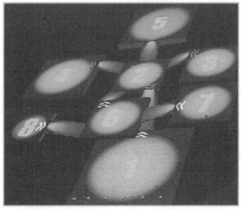

The 3D models were designed in 3D Studio Max and exported in W3D format for Director – most professional level 3D modeling applications can now export to this format. Director links to models in a 3D world by referring to the name of each model, which is defined by grouping the components together and assigning a name to the group when creating the model in the first place. So, in this case, the main model names are car1 to car6, and the world contains various other models – lights, floors, position markers, and so on.

> *We haven't got room for an extended conversation about 3D here, but if you want to find out more, check out some of the other friends of ED Director titles. It's also possible to obtain W3D models from various sources on the Web, so it's not necessarily essential to have expensive 3D modeling software when embarking on Director 3D projects.*

Other design issues

Having made some decisions about the game-play, and how the user will interact with the game, there are several other decisions that need to be taken before production can begin. Here, these are the login procedure, handling groups; and dealing with "play again" requests, lag, and collision detection.

I won't even attempt to pretend that we made a final decision on all these issues before starting development – many important elements of a good end product (both in terms of ideas and game-play) will emerge in the course of the production process. Even by the time you have a working prototype, unforeseen issues can still raise their ugly heads. Where this has happened here, we've come clean and described both the version we initially planned and the version we finally went with so that you can see the commercial reality of an evolving application.

Login procedure

First impressions count: login is likely to be the first thing a prospective user will see of your application, so you need to make it friendly and accessible. Each field is a potential put-off, so keep them to a minimum. In this case, the application is a quickfire game, so we have opted for no visible login at all; you go straight to play mode. You are allocated one of six cars, and that is it. If you're playing with friends, you can identify yourself through the chat interface.

Handling groups

The maximum number of people you allow to join a group is key to each player's experience. Too many players and there could be bottlenecks for data flow, increased lag and too much work at the client computer end to process each other player. But too few can result in a massive amount of small groups (problematic if players are asked to chose a group to join), frustration for players if they want to play against their friends, and a feeling of empty space where there should be other players.

The best way to arrive at a good group limit is trial and error, combined with some back-of-an-envelope calculations to ensure that data transfer requirements don't come too close to available bandwidth. We have chosen six as the maximum number of players allowed per group, but if you disagree with that number, just go ahead and change it!

Play again?

Most games have a beginning, middle, and end. In multiplayer games, this creates a few issues that are worth considering from both the construction and players' points of view.

How does a round start and finish? Does everyone have to begin at the same time? If a game ends, do players remain logged onto the same group while deciding whether to play again or submitting a high score? If not, then they are likely to find their place in a group has gone and they have to join a different group of players. This can be a confusing and frustrating experience.

It's also important to work out what happens if a player joins part way through a game when defining the game-play. In most cases, it isn't a good idea to have people waiting around with nothing to do.

Lag and collision detection

This is a crucial element in the success or otherwise of our enterprise – any multiuser game that does not take lag into account will fail. We made a classic and elementary blunder with an early prototype of this game. Initially, we'd envisaged a game with a single crate. The first car to collide with it would carry it around until getting hit by someone else, and then the crate would pass on – a variation on tag. A nice simple game, but one that swiftly proved impossible to play on anything but a local network, simply because of Internet lag. Its problem was that it relied on two players both being in the same place at the same time, when in fact there could be several seconds between each user's experience.

Say that player 1 sees the avatar of player 2, but this signal is old because of lag. This means that player 2 will also have an old position for player 1. Following this, what player 1 considers to be a successful collision to claim the crate might look completely different to player 2, leaving at least one party confused.

Collision detection in web-based multiplayer environments is still on very shaky ground. As a rule of thumb, it's best if lag has marginal effect and is determined at the client's level. In this case, player 1 may see a collision that player 2 does not see.

For example, if the result of a collision is to slow you down, but have no effect on your opponent, there is no real need for your opponent to see that explosion, and therefore it need not be dependent on the multiuser server. Instead, it can take place on your local machine, and as long as your position within the game is updated on the multiuser server, you will still serve the time penalty for the collision within the game, but avoid problems of lag by not trying to actually display the collision on other machines at the exact point it occurs on yours.

Another way to get round lag is to use projectiles to shoot at each other. As a projectile has a time element to it (it takes a while to go from the gun to the target), that can be used to counteract lag.

But back to our game: what happens if player 1 and player 2 both think they hit the same crate first? There are several possible solutions to this:

- A server-side script that awards the points to whichever player's signal is received first. A particle emitter at impact will obscure the view for sufficiently long to cloud the visual details and not create too much dislocation.

- A client-side script that tells everyone that you hit the chest with a TimeStamp from the multiuser server. If several players think they hit the same crate then the person with the earliest TimeStamp gets the points. This is the same solution, effectively, but without server-side scripting. This is how it would have to be done with earlier versions of the multiuser server.

- Both players get the points – does it really matter that there are more points than crates?

Our finished game uses the first option, because we felt that scoring needs to be as fair as possible.

Coding structure

Before going on to discuss the multiuser aspects of our game, we'll take a look at how the game itself is created. We'll begin with an outline of the objects used in the game and the setup of the score, and then go into a more in - depth look at how the game is constructed. More specifically, we'll cover:

- The objects used in the application, and how the score is set up

- How to import the world and the car into Director, and how to set up the objects

- The car and its properties

- How the car and the 3D world are set up and initialized

- All the active objects involved

- How to standardize the game experience for people using slower machines

- Placing the car in the world, telling it where the floor is, and how to move across it

- How to set up the camera object, and how it works

The game is built within an object-oriented structure, using the `actorlist` to control a series of objects. This determines which child objects are active at any given time. Frame commands for objects used this way are placed in the `stepframe` handler.

Objects

The objects used in the finished game are:

- `CarObj` – the car object that controls your car.

- `AvatarObj` – the avatar object that controls the way you see other peoples' cars. There is one instance of `AvatarObj` per person online.

- `CrateObj` – controls the crates.

- `Stringcycle` – a chat object.

- `ServerObj` – is created at the beginning of the movie, and remains active regardless of whether or not there is a connection to the multiuser server.

- `CameraObj` – controls the camera, or view.

The Score

The score has four active frames: two setup frames, a frame to initialize connection to the multiuser server, and the normal status run frame.

Almost all the action happens in sprite 1, which is the 3D sprite; other sprites are used only for interface display. In the event of a connection to the server being absent or lost, a timeout script will poll the server every few seconds to try and re-establish connection. In the meantime, the game is playable in single user 'practice' mode. The casts are loosely structured around themes: the cars, interface, chat and the internal cast, which holds the multiuser and setup scripts.

The server controls group management, car allocation, the dropping of the crates, and communication between the players with server - side scripts.

Setting up the visuals

This section deals with the visual setup of the 3D space, putting the car in it and making it interactive. The active game-play is defined here, and at the end, you will have a 3D driving space and a car that can be driven around within the space. The object scripts `CarObj` and `CameraObj` will control the car and the camera.

> *Whilst running through this section of the game's creation, refer to KARZ_1.dir, downloadable from the web site in the usual way, which shows the end results of the stages discussed here without any other confusing elements being present.*

Importing the world and the car and setting up the objects

3D objects are imported into Director and treated as a single sprite, irrespective of the amount of objects within the world and what has been done to them. In that sense, the information is treated more like a single piece of video footage than a set of interactive graphics. Like QuickTime video in Director, a 3D world is rendered by default as direct to stage, though this can be turned off if the performance hit is acceptable.

This means that 3D sprites can use hardware acceleration (both DirectX and OpenGL), and a very high level of Lingo control can be applied to the world by accessing the cast member directly.

Before we can start playing around with our models though, we need to bring them into Director. The first few steps of putting the game together began with a new Director movie, and a new cast called cars. Everything to do with cars, 3D, and movement goes in here. The world and first car were imported (cars1-6 and the world, called gworld, can be downloaded from the web site), and named gworld and car1 respectively.

gworld was then dragged into the score in the first sprite channel, and placed in frames 3 to 8 (3D sprites are entirely stretchable).

We need to control the camera and the car, and two movie scripts in the car cast (CameraObj and CarObj) are used for this. We will look at these in a moment but we will initialize the objects with the script first. We do this in frame 2 (before the 3D world appears):

```
on exitFrame me
 global CarObj, CameraObj
 CarObj = new(member("CarObj").script)
 CameraObj = new(member("CameraObj").script)
end
```

The single user car object

The car object covers all aspects of your car; its movement, the way you interact with it, and the information it sends to the multiuser server. It captures the keystrokes that form the basis of the interactivity and determines how the car reacts to its environment and your input.

To understand how it works, it's probably easiest to look at the car control first. By stripping out the multiuser component of the car object, we're left with an interactive space containing a controllable car.

The first thing to do is set up a bunch of variables – the following is placed in the CarObj script member. Most of these are properties, as they will generally only be accessed within the object.

```
property Car — the car itself
property MyWorld — reference to the world
property TotalRotation — total amount of rotation around Y
property MyResource — which car i am using
property MyDirection — direction that i am moving in
property UpVector
property ForceD — magnitude of ForceD - = forward
property ForwardVector — vector of direction
property Steer — angle to turn
property XVector
property LastForwardVector — last direction forward to use for lag
property TiltAngle —angle to be used with up down angle of car
global FrameDiff displaycarincr —FrameDiff= factor \
     difference between frames , and display spritenum
global  CarShaderList,  CarResourceList — all the car \
     shaderlists and resources
```

Car and MyWorld are used as shorthand references to the car and the world respectively. As with the other variables, their value is determined in the on new me script.

TotalRotation keeps track of the absolute rotation angle of the car about the y axis (in degrees).

UpVector, ForwardVector, and all of the following are relative to the position of the car:

- XVector (a unit vector going horizontally out from the side of the car)

- LastForwardVector (stored forward vector from the last frame, used for momentum and lag)

- ForceD (magnitude of force forward)

- MyDirection (direction of current movement)

- Steer (the incremental angle to turn)

- TiltAngle (vertical tilt angle about XVector)

MyResource will eventually be used to differentiate between the different cars; it is set to 1 by default.

FrameDiff will be used to make the movement independent of the performance of your machine, and CarShaderList and CarResourceList refer to properties of the car described below.

Setting up the car

The on new me function, called when the objects are first declared (see the exitframe script above), defines initial values for each variable, and makes a few initialization changes to the world itself. It also sets the car up within the world:

```
on new(me)
...
  — set up resources
  carlist = []
  CarShaderList = []
  CarResourceList = []
  repeat with i = 1 to 1 —6
    add carlist, MyWorld.clonemodelfromcastmember("car"&i, \
      member("car"&i).model[1].name, member("car"&i))
    add CarShaderList, carlist[i].shaderlist
    add CarResourceList , carlist[i].resource
    MyWorld.deletemodel("car"&i)
  end repeat
```

The cars are not directly imported in the on new me script. Instead, lists are created that reference the resource and the shader list for the car (CarResourceList and CarShaderList). The resource is the blueprint for the actual 3D model, and a 3D model's shader properties define its surface – textures, reflectivity, and so on.

This is set up in a repeat loop of 1. The lists and repeat loops are set up this way so that they can be easily adapted for multiuser play later.

The repeat loop makes a clone of the model in member "car1", calls it "car1" and adds the shader and resource properties from the original model onto the cloned model. These properties are stored in lists: CarShaderList and CarResourceList. The original model itself is then removed, as it will be created again from the model list. It's done this way because in the multiuser version, car allocation needs to be dynamic to respond to players coming and going in mid-game, and connections being lost and re-established.

Setting up the 3D world

As this is the first time we actually affect the 3D world, it is as good a place as any to make a few tweaks to the 3D world generally. These could be placed in a separate setup handler, but as this is the first initialization script, they can be placed in here as well.

```
—the surrounding globe must be only visible from the inside
  MyWorld.model("geosphere01").visibility = #back
...
  — make invisible position markers
  repeat with i = 1 to MyWorld.model.count
    if  MyWorld.model[i].name contains "start" then
      MyWorld.model[i].visibility  = #none
    end if
    —rotate world -90 about x
    MyWorld.model[i].transform.rotate(vector(0,0,0), \
      vector(1,0,0), -90.0)
  end repeat
...
return me

end
```

This code grabs hold of the background sphere within which all the action takes place (called `geosphere01` in the 3D world), and makes the outside invisible. Options for the visibility property are #back, #front, #both, #none. These options refer to the way the polygons are facing, so for the inside of an object you need to see the back of the polygons.

There are also some markers used later for initial positioning of the cars, which need to be made invisible – these models all contain the string "start" in their name.

The imported models were made in 3D Studio Max, which uses different x, y and z axes to Shockwave3D. Because the axes are different in Max and Lingo, the entire space needs to be rotated by 90 degrees about the x-axis.

An `on new me` handler is a function that needs to pass back object references as variables, and so the 'return me' call is required at the end of the handler.

Note that naming conventions are essential when building 3D worlds for use with Lingo, as the name of each model or group is the hook that Lingo uses to access it.

The frame script

Let's take a look at the `actorlist`, before taking a look at frame rate issues.

The actorlist

The actorlist is a list of objects that are active at any given time. Any objects in the actorlist will have their `stepframe` command executed each time a frame is entered.

This is the main frame script – in the example it's in frame 8, the last frame of the movie. It defines `CarObj` as the only active object at the moment, but more will be added. It also sets up `FrameDiff`, used throughout to make movement work according to the timer independently of the framerate of the movie (and hence the power of the computer).

```
on prepareframe me
  global FrameDiff, CarObj, CameraObj, fps

  global lastdiff , avatarobjectlist
  FrameDiff =  (the milliseconds - lastdiff)*0.034
  lastdiff= the milliseconds

  deleteall(the actorlist)
  add the actorlist, CarObj
  sortcam CameraObj, "fastcar"
  fps = fps + 1
end

on exitFrame me
  go the frame
end
```

This script also links the camera to your car.

Timer-based play

The 3D multiuser browser game is open to most people on the Web. Mac users, PC users, people running DirectX or OpenGL or neither – a very broad spectrum of processing power. It is imperative for fair play that, within limits, everyone gets a similar experience.

There is nothing that can be done about framerates; it is a fact of life that a player with a Pentium 4 and a 64MB video card is going to have a faster framerate than somebody with an iMac – and we don't want to reduce the P4 to a paltry performance level either. In Director, you can set the maximum framerate, but that does not define the minimum.

Assuming that the framerate does not go below playable levels (i.e. around 8 frames per second), we need to create code that works identically over time, independent of the fps rate.

If my car travels at a top speed of 8 units of distance per frame and has been built on a machine that runs the program at 25 fps, then that is equivalent to 25*8= 200 units per second. So, if my car were traveling at full speed, its next position would normally be

$$currentpos = lastpos+8$$

a framerate-independent version of that would be

$$currentpos = lastpos+ (200*(currentframetime-lastframetime))$$

where *currentframetime - lastframetime* is the time between frames in milliseconds.

By implementing this throughout in 3D, we can set the desired framerate as 999 fps (the maximum allowed). This way it will take full advantage of the fastest machine.

Controlling the car

The resources and shaders for the car are now available for instant use, but do not yet exist within the world. The reason for this apparently round-about technique is to give players a smooth experience; they can carry on driving even if they lose connection, and then continue again when connection is re-established.

Placing the car in the world and telling it how to move

The property variable MyResource is only <> 0 for a single frame at a time. This happens at the start, to establish a player's car, and then whenever connection is reestablished to the server after being lost.

This script, contained in the on stepframe me function back in the CarObj script member, is almost like a setup script. It's only run when MyResource <> 0 which, in normal connection situations, would be only when you first join.

First, the script checks to see whether or not you have a car model. If you don't, it creates one called "fastcar", rotates the car by 90 degrees (because Max and Director use different axes – whether or not this is required depends on the orientation of the car model) and places it in one of the six invisible markers used as random starting locations.

The markers are models within gworld that have a name including the string startpos. As MyResource is currently the number of your car (1 now, 1 to 6 in the multiuser version), it then takes the model resource and the model shaders from the lists created earlier, and applies them to your car. Finally, MyCar becomes the variable that holds your car number and MyResource is set back to zero:

```
on stepframe me
  if MyResource <> 0 then
    —does the model exist if not create one
    if  voidP(MyWorld.model("fastcar")) then
      car = MyWorld.newmodel("fastcar")
      car.transform.rotate(car.worldposition, vector(1,0,0), \
        -90.0)
      TotalRotation = 270
      car.translate(MyWorld.model("startpos"&random(6)). \
        worldposition ,#world)
    end if

    mycar = MyResource

    —-set the resource and shader list
    CarRes = CarResourceList[MyResource]
    car.resource = CarRes
    CarShaders = CarShaderList[MyResource]
```

continues overleaf

```
car.shaderlist =CarShaders
MyResource = 0

end if
```

Assuming the car model exists, we are now ready to start coding the interaction. (We're still in the `CarObj` script member at this point.)

The first thing to do is to set the car flat again, so that up and down are vertical. This won't be visible in game-play, but makes visualization and coding much simpler at this point.

```
—if the car model exists
if car <> 0 then
  acc = 0
  turn = 0
  car.transform.rotate(car.worldposition, XVector, -TiltAngle)
```

The car is going to be steerable using the arrow keys. These are defined by their ASCII code (123-126), and if a key is depressed it will affect either `Steer` or `Acc` – local variables for acceleration and turning.

```
if keypressed(125) then —downarrow
 Acc = 0.15
end if

if keypressed(124) then —rightarrow
 if Steer > 0 then
  Steer = 0
 end if
 Turn = -0.1
end if

if keypressed(123) then  —leftarrow
 if Steer < 0 then
  Steer = 0
 end if
 Turn = 0.1
end if

if keypressed(126) then  —uparrow
 Acc = -0.15
end if
```

The key interaction then needs to be transformed into movement. This could be done very simply, but a strong part of what determines whether a game is enjoyable or not – let alone addictive – is the 'feel' of the game. In this case, that means how the car reacts to your input.

The following routines apply a sensation of movement and friction to your car. `forceD` is the magnitude of the force applied to the car to make it react to your control; it is a simplified version of combining the throttle, the brakes, and friction to the car movement. It is also frame-independent. This is not based on a real physics simulation, but an intuitive interpretation of the real world.

```
— what to do with the keys
if turn <> 0 and ForceD <> 0 then
  acc = acc*0.75

  — decelerate
  if ForceD < 0  then
    ForceD = ForceD +0.1*FrameDiff
  else
    ForceD = ForceD -0.1*FrameDiff
  end if
end if

—don't let the acceleration go past max speeds (magnified
—by frame time factor)
if acc <> 0  then
  if ForceD + acc*FrameDiff < 6.5 and ForceD + \
    acc*FrameDiff > -12.0 then
    ForceD = ForceD + acc*FrameDiff
  end if
else
  if ForceD > 0  then
    if ForceD - 0.1*FrameDiff > 0 then
      ForceD = ForceD - 0.1*FrameDiff
    else
      ForceD =0
    end if
  end if
  if ForceD < 0  then
    if ForceD + 0.1*FrameDiff < 0 then
      ForceD = ForceD + 0.1*FrameDiff
    else
      ForceD =0
    end if
  end if
end if

if ForceD = 0 then
  LastForwardVector = ForwardVector
end if
```

The following ensures that the direction of turn stays within certain limits, that the amount of turn is related to speed (as with a real car), and that it is frame-independent.

```
—to make turning factor according to speed
movefact =sqrt((ForceD/4.0)*(ForceD/4.0))
```

```
—don't go past max turn
if turn <> 0 then
  if Steer + turn*movefact < 6.0 and Steer + turn*movefact \
      > -6.0 then
    Steer = Steer +turn*FrameDiff*movefact
  end if
else
  Steer = 0
end if

if ForceD <= 0 then
  aSteerfact = 1.0
else
  aSteerfact = -1.0
end if
```

These variables are then applied to the car in the 3D space. A rotation transform is created (an identity transform is a unit matrix) and applied to the car for the rotation, and the car is then moved by vector `MyDirection`. The vector `LastForwardVector` provides the direction, and `ForceD` gives the amount.

```
— apply rotations before movements
— make a transform to rotate the vectors
at = transform()
at.identity()
at.rotate(vector(0,0,0), UpVector, \
  aSteerfact*Steer*FrameDiff)

—rotate vectors by transform
XVector = at*XVector
ForwardVector = at*ForwardVector

—rotate the car
car.transform.rotate(car.worldposition, UpVector, \
  aSteerfact*Steer*FrameDiff)
TotalRotation = TotalRotation + aSteerfact*Steer*FrameDiff

—implement total absolute rotation
if TotalRotation > 360 then
  TotalRotation = TotalRotation - 360
end if
if TotalRotation <= 0 then
  TotalRotation = TotalRotation + 360
end if

—how far are we moving and in wnat dir
MyDirection = (( LastForwardVector*ForceD ) )*FrameDiff

—move the car
car.translate(MyDirection ,#world)
```

```
        —do the seek floor thing and at same time implement
     —directional movement
     afl = seekfloor(me)
```

The seekfloor handler

There is a self-contained script routine in the script member `CarObj` called `seekfloor`. Its purpose is to angle the car according to what is beneath it. It does this by sending a ray directly down from the center of the car, and creating a list (`alist`) of the models that the ray encounters.

In this case, the `ModelsUnderRay` command will return up to 5 models with full details (e.g. intersect position) for each in list form. It is looking for models called 'floor'. If it finds one, it first checks that it is below or just above the car (if not, it sets `flag` to zero), then it finds out the angle of tilt of the floor. This is done by measuring the angle between `UpVector` (vertical unit) and `alist[i].isectnormal` (a line at right angles to the plane of the floor).

It then checks the magnitude of the distance between car and floor to determine whether the car is on the ground or flying through the air, and applies an appropriate vector. Finally, it applies a gravitational force to the car if `flag` = 0 (in other words, if it hasn't found a floor underneath the car):

```
        —seek floor for this car
     on seekfloor me
       TiltAngle = 0
       alist = []
       ok = 1

       alist = MyWorld.modelsUnderRay(car.worldposition + \
         UpVector*200   ,-UpVector,5, #detailed)
       thisone = 0

       repeat with i = 1 to count(alist)
         if alist[i].model.name contains "floor"  then
           a = alist[i].isectposition
           av = vector(0,(-car.worldposition.y + \
             alist[i].isectposition.y + 20.0), 0)
           am =  MyDirection
           — car.boundingsphere[2] is the radius of model of car
           —(look up)
           if a.y > car.worldposition.y + car.boundingsphere[2]   then
             flag = 0
           else
             flag = av

             —the angle between the normal of picking and the vector
             —straight up
```

continues overleaf

```
        TiltAngle = -UpVector.anglebetween(alist[i].isectnormal)

        —the vector for the angle
        XVector = alist[i].isectnormal.perpendicularto(UpVector)
        if av.magnitude > 5.0*FrameDiff then
          ab = av/av.magnitude*5*FrameDiff
          car.translate(ab, #world)
        else
          car.translate(av, #world)
        end if
        exit repeat
      end if
    else
    end if
  end repeat

  —do we need to add gravity
  if flag = 0 then
    car.translate(0,-2.0*FrameDiff, 0, #world)
  end if
  if flag = 1 then
    flag = 0
  end if
end
```

Transferring seekfloor script information back to the stepframe script

Returning to the main stepframe script, we now need to update LastForwardVector, the lagged forward vector, so that it can be used in the next frame call.

```
  —make acceleration lag
  if acc = 0 then
    LastForwardVector =(LastForwardVector)
  else
    LastForwardVector =(ForwardVector + LastForwardVector)/2.0
  end if
```

Seekfloor delivers values for TiltAngle (the tilt angle) and XVector (the vector for the angle). This information is easily applied to the car as a rotation transform:

```
  —apply floor rotation
  car.transform.rotate(car.worldposition, XVector, TiltAngle)
```

The only thing left to do to the car is to decide what happens if it falls completely off the structure. The easiest thing is to say there is an invisible floor just below the bottom level of the car park structure and let people drive around forever, but another option is to reset the car if it falls off the edge. The car is beyond hope if it falls below the lowest level of the structure, (if its global y position falls below 100).

```
—if the car has fallen too low we will have to reset its
—position and variables
  if car.worldposition.y < 100 then
    MyDirection = vector(0,0,0)

    car.transform.rotate(car.worldposition, XVector, \
      -TiltAngle)
    car.transform.rotate(car.worldposition,UpVector, \
      -TotalRotation)
    car.transform.rotate(car.worldposition,UpVector, -90)
    TotalRotation = 270
    car.translate(-car.worldposition /
    +MyWorld.model("startpos"&random(6)).worldposition,#world)
    UpVector = vector(0,1,0)
    ForwardVector = vector(0,0,1)
    XVector = vector(1,0,0)
    TiltAngle = 0
    ForceD = 0
    Steer = 0

  end if
end if

end
```

The camera object

This script is placed in a new movie script member in the car cast, called `CameraObj`. The `on new me` function sets up a few variables (including `MyCamera`, which refers directly to the default camera), and also creates a new model called `MyCameraModel`, which will be used in the frame script to control the camera. This is the best place to define camera settings: fog, projection angle (wide angle, telephoto...), and so on.

```
—CAMERA OBJECT
—simple camera object follows your car
—not complex you may wish to update this object
property MyCamera, MyCameraModel, MyWorld, MoveTime
global CarObj
on new me
  —this is where you may wish to put fog settings near and far
  —hither and thither, play with these
  MyWorld = member("gworld")
  MyCameraModel = MyWorld.newmodel("MyCameraModel")
  MyCamera = MyWorld.camera[1]
  MyCamera.projectionangle = 65.0
  MoveTime = the milliseconds
  return me
end
```

This object is always called on the main `prepareframe` script, so there is no need to put it in the actorlist.

```
SortCam CameraObj, "fastcar"
```

This calls the `sortcam` handler, in the `CameraObj` object script member:

```
on sortcam me ,modname

    secs = the milliseconds - MoveTime
    MoveTime = the milliseconds

    —if the model exists then transform camera
    if voidp(MyWorld.model(modname)) then
    else
```

`modname` is a reference to the player's car (`fastcar`, defined in the `CarObj` object) to make sure the camera follows your car, and not somebody else's.

The script creates its own simplified timer script, where `secs` is the time since the last call, and then checks that the player's car has been defined before positioning the camera.

The camera model (not the camera itself) is placed at the same place as the player's car. It is then moved back by 100 units (relative to the car), up by 20, and finally pointed at the car again.

```
MyCameraModel.transform.interpolateto(MyWorld.model(modname).getwo
rldtransform(), 100.0)

—100 upwards from car
MyCameraModel.translate(CarObj.UpVector*-100.0, #self)
—back a bit
—not a great cam function haven't worked much on it, feel free
MyCameraModel.translate(0, 20, 0, #world)
MyCameraModel.pointat(MyWorld.model(modname).worldposition)
```

So `MyCameraModel` is now constantly just above and behind the car:

The reason we've used a model to attach the camera to is that it is then much easier to take advantage of the `interpolateto` function, which moves a model towards another model in increments. If the `interpolateto` lag is set to 100 (done above) then the model will be immediately moved onto the target. If, on the other hand, a lower figure is used (it must be at least 1) then the model will move that percentage of the way towards the target.

The following routine creates that percentage as a function of the timer rather than the framerate, and then uses it to interpolate the camera to `MyCameraModel`. If `ap` were set to 100, the camera would be rigidly fixed just above and behind the car.

```
—make percentage for lag
ap = secs/4.0

if ap < 1.0 then
  ap = 1.0
end if
if ap > 100.0 then
  ap = 100.0
end if
    MyCamera.transform.interpolateto \
                  (MyCameraModel.getworldtransform(), ap)
  end if
end
```

Going multiuser

We now have a working interactive setup – the car can be driven within the world, and the scripting has been structured in such a way that it can be fairly easily transformed into a multiuser engine. This section will turn the program into a multiuser car driving experience.

It's divided into six main parts that cover the groundwork needed to prepare for, and actually make the connection to the server, before looking at how other players' cars are initialized and controlled. Specifically, we'll be looking at:

- How to prepare for a connection: setting up your timeout script and establishing the server object.

- Making contact with the server.

- How the server responds to the connection.

- What the player receives from the server and how it's handled.

- How information about your car's movement is packaged up and passed to the server.

- How the server deals with and represents that movement information.

- How the server represents other players' cars on your machine and vice versa.

- The actions taken when a player leaves the game.

> *Whilst running through this section of the game's creation, you should refer to* KARZ_2.dir. *This shows the results of the completion of this section, without any other confusing elements.*

Preparing for connection

There is a handler, startit, which is called from an early exitframe script. This is where the multiuser instance begins. It sets up a timeout script and initializes the ServerObj object.

```
on startit me
  secs = the milliseconds
  thenetid = 0

  sendlist = []
  OnlineConnect = 0
  checker = timeout("looker").new(10000, #looker, me)

  ServerObj = new(member("ServerObj").script)
end
```

The server object is the heart of the multiuser data machine – and the first step is the on new me handler, which sets up the basic parameters and properties of the object. At this point, the parts to focus on are the connection details; movie ID, IP address, port number, and user ID. Because we will be instituting automated login, the user ID is appended by a random number – the chances are literally a million to 1 that these will be duplicated.

```
on new me
  AvatarList = []
  AvatarObjectList = []

  CrateState = "noconn"

  MyState = "offline"

  myconnection = void
  movieid = "karz"
  MyMovieID = movieid
  userid = "car"&random(999999)
  MyUserName = userid
  myConnectionType="server1"

  -the ip address
  ip = "127.0.0.1"
  MyServerName = ip
```

```
          —the port to be used
          port = 1626
          MyPortNum = port

          —timer for checking groups
          LastGroupUpdate = the milliseconds


          —set up a timeout to check server state and resolve it
          ServerTimeout =  timeout("serv").new(3000, #updateserver, me)

          return me
      end
```

From within our `startit` handler, `checker` sets up a timeout script that is automatically called at regular intervals. The script called here is named `looker`, and is called every 10,000ms, or every 10 seconds, regardless of what else is going on. `looker` is in the `beginscript` script, and its function is simply to check that a connection has been made, and if not, to automatically go to frame `con` (frame 5) and attempt to connect every 10 seconds.

```
      on looker me
        if ServerObj <> void and ServerObj <> 0 then
          if OnlineConnect = 0 and ServerObj.MyState <> \
          "waitinggroup" and ServerObj.MyState <> "waitinggroup2" then
            go "con"
          end if
        end if

      end
```

Whether called by `looker` or as part of the initial setup, the script that is used is the same: it is the on `connect me` handler in `ServerObj`. It is called from the `prepareframe` script on the `con` frame:

```
      on prepareframe me
        global ServerObj, chatstuff, fps
        if ServerObj.myconnection <> void then
          ServerObj.myconnection = void
        end if
        connect ServerObj
```

Attempting connection

This script is familiar territory, it is taken from the multiuser behavior library in Director. It creates the multiuser Xtra instance, and performs various checks. If there is already a connection, the username, server name, and port number are checked for validity. If the connection is invalid or does not exist, a new one is created. Once the instance is successfully created, a series of handlers are defined to deal with incoming messages from the server.

```
on connect me

  myPassword = "none"
  — make sure that a connection doesn't already exist
  set   existingConnection = \
    locateExistingConnection(myConnectionType)
  if existingConnection <> VOID then
    — see if we can just use the existing connection
    if existingConnection.MyUserName <> MyUserName then
      report(me, "Can't connect \
        since"&&existingConnection.MyUserName&&"is already \
        connected using" && myConnectionType)
    else if existingConnection.MyServerName <> MyServerName then
      report(me, "Can't connect since" &&\
        existingConnection.MyUserName && "is already connected \
        to server"  && existingConnection.MyServerName && \
        "using" && myConnectionType)
    else if existingConnection.MyPortNum <> MyPortNum then
      report(me, "Can't connect since" && \
        existingConnection.MyUserName && "is already connected \
        to port"  && existingConnection.MyPortNum && "using" &&\
        myConnectionType)
    else
      — since all the conneciton parameters are the same, we
      —can just use that
      — connection object and do nothing here
    end if
  else

    if ilk( myConnection ) <> #instance then
      — no multiuser xtra instance, so let's create one:
      set myConnection = new( xtra "multiuser")

      if not objectP( myConnection ) then
        alert"problem creating the mutiuser xtra"

      else
        —add the actorlist , me
        —here check for if the name exists
        —set up a handler to respond to the connection message
        —from the server
        setamessagehandler(me, #responsetoconnection, me, \
          "ConnectToNetServer", "", 0 )
        setamessagehandler(me, #sortmessages, me, "","", 1)

        setamessagehandler(me, #gettingusers, me,"getusers", \
          "",1)
        setamessagehandler(me, #getcar, me,"getcar", "", 1)

        setamessagehandler(me, #jointhis, me,"jointhis", "", 1)
        setamessagehandler(me, #joining, me,"joingroup", "", 1)
```

We'll look at each handler as it is used. The first call to the server is now made. The connectToNetServer command sends your user name, password (in this case "none"), the IP address of the server you're trying to connect to, the port number you are using, and the movie name.

```
set err = myconnection.connectToNetServer \
          ( MyUserName, "none", MyServerName, MyPortNum,
MyMovieID )

        if err <> 0 then
          — problem connecting...
          set errString = GetNetErrorString( myConnection, err )
          alert errString
          —          destroy me true
          —          quit
        end if
        set MyState = "connecting"

      end if
    end if
  end if
end
```

On the server

> You'll need to refer to SERVERSIDE.dir for much of the code under
> this heading.

So connection has been attempted using connectToNetServer. If nobody else is connected (as is the case in the above response), the server movie will be created and initialized on the server:

```
on new me
  sscriptText =gDispatcher.pScriptObjectList[1]
  me.initGame()
  return me
end

on initGame me
  groups = []
  groupnamelist = []
  grcount = 1
  maxusers = 6
end
```

Dispatcher.ls will then check scriptmap.ls for additional scripts to use with the movie:

```
on scriptMap
 theMap = []
 theMap.append( [ #movieID: "karz*", #scriptFileName: "cargame.ls"
] )
 return theMap
end
```

An additional script object has also been appended to the scriptObjectList:

```
on scriptObjectList
 theList = []
 theList.Append( "cargamegroupobj.ls" )
 return theList
end
```

Back in the cargame movie script, the server has detected that you want to log on, and so sets about finding you a group to join, in on findplacem.

```
on userLogOn (me, movie, group, user)
 —a user has just logged on to the movie call this hadler to
 —find a group for them
 findplacem (me, user, movie)
end
```

This goes through each existing group in turn until it finds one that has some space left in it. If it doesn't find any groups with space in them, the thisgroup flag will still be 0 and a new group needs to be created. This would happen if all groups have six players in them, or if there's nobody there.

```
on findplacem me, user, movie
 —set up a flag
 thisgroup = 0
 —  check existing group objects for numbers of users
 repeat with i = 1 to count(groups)
   if groups[i].usercount < maxusers then
     thisgroup = i
     exit repeat
   end if
 end repeat
 if thisgroup = 0 then
```

Creating a new group consists of defining a number to append to the group name, creating a new group script object, adding it to the groups list, and adding the name of the group to groupnamelist.

Whether or not a new group has been created, the player now needs to log on to the group and be assigned a car number (with the userLogOngroupobj) before the information is then sent back to him.

```
                    —if no  groups with spare room exist
                    grcount = grcount + 1

                    —    lets not let this number get out of hand
                    if grcount > 9999 then
                      grcount = 1
                    end if

                    —create a new group script obj and add to list groups
                    add groups, new(sscriptText, grcount, \
                                        "@cgamegroup"&grcount , myMovie)
                    —add the name of that group to a namelist for
                    —position reference
                    add groupnamelist,   "@cgamegroup"&grcount

                    —call handlers for this group obj to set it up
                    moviecreategroupobj(groups[count(groups)],
      movie,"@cgamegroup"&grcount, user)
                    userLogOngroupobj (groups[count(groups)], movie, \
                                        "@cgamegroup"&grcount, user)

                    —-tell the user what group they must now join
                    myMovie.sendMessage ( user.name, \
                                "jointhis","@cgamegroup"&grcount )

                  else
                    —-if a group exists

                    —tell the groupobject that a new user is about to join
                    userLogOngroupobj (groups[thisgroup], movie, \
                                groups[thisgroup].mygroup, user)

                    —-tell the user to join the group
                    myMovie.sendMessage ( user.name, "jointhis", \
                                groups[thisgroup].mygroup )
                  end if
                end
```

Having been assigned to a group, the following scripts in `cargamegroupobj` keep count of how many players there are in that group, and then assign a car number (ac). If there are no crates in the space, it adds one (more on that later) and then sends the assigned information back to the player that just joined:

```
                —some one has joined so set up their details and asign them a
                —car
                on userLogOngroupobj (me, movie, group, user)
                  mput user.name&"<——user logged on ..."
                  usercount = usercount + 1
                  findplace (me, user, movie)
                  —  send to group
```

continues overleaf

```
    end
    on findplace me, user, movie
      add namelist,user.name
      if count(availcars) >= 1 then
        ac = availcars[1]
        deleteat (availcars, 1)
        add takencars, ac
      else
        ac ="groupfull"
      end if
      add positionlist, [user.name, ac, 0]
      if cratestate = 0 then
        makecrate me
      end if
      —tell the new user what car they are to be and where the
      —crate is
      myMovie.sendMessage ( user.name, "getcar", [ac, cratestate] )
    end
```

What the player receives and how it's handled

By the time the server has done all of the above, it will have sent three messages back to you, the player. First, assuming the data you sent checks out with the server, you will get a message response with subject connectToNetServer. Then, when a group has been assigned, you get a jointhis message. Finally, when you've been assigned a position, you are sent a getcar message. Here, we'll look at how you'll process these messages.

connectToNetServer

A message handler (set up in on connect me from the Shockwave movie) passes this to on responsetoconnection me. This handler checks the error code (hopefully '0'), and then sets the MyState variable to waitinggroup.

```
        —did we get connected?
        on responsetoconnection me
          set newmsg = myconnection.getnetmessage()
          —put newmsg
          case(newmsg.errorCode) of
            0:
              OnlineConnect = 0
              timeoutconnect = the milliseconds
              set MyState = "waitinggroup"
            otherwise
              OnlineConnect = 0
              set MyState = "offline"
              myconnection = void
          end case
        end
```

```
jointhison jointhis me, msg
  ng = msg.content
  errCode = myconnection.sendNetMessage("system.group.join", \
    "joingroup", ng)

end
```

The script above returns confirmation that you have joined the group (if required, a group will have been created) from the server. It also triggers the following script from the joingroup subject, which confirms the group name, and, unless there's a problem, sets MyState to connected:

```
—now i have joined a group ...or have i?
on joining me, msg
  case(msg.errorCode) of
    0:
      MyGroup = msg.content
      OnlineConnect = 1
      set MyState = "connected"
    otherwise
      OnlineConnect = 0
      set MyState = "offline"
      myconnection = void
  end case
end
```

getcar

Having been assigned a car number, the number is now applied to variable MyResource, which is used in the CarObj stepframe script to assign you the correct car:

```
—what car am i going to be?
on getcar me, msg
  global CarObj
  CarObj.MyResource = msg.content[1]
  CrateState = msg.content[2]
end
```

We've said that our limit is six cars per group. In the on new me script in CarObj, we created lists for CarResourceList and CarShaderList in a repeat loop of 1. These must now be changed to 6 to allow up to six cars in the environment.

Defining and sending movement data

Other players need to know your position. The information that needs to be sent is: who you are, where you are, and what group you belong to. This needs to be updated regularly – but not so often as to block up the pipe with too much data.

These details are added to the `CarObj` stepframe, where `SendTimer` is set at 800 – meaning that your position is sent to the server every 800ms. `MySender` was the time (in milliseconds) that the last position message was sent to the server.

```
if the milliseconds - mysender > SendTimer then
 SendCar me
 mysender = the milliseconds
end if
```

`SendCar` controls the collecting and sending of information to the server. As this game also runs in a standalone (non-MUS) version, and can slip from one state to the other without interrupting game-play, all multiuser calls must be prefaced by a check on whether the connection is there or not.

In addition to just sending our information, we have also implemented a simple method to compensate for time lag. Rather than sending the actual location of the car at the time of sending, you can predict where it will be in the future if you assume that it will continue in its current direction. As lag is indeterminate and variable (especially on somebody else's computer) this is a process of trial and error, but our tests show that this creates a more lifelike experience than simply sending the current position of the car.

The data is sent in as compact a fashion as can reasonably be produced; it sends the x, y, z coordinates as three comma-delimited integers. The default of floating-point numbers adds surprisingly to the bandwidth requirements as the numbers contain significantly more digits – and with six cars sending data more than once a second, this is not negligible. It also sends car name, score, and rotation about the y axis. Data, although normally sent every 800 ms, is only sent every 3 seconds if the car is static – this, again, avoids data buildup.

```
on sendcar me
  —make sure server obj exists
  if not voidp(ServerObj)  then
    —MyDirectionPlus is magnified by the time lag in the sense
    —i will not send for another 800 mils
    avts = car.worldposition + \
      MyDirectionPlus*(SendTimer/1000.0)*30.0

    —sending [[car position as integers in a list] , which
    —car, score , absolute rotation around y]
    tosend = [[integer(avts.x),integer(avts.y), \
      integer(avts.z)], MyCar , MyScore,  TotalRotation]
    —if set has not changed ie is still send lest
    —frequently(this can be played with for optimization
    if LastSentPosCheck <> tosend  or the milliseconds \
      - LastSentPos > 1500 then
      if  not voidp(ServerObj.myconnection) then

        —the sending function
        sendit(ServerObj, ServerObj.MyUserName&"newpos",tosend)
        —last time i sent
```

```
                LastSentPos = the milliseconds
            end if
            — what did i just send?
            LastSentPosCheck =tosend
        end if
    end if
end
```

Implementing received movement data

The format of the message sent back from the server is a property list with five properties. The #content property is also a list in its own right (as defined in SendCar). For example, see the following, which is the data format of what is sent and received by all cars defining their position:

```
[#errorCode: 0, #recipients: ["@cargamegroup1"], #senderID:
"car199536", #subject: "car199536newpos", #content: [[870, 531,
728], 1, 0, 270.0000], #TimeStamp: 62840427]
```

As a received message, this is passed to the sortmessages handler in your ServerObj movie script, as it has an unrecognized #subject (your id and newpos):

```
on sortmessages me, msg
    if msg.subject contains "newpos" and msg.SenderID  <> \
      MyUserName then
      alist = msg.content

      set anum = getone(AvatarList,msg.SenderID)
      if anum  = 0 then
        —if msg.SenderID  <> MyUserName then
        makeav me , msg
        —end if
      end if
    end if
end
```

Sortmessages checks to see whether the message is simply being returned to you, the sender. If so, then it's ignored. If you remove the and Message.senderid <> MyUserName from sortmessages, it will think you are somebody else, so you will see your own avatar as others will see it. This is very useful for fine-tuning performance! It also double-checks to see whether the sender's user ID is already in the list of existing players (AvatarList), before calling Makeav.

Makeav adds the sender's ID to AvatarList and AvatarObjectList, and calls the AvatarObj on new me function:

```
on makeav me, message
    set sender = message.SenderID
    if getone(AvatarList, sender) <> void then
      nothing
    else
```

continues overleaf

```
        add AvatarList, sender
        add AvatarObjectList, [sender, \
          new(member("AvatarObj").script, message)]
     end if
  end
```

The new information is then added to the main `prepareframe` script, to incorporate the objects in `AvatarObjectList` into the `actorlist`:

```
     if ilk(AvatarObjectList) = #list then
     repeat with i = 1 to count(AvatarObjectList)
        add the actorlist, AvatarObjectList[i][2]
     end repeat
  end if
```

The remote car object (AvatarObj)

`AvatarObj`, the object that controls other people's cars, has now been initialized and is running. Each player in your group, except yourself, will create an instance of `AvatarObj` in your game. The instances are held in the `AvatarObjectList` list, which is updated in the main `prepareframe` script in frame 8.

`AvatarObj` controls the movement and position of the other cars in the game, based on the incoming position messages from other players. It applies a bit of intelligence to this, predicting (to an extent) where each car probably is from what it knows about lag, when the last position was sent and received, the direction of travel and so on.

Initialization

The `on new me` function sets up various properties of the car (`KillMe` is used to delete cars when they leave – more on this later). `Avatar` is the reference name given to the avatar. The `ExtraBit` is used simply to deal with a feature of Director. If car326818 loses connection then reconnects, your movie will delete model car326818 then try to recreate it. This will generate a 'model has been deleted' error. `ExtraBit` just ensures that in this case, the model name will be different on each connection.

```
on new me,  msg
   TimeStamp = msg.TimeStamp
   NetTime = the milliseconds
   MyWorld = member("gworld")
   KillMe = 0
   —make amodel for the av
   SendID = msg.SenderID
   ExtraBit = string(random(999999))
   Avatar = MyWorld.newmodel(SendID&ExtraBit)
```

Following on from this in `AvatarObj`, `ResourceList` and `ShaderList` are lists generated by `CarObj` (see earlier) that contain all six available cars' model resources and shader properties. As

Message.content[2] represents the number (from 1 to 6) of this car, it simply pulls the appropriate properties from the lists.

```
—fill with the ressources
MyResource = 0
if MyResource = 0 then
  Avatar.resource = CarResource[msg.content[2]]
   Avatar.shaderlist = CarShaderList[msg.content[2]]
  MyResource = msg.content[2]
end if

 —needed vectors
UpVector = vector(0,1,0)
XVector = vector(1,0,0)
 —  how much to rotate
TotalRotation =msg.content[4]
```

The car is then positioned in the space in two steps; first it is correctly orientated, then it is translated to the position defined in the received message (item 1 of #content – remember that we turned the vector into three integers to save on bandwidth in SendCar). XVector and TargetTotal are variables needed later.

```
—initialize the avatar car
Avatar.transform.rotate(Avatar.worldposition, XVector, -90.0)

Avatar.transform.rotate(Avatar.worldposition, UpVector,90)

Avatar.transform.rotate(Avatar.worldposition, \
  UpVector,TotalRotation)

—transform to rotate vectors
at = transform()
at.identity()
at.rotate(vector(0,0,0), UpVector, TotalRotation)

XVector = at*XVector

targettotal = TotalRotation
—make a varialble
atrans = msg.content[1]
MyTrans = [vector(atrans[1],atrans[2],atrans[3]),void]

—put to told position
diffvector = -Avatar.worldposition + MyTrans[1]
Avatar.translate(diffvector, #world)

—set up timers
LastSecsF = the milliseconds

MoveTime = the milliseconds
```

You also need to create a new message handler for future calls from this car, with `SendID&"newpos"` as the subject. This way, incoming messages with that subject will always be transferred to this `AvatarObj` object. And at some point, the player will leave; you need to be able to deal with this too!

```
—see ServerObj, i need to make the server obj know where to
—tell the MU xtra to send future messages about movement
  —send them here
  setamessagehandler( ServerObj, #newpositioncar, me, \
    SendID&"newpos", SendID, 1)
  —to collect messages about avatar if left
  setamessagehandler( ServerObj, #destroyav, me, \
    SendID&"KillMe", "System.Script", 1)
  return me
end
```

Updating a car's position from the server

Every time your movie receives a position update from the server for an initialized car, the message is forwarded to that avatar's `newpositioncar` handler. This defines the target positions that the car is aiming at. Iterating to that position is performed every frame on the `stepframe` handler discussed below. Without this approach, other cars would simply leap from one position to the next every 800ms or so, when you got a position update for it.

`NetTime` is used to ensure that users remain connected; its value is checked in the `stepframe` handler against the actual time – see below. Then, assuming that the avatar is still alive, the new target angle of rotation (`TargetTotal`) and position (`mytrans`) are stored. A bit of deft footwork ensures that the car turns in the right direction (e.g. if it goes from 90 degrees to 110 degrees it should take the shortest route, clockwise).

```
on newpositioncar me, msg
  —not useing but i wanna know how long from sending to
  —recieving
  TimeStamp = msg.TimeStamp -TimeStamp
  TimeStamp = msg.TimeStamp

  —cancel the time out net function
  NetTime = the milliseconds

  —if i am alive do this
  if KillMe = 0 then

    targettotal  =msg.content[4]
    adif = targettotal - TotalRotation
    —we always want the rotation to be with in 0 to 360 but we
    —also want it to turn the right way this bit handles if
    —total rotation is 10 and target is 350 it only rotate - 20
    —not + 330
    if adif > 180 then
```

```
      TotalRotation = TotalRotation + 360
    end if
    if adif < - 180 then
      TotalRotation = TotalRotation - 360
    end if

    --store the position for later
    atrans = msg.content[1]
    MyTrans = [vector(atrans[1],atrans[2],atrans[3]),void]
```

The next procedure is to move the car to an appropriate position. `SetDiff` establishes how bad the lag is, by comparing the time since the last position and the expected time (800ms). If there is a lag, then the car is moved instantly (in a single jump) to a position between where it was and where it should be. For example, if the lag is twice the expected time or greater, `ap` is 100% and the car is moved directly to the new received position.

```
    --work out a time percentage
    setdiff = (the milliseconds - LastSecsF) - SendTimer
    if setdiff > 0 then
      ap = (setdiff/SendTimer)*100.0
      if ap > 100 then
        ap = 100
      end if
      if ap <= 0.0 then
        ap = 0.0
      end if
    else
      ap = 0.0
    end if
    LastSecsF = the milliseconds
    dv = -Avatar.worldposition + MyTrans[1]
    tv = (dv/100.0)*(ap)
    - trans late towards dest by that percentage
    Avatar.translate(tv, #world)
```

Due to the dynamic nature of the login procedures here, it's worth checking that the car has not changed identity. If it has, we update its model resource and shaders from the lists:

```
    if MyResource <> msg.content[2] then
        Avatar.resource = CarResource[msg.content[2]]
        Avatar.shaderlist = CarShaderList[msg.content[2]]
        MyResource = msg.content[2]
      end if
    end if
  end
```

Iterating the car's position

The first thing to do here is ensure that you are still receiving information from the car. NetTime is updated whenever you receive this kind of information, so if the last message was received over 40 seconds ago, they are considered dead and removed using destroyav.

If this was actually just a bad bit of lag, the car will then reconnect using the sortmessages and MakeAvatar handlers. mytrans is the target location received, and ap is calculated as a variable proportional to the time between frames. dv is the vector between where the car is in your world and the last position it sent; the car is then moved by a percentage of that vector.

```
on stepframe me
  if the milliseconds - NetTime > 40000 then
    — if it has been idle for 40secs kill it
    destroyav me, ""
  else
    — if it's alive then
    if KillMe = 0 then
      — make sure there is info to use
      if MyTrans <> 0 then
        —make a vector for the avatar to move to
        —interpolating with a time based percentage
        secs = the milliseconds - MoveTime
        MoveTime = the milliseconds
        ap = secs/5.0
        if ap < 1.0 then
          ap = 1.0
        end if
        if ap > 100.0 then
          ap = 100.0
        end if
        dv = -Avatar.worldposition + MyTrans[1]
        tv = (dv/100.0)*(ap)
        Avatar.translate(tv, #world)
```

You also want to iterate the angle of rotation of the car. This is done by removing the existing rotation, and then reapplying an absolute rotation. This rotation comprises of the old rotation angle plus fraction ap (calculated above) of the difference between the old and the target rotation angle.

```
—cancel last rotation for vectors and the model avatar
Avatar.transform.rotate(Avatar.worldposition , \
  UpVector, -TotalRotation )
—use the percentage to calcutate absolute rotation
TotalRotation = TotalRotation + (( targettotal - \
  TotalRotation)/100.0)*ap
—use that rotation on vectors and model
Avatar.transform.rotate(Avatar.worldposition , \
  UpVector, TotalRotation )
```

```
                —check the floor same as seek floor
               upfloor me
            end if
          end if
       end if
    end
```

UpFloor is very much like the seekfloor handler on CarObj. It detects whether there is a floor below or near the car, and tells the car to act accordingly. However, UpFloor is not concerned with tilt, only height.

The additional accuracy of putting tilt on other players' cars seems less desirable than the performance improvement – because the cars move quickly it is in fact hardly noticeable. However, the full seekfloor could easily be adapted for use here, if you wanted to use it.

```
on UpFloor me
 aList = MyWorld.modelsUnderRay(avatar.worldposition + \
            vector(0,1,0)*200 ,-vector(0,1,0),3, #detailed)

 thisone = 0
 repeat with i = 1 to count(aList)
  if aList[i].model.name contains "floor" then
   a = aList[i].isectposition
   av = vector(0,(-avatar.worldposition.y + \
                  aList[i].isectposition.y + 20.0), 0)
   if a.y > avatar.worldposition.y + avatar.boundingsphere[2]
then
     else
      avatar.translate(av, #world)
      exit repeat
     end if
   else
   end if
 end repeat
end
```

When people leave

There is some tidying up that needs to be done when people leave; their car needs to be removed from the group, and the group itself may need to be deleted if that user is the last to leave.

Removing a car

If a car leaves, the on groupleave handler detects it on the server:

```
on groupLeave   (me, movie, group, user)
  —someone left the group notify the object
  agname = group.name
  apos= getone(groupnamelist, agname)
  if apos <> 0 then
    groupleavegroupobj   (groups[apos], movie, group, user)
  end if
end
```

This handler calls the GroupLeaveGroupObj group object script. aNum is the name of the exiting car, and it checks to see whether the car's position is available or not. If it is taken, it's deleted from the taken list and added to the list of available cars again (availcars). The car (or at least its name) is also removed from the position and names lists. Finally, it sends a message to everyone in the group saying that a car has left:

```
on groupLeavegroupobj   (me, movie, group, user)
  —this lets us know which cars to make free for other users
  anum = getone(namelist, user.name)
  if anum <> 0 then
    p =  getone(availcars, positionlist[anum][2])
    if p = 0 then
      g = getone(takencars, positionlist[anum][2])
      if g <> 0 then
        add availcars , positionlist[anum][2]
        deleteat takencars, g
      end if
    end if
    deleteat(positionlist, anum)
    deleteat(namelist, anum)
    —tell every one to kill this user from their game
    myMovie.sendMessage ( mygroup,  user.name&"killme", \
      user.name )
    usercount = usercount - 1
  —if usercount <=0 then
  —kill off group
  —end if
  end if
end
```

When an avatar object is initialized, a message handler is created to sort messages with a sender ID and a subject of `KillMe`.

```
setamessagehandler( ServerObj, #destroyav, me, \
          SendID&"KillMe", SendID, 1)
```

This will either be called from the server, or as a secondary safety measure if no signal has been received from a car for 40 seconds (this is checked in the `stepframe` script above).

When a player leaves, the `DestroyAv` handler in `AvatarObj` is called. This sets the variable `KillMe` to 1 to ensure that no other `stepframe` or other scripts are run that could generate errors. It then deletes the model and removes the car's name from the `AvatarList` and the object from `AvatarObjectList`. The message handler reference that detects position calls from the car is cancelled, the object is removed from the `actorlist`, and it sets itself to void.

```
on destroyav me, msg
  —if KillMe = 1 then it won't try to run any error making
  —scripts
  KillMe = 1
  MyWorld.deletemodel(SendID&ExtraBit)
  aget = getone(AvatarList, SendID)
  if aget<> void then
    deleteat( AvatarList  , aget)
  end if
  aget = getone(AvatarObjectList , [SendID, me])
  if  aget <> void then
    deleteat(AvatarObjectList, aget)
  end if
  setamessagehandler( ServerObj, 0, me, SendID&"newpos", \
    SendID, 0)
  setamessagehandler( ServerObj, 0, me, SendID&"KillMe", \
    "System.Script", 0)
  aget =getone(the actorlist, me)
  if aget<> 0 then
    deleteat(the actorlist, aget)
  end if
  me = void
end
```

Deleting groups

The server automatically deletes groups if they're empty but – as we've made our own lists to control and monitor the groups – the references to the empty group need to be removed from them. This is done on the server side in `cargame`:

```
on groupDelete (me, movie, group, user)
 anum = getone(groupnamelist, group.name)
 if anum <> 0 then
   groupdeletegroupobj groups[anum]
```

continues overleaf

```
    deleteat (groups, anum)
    deleteat (groupnamelist, anum)
  end if
  mput "cargame groupDelete "&group.name
end
```

Checking for net congestion

Another timeout script was created in the `on new me` handler of the server object, called `ServerTimeout`. The script called here is `updateserver`, and it is called every 3,000ms, or every 3 seconds, regardless of what else is going on. `Updateserver` is used to check whether there is a buildup of unread messages from the server.

`getnumberwaitingmessages` returns an integer; if this number is greater than 5 (there are more than 5 messages queued) these are processed immediately. Similarly, `LastGroupUpdate` denotes the time of the last received message – if this exceeds 6 seconds, then an immediate call is made to the server.

```
on updateserver me
  tfps = fps/4.0
  fps = 0
  if MyState = "connected" and OnlineConnect = 1 then
    if myconnection <> void then
      set anum = myconnection.getnumberwaitingnetmessages ()
      if anum > 5 then
        myconnection.checknetmessages (anum)
      end if
      if the milliseconds - LastGroupUpdate > 6000 then
        set err = /
          myconnection.sendnetmessage ("system.group.getUsers", \
          "getusers", MyGroup)
        if UpdateLag = "wait" then
          UpdateLag = the milliseconds
        end if
        if err = -2147216214 then
          OnlineConnect = 0
          myconnection = void
        end if
      end if
    end if
  end if
end
```

Making it a game

You now have a working multiuser car environment; it works and it's interesting, it's the biggest part of the game done, but it ain't a game yet! We need to add in the game-play element and the interface. The rules of this game are that crates of contraband drop out of the sky, and it's your job to get them before anybody else. It's a case of smash and grab as you race towards the next crate, trying to drive through it and make it explode before anyone gets it.

We'll cover how the crate is initially created and positioned, and how its state is monitored. We'll then see how the server responds to a collision with a crate, how scores are calculated and updated on the player's machine, and how the particle emitter is used to create an explosion effect.

> *While running through this section of the game's creation, refer to* `KARZ_3.dir`.

Creating the crate

The first crate appears when the first car logs onto a group.

The crate sits where it lands until someone collides with it, at which point a message is sent to the server that the crate has been collected. The server checks this message (in case, for example, two cars both think they have hit the crate) and at that point, the next crate is dropped at a new location. And so the process goes on until the last person leaves the group.

There is in fact only one crate. The model and the crate object are created in the client's world at the same time as the car and the camera, in the first `exitframe` script:

```
CrateObj= new(member("CrateObj").script)
```

This calls the `on new me` function in the `CrateObj` object. The cast member that includes the parachute as well as the crate itself is imported into the world in two parts, `chute` and `cratemod`, both made invisible as they are not yet in use. A message handler is also set up, ready to respond to server calls with subject "`crate`".

```
on new me
  explosions = []
  expcount = 0
  boxheight = 32
  MyWorld = member("gworld")
  crategrav = -3.0
```

continues overleaf

```
      chute = MyWorld.clonemodelfromcastmember("chute", \
        member("parachute").model[2].name, member("parachute"))
      cratemod = MyWorld.clonemodelfromcastmember("cratemod", \
        "box01", member("parachute"))
      chpos = chute.worldposition
      chute.transform.rotate(chpos, vector(1,0,0), -90.0)
      cratemod.transform.rotate(chpos, vector(1,0,0), -90.0)
      chute.visibility = #none
      cratemod.visibility = #none
      aTexture = MyWorld.newtexture("exptex", #fromcastmember, \
        member("exptex"))
      aTexture.renderformat = #rgba8888
      lastcrate = 0
      expready = 0
      setamessagehandler( ServerObj, #anewcrate, me, "crate", "", 1)
      return me
    end
```

When you log on to the server, the on findplace me script in cargamegroupobj checks to see if there's already a crate in the world. The variable CrateState will only be zero if you're the first person to enter a group; and if this is the case, the MakeCrate server script is called. This creates the crate. As you're a new player, you also need to be informed of the location of the crate – this is included in the getcar information you receive. ac is the first available car in the server side list of available cars AvailCars.

```
    if cratestate = 0 then
        makecrate me
    end if
    —tell the new user what car they are to be and where the
    —crate is
    myMovie.sendMessage ( user.name, "getcar", [ac, cratestate] )
```

MakeCrate is a simple server script that defines the location of the new crate drop as a two dimensional location. There is no need for a height, as the crate is dropped vertically until it hits something. The location is randomly selected from one of eight 300x300 squares. An initial location is selected at random from cr, and a random addition (300x300) is added to it. This 2D coordinate is then sent to the group under subject "crate".

```
    on makecrate me
      —make  a randomized crate position and send it to the group
      cr = [[-88.9078, 957.1812], [-1502.6875, -540.0601], \
        [-364.4865, -539.6384], [657.6740, -537.3918], [-364.4866, \
        -1711.8447], [-1418.0785, 686.1290], [-364.4866, 466.9032],\
        [785.1597, 438.2143]]
      cr =cr[random(count(cr))]
      cr[1] = cr[1] + random(300) - 100
      cr[2] = cr[2] + random(300) - 100
      cratestate = cr
      myMovie.sendMessage ( mygroup, "crate", cratestate )
    end
```

Now we go back to your movie. The message handler will call the `on anewcrate me` script when you receive the `crate` message, which sets your `crateState` variable to the new coordinates in list format.

```
on anewcrate me, msg
   CrateState = msg.content
end
```

The crate object detects this change next time the `stepframe` handler is called (i.e. on the next frame). Any change to `CrateState` will therefore send a message to the interface informing you that there is a new crate:

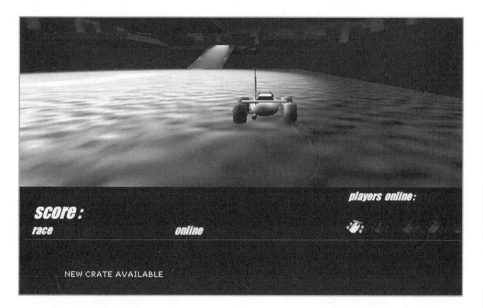

It will also reposition the crate at the new location, adding a y-coordinate (800 for the crate) as the height from which the crate is dropped, and it makes the chute and the crate visible. `targetcrateloc` is calculated from the `myseekfloor` function (for more details on this function, see 'Controlling the car' earlier in this chapter).

If, for some reason, the crate misses the structure, `myseekfloor` will return a value of –500 for `targetcrateloc`. In order to avoid the crate being lost forever and the game becoming stalled, you can make this event trigger a win for the player; it's pot luck as to who gets the prize as it'll be awarded to the first person to hit the server with their `WinCrate` call.

```
on stepframe me
   case (ilk (CrateState)) of
      #string :  nothing
      #list:
         if lastcrate <> CrateState then
```

continues overleaf

```
docarchat(ServerObj, [#content: "NEW CRATE AVAILABLE"])
av = vector(CrateState[1], 800, CrateState[2])
cratemod.translate(-cratemod.worldposition + av, #world)
chute.translate(-chute.worldposition + av + \
  vector(0,32,0), #world)
targetcrateloc =  myseekfloor("cratemod", "floor", \
  "gworld", 0, vector(0,-1,0))
chute.visibility = #both
cratemod.visibility = #both
lastcrate = CrateState
expready = 1
incar = 0
—check to make sure it has landed on one of the floors
—targetcrateloc[4] will be -500 if it doesn't detect a
—floor
—so send a signal saying it has been won, this will
—create a new crate(kind of a bonus if you get the
—points for it)
if targetcrateloc[4] = -500 then
  sendit(ServerObj, "wincrate", CrateState, \
    "system.script")
  makeexp me, cratemod.worldposition
end if
```

From now on, there are no server calls regarding the crate until someone hits it. movecrate controls the behavior of the crate within your movie once it has been created, as it is called from the stepframe script if nothing changes. First, it drops the crate until it hits the ground (targetcrateloc[4]), at which point the chute disappears.

```
      else
       MoveCrate me
       if CheckProximity(me) = 1 then
        SendIt(ServerObj, "WinCrate", CrateState, "system.script")
        MakeExp me, cratemod.worldposition
       end if
      end if
    end case
  end

  on MoveCrate me
   dv = vector(0,CrateGravity*FrameDiff, 0)
   cv = vector(0,cratemod.worldposition.y, 0)
   if cv.distanceto(vector(0,targetcrateloc[4],0)) < 30.0 then \
   chute.visibility = #none
    cratemod.translate(vector(0,-cratemod.worldposition.y,0) \
+vector(0,targetcrateloc[4],0), #world)
   else
    chute.translate(dv, #world)
    cratemod.translate(dv, #world)
   end if
  end
```

Grabbing a crate

So somebody – let's say it's you – hits a crate. This is triggered from some basic collision detection called from the `CrateObj` stepframe handler.

```
on checkproximity me
 flag = 0
 ad = CarObj.car.worldposition.distanceto(cratemod.worldposition)
 if ad < 50 then
  flag = 1
 end if
 return flag
end
```

If `checkproximity = 1` in the `stepframe` script, then two things happen. First, there is a server call triggered from the server object `sendit` script that sends the data with subject heading `WinCrate`, and second, `MakeExp me` creates a particle emitter explosion at the position of the crate.

```
if checkproximity(me) = 1 then
  sendit(ServerObj, "WinCrate", CrateState, "system.script")
  MakeExp me, cratemod.worldposition
end if
```

The server detects subject `WinCrate` and checks that the content – the current crate location – matches what the server says are the coordinates. This will be true for the first player to send the message, and at this point, the server notifies everyone that you won the crate, and we go round the loop again from the `on MakeCrate me` handler we saw above.

Anybody else who thinks they have won a crate will get bounced, as `CrateState` will have changed and no longer match the content of the sent message.

```
on incomingMessagegroupobj (me, movie, group, user, fullMsg)
  if fullmsg.subject = "wincrate" then
    if cratestate = fullmsg.content[1] then
      mymovie.sendmessage(mygroup, "wincrate", \
        [ fullmsg.senderid, cratestate])
      —then make another carte
      makecrate(me)
    end if
  end if
end
```

So, each player will receive the server message with `WinCrate` in the subject, and the winner in the content. The code then calculates the additional points locally in the `ServerObj` movie script – a crate gets the recipient (the number of people playing + 1) points – and extracts the name of the winner to put this information together for display. If the winner is somebody else, the crate explodes (`MakeExp`), and if you are the winner, the extra points are added to your score.

```
on wincrate me, msg
  —content = [winnerid, cratesate]
  collectedcrate = msg.content[2]
  winner =msg.content[1]
  tempnumusers = 1
  —who is the winner?
  if ilk(AvatarList) = #list and ilk(AvatarObjectList) = \
    #list then
    set alistref = getone(AvatarList, winner)
    tempnumusers = tempnumusers + count(AvatarList)
    if alistref <> 0 then
      if count(AvatarObjectList) >= alistref then
        winner = getname(AvatarObjectList[alistref][2])
      end if
    end if
  end if
  —if you did not explode it and someone else won it
  if winner <>  MyUserName and collectedcrate = CrateState then
    makeexp CrateObj, CrateObj.cratemod.worldposition
  end if
  if  winner = MyUserName then
    CarObj.MyScore = CarObj.MyScore +  tempnumusers
    if  CarObj.MyScore <> value(member("MyScore").text) then
      member("MyScore").text = string( CarObj.MyScore)
    end if
    winner = "You"
  end if
  put winner&" won "&tempnumusers&" POINTS" into member
"infotext"
end
```

Scores and interface display

As we mentioned earlier, this game uses a fairly primitive scoring system. Each crate that a user gets awards them a certain number of points: the number of current players + 1. There is no account taken of time and so a high score table would reward the people who stayed in the game world for longest, rather than those with the most skill. There are many alternative scoring mechanisms: the tools are here to build your own.

Each player distributes his score to others every time they send their position – see on SendCar me in CarObj – and this is received and loaded into the interface fields by part of the script newpositioncar in AvatarObj:

```
MyScore = Message.content[3]
  – update score etc
  if MyScore <> value(member("scr"&MyResource).text) then
    member("scr"&MyResource).text = string(MyScore)
  end if
  set the blend of sprite(MyResource + DisplayCarincrement) /
    = 100
  end if
end
```

A quick look at the score will help here. So far, we have only used sprite 1, the interface elements are in sprites 3 to 24.

Sprites 3 and 4 display whether the game is running in multiuser mode or not (a behavior checks ServerObj.mysatate). Sprites 5 and 6 do exactly the same. Sprite 10 is used at various points to display game information. Sprite 12 displays your score, and sprites 13 to 18 show all car scores. Sprites 19 to 24 show the cars that are currently in play.

Sprites 78 to 88 control the chat; all the chat code is in the chat cast. As chat has been covered quite comprehensively throughout the book so far, the methods used here should be fairly self-explanatory.

Explosions

A great feature of Shockwave3D is the way that particle emitters have been implemented.

We have used them in a limited way here, but they could be used to simulate exhaust, skidding against the ground, engine smoke, dust in the air and so on – particles can really add life to a 3D space. This handler creates a particle explosion at location `cr`, with the parameters set out in the script.

This script also makes the crate invisible and resets the relevant variables. When the explosion is over, the `doit` handler (setup as a timeout script to go off 2.5 seconds after the explosion), deletes the particle emitter, and then deletes itself.

The texture used is a bitmap with an alpha channel, defined as `aTexture` in the 'Creating the crate' section above.

```
on MakeExp me, cr
  if cr <> 0 then
   aloc =cr
   arec = MyWorld.newmodelresource("part"&expcount, #particle)
   arec.lifetime = 2000
   arec.emitter.numparticles =15
   arec.sizerange.start =90.0
   arec.sizerange.end = 5.1
   arec.emitter.minspeed = 10.0
   arec.emitter.maxspeed = 100.0
   arec.blendrange.start =60.0
   arec.blendrange.end = 0.0
   arec.emitter.direction = vector(0,1,0)
   arec.emitter.angle = 50.0
   arec.texture = aTexture
   arec.emitter.loop = false
   arec.emitter.distribution = #linear
   arec.emitter.mode = #burst

   amod = MyWorld.newmodel("partmod"&expcount)
   amod.resource = arec
   amod.translate(aloc,#world)
   add explosions, [amod, expcount]

   at = timeout("parttime"&expcount).new(2500, #doit, me)
   expcount = expcount + 1
  end if

  chute.visibility = #none
  cratemod.visibility = #none
  CrateState = "none"
  LastCrate = CrateState

end


on doit me
```

```
      anum = explosions[1][2]
      MyWorld.deletemodelresource("part"&anum)
      MyWorld.deletemodel("partmod"&anum)
      timeout("parttime"&anum).forget()
      deleteat explosions, 1
   end if
```

Conclusion

In this chapter, we've followed the creation of a major multiuser online game. We've discussed the design issues, what's involved in constructing the game as a single-player application, and how to build in the multiuser components.

You should have had a lot of fun playing with KARZ along the way, and now would be a great time to add your own unique touch to it. In particular, the game needs a better scoring system, a high scores table, and some sound. Done that? Well, how about making more of the particle emitters, and calculating (and reacting to) the collision between cars locally, without recourse to the multiuser server at all?

Still not satisfied? Well, you could add some automated cars to the environment so that players in single user mode can compete against robots rather than driving around an empty space. The multiuser server and server - side scripting to control robots in a multiuser playing field would also be a fascinating experiment – does it matter whether you are playing against people or computers? Can you even tell them apart?

The next chapter takes a look at some other approaches to Director-based multiuser apps, but – as this chapter has shown – the Multiuser Server allows you to achieve some mighty impressive results, and we hope that this book has unlocked some of the secrets behind achieving these results.

You probably need to take another careful look at KARZ – the idea behind this chapter was to show you the extent of what was possible, and as such, it's not easy stuff – but, if you can even follow most of this chapter, you're several steps ahead of the rest. You're now well able to go and create the ultimate web application – one that takes advantage of the visual cutting-edge offered by Director or Flash, but adds in the magic ingredient of human interaction.

Chapter 15

New Directions

Throughout the Director section of this book, we've taken the use of Director's Multiuser Server as a given. We've done this because this is by far the easiest, quickest, and cheapest way to start when developing multiuser web applications with Director. That's not to say that you always have to do things this way, so before we bid you a fond farewell as you set out on your own individual multiuser adventures, we're going to discuss the server choices that you have when developing your applications.

We also recognize that, in this section of the book, we've concentrated mainly on chat applications – although the game in the last chapter hopefully opened up your eyes to a few other possibilities. Again, we've done this because this is the best and most useful model to show you the mechanics of a multiuser application. That's not all there is to it, though. By reaching this stage in the book, you have the key to many exciting possibilities in your hand.

How far can multiuser applications be taken? The concepts and technologies can be expanded as far as the imagination can take them. The idea that many people can communicate by sharing data over the Internet is so broad that it most certainly is not limited to chat lobbies.

Server alternatives

In Director, the Multiuser Xtra is the software component used to make a socket connection to a given server. As we know, a socket connection is a connection to a server on a port and almost all communications on the Internet are done through sockets. For example, when you go to a web site, let's say www.setpixel.com, a socket connection is made to setpixel.com, port 80. Port 80 is the standard HTTP port. Once the connection is made, a request command is given, and the server responds with the HTML data. When the data is finished being transferred, the socket connection is closed.

The Multiuser Xtra can connect to virtually any text-based server. FTP, HTTP, SMTP Mail, and IRC are just a few popular server daemons that the Xtra can be used to connect to. Every server daemon operates on a certain port, and the table below sets out a few of the common sever daemons.

Server daemon	Port
DNS	53 53
FTP	20, 21
IRC	6661 - 6667
HTTP	80
HTTPS	443
NNTP	119
POP3	110
SMTP	25
Telnet	23
Counter-Strike	26000 – 30000
Dial Pad	51210
ICQ	4000
ALL ms directx games	47624, 2300 – 2400
Netmeeting	389, 522, 1503, 1720,1731

Novell VPN software	353, 2010, 213
PC Anywhere 2.0-7.51	65301
PC Anywhere 7.52+	5631
Quake 2, 3 Server Only	26000 – 30000
SSH	22, 1019 – 1023
VNC	5800

What does this mean in practical terms? It means an application can be written in Lingo to connect to a SMTP Mail server and send some mail through your application without using any other software. While writing your own outgoing mail client has useful applications, it simply illustrates that you are not relegated to using Macromedia's Multiuser Server.

Macromedia Multiuser Server

Macromedia's Multiuser Server is a very acceptable server for the development and small-scale deployment of projects. Macromedia boasts being able to support up to 2,000 concurrent users and reasonably dependable and reliable code. However, the software only runs on the Windows and Macintosh platforms. Those people who are running business grade Windows and Macintosh Servers on T3 lines should have no problem; the majority who don't will in all probability face problems.

Why? Because many hosting service providers are reluctant to host non-standard servers. Furthermore, because Multiuser Server was not written as a service, most hosting companies will refuse to even consider hosting MUS. MUS has been known to lock up and commandeer much of the system resources on a server if the application is not developed correctly, and owners of servers aren't particularly keen to invite that kind of an eventuality.

For the majority of developers Multiuser Server will fill their needs, but sometimes it just doesn't cut it. Whether the problem is hosting issues, reliability, speed, or expandability, an alternative to Multiuser Server will be needed. Fortunately, there are many solid options. Three options are: using an existing socket server like IRC, using alternative servers written specifically for use with the Multiuser Xtra, or writing your own custom server. Let's take a look at these options.

IRC

IRC, or Internet Relay Chat, was developed as a simple text-based chat server in the 1980s. It was built to support as many users as the server could handle, and perform with total reliability. The original IRC net regularly had more than 32, 000 users logged on at once, as strings of IRC servers can be linked together to support a theoretically infinite amount of users. IRC daemons are available for Linux, and IRC is a standard server so many hosting companies support it.

There is an RFC (Request for Comments) document downloadable from rfc.net for pretty much every aspect of IRC, and some of these documents can be used to build a framework for a custom technology. For creating a fully functional IRC client using the Multiuser Xtra, for example, you'd need to take a look at "1459 Internet Relay Chat Protocol" by J. Oikarinen and D. Reed (May 1993).

The drawback to using IRC is that there is no built in provision for server-side scripting. IRC was developed as a chat server, so message-relaying functions aren't supported, and neither are functions like connecting to a server-side database. These functions are not impossible to achieve, however. A robot or "bot" can be set up to perform any server-side function it is programmed to do. Essentially, a bot resides on the server just as any other client does. The only difference is that the bot does not have a human operating it, and relies entirely on commands you send it. For example, you might want a list of the highest scores for a game so you could program the bot to listen for commands like "botShowHighScores". Once the bot receives the message, it will process the command, and return a result.

The model of a bot performing functions has its pros and cons. Because the bot exists just as any other client on the network, the message is sent first to the IRC server, and then to the bot, which is not running on the same process. The result can sometimes be that the bot's responses are lagged thus affecting the game play, but there shouldn't be any noticeable lag if the bot is running on the same physical machine as the IRC server.

Unfortunately programming a bot is often done in languages foreign to most Flash/Director developers and can be complicated. On the upside, being detached from the actual IRC daemon makes bots modular. Much like the way Xtras work in Director, you can use or, in this case, create only what you need. Because bots act just like any IRC client, they can be programmed in any language supported by the server.

The most popular implementation of an IRC bot is using an Egg drop client. The Egg drop client is a small, easily configurable IRC client that allows scripts to be run. Scripts can be written in TCL or PERL. Egg drops are attractive because the IRC client is already written, optimized and tested by the many people that use it. But, just as an IRC client can be written in Director, it's possible to write one in Java, C++, or any language of your preference.

The popular music sharing software "Napster" was entirely based on IRC technology. The Napster servers were modified IRC daemons with bots that would store and retrieve the index of MP3s on a user's computer in a database. When a user first started Napster, it connected to the IRC server. The Napster client then sent the list of its MP3s to the bot, which stored it in a database. When someone searched for a particular song, the search query is sent to the bot. The bot searched the entire database and returned all the appropriate records. When a user selected an MP3 to download, a direct (peer-to-peer) connection was made with the person in possession of that particular MP3, and the transfer was started. The concept is so simple that similar applications have been creating using IRC and a Shockwave/Lingo client.

Alternative Multiuser Servers

There are server alternatives like IRC, but there are also servers designed specifically to work with Macromedia Multiuser Xtra. Because the main drawback of Macromedia's Multiuser Server is that it only runs on Windows and Macintosh platforms, these servers fill a void by running on Linux or other platforms.

FUSE Light by Sulake

http://www.sulake.com/fuselight/

Sulake, the developers of Habbo Hotel, created an open-source, pure Java server that provides the most important features of Macromedia's Multiuser Server. Because the server is written in Java, it runs on every platform.

FUSE Light provides the ability to connect to relational databases using standard SQL syntax. Currently, FUSE supports MySQL. MySQL is an excellent database server for the price, which is free. With slight modifications, the server can be used to connect with any data source because it uses the JDBC database model (JDBC is very similar to OBDC, and simply provides a connection between a Java application and the information in a database).

This is very powerful, because the data used in the multiuser applications can be used/manipulated by other applications. For example, users can sign up for your multiuser application, which creates an entry in the database. This data can be modified by a web-based administrative tool, or used on the application's web site. "UserXYZ has just joined the MUWorld" could appear in the news section of the site.

Some other advantages include:

- automatic connection monitoring (to remove dead connections automatically)

- statistics collection

- the ability to refuse certain connections

- a high level of stability

- basic-key security mechanism to protect against hackers

The biggest advantage by far, is the fact that the server is open source and free. This allows for customizations, additions, and the chance to use it as a framework for building your own server. For example, with a few changes, Oracle databases can be supported. Additions to the server can also be made to allow server-side logic, which is important to the architecture of a well-developed multiuser application. Furthermore, because Java is much faster than Lingo, performing some functions on the server and sending the results back to the client is no longer so slow.

There are a few downsides to FUSE Light. There is no support for binary messages, while Macromedia's Multiuser Server supports sending any cast member type (images and sounds for example) to and from the server. There is no support for peer-to-peer connections or for UDP. The last drawback, which is both a pro and a con, is that it is written in Java and customization may be difficult. Most Director and Flash developers aren't very familiar with Java; there may be a steep learning curve involved in customization of the server.

Nebulae MultiUserServer by Tabuleiro

http://xtras.tabuleiro.com

Tabuleiro Nebulae MultiUserServer is a server application that runs on Linux, Solaris, MacOSX, FreeBSD and almost any Java-enabled operational system. Nebulae is dependable, and supports remote administrative functions from, for example, a web browser.

Because Nebulae is 100% compatible with Shockwave Multiuser protocol published by Macromedia, movies authored for the Shockwave MultiUserServer versions 2 and 3 can connect seamlessly to a Nebulae server without the need for any modifications. A nice working example would be to use Macromedia's Multiuser server locally on the same Windows machine during development, and replace it with the reliable Nebulae server running on Linux when the application is deployed.

There are two main advantages to Nebulae over FUSE Light. Firstly, UDP and peer-to-peer connections are supported; and secondly, transfers of all cast member media types are supported. So sending an image, a vector, some sound, and so on is as easy as it is in Multiuser Server.

The only major drawback is that Nebulae costs nearly $500. This drawback is minor in comparison unless you're working on your own application, the cost of the server can be worked into the cost to the client. $500 is pretty negligible compared to the overall budget for most multiuser applications in any case. Furthermore, you may be able to find a hosting facility that offers a special deal for Nebulae users.

Custom Servers

In some cases, the best server solution is the one you make yourself. Because you, as the developer of your multiuser application, know exactly what is needed in a server and how it may expand in the future, you are the best judge whether the other servers aren't enough.

Many Shockwave applications use their own custom developed servers. Some examples are SissyFight (www.sissyfight.com), Habbo Hotel (www.habbo.com), and Tildruin (www.tildruin.com).

There are a number of reasons why a developer would develop a custom server. Sometimes the server needs to run on a specific server platform. Perhaps the existing servers don't provide enough functionality. Security may be a very important issue, as none of the previously described servers have great security options.

The primary reason for writing custom servers for fast "twitch" multiuser game applications is speed. In some cases, quite a bit of processing is done on the server-side. It is absolutely important in fast applications that functions are executed and data is transferred as quickly as possible.

Many multiuser games like Counter Strike and Quake use their own servers. As more people continue to use Shockwave3D, it should be expected that a first person shooter server will be developed specifically for Shockwave applications.

For many server developers, Java is the development platform of choice because Java runs on all system platforms, removing a huge step in finding the right host for your server application. However, a socket server can be written in C++, or any other language that supports socket connections.

The obvious downside to creating your own server is that you have to know how in the first place. The learning curve is not only steep for the language, but also the way to go about it. If you're a first time server developer, check out the source of FUSE Light and review existing RFC documents on socket servers before taking the plunge.

Hosting

The process of finding hosting for small to medium sized applications is usually a nerve wrecking one. For large businesses with their own hosting facilities, this is generally an easy task. For Shockwave multiuser applications, the Shockwave file must reside on the same domain as the multiuser server, or a securities alert will pop up for your users. The objective is to find a hosting service that will meet your web hosting needs, and your multiuser server needs. Most people want hosting so that it is set up, reliable, and they don't have to perform maintenance to keep it going.

One route is dedicated hosting. In most cases, you pay for the use of a single dedicated machine physically at the hosting company's facility, which you have total control over. Network maintenance is performed by the hosting company. You are free to install any services on the machine. This should only be attempted if you have experience in managing a server. If for some reason, something stops functioning as a result of something you did, that service might be down until you can find someone who can fix it.

Most small to medium sized companies go with a shared hosting of some sort. This is where many different sites exist on one server. In most cases, you have no control over installing services or system maintenance. You just upload your files, and administrate your database. This is very attractive for the majority of people that require web hosting. For most hosting companies, it is in their best interest to only install services that the majority of their hosting tenants need. If one person wants to install a multiuser server for example, the request will be denied in most cases.

This means that finding a hosting company that will fit your web hosting needs, and provide multiuser services to a shared hosting account is very difficult, if not impossible. Examine all the options and do research before choosing a company.

One such company is Media Temple (www.mediatemple.net), known for the hosting of k10k.org and many other popular design portals. Media Temple offer hosting of Fortress, and plan to offer Nebulae MultiUserServer to their Appliance, or Dedicated-Servers at a relatively cheap cost compared to buying full licenses. Media Temple's Appliance servers are interesting because they offer the security, performance, control, and reliability of a dedicated Linux server.

Developing your ideas

A fledgling idea for a multiuser application should be developed to the fullest extent possible. You should brainstorm first, define your target audience, and build the idea around them. Then envision everything the application will do without questioning exactly how to do it. This allows you to identify processes and define them before examining how the application will talk to the server. Most importantly, write **everything** down.

Once the first brainstorm is complete, there should be enough content written to form a loose document. Many developers are in the habit of just diving in and creating the application while it is fresh in their head. This approach is not a bad one, especially for proof of concept or a rough build of their idea, but keep your application well documented at all times.

As you continue to work on the application, update the document. Every time you add a function or a process, write it down and explain how and why it exists within the framework of your application. This will structure your thinking and save you a lot of valuable time when things go wrong.

Why think everything through before questioning how to do it? The technology applied is admittedly important to the framework of the multiuser application, but the specific technology is just a tool in the application of the concept. Often, heavy emphasis is placed on the technological aspects of an application and not the application itself, creating some expensive white elephants along the way. How often have you seen a visually stunning game that's totally unplayable?

Multiuser applications depend on having people visit them to work, so this is even more important. With a focus on technology and not on concept, we could all too easily develop an application with very powerful communication capabilities but with no focus or reason to be there in the first place.

The concept is the most important element in your multiuser application, and multiuser applications offer almost unlimited scope for imaginative exploitation. Let's take a look at some of the most interesting routes down which people have already taken multiuser applications.

Community Applications

By definition, any multiuser application is a community application but for our purposes, these are applications with the purpose of communication for the sake of communication. The "hello world" example of multiuser is chat. It is the most primitive form, yet for its simplicity, is also the most effective.

In its most simple form, chat communication is relayed by a typed message and the username property of the user. So in IRC, an example of a communiqué might be:

<cforman> Hi. How are you?
<jim> I am fine. What did you eat for lunch?
<cforman> I ate a hamburger

Within this form, the communication is limited to the use of language, and the username property of the user. Creative use of language can go a long way towards enabling communication between people, but in real-life peer-to-peer communications, much more is involved in a message than just the spoken word.

Facial expressions, body language, tone of voice, location, and gestures are just a few of the properties of a person's communication. In some cases, the non-verbal communication contains more of the message than the verbal. The logical progression in chat is to add more properties that are controllable by the user to simulate real-life communications.

MUDs and MOOs

One of the first ever multiuser applications was created in 1980 at Essex University as an online adventure game where users could log in and interact with each other (earlier MUDs went back to using a system called PLATO across a network of mainframes in the early seventies). At the time, there was an experimental packet-switching system (EPSS), which linked Essex University in Great Britain to Arpanet in the USA. This network would later become popularly known as the Internet.

The application was called a MUD, standing for Multiple User Dimension, Multiple User Dungeon, or Multiple User Domain depending on whom you ask. A MUD is a text-based multiuser server application, where you are given extended properties such as characteristic attributes and location. Its primary and most popular purpose is for a role-playing game. A MUD lets you walk around, chat with other characters, explore dangerous monster-infested areas, and solve puzzles.

MOO stands for MUD, Object Oriented. MUDs are fixed virtual environments controlled by programmers, while MOOs allow users to create their own virtual environment by creating their own rooms, objects, and personal attributes. The most attractive feature of a MOO is unquestionably the built in object-oriented programming that allows the users to create their own functionality – a user could program a pet dog to walk around even when the user is not logged in, for example.

The drawback to both MUDs and MOOs is the learning curve involved. Both are text based and visually unattractive, and require you to be familiar with most of the functions of the application in order to participate. MOO's language, while laid out extremely well, has a very steep learning curve for non-programmer users.

Avatar Chat

An Avatar is defined as a representation of a user in shared virtual reality. Technically, in the simple chat example mentioned before, the user "cforman" is an avatar within the IRC server, but avatar chat popularly refers to a graphical multiuser application where users are represented by characters or icons.

Imagine a room with five people in it. Each person can walk around the room as they please. They can talk to each other, they pick up objects, and they can even smile and dance. Each has a different skin tone, different clothes, and different accessories. This shouldn't be so hard to imagine. Unless you've been living in a cave, you've probably witnessed scenes like this millions of times in your life. Now imagine a similar scene on a computer application where a human user on another computer somewhere on the Internet is controlling each person.

Many people falsely believe the popular use of the word avatar in relation to chat originates from a CMU hacker disliking the word "root", which is the most powerful user (super user) on a Unix system. He decided to use a word that was more befitting of the respect he demanded as a powerful and unique user. The popular word "avatar" as it applies to chat is actually a Dungeons'n'Dragons reference, which in turn probably stems from the use of avatar as a term for the self's higher being in the religious pantheon of central Asia.

Habbo Hotel

http://www.habbohotel.com

One of the most popular Avatar Chat applications is Habbo Hotel. The first step to Habbo Hotel or any avatar chat for that matter is to create an avatar. The user can select the hair, face, upper body, lower body, and shoe types and colors. This information is stored on the server database.

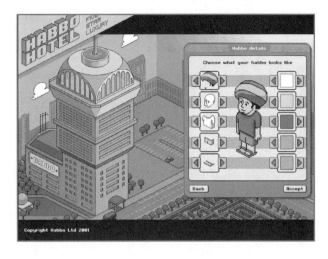

The next step is to log in. Once logged in, the user is presented with a list of available rooms, or virtual spaces. These spaces are created by the developers, and stored in a database on the server. If any changes need to be made to the room, they can be made easily and changed instantaneously.

Once logged into a room, the room will be displayed, as well as everyone in the room. Each user appears unique, as he or she has selected the way they would like to be displayed, and this information is pulled from the database and shown on screen by the application. Chatting is represented by cartoon like text bubbles that appear over your avatars head.

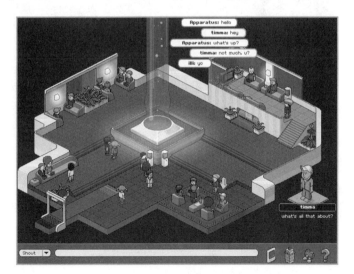

Habbo Hotel was developed by Sulake. We discussed their FUSE Light server earlier in this chapter, and they used this to develop a custom multiuser server specifically for use with Habbo Hotel.

Habbo Hotel needed a server that would run dependably under heavy traffic, support server side custom programming and execute very quickly. Unfortunately, this is a case in which Macromedia's Multiuser Server did not fit their needs.

It is not always very easy to see what is going on behind the scenes in Habbo Hotel, but there are some nice touches. Certain key role characters in rooms are not real people, but programmed avatars, or "bots". For example, behind the bar, there are two bar tenders who appear to be very lively and talkative. You can order a drink, or even make small talk. The bartenders are programmed to be "smart" and respond to everyone at the bar. They run on the server, so all the users get the same message, and everyone sees the same thing.

Habbo Hotel's predecessor, Mobiles Disco (www.mobilesdisco.com), also used a custom version of FUSE Light, and can be viewed as a watered down version of a similar avatar chat application. This was the first Shockwave multiuser application with "smart" bot avatars. A user could ask the bartender if she had seen another user around lately. Based on database records, the bartender would respond accordingly. If someone were looking for you, the bartender would tell you about it when you ordered a drink.

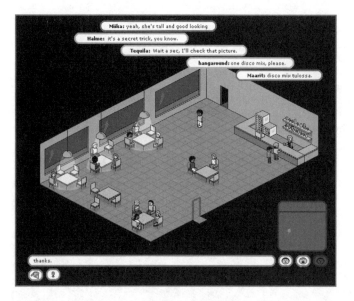

These types of avatar chats are never going to replace the utilitarian efficiency of an IRC style chat or instant messaging, but that's not the point. Avatar chats like Habbo force the user to pay attention to exactly everything that is going on as it happens and play an altogether different, more immersive role.

RobotDuck's MUMOO

http://www.mumoo.com

Robotduck (www.robotduck.com), known for some of the best Shockwave games on the Web, created an avatar chat that in some ways exceeded Habbo Hotel's model. The multiuser server being used is a MOO server and most functions of a MOO, as previously described, are implemented graphically. Users can modify worlds; objects can be created and given to people. It is a much more radical world, where users decide what's going on and what exists.

Taking Avatar Chat Further

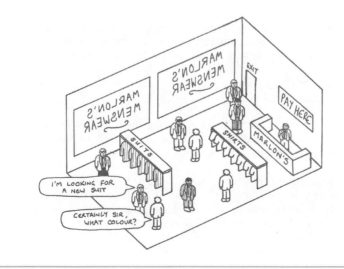

Avatar chat has been a great and novel way of giving people graphical representations of themselves in a virtual world. However, very few applications have explored the use of avatars outside the realm of simple avatar chat.

Applying the avatar chat model to existing activities that people do as a community is very possible. Imagine a retail store for example. So much more is illustrated by the people shopping than just the store itself. The number of people in the store gives you a good idea of its popularity. The appearance of the people gives you an idea of what type of goods are sold by that store. In a real retail store, you can even go up to a person and ask them what they think of a particular item, or the store service.

After seeing an avatar chat like Habbo Hotel, it's easy to see how e-commerce or online shopping would apply perfectly to a particular store. Now, imagine something even larger. Perhaps a mall, full of independently functioning stores.

Similar to the way that Habbo Hotel and Mobiles Disco use "smart" bots, the shopping mall and the stores could use "smart" bots to roam the store helping people out, announcing specials, and so on. If a user has a question, they can go up to the bot, disguised as a store employee, and ask it a question. The server would have logic in which it would use to generate the best answer. For example:

```
User:        "Hi. Do you know where I can find a nice sweater?"
Bot:         "Hi. Sweaters are in section 9 next to the scarves.
There is a special on them today."
User:        "Thanks."
Bot:         "Have a great day."
```

In the event that the server-side logic could not answer a user's question, a team of customer representatives could be waiting to help the user out. Take this example:

User: "Hi. Do you know where I can find a nice sweater?"
Bot: "Hi. Sweaters are in section 9 next to the scarves. There is a special on them today."
User: "Well, I'm shopping for my daughter, what kind of sweaters are in style this year?"

At this point, the server-side logic couldn't possibly answer this question unless it has already been entered in the frequently asked questions database. A customer representative would be alerted. The conversation would be sent to their computer, and he/she would give a human answer:

Customer Representative: "It's just about the holiday season. Is this for Christmas? Red cardigan sweaters are very popular right now."

The customer representative would, in a sense, assume the body of the "store employee" bot. He/she could even walk around and show the user exactly where the sweater is. The result is a seamless, and responsive model of customer service.

Most people still go shopping with their friends, or their families, and shopping is more of a communal experience than most think. This means that the element of community in online shopping could give all of the benefits of Internet shopping (no hassle, no parking problems...) with none of the minuses (no-one to talk to, no fun...).

Our customer service example is almost non-existent in online shopping today, and this could be developed even further. Applications like shopping agents could be hired to do the shopping for you based on your shopping habits and general shopping trends. You could see something that someone has in his or her shopping cart, and want one too, so just copy it into your cart. The possibilities are endless.

Games

Since the beginning of time, the majority of games have involved more than just one player. Whether the game was a sport or a game of checkers, most required a communal, multi-player effort. A lot of computer games from the last twenty years have been single player but this is surely because of technical limitations, rather than because computers are so fast and "smart" that another human as an opponent is obsolete.

The popularity of the existing multiuser games like Doom, Quake, Counterstrike, Warcraft, and Command and Conquer is truly remarkable. Take away the multi-player capability of the game, and a very large chunk of the popularity would be removed. With the rising popularity, and speed, and lowering price of the Internet we can only expect the popularity of multiuser games such as these to increase. There must be a wealth of ideas to exploit in this field.

Turn-based games

Turn-based games are multiuser games in which each person makes an action, one turn at a time. A good example of this would be a game of checkers. The game opens; the first player makes a move, while the second player waits until the first player's move is over. The second player moves. This is repeated until the game is over.

The first multiuser application of a developer is usually a turn-based game. Turn-based games are extremely attractive to developers because all the logic in the game can be done on the client – side. This doesn't require the developer to create a server-side script to moderate the game. Most turn-based games are usually nothing more than simple versions of board games. The model may be simple, but that doesn't necessarily mean the game is.

Sissy Fight

http://www.sissyfight.com

Sissy Fight is a turn-based multiuser game, which, unlike online games that focus solely on action or mechanical game play, revolves around social strategy and manipulation. For each turn, you have about a minute to choose a single action. When the timer runs out and the turn is over, a series of snapshots will pop up on the screen and you can click through them to see what happened to everyone. The game normally continues until all but two girls have lost all of their self-esteem.

Multiplayer Mini Golf

http://www.electrotank.com

Developed in Flash, this is one of the better, certainly more popular, multiuser games on the Internet. The game is an isometric mini golf dual. The strength of this game is that, on its own, without the multiuser aspects, it is a great game. This turn-based multiuser game is simple and easy to understand; yet you can easily play it for hours, like a game of pool.

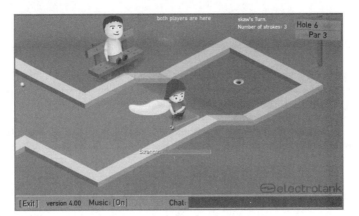

Realtime games

Realtime games evaluate actions for the users as they happen as quickly as possible. The most popular example of a realtime game is a multiuser first person shooter such as Quake or Doom. Each player moves around independently trying to shoot each other and while doing so, data is sent to the server so that it can be sent to the other players for display. These are much more difficult to create and run properly than their non-realtime equivalents but the results can be well worth it, as we saw with the rather lovely racing game in the last chapter.

Coop

Coops are traditionally single player games where other players play the same game along side each other. For example, take a look at a platformer type game like Hamster Xcape (www.hamsterx.com). The objective of the game is to find the end of the level without inconveniently dying first. Now imagine that, as other people play the game, you can see them on your screen as ghosted players.

The other players do not have to influence your game, but you are aware of their movements. Perhaps the other players will choose to chat with you and give you some tips. While making a game coop does not add much to the actual game play, it does add an organic, realistic dimension to the game that would be near impossible to achieve artificially.

This is also a model that can be combined with other approaches. For example, you could have a wargame of some type with two coops playing against each other. Each coop would have to communicate with their fellow team members and be aware of their position to function - it's always embarrassing, not to mention unhelpful, to shoot your own troops. Such a game would have the built-in need for a great deal of multiuser communication that creates a compelling web experience.

Experimental

Some members of the art community have created multiuser applications as artistic experiments. Artists use kiosk installations (generally using Projector files on a dedicated machine) not only as the piece of art, but also as means to communicate with other kiosks.

For example, you could have a setup where input data is polled from sensors placed around the kiosk. These sensors may be pressure sensors in the floor, proximity sensors, light sensors, and so on. The sensors record every physical action the user makes, and this information is collected and sent to a server, and then sent to the other kiosks.

The other kiosks could use the data to display a light show on the screen of the kiosks. Each movement from another kiosk could generate a display on every kiosk. You could even have a robotic device in the center of the room, affected by the action from the kiosks.

Goodbye!

This brings us to the very end of our book. This last section should have given you just the inspiration that you need to add to the skills you've learnt in the rest of the book in order to go out and design your own killer multiuser application. We hope that you've enjoyed the book, and look forward to seeing you talking about it and your projects at friendsofed.com.

Appendix A

XML object method and properties

XML Object methods

This appendix will cover some of the ActionScript methods and properties that are part of the Flash XML object, and are used to read, write, and manipulate XML contained in the object.

Arguments

Arguments are parameters that you can pass to functions or objects. The only argument that you can pass to the XML object is XML source. This is a string of well-formed XML that is to be parsed into the XML object hierarchy. This is passed when you define a new XML object, and is completely optional.

If I wanted to create an XML object from a string of XML in one step, I could use the following syntax:

```
MyXML = new XML("<USER name=\"Timothy\"><MESSAGE>Hello
➥World!</MESSAGE></USER>");
```

Note that I've escaped the quotes on the '*name*' attribute. Since these quotes are contained within a string, we need to add a slash before the quotes, so that they do not prematurely terminate our string.

Properties

The following are properties that apply to an XML object. Each of these properties can be accessed using the syntax, myXML.property, unless otherwise stated.

loaded
A Boolean value that indicates whether XML has been successfully loaded into this object.

status
An integer value that indicates whether or not there were any errors encountered during the parsing of XML source. The status codes are as follows:

> 0 – No error. Parsing was successful.
> 2 – A CDATA section was improperly terminated.
> 3 – XML declaration not terminated.
> 4 – DOCTYPE declaration not terminated.
> 5 – A comment was not terminated.
> 6 – An XML element was malformed.
> 7 – Not enough memory was available to parse the XML.
> 8 – An attribute was not properly terminated.
> 9 – A starting tag didn't have a matching end tag.
> 10 – An ending tag didn't have a matching starting tag.

ignoreWhite

We mentioned this property early in the book (chapter 3). Set this to `true` before you parse your XML, and whitespace will be ignored. This only works in build 41 or later of the Flash 5 player, and does not work in the Flash authoring environment.

Node properties

The following are properties that apply to XML nodes. Each of these properties can be accessed using the syntax `myXMLnode.property`, unless otherwise stated.

nodename

The name of the current node as defined by the name of the XML Element. The name of the element `<FOOD/>` is `'FOOD'`.

nodeValue

The value of the node. Only text nodes have a value, which is a string containing the text in the node.

nodeType

An integer denoting the type of the node. Flash only understands two node types; element nodes and text nodes. Element nodes are of `nodeType 1`, and text nodes are of `nodeType 3`.

attributes

In XML source, each XML node contains an object within it called 'attributes'. This is an object that contains all of the attributes defined for that XML element. You can access them by using the following syntax:

```
myXMLnode.attributes.attributename
myXMLnode.attributes["attributename"]
```

For example, if I am accessing a particular node defined by the following XML:

```
<DOG name="scruffy" breed="mutt">
```

I could access the 'breed' attribute by one of two ways,

```
myXMLnode.attributes.breed
```

Or,

```
myXMLnode.attributes["breed"]
```

Navigating XML trees

The following are properties used to 'navigate' an XML tree. These are properties that refer to other nodes relative to the current node. These can be applied to both XML nodes, and the root XML object.

childNodes
This is an array of references to all of the children of a particular node. Arrays are zero-based, so `myXMLnode.childNodes[2]` would access the third child of the node.

firstChild
A reference to the first child of the node.

lastChild
A reference to the last child of the specific node. If the node only has one child, then it returns the same reference as firstChild.

nextSibling
A reference to the next element in the current level of the XML hierarchy. Basically, it returns a reference to the next child of the parent of the current node. If the current node is the last child of the parent node, then it returns null.

previousSibling
Likewise, this returns a reference to the previous element in the current level. If this is the first child, then it returns null.

parentNode
This returns a reference to the parent of the node. If this node is the root, then it returns null.

Methods

The following methods apply to the XML class of objects. Use the syntax `myXML.method`, unless otherwise stated.

load(URL)
Imports external XML source, parses it, and converts it into an XML object hierarchy.

parseXML(source)
Takes an argument that is a string of XML source, parses it, and then converts it into an XML object hierarchy. This will not take external sources, only strings of XML that exist within the movie.

send(URL, window)
Converts an XML object back into a string of XML source, and sends it to an external server. You must specify a URL, and a 'window' argument, which will be the location where the server response is sent. This may be a custom window name, or one of the four reserved window names `"_blank"`, `"_parent"`,`"_self"`, or `"_top"`.

sendAndLoad(URL, responseXML)
This is similar to the `send()` method, but it allows you to specify a reference to another XML object, which will accept a response from the server in XML format. It will then be parsed, and converted into the XML hierarchy.

createElement(nodename)

This method allows us to create new elements in an XML object with the specified node name. This method does not actually insert the new node into our XML hierarchy. Use either the appendChild, or the insertBefore method to attach our new node to the XML tree.

createTextNode(nodevalue)

This method allows us to create new text nodes in an XML object. The argument sent to this method is either a string of text, in quotes, or the name of a variable containing a string of text. For example:

```
mytext = "This is fun!";
myNewNode = myXML.createTextNode(mytext);
```

Would be the same as:

```
myNewNode = myXML.createTextNode("This is fun!");
```

Just like the createElement method, this method does not insert the new node into our XML hierarchy. We must use the appendChild, or the insertBefore method to attach our new text node.

Methods that apply to both XML objects and nodes

As above, the following methods apply to the XML class of objects. They also apply to XML nodes. Use the syntax myXML.method, or myXMLnode.method, unless otherwise stated.

appendchild(childNode)

Appends a new node after this node's last child. The childnode argument is either a reference to a new node created with createElement or createTextNode, or a reference to an existing node in an XML object.

When we create a new node using createElement or createTextNode, we must assign a reference to that new node at the same time, like so:

```
myNewNode = myXML.createElement("Bob");
```

myNewNode is now referencing this new node in the myXML XML object. In order to insert it into the XML object's hierarchy, we can use the appendChild method.

```
myXML.firstChild.appendChild(myNewNode);
```

The new node is now the last child of the first child in the XML object.

If we want to move a particular node from another document, we can make a reference to that node, and send it as an argument to the appendChild method.

```
// Reference existing node
NodeToMove = myXML.firstChild.firstChild;
// Move existing node to myOtherXML
myOtherXML.appendChild(nodeToMove);
```

Any child nodes of the existing node will be moved along with it.

cloneNode(deep)

Creates a clone of the specified node. This takes an argument, `deep`, which is a Boolean value. When set to 'true', this will also create a clone of all of the child nodes inside this node.

Just like the `createElement` and `createTextNode` methods, this method does not insert the new node into our XML hierarchy. We must use the `appendChild`, or the `insertBefore` method to attach our new text node.

The procedure is similar to `createElement`, where we make a reference to the new node, and then insert it into the XML hierarchy using `appendChild`.

```
// Clone node and create a reference, myClone.
myClone = myXML.firstChild.cloneNode(true);
// Append to myOtherXML
myOtherXML.appendChild(myClone);
```

removeNode

This method simply removes the node and all of its children from the XML object, and deletes it. The XML object structure automatically updates, so there is no 'hole' left in the XML structure. For instance, if we delete the second child from a parent node that has three children, the third child will automatically become the second child.

insertBefore(childNode, beforeChild)

This method is similar to `appendChild`, the only difference is that it allows us to specify where in a node's set of children to place the new node. The method takes an additional argument, which is a reference to the child we want to place the new node before. Take a look at the following example:

```
// create a new XML document
MyXML=new XML("<BEGINNING/><END/>");

//Create a new node
myNewNode = myXML.createElement("<MIDDLE/>");

//insert the new node before the last node
myXML.insertBefore(myNewNode, myXML.lastChild);
```

A trace would reveal our XML document to look like this:

```
<BEGINNING/><MIDDLE/><END/>
```

hasChildNodes()

This is a simple method that returns a Boolean value. It returns `true` if the specified node has any children, and `false` if it does not.

toString()

This simply converts an XML object back into a string of XML source. If this method is executed on a node within an XML document, it returns a string of XML describing that element and all of the child elements within that node.

Appendix A
Appendix B

Appendix B
The multiuser.cfg file

This section is a reference for the `multiuser.cfg` file. We will go through the file, breaking it down into sections, giving explanations and reasons for possible modification.

```
#================================================================
# Sample and specification for the Multiuser.cfg file used
# to configure the Shockwave Multiuser Server version 3.0.
#
# This file must be placed in the same directory as the
# server application.
#
# Comment lines begin with a pound sign. Some lines are
# commented in this file because they are designed to be used
# optionally.
#
# To change a setting, remove the pound sign and edit the value.
#
# Variables are set using a variable = value syntax.
#================================================================
# Echo statements get displayed in the server window. Add an
# echo to the beginning of a line to verify that it has been
# read by the server.

echo Reading the Multiuser.cfg file.
```

As we've seen in several chapters, it's useful to modify the echo commands when you make other alterations to the file, in order to check that your amendments are being read by the server.

```
echo Reading my modified configuration file

#==============================================================
# Director users licensing information
#
# If you have purchased a copy of Director 8.5, uncomment the
# following two entries and enter your serial number
# and name below.  This will allow the server to accept
# up to 1000 incoming connections.
#
# For some Windows computers, you may need to reconfigure the
# system to allow more connections.  Read TechNote #14107 on
# http://www.macromedia.com/support/director for more
# information.
#==============================================================
```

The hash signs (#) keep the line concerned commented. If you leave lines like this, then the server uses the default value – usually the best option unless you need to make a change for a particular reason.

Number of users

There is an error in the comment shown above for SMUS 3.0 - the server can handle up to 2000 incoming connections, not 1000.

By default, the Multiuser Server only handles 50 connected users at a time. To enable 2000 maximum connections you need to enter your name and serial number in these lines. As with all changes, remove the hash sign from the beginning of the line to allow the settings to take effect.

```
# ServerOwnerName = "Enter Your Name Here"
# ServerSerialNumber = DRW850-12345-12345-12345
```

There is no separate serial number for the SMUS, so use your Director serial number. Unlike the Director application the SMUS will accept any valid serial number, so Windows servers can use a Macintosh serial number and vice-versa.

Connections

```
#============================================================
# General server configuration information.
#============================================================
# The default ServerPort value is 1626
# ServerPort = 1626
```

Here, you can customize the TCP/IP port that the server will use to listen for connections. The default is a good option, since it is used by most multiuser movies and does not conflict with any other TCP services that may be installed on the server machine.

```
# Server IP address.  This is optional, but must be specified if
# the server runs on a multihomed system or if listening on
# multiple ports.  Specify the IP address plus a colon and the
# port number.
# If listening on multiple addresses, specify them each here.
# ServerIPAddress = 123.45.67.90:1626
# ServerIPAddress = 123.45.67.90:1627
```

This above option is useful if you are running on a Windows machine with multiple network cards or more than one IP address assigned to it. It is not necessary to set this property in most cases, and when it is set, the ServerPort option is ignored.

UDP

If your movies are going to use the UDP protocol, then you have to specify the UDPServerAddress. This setting includes the IP address for your server and the starting UDP port number.

```
# Server UDP address and starting port number.  This is
# optional, but must be specified if the server uses the UDP
# protocol.  Enter the ip address plus a colon and the starting
# port number.  Only one address should be entered
# UDPServerAddress = 123.45.67.89:1627
```

The Multiuser Server will allocate one UDP port for each possible user connection to the server, starting at the port specified. If your server is configured for 2000 connections the server can end up sending traffic through ports 1627 to 3627, for example.

If you want to use the UDP protocol you also need to uncomment this line:

```
# Enable UDP for incoming connections.  This is by default off,
# and can be set on here or in a movie's configuration file
# EnableUDP = 1
```

Message Size

The MaxMessageSize option should only be tweaked if your movies send very large data – pictures or sound, for example - to the server. The default is OK for most multiuser applications, and holds 16 KBytes of data for each message. Remember to also use the setNetBufferLimits command in your multiuser movies if you want to send data larger than 16 KBytes.

```
# Maximum size of messages we allow.  The server will allocate  #
# twice this number of bytes for each connection.
# MaxMessageSize = 16384
```

TCP

By default, the tcpNoDelay setting is used on all TCP connections. This disables the Nagle algorithm used in most TCP implementations to prevent a large number of small packets from being sent, and increases message speed.

```
# Disable packet gathering for TCP.  In some cases, this will
# increase messaging speed, but will cause greater network
# traffic.
# tcpNoDelay = 1
```

The Nagle algorithm caches very small messages and sends them in one larger packet. This minimizes network traffic but may introduce a delay of up to 200 ms on your messages. Most chat and multiuser servers including the Multiuser Server use the default `tcpNoDelay` setting to disable the algorithm and prevent the delay from taking place.

Limiting Connections

```
# Number of connections the server will handle (up to the
#license limit)
# ConnectionLimit = 50
```

We've seen how to enter the serial number to allow us to exceed 50 connections, but you may well not want your server to be taken all the way up to the 2000 limit. Edit this line to set a limit for the number of connections allocated by the server.

Encryption

```
# Encryption key - if used, the connecting machine must use the
# exact same key in ConnectToNetServer()
# EncryptionKey = SomeVerySecretSequenceWithoutSpaces
```

By default, all login messages sent to the server are encrypted to protect passwords. For additional protection you may want to specify your own encryption key by modifying these lines. If you decide to use a different key, you have to make sure all your multiuser movies specify the same encryption key in the `ConnectToNetServer` function, or server connection will fail.

User Levels

This will be fairly familiar to those of you who have read the chapter on using the Multiuser Server database.

```
#=============================================================
# Default user level for someone logging on to the server.
# This is used if you do not specifically authorize logons
# with a database.
#=============================================================

# DefaultUserLevel = 20
```

This is the default user level that will be assigned to users that connect to the server and do not have an entry on the database. It will also be used if you configure your server not to authenticate users using the database. The authentication behavior is controlled by a different setting, which we'll be looking at later on in this appendix.

```
#=============================================================
# The user levels required for various server commands.  Note
# that the new dot syntax replaces the old syntax of the
```

continues overleaf

479

```
# commands.  The old syntax will still function in this release,
# but is supported in this release only for backward
# compatibility and will be phased out in a future release of
# the server.  There are some new commands; refer to the
# documentation for syntax and examples.
#==============================================================
# Server commands
UserLevel for System.Server.GetMovies =      20
UserLevel for System.Server.GetMovieCount = 20
UserLevel for System.Server.GetTime =        20
UserLevel for System.Server.GetVersion =     20
```

These entries indicate the userlevel necessary to perform each server command. By default all connected users (userlevel 20 or higher) can use these functions.

```
# Movie commands
UserLevel for System.Movie.Enable =          80
UserLevel for System.Movie.Disable =         80
UserLevel for System.Movie.Delete =          80
UserLevel for System.Movie.GetGroups =       20
UserLevel for System.Movie.GetUserCount =    20
UserLevel for System.Movie.GetGroupCount =   20
```

Notice that some functions are only available to users connected with a userlevel of 80 or higher. These are usually administrators of the server, and they have the power to enable, delete, and disable movies.

```
# Group commands
UserLevel for System.Group.GetUsers =          20
UserLevel for System.Group.GetUserCount =      20
UserLevel for System.Group.CreateUniqueName = 20
UserLevel for System.Group.Join =              20
UserLevel for System.Group.Leave =             20
UserLevel for System.Group.Enable =            80
UserLevel for System.Group.Disable =           80
UserLevel for System.Group.Delete =            80

# User commands
UserLevel for System.User.Delete =             80
UserLevel for System.User.GetGroupCount =      20
UserLevel for System.User.GetGroups =          20
UserLevel for System.User.GetAddress =         80
```

Again, some group and user commands are reserved for users with a userlevel of 80 or higher, as free access to them would pose a security risk.

Multiuser.cfg file location

The `MovieCFGPath` setting is useful if you need to keep your `multiuser.cfg` file and movie specific configuration files in a different folder rather than in the folder where the Multiuser Server resides.

```
#=============================================================
# This indicates where to look for movie configuration (.cfg)
# files. Provide a path to the directory the movie cfg files are
# stored.
# You may also express a path like "@\ConfigFiles\"
# to access a path relative to the server program.
#=============================================================
# Example Mac pathname:
#      MovieCFGPath = "HardDisk:Multiuser Server:Database:"
# Example Win pathname:
#      MovieCFGPath = "C:\Program Files\Multiuser
# Server\Database\"
```

Log Files

A log file is optional in the Multiuser Server. If you want to keep a record of all messages exchanged, you can specify the name of a log file using this property. Keep in mind that log files can get very large very quickly and use a lot of disk space, which is why this isn't switched on by default.

```
#=============================================================
# Location of the Log file - all messages will be recorded in
# this text file.  Provide the path and name for the log file.
# You may also express a path like "@\Logs\ServerLog.txt"
# to access a path relative to the server program.
#=============================================================
#Example Mac pathname:
#      LogFileName = "HardDrive:ServerLog.txt"
#Example Win filename:
#      LogFileName = "C:\Temp\ServerLog.txt"
```

Specifying movies that can connect to your server

The following property was designed to restrict access to your server, by specifying the names of movies that are allowed to connect. Unfortunately there are a couple of problems with this approach. The first is that other developers can use a different movie with the same name, and defeat this simple protection.

```
#===============================================================
# The AllowMovie value indicates a movie that can connect to
# the server.  If not set, any movie can connect.  It may
# be set multiple times to allow multiple movies.
# Continue with additional lines with a "\".
#===============================================================
# AllowMovies =    YourMovieName  \
# AnotherMovieName
```

Another, slightly more notable problem is that AllowMovies doesn't work in version 3 of the Multiuser Server, as released with Director 8.5. Check technote # 15602 at Macromedia's web site support center for a Lingo based work-around.

There is, however, an optional server property to control movie access to the server that is not well known. It is listed in the Director online help for Shockwave 8.5, and can be used to authenticate the movies that are able to connect to this server in a secure way, making it a potentially better option than the one shown above. This option is MoviePathName. It takes the format:

```
MoviePathName = http://www.yourserver.com/movie.dcr /
http://anotherserver.com/movie.dcr
```

This setting is not listed in the default multiuser.cfg file or in the Multiuser Server 3 PDF documentation. It seems to work reliably, although extensive testing is recommended if you do use this. Check the Director online help for more information about this property and the format of the ConnectToNetServer necessary to use it.

Idle time

Sometimes a user will lose their Internet connection in a way where is not possible for the server to detect this immediately. In this case the server will drop the connection after the number of seconds indicated in the IdleTimeOut property if it doesn't receive any data from the user during this period.

```
#===============================================================
# This is an idle timer for connections - if they have not sent
# any data before this many seconds, the connection will be
# dropped.
#===============================================================

IdleTimeOut = 600
```

It's not a good idea to set this value too low, or users that don't interact much with the server will end up being dropped as well. The default 10 minutes value is reasonable for most applications but remember that in some applications – chatrooms for example – users may be idle for long periods of time while they wait for another user to log in, or for an interesting topic of conversation to arise. Users may not want to find themselves dropped and have to log back in every ten minutes just because they haven't said anything.

Message display settings

```
#================================================================
# These flags control what messages the server will display at
# startup.  A "0" flag turns off messages.
#================================================================

ShowLogonMessages = 1
ShowCreateMovieMessages = 1
ShowScantimeMessages = 0
ShowCreateGroupMessages = 0
ShowJoinGroupMessages = 0
```

This is a cosmetic setting that controls the appearance of messages in the server console window. The options are equivalent to the items in the View menu of the server application.

Message time performance

```
#================================================================
# This set the number of seconds between scan time reports.
#================================================================

ScanTimeReportInterval = 10
```

This is another setting that doesn't impact user connections to the server. This value controls how frequently the server will report message time performance in the console window.

Xtras

```
#================================================================
# Load the xtras for the server.  If you don't need the commands
# these xtras provide, you can omit them from this file.  Custom
# server xtras should be included here.
#================================================================

ServerExtensionXtras = RuntimeAttributes DatabaseObjects LingoVM
```

Some functions of the Multiuser Server are implemented as Xtras, and you may want to install third party Xtras to enhance your server. The ServerExtensionXtras line controls the Xtras that will be loaded when the server starts. You may want to remove one or more Xtras from the list if you do not use their functionality on your movies. The default Xtras are:

- RuntimeAttributes: this provides the group attributes functions.

- DatabaseObjects: this provides DBAdmin, DBUser, DBApplication and DBPlayer commands. It is also necessary if you use the database for login authentication.

● LingoVM: this is used for server side scripting. This Xtra is also used by the Multiuser Server for some of its message routing routines, so it should not be removed.

```
#===============================================================
# Configuration commands for the LingoVM xtra.   Set
# up a debugging script to enable the debugger functions
#===============================================================
# XtraConfigCommands for LingoVM
# XtraCommand = "DebugScript Debugger.ls"
```

Each Xtra is configured with an XtraConfigCommands line, followed by several XtraCommand ones. It is not usually necessary to edit these settings. The LingoVM Xtra shown above supports the DebugScript property. If you want to enable a server side script for debugging purposes then I'd recommend that you check Macromedia's support center for more information on debug scripts and how to enable them. Production servers probably should not have debug scripts running.

```
#===============================================================
# Configuration commands for the RuntimeAttributes xtra.   Sets
# the userlevels required to execute various commands
#===============================================================

XtraConfigCommands for RuntimeAttributes

XtraCommand = "System.Group.SetAttribute       20"
XtraCommand = "System.Group.GetAttribute       20"
XtraCommand = "System.Group.DeleteAttribute    20"
XtraCommand = "System.Group.GetAttributeNames 20"
```

Since the group attribute commands are implemented by the RuntimeAttributes Xtra, they too need to be configured with an XtraCommand line, as shown.

The database xtra

```
#===============================================================
# Configuration commands for the DatabaseObjects xtra.   Defines
# the base filename of various tables holding database
#information.
#===============================================================

XtraConfigCommands for DatabaseObjects

XtraCommand = "AppFile Applications"
XtraCommand = "AppDataFile AppData"
XtraCommand = "AttrFile Attributes"
XtraCommand = "AttrIDFile AttrList"
XtraCommand = "IDFile IDTable"
XtraCommand = "PlayerFile Players"
XtraCommand = "RawDataFile RawData"
```

```
                  XtraCommand = "UserFile Users"
```

The commands shown above configure the name of the DBF files that hold the internal database information. Since data is stored in an undocumented format and there is a strict relationship between tables, altering the defaults is not something I'd recommend!

```
        #===============================================================
        # Define the path where database files should be stored,
        # otherwise use the working directory of the server.  Spaces
        # are supported in Mac paths.  Only use quotes around the entire
        # path name.
        # You may also express a path like XtraCommand = "DBFolder
        #@\TempDB\"
        # to access a path relative to the server program.
        #===============================================================
        # Example Mac path to database folder:
        #       XtraCommand = "DBFolder MyHardDrive:DBFolder:"
        # Example Win path to database folder:
        #       XtraCommand = "DBFolder C:\DBFolder\"

        XtraCommand = "DBFolder @\DBObjectFiles\"
```

Alter these settings if you want the database files created on a different location on your server. The exact syntax is different for Macintosh and Windows systems, as shown.

```
        #===============================================================
        # This option defines the value of the #status
        # attribute of DBUser objects when they are created.
        #===============================================================

        XtraCommand = "DefaultUserStatus 20"
```

It *is* possible for a multiuser movie to create a user with the DBAdmin.createUser function without assigning a #userlevel property in the contents section of the message. In this case the DefaultUserStatus value specified in this XtraCommand shown above will be used and assigned to the newly created user.

```
        #===============================================================
        # Set the authentication level that determines who can log on
        # to the server.  Possible values are:
        #     None - anyone may log in with any name and password
        #             (as long as another user has not already connected
        #             to the movie using the same name)
        #     UserRecordRequired - users may only log in if they
        #             have a DBUser record in the database
        #     UserRecordOptional - if a DBUser record exists for the
        #             the given name, then the correct password is
        #             required.  If there is no record, then the
        #             connection is allowed.  (user level set to the
        #             value of "db_default_userlevel")
```

continues overleaf

```
#================================================================

XtraCommand = "Authentication UserRecordOptional"
```

The Authentication XtraCommand is discussed at greater length in the database chapter, but it's interesting to note that if the None option is used then all users will be logged with the DefaultUserLevel as specified in this configuration file. The UserRecordOptional default setting is adequate for most servers.

Packing the DBF files

```
#================================================================
# This option controls how often the RawData datafiles are
# packed automatically. Reusing deleted records works for
# everything except "memo" type fields, which are present in
# the RawData table.
#
# In order to reclaim the space, a pack must be done
# periodically.
#
# Packing the datafile every few deletions helps keep the file
# size down. If the pack period is too small, then the datafile
# is packed too often, which will cause the server to "freeze"
# briefly. If too large, then too much disk space will be
# wasted.
#================================================================

XtraCommand = "DataPackPeriod 50"
```

The DBF files used by the internal database need to be packed periodically. The default setting provides a good balance between too many packing operations and too much disk space wasted. If your application does not delete database records frequently, you can increase this setting as more frequent re-packing will have no effect.

Directly declaring database attributes

```
#================================================================
# Attributes can be declared in the configuration files
# using the syntax:
#
#   XtraCommand = "System.DBAdmin.DeclareAttribute myAttribute"
```

In most cases, you would use the DatabaseAdministrator tool presented in the database chapter to declare an attribute for the database. Should you want to, you can do this directly, using the format shown above. If you've already declared the attribute, then this line will be ignored.

User levels for database commands

```
#=================================================================
# Set the userlevels required to execute various commands
#=================================================================
# Admin commands
XtraCommand = "System.DBAdmin.CreateUser 80"
XtraCommand = "System.DBAdmin.DeleteUser 80"
XtraCommand = "System.DBAdmin.CreateApplication 80"
XtraCommand = "System.DBAdmin.DeleteApplication 80"
XtraCommand = "System.DBAdmin.CreateApplicationData 20"
XtraCommand = "System.DBAdmin.DeleteApplicationData 20"
XtraCommand = "System.DBAdmin.GetUserCount 80"
XtraCommand = "System.DBAdmin.GetUserNames 80"
XtraCommand = "System.DBAdmin.DeclareAttribute 80"
```

Userlevels required to execute DBAdmin commands are specified in this section of the configuration file. By default, only administrative users with userlevel 80 or higher can use these functions.

```
# User commands
XtraCommand = "System.DBUser.SetAttribute 20"
XtraCommand = "System.DBUser.GetAttribute 20"
XtraCommand = "System.DBUser.SetAttribute#Password 100"
XtraCommand = "System.DBUser.GetAttribute#Password 100"
XtraCommand = "System.DBUser.GetAttributeNames 20"
XtraCommand = "System.DBUser.DeleteAttribute 20"
```

These lines configure the DBUser commands. Notice that only administrators with the maximum userlevel can set and get the #password attribute. Any user connected to the database can use the remaining functions. The same is true for DBPlayer and DBApplication commands:

```
# Player commands
XtraCommand = "System.DBPlayer.SetAttribute 20"
XtraCommand = "System.DBPlayer.GetAttribute 20"
XtraCommand = "System.DBPlayer.GetAttributeNames 20"
XtraCommand = "System.DBPlayer.DeleteAttribute 20"

# Application commands
XtraCommand = "System.DBApplication.SetAttribute 20"
XtraCommand = "System.DBApplication.GetAttribute 20"
XtraCommand = "System.DBApplication.GetAttributeNames 20"
XtraCommand = "System.DBApplication.DeleteAttribute 20"
XtraCommand = "System.DBApplication.GetApplicationData 20"
```

The format of the CreateUser command should be familiar if you've read the database chapter. This is very useful for creating the first administrative user in a database, as we did in that chapter. Additional user accounts can be created with the DBAdministrator tool.

```
#=================================================================
# Use the following commands to create extra user accounts
# in the database when the server starts up.  These accounts
# are permanently added to the database, so future modifications
# to a username are not effective.  Once that user is created,
# you could remove the line from the config file.  The user
# level must be an integer value, do not use spaces.  The
# template for setting this is:
#
#      XtraCommand = "CreateUser <userName> <password>
# <userLevel>"
# Examples:
#      XtraCommand = "CreateUser Marge Homie! 100"
#      XtraCommand = "CreateUser Homer doh!  25"
#      XtraCommand = "CreateUser Apu nono   80"
```

Packing the database at startup

We saw a short while ago that packing the database file at a regular interval helps keep file size down. The following command is used to remove empty space from the database files when the server starts:

```
#=================================================================
# Pack the databases on server startup.

  XtraCommand = "PackDatabase"
```

Everything else

The remaining section of the multiuser.cfg file is there to support database commands used with version 1 of the Multiuser Server application. You can safely ignore these lines since they are no longer useful for the DBObject commands first implemented in version 2.

It is recommended that old movies are updated to use the new DBObject commands, since the old syntax is considered obsolete and will probably not be supported in future versions of the Multiuser Server.

```
#=================================================================
# The following sections are used in working with earlier
# database commands.  This functionality will be phased out in
# future versions of the server.  These sections are included
# as a reference only.  It is suggested that the new database
# objects be used instead.
#=================================================================
```

Index

Index

The index is arranged hierarchically, in alphabetical order, with symbols preceding the letter A. Many second-level entries also occur as first-level entries. This is to ensure that users will find the information they require however they choose to search for it.

friendsof

D E S I G N E R   T O   D E S I G N E R™

friends of ED writes books for you. Any suggestions, or ideas about how you want information given in your ideal book will be studied by our team.

Your comments are valued by friends of ED.

For technical support please contact support@friendsofed.com.

Freephone in USA	800.873.9769
Fax	312.893.8001
UK contact: Tel:	0121.258.8858
Fax:	0121.258.8868

Registration Code : [   ]

friendsof

D E S I G N E R   T O   D E S I G N E R™

NB. If you post the bounce back card below in the UK, please send it to:

friends of ED Ltd.,
30 Lincoln Road,
Olton,
Birmingham.
B27 6PA

BUSINESS REPLY MAIL
FIRST CLASS   PERMIT #64   CHICAGO, IL

POSTAGE WILL BE PAID BY ADDRESSEE

friends of ED,
29 S. La Salle St.
Suite 520
Chicago Il 60603-USA